W9-CBU-480

THE
EXTRAORDINARY
CONVERSION,

AND

RELIGIOUS
EXPERIENCE

OF

DOROTHY RIPLEY,

WITH

HER FIRST VOYAGE

AND

TRAVELS IN AMERICA.

―――――――

"Seek first the kingdom of God, and his righteousness."

MATT. 6 c. v. 33.

―――――――

[COPY-RIGHT SECURED ACCORDING TO LAW.]

New-York:

PRINTED BY G. AND R. WAITE, FOR THE AUTHOR.

1810.

The Extraordinary Conversion, and Religious Experience of Dorothy Ripley
(title page)

Saving Women
Retrieving Evangelistic Theology and Practice

Laceye C. Warner

BAYLOR UNIVERSITY PRESS

Scripture quotations are from the New Revised Standard Version Bible, copyright 1989, Division of Christian Education of the National Council of the Churches of Christ in the United States of America. Used by permission. All rights reserved.

Cover Design by Stephanie Blumenthal

Cover and Interior Images: Julia A. J. Foote is used by permission of the Robert W. Woodruff Library of the Atlanta University Center. Helen Barrett Montgomery is from the collection of the Rochester Public Library Local History Division and used with permission. Angelina Grimke Weld [LC-USZ61-1609], Sarah Moore Grimke [LC-USZ61-1608], Frances Willard [LC-DIG-ggbain-02864], Mary McLeod Bethune [LC-USW3-014846-C] are all public domain via Library of Congress, Prints & Photographs Division.

Library of Congress Cataloging-in-Publication Data

Warner, Laceye C.
  Saving women : retrieving evangelistic theology and practice / Laceye C. Warner.
     p. cm.
  Includes bibliographical references and index.
  ISBN 978-1-932792-26-3 (cloth/hardcover : alk. paper)
  1. Evangelistic work. 2. Women in church work. I. Title.

  BV3793.W375 2007
  226'.2082--dc22

                          2007014015

Printed in the United States of America on acid-free paper with a minimum of 30% pcw content.

This book is dedicated to

the Duke Divinity School students of PA 178
"Women and Evangelism" 2001–2004

with gratitude for

the immeasurable blessings and unexpected lessons.

Frances E. Willard, Woman's Christian Temperance Union

CONTENTS

LIST OF ILLUSTRATIONS

PREFACE

When reflecting upon existing resources with colleagues teaching evangelism in United Methodist theological seminaries, we quickly realized the substantial need in a number of areas—for example, women's contributions. In light of the recognized need, this project has developed from the encouragement and counsel of many friends and colleagues. Bishop Scott Jones, William Abraham, Stephen Gunter, Bryan Stone, and Carolyn Gifford were particularly persuasive and influential in this project's early development. Most significant to my vocational work, making it possible for me to teach seminary students, is the support and prayers of the Foundation for Evangelism staff and Board of Trustees, specifically Paul and Kitten Ervin and Royce and Jane Reynolds. As mentioned in the dedication, seminar discussions related to this material in the PAR 178 "Women and Evangelism" courses over the last several years have brought much learning and joy.

The early stages of this research were made possible through the Lilly Theological Research Grants program, enabling travel and access to primary source documents. The conversation among other grant recipients and guidance from experienced scholars within the context of that program offered both framework and motivation, including an introduction to Carey Newman, director of Baylor University Press—an intrepid, insightful, and visionary editor whose expertise has immensely improved this project and whose company made for an enjoyable and educational process. Another fruitful venue for conversation was the Summer Wesley Seminar convened by

Richard Heitzenrater at Duke Divinity School. Most recently, the Louisville Institute, through a Summer Stipend Grant, provided the opportunity for carving space to bring closure to this work. The grants, with additional research support from Duke Divinity School, enabled research assistance throughout the project's development. I am grateful for the distinctive contributions of Nathan Kirkpatrick, Dan Rhodes, Mandy McMichael, and Amy Beth Hougland in assisting with research and editing tasks. A special mention must go to Anne Weston for seeing and listening beyond the page. While Duke University Libraries—specifically the Divinity School, Perkins Library, Special Collections, and the Law School—provided substantial resources and services, several others and their staff were instrumental: Garrett-Evangelical Theological Seminary United Library and Dr. David Himrod, Woman's Christian Temperance Union Archive and Ms. Virginia Beatty, as well as John Rylands Library, University of Manchester, and Dr. Peter Knockles.

The process of discovery in research benefited from many presentations and their gracious audiences outside the classroom, such as the Academy for Evangelism in Theological Education, American Academy of Religion, Congress on Evangelism, South Indiana Annual Conference (especially Deborah Cronin), Professional Association of United Methodist Church Secretaries', and numerous local church venues. These presentations and responses helped clarify material that appeared in print: "Saving Women: Re-visioning Contemporary Concepts of Evangelism," in *Considering the Great Commission: Evangelism and Mission in the Wesleyan Spirit*, ed. W. S. Gunter and E. Robinson (Nashville: Abingdon, 2005), 119–33; "Saving Women: Re-visioning Contemporary Concepts of Evangelism," *Journal of the Academy for Evangelism in Theological Education* vol. 18 (2003): 16–31; "Kingdom Witness and Helen Barrett Montgomery's Biblical Theology," *RevExp* vol. 101, no. 3 (2004): 451–71; and "Redemption and Race: The Evangelistic Ministry of Three Women in Southern Methodism," *Wesleyan Theological Journal* vol. 40, no. 2 (2005): 7–29. Thanks to Abingdon Press, *Wesleyan Theological Journal*, and *Review and Expositor* for allowing revised materials to be reprinted in this volume.

I now comprehend more fully the notion that such research and writing are truly shared projects informed by individuals and communities over time beyond the confines of grant support or deadlines. I am appreciative to the following key figures in this process: Stephen Chapman (for, among other things, a more interesting title than I could ever compose on my own) and Amy Laura Hall (for the essential push needed to begin). Most of all, I am grateful for the blessings of a wonderful spouse, Gaston, who continues to share with me our many sojourns with unwavering love, friendship, and winsome humor!

INTRODUCTION

That if the disciples had watched with the same assiduousness, as Mary did at the Sepulchre, they would have had the joyful tidings to preach.[1]

Early Christian tradition focuses attention primarily on the roles of Peter and Paul in the spread of the gospel and birth of the Christian church.[2] However, in the resurrection accounts of the synoptic gospels, women were not only present but they were entrusted with this crucial task.[3] In spite of the participation of women in the initial proclamation of Jesus Christ's resurrection, a precise connection between the women at the tomb and the growth of Christianity remains elusive. This elusive connection between women and their participation in practices of evangelism is merely one example of the neglect of women's religious history within the larger Christian tradition. Women's contributions to the history and theology of the Christian church remain largely unclaimed. The first—and in some sense, primary—aim of this project is to contribute to research about women's historic contributions to the

---

[1] D. Ripley, *The Bank of Faith and Works United* (Philadelphia: J. H. Cunningham, 1819), 112.

[2] For example, O. Cullmann, *Peter, Apostle, Disciple, Martyr: A Historical and Theological Study* (Philadelphia: Westminster, 1953).

[3] See E. S. Fiorenza, *In Memory of Her: A Feminist Theological Reconstruction of Christian Origins* (New York: Crossroads, 1983), and A.-J. Levine, ed., *"Women Like This": New Perspectives on Jewish Women in the Greco-Roman World* (Atlanta: Scholars Press, 1991). See also W. Liefeld, "Women and Evangelism in the Early Church," *Missiology: An International Review* 15 (1987): 291–98.

theology and practices of the church by throwing light on the religious life of a select number of extraordinary women.

Saving Women

The deficiency of research attuned to contributions of women's evangelistic ministries is especially acute. Throughout Christian history, women's practices of discipling have remained largely unnoticed, even if women have accounted for over half of the church's constituency for much of that history.[4] Although a limited number of studies focusing on women's contributions to this vital area are beginning to appear, resources with theological themes are still needed within discussions related to the study of evangelism.[5]

An underlying reason for this lack of attention to women's evangelistic ministries relates in part to terminology. Scholars writing in American religious history recognize the synonymous use of evangelism with verbal proclamation in the nineteenth century.[6] As a result of the persistent usage of *evangelism* to mean "preaching" ministries

---

[4] A. Braude, "Women's History *Is* American Religious History," in *Retelling U.S. Religious History*, ed. T. A. Tweed (Berkeley: University of California Press, 1997), 88–92. The language of "discipling" is a more accurate translation than "make disciples" in Matthew 28:19-20a with its more complex reference to the roles of God as well as the baptized in the process of Christian initiation. For a thorough exegetical treatment of the Great Commission, see D. Bosch, "The Structure of Mission: An Exposition of Matt. 28:16-21," in *Exploring Church Growth*, ed. W. Shenk (Grand Rapids: Eerdmans, 1983), 218–48, specifically 230–33.

[5] For example, R. Nixson, in *Liberating Women for the Gospel: Women in Evangelism* (London: Hodder & Stoughton, 1997), hopes to empower women for the practice of evangelism. N. Hardesty, in *Women Called to Witness: Evangelical Feminism in the Nineteenth Century* (Nashville: Abingdon, 1984), provides a thematic historical background to women's evangelistic social ministries alongside their struggles for ecclesiastic privileges, and P. Pope-Levison, in *Turn the Pulpit Loose: Two Centuries of American Women Evangelists* (New York: Palgrave Macmillan, 2004), offers a collection of primary source excerpts from women evangelists.

[6] For example, B. Collier-Thomas, in her text on women preachers in African-American traditions, *Daughters of Thunder: Black Women Preachers and Their Sermons, 1850–1979* (San Francisco: Jossey Bass, 1998), 21, and N. Hardesty in her study of the reform work of nineteenth-century evangelical women *Women Called to Witness*, 82, 85, use the terms *evangelism* or *evangelists* synonymously with *preaching* or *lay preachers*, usually as distinct from those holding ordination. Scholars of women's religious history use alternative terms, such as *mission, outreach*, and *reform*, to represent practices other than preaching. C. Brekus demonstrates that connotations of female evangelism merely as preaching too narrowly construe the contributions of women

and verbal proclamation, women largely have been excluded from studies of evangelism.[7] Even when women have participated in proclaiming the message of salvation and practices of Christian discipling, their contributions mainly have been overlooked. As visitors, nurses, and teachers, for example, many women have proclaimed the Christian gospel in their words and lives, helping to initiate persons into the reign of God. The purpose of this project is not to argue that women's evangelism is innately different from or better than men's. It is, rather, to take the opportunity to uncover evangelistic theology and practices of select representative women. The objective of this study is to retrieve the ministries and writings of these "saving women," for the purpose of preserving their voices and examples for inclusion in the contemporary discussion related to evangelistic theology and practice.

Women have contributed significantly to the spread of Christianity and the nurture of individuals in the faith throughout Christian tradition, such that the women in this study are not unique despite a truncated understanding of evangelism as solely verbal proclamation. For example, Elizabeth Schussler Fiorenza, in her now classic text *In Memory of Her: A Feminist Theological Reconstruction of Christian Origins*, theologically conceptualizes the stories and history of women in early Christianity "as an integral part of the proclamation of the gospel."[8] Aime Martimort extends the observations of Fiorenza in her critical examination of the diaconate ministry of

---

and hinder the implications of women's examples for contemporary evangelistic theology and practice. According to C. A. Brekus, "A Mother in Israel or Sister in Christ was not a crusading evangelist who traveled from town to town preaching the gospel, but a Sunday school teacher, a temperance reformer, or an antislavery activist who deferred to the authority of her local pastor" (*Strangers and Pilgrims: Female Preaching in America 1740–1845* [Chapel Hill: University of North Carolina Press, 1998], 294). See also C. Brekus, "Female Evangelism in the Early Methodist Movement, 1784–1845," in *Methodism and the Shaping of American Culture*, ed. N. Hatch and J. Wigger (Nashville: Kingswood Books, 2001), 135–73. Likewise, J. M. Schmidt acknowledges the significance of such activities beyond preaching for Christian witness in her description of Phoebe Palmer's encouragement of urban mission work at the Five Points Mission in New York City. According to Schmidt, Palmer "was convinced that something more than evangelism [as only verbal proclamation] was required" (*Grace Sufficient: A History of Women in American Methodism 1760–1939* [Nashville: Abingdon, 1999], 142).

   [7] D. L. Robert, ed., *Gospel Bearers, Gender Barriers: Missionary Women in the Twentieth Century* (Maryknoll, N.Y.: Orbis Books, 2002), 20.

   [8] Fiorenza, *In Memory of Her*, xv.

women beginning in the early church and its evangelistic trajectory demonstrated in catechesis and visitation of the sick.[9] Monastic *ammas* of the patristic church followed by sisters of the medieval church living in community proclaimed the gospel and nurtured disciples in the Christian faith through their pursuit of virtue and spiritual disciplines that included compassion, service, and hospitality.[10] Medieval beguine women offered inspiration to deaconesses and missionaries of the modern period through their proclamation of the gospel alongside care of the infirm and disenfranchised.

Studies in American women's religious history feature the evangelistic ministry of women. For example, Catherine Brekus uncovers among Methodist and Baptist denominational traditions the preaching ministry of numerous women beginning in the eighteenth century.[11] Bettye Collier-Thomas and William Andrews enhance the accessibility of primary sources from African American preaching women.[12] While each of these projects focuses upon preaching, close attention to the writing and practices of the women reveals a more varied range of evangelistic ministries. In an exhaustive study of American women missionaries, Dana Robert narrates the textured evangelistic ministries of women in a spectrum of roles such as teachers, nurses, and preachers.[13] Nancy Hardesty explores the evangelistic motivations for advocacy of women's ecclesiastic rights as well as other social causes, such as abolition and temperance.[14] Similarly, *Saving Women* begins with American women's religious history while intentionally connecting the study of evangelistic theology and practice through a focused analysis of seven representative Protestant women and their evangelistic ministries.[15]

---

[9] A. G. Martimort, *Les Diaconesses: Essai Historique* (Rome: CLV Edizioni Liturgiche, 1982).

[10] R. Bondi, *To Pray and to Love: Conversations on Prayer with the Early Church* (Minneapolis: Fortress, 1991).

[11] Brekus, *Strangers and Pilgrims*.

[12] Collier-Thomas, *Daughters of Thunder*; and W. Andrews, ed., *Sisters of the Spirit: Three Black Women's Autobiographies of the Nineteenth Century* (Bloomington: Indiana University Press).

[13] D. Robert, *American Women in Mission: A Social History of Their Thought and Practice* (Macon, Ga.: Mercer University Press, 1997).

[14] Hardesty, *Women Called to Witness*.

[15] For a comprehensive resource related to American women's religious history, see R. S. Keller and R. R. Ruether, eds., *In Our Own Voices: Four Centuries of American Women's Religious Writing* (San Francisco: HarperSanFrancisco, 1995; repr., Louisville, Ky.: Westminster/John Knox, 2000).

By retrieving historical precedents for evangelistic practices broadly conceived, significant models may be cultivated for a contemporary church that often struggles with its identity and purpose. Critical reflection on the theology and practices of evangelism provides a vital resource, particularly among mainline Protestant traditions in the United States whose total memberships have suffered declines from the 1960s. The recent study of evangelism, grounded in the interaction among scholars and practitioners, has resulted in a deeper critical theological reflection.[16] While a number of questions arising from this interaction motivate research focused on the theology and practices of evangelism, two are primary: (1) What is the *content* of the gospel of Jesus Christ? Beginning with reflection upon biblical texts, particularly the gospels, but in the context of the whole canon, foundation may be gained for further historical and theological study related to the content of the gospel and substance of evangelism. (2) What *practices* faithfully share this gospel?[17] Indeed, several recent studies thoroughly address biblical foundations and provide theological analysis related to the content of the gospel and methods of sharing. This has led to further topics: (3) the faithful and effective practices of sharing the gospel by and among various constituencies

---

[16] For example, W. Abraham's text, *The Logic of Evangelism* (Grand Rapids: Eerdmans, 1989), in many ways initiates the academic study of evangelism by providing a theological and philosophical framework to pertinent and significant questions. S. Jones, in *The Evangelistic Love of God and Neighbor: A Theology of Witness and Discipleship* (Nashville: Abingdon, 2003), continues this trajectory, building on Abraham's assertions. W. Brueggemann, in *Biblical Perspectives on Evangelism: Living in a Three-Storied Universe* (Nashville: Abingdon, 1993) and W. Klaiber, in *Call and Response: Biblical Foundations of a Theology of Evangelism* (Nashville: Abingdon, 1997), also contribute to the shape of biblical foundations for evangelism. M. Arias, in his texts *Announcing the Reign of God: Evangelism and the Subversive Memory of Jesus* (Philadelphia: Fortress, 1984; repr., Eugene, Ore.: Wipf & Stock, 1999) and with A. Johnson, *The Great Commission: Biblical Models for Evangelism* (Nashville: Abingdon 1992), as well as D. Bosch, *Transforming Mission: Paradigm Shifts in Theology of Mission* (Maryknoll, N.Y.: Orbis Books, 1991); D. Guder and L. Barret, eds., *Missional Church: A Vision for the Sending of the Church in North America* (Grand Rapids: Eerdmans, 1998); B. Kallenberg, *Live to Tell: Evangelism for a Postmodern Age* (Grand Rapids: Brazos, 2002); S. Bevans and R. Schroeder, *Constants in Context: A Theology of Mission for Today* (Maryknoll, N.Y.: Orbis Books, 2004); and C. Braaten and R. Jenson, eds., *The Strange New Word of the Gospel: Re-Evangelizing in the Postmodern World* (Grand Rapids: Eerdmans, 2002) explore theological implications for the church's practices of evangelism and mission.

[17] These questions are reminiscent of those with which Jones opens his study (*Evangelistic Love of God and Neighbor*, 13).

within the Christian tradition, and (4) the impact of these practices upon the understanding and theology of evangelism in various times and contexts. While the gospel's content is constant, its implications for communities of faith and their practices may shift as a result of changing or diverse circumstances.

Although this research engages in historical reconstruction, the second aim of the study is to provide a historical theology of women's contributions to evangelistic ministry. By attending to primary sources (e.g., autobiographies, letters, personal journals, periodicals, essays, and other materials) to understand the actual practices of evangelism of the selected women, this study exposes the biblical sources, the theological influences and motivations, as well as the social location and consequences for the evangelistic ministries of these women.

Each of the women was motivated by a desire—more specifically, spiritual doubts and anxiety—to receive and nurture her own faith, most often cultivated by good works as an appropriate response in faith to God's grace in Jesus Christ. While the women were largely not formally educated or trained in theological disciplines, they each ably connected their personal faith and understandings of biblical foundations to moral issues of their time and context, creating nuanced evangelistic theology and practices. Although from a variety of ecclesiastical traditions, most of the women relied less on a highly developed ecclesiology and more on biblical interpretation ideally discerned in spirit-filled communities of faith. However, several of the women endured uneasy relationships with local churches and denominations, often leaving such interpretation to the individual women.[18] This sustained attention to the influences, language, and images related to their ministries provide a "thick description" of theology and practices of evangelism.

This study navigates the historical and theological landscape upon which the women's faith journeys led them to innovative and textured understandings and practices of evangelism. The evangelistic practices of the selected women provide a much needed balance to contemporary concepts and practices that have long focused upon verbal proclamation to the exclusion of evangelism's relatedness to other ministries. The third aim is therefore to propose components of a constructive practical theology of evangelism. Focusing upon the evangelistic ministry of these women provides an opportunity for their voices to contribute to the formation of understandings, theol-

---

[18] Brekus, *Strangers and Pilgrims*, 284.

ogy, and practices of evangelism within the contemporary church. The purpose of this project is to retrieve women's voices and create a space for them to be heard on the topic. While this project aims at incorporating examples of representative voices among modern Protestant women, it is my position—and hope—that this argument and its revisions will continue to be voiced through the particularities of constituencies currently excluded in variable degrees from discussions related to the study of evangelism.[19]

Evangelism Truncated

In America, the contemporary Protestant church's emphasis upon verbal proclamation of the gospel tends to conceptualize evangelism as a practice distinct from social reform and works of charity or mercy.[20] In contrast, two of the most influential practitioners and scholars of their eras in British and American contexts (and on the women in this study), Wesley and Finney integrated evangelistic theology and practices. John Wesley (1703–1791) and Charles Grandison Finney (1792–1875) used language related to the term *evangelism* to describe the ministries of verbal proclamation assumed by preachers. Wesley did not apply the term evangelism within the Methodist renewal movement. This noun was simply not in use in his day.[21]

---

[19] While this study focuses upon select women within American Protestantism, it seems that other historical periods and constituencies would offer similar themes with distinctive emphases.

[20] In his reflections upon the International Congress on World Evangelization held in Lausanne, Switzerland, July 16–24, 1974, a groundbreaking gathering in the accomplishment of placing both "evangelism" and "social action" on the table for consideration together, Stott clarifies the priority of "evangelism" over "social action," leaving little room for a comprehensive understanding of evangelism among evangelicals that could reach beyond a myopic focus upon verbal proclamation. J. Stott, "The Significance of Lausanne," *International Review of Mission* 64 (1975): 290–91.

[21] According to the *Oxford English Dictionary* (2d ed., s.v. "evangelism"), although there exists an early use (1600s) of a form of the term *evangelism*, its broad usage seems demonstrable beginning in the nineteenth century. According to Bosch, terms related to evangelism fell into almost complete disuse during the Middle Ages. Even today they are seldom used in English Bible translations; alternatives include "good news," "gospel," and "preach the gospel." Since the early nineteenth century the verb *evangelize* and its derivatives *evangelism* and *evangelization* have been rehabilitated in church and mission circles. They became particularly prominent around the turn of the century because of the slogan "The evangelization of the world in this generation." Bosch, *Transforming Mission*, 409.

Wesley did refer to his itinerant preachers on occasion as *evangelists*, indicating their main responsibility to preach.[22] "Finneyites" used the language of evangelism similarly, adding a subtle nuance by claiming reform lectures as a corollary to evangelism.[23] Despite the connotation of the term evangelism by Wesley, Finney, and their immediate followers, as preaching or verbal proclamation, they both practiced and understood other ministries as evangelistic ranging from small discipleship groups to various forms of compassionate ministries and social reform efforts.

Wesley and Finney led movements that assumed a variety of ministries in addition to verbal proclamation to share the gospel for the purpose of Christian initiation and discipling.[24] This complexity is often not demonstrated by contemporary understandings or practices of evangelistic ministries that trace their foundations to the late nineteenth century. A reason for this truncation is a shift away from theological reflection among those committed to practicing evangelistic ministry.[25] John Wesley and Jonathan Edwards (1703–1758) are among the last serious theologians associated with the practice of evangelism.[26] Although a respected thinker and significant practitioner of evangelistic ministry, Finney's impatience with the academy represents the beginning of a major shift from serious theological reflection upon evangelism by its practitioners.[27] This shift away from theological reflection has drastically minimized the church's resources to shape its understanding and practices of evangelism. Study in the use of language related to the term evangelism emphasizes the clear connection of evangelism with the practice of preaching the gospel.[28]

---

[22] J. Logan, "Offering Christ: Wesleyan Evangelism Today," in *Rethinking Wesley's Theology for Contemporary Methodism*, ed. R. Maddox (Nashville: Kingswood Books, 1998), 118.

[23] Hardesty, *Women Called to Witness*, 84.

[24] See T. Smith, *Revivalism and Social Reform in Mid-Nineteenth-Century America* (New York: Abingdon, 1957).

[25] See M. Noll, *The Scandal of the Evangelical Mind* (Grand Rapids: Eerdmans, 1994), 60–62. See also W. Leonard, "Evangelism and Contemporary American Life," *RevExp* 77 (1980): 493–506. Leonard's article examines the historical implications related to confusion that exists between the terms *evangelism* and *evangelicalism* as separate but related concepts.

[26] Abraham, *The Logic of Evangelism*, 9.

[27] Abraham, *The Logic of Evangelism*, 9.

[28] For example, a popular study often cited in texts related to evangelism is D. Barrett, *Evangelize! A Historical Survey of the Concept* (Birmingham, U.K.: New Hope, 1987), 11. Although there is no Aramaic version of Jesus' commission to the disciples

However, Luke and Paul predominantly developed the term *evange-lizo* to explain the mission *and* message of Jesus. Therefore, to focus too narrowly on evangelism as verbal proclamation alone, rather than as an all-inclusive description of Jesus' whole work of ministry, includ-ing complementing practices, is to neglect the biblical foundations for a faithful theology and practice of evangelism.[29]

Indeed, the language of evangelism throughout Christian tradi-tion has highlighted verbal proclamation over other nonverbal prac-tices. In the English language, for example, in his second translation of the Bible, Wycliffe in many cases replaced words beginning with *evangel-* with terms related to preaching. In 1525 Tyndale retained terms related to preaching instead of terms related to evangelism. Tyndale used the term *preach* instead of *evangelize* in an effort to make the biblical text more accessible by using less scholarly and more ver-nacular language.[30] This practice has continued to the present in many biblical translations. According to many, the American Protestant church has largely inherited the sixteenth-century reformers' empha-sis on proclamation. As a result of this emphasis upon proclamation, the richness of the language related to evangelism has been lost. This bereavement has contributed to the characterization of evangelism as technique or strategy related to practices of verbal proclamation addressed to individuals such as mass religious gatherings and door-to-door visitation often displaced from communities of faith. William Abraham clarifies the problem: "[A]t issue is the appropriation of what evangelism has actually meant in the early church and in history, not judged by the etymology of the word *evangelism* and its rather occasional use in Scripture, but by what evangelists have actually done in both proclaiming the gospel and establishing new converts in the kingdom of God."[31]

Retrieving the history of women in evangelism not only con-tributes missing voices to the chorus of church history, but also

---

in the gospels, according to Barrett the Greek term *euangelion* was most likely trans-lated from the Hebrew term *sabarta* meaning "good news," with the related verb *sabar* meaning "to tell good news." The Hebrew counterpart to this term is *basar* from the root *bsr*, which in Old Testament usage is often translated "to proclaim good news."

[29] Barrett, *Evangelize!* 12. Barrett offers an example of a study too narrowly focused on verbal proclamation. Based on his research Barrett argues that the six clos-est English synonyms to the term *evangelize* are *preach, bring, tell, proclaim, announce,* and *declare,* thus perpetuating the emphasis upon verbal proclamation.

[30] Barrett, *Evangelize!* 22.

[31] Abraham, *The Logic of Evangelism,* 69.

reclaims a lost harmony muted by the solo of long-held, deeply entrenched, but entirely insufficient concepts of evangelism toward resonance with biblical foundations and theological reflection.

Women Saving

The women in this study ministered primarily within Protestantism in the United States, most often influenced by Wesleyan and Arminian traditions, from the late eighteenth through the early twentieth centuries. The time frame of the study begins with the First Great Awakening and extends through the early twentieth-century fundamentalist-modernist controversy, a particularly influential time frame for contemporary understandings and practices of evangelism. The selection of these women takes into consideration theological and racial diversity among available primary sources that offer substantial materials for reflecting upon evangelistic theology and practices.[32] In order to offer representation of mainline and other prominent denominational traditions, the women selected are affiliated with Episcopal, Methodist, Presbyterian, Baptist, and Quaker traditions. Each of these traditions supported significant, if at times limited, opportunities for women's ministry roles including preacher, minister, social reformer, class leader, visitor, nurse, and deaconess. In the ministries of these women a profound synthesis of verbal proclamation and other evangelistic practices embodied the gospel message, offering resources to broaden contemporary concepts.

In chapter 1, strongly influenced by her father, a Methodist preacher, and desiring the endorsement of the Society of Friends, Dorothy Ripley embarked upon a transatlantic itinerant ministry that took her throughout the newly formed United States, particularly the South. In addition to documenting her spiritual autobiography and ministry journeys in two lengthy volumes, Ripley's evangelistic ministry could not ignore the sins of racism. Through political action—including the first known sermon by a woman preached to the U.S. Congress, a meeting with President Jefferson, and advocacy against capital punishment—Ripley's evangelistic ministry offers a provocative opening study.

---

[32] However, as a result of a variety of circumstances there remains a lack of primary resources from women and people of color specifically related to understandings and practices of evangelism.

In chapter 2, Angelina and Sarah Grimké participated in the American Anti-slavery Society as the only two southern white women. Raised in South Carolina in an affluent and politically active slave-owning family, both Angelina and Sarah received baptism in the Protestant Episcopal Church, evangelical conversions while worshiping with Presbyterians, and membership in the Society of Friends, from which they both grew estranged later in life. In select writings, the Grimké sisters outlined an evangelistic theology with a textured understanding of sin that confronted not only the injustices of racism embodied in the institution of slavery, but the disenfranchisement of women and the implications for slave-owning Christian women's complicity in sinful social structures.

In chapter 3, the evangelistic ministry of Julia Foote, the first woman ordained in the African Methodist Episcopal Zion Church, described in her autobiography demonstrates the implications of entire sanctification for real change in individuals and communities of faith. As a result of her experience of entire sanctification, a culmination of several dramatic religious experiences, Foote answered a call to evangelistic ministry that included advocacy of women's ecclesiastic rights and racial reconciliation—a courageous witness in her time and context.

In chapter 4, Frances Willard's frustrated vocation to ordained ministry in the Methodist Episcopal Church led her to facilitate women's evangelistic ministries within the National Woman's Christian Temperance Union, in which she served as a longtime and influential president. An educator and social reformer, Willard led the NWCTU at the end of the nineteenth century with a platform for woman's suffrage. Willard's frustrated vocation and leadership in the NWCTU converged in elements of a "woman's church," creating opportunities for women's evangelistic ministry.

In chapter 5, Helen Barrett Montgomery's love for biblical texts and ministry vocation to engage the disenfranchised contributed to her leadership in the ecumenical women's missionary movement. Strongly influenced by her father, a teacher and later Baptist minister in Rochester, New York, Montgomery's evangelistic theology and ministry were most clearly demonstrated in her publications, particularly a biblical theology related to the ecumenical women's missionary movement.

In chapter 6, raised in a Methodist home, educated among Presbyterians, and the first African American to attend what would become Moody Bible Institute, Mary McLeod Bethune in her youth discerned a vocation to the mission field. When she was not accepted as a missionary, Bethune turned her attention to African American youth, particularly girls, in the South. Arguably the most influential African American individual of her era, Bethune claimed the significance of her Christian faith. Throughout her writings, including the curriculum of the educational institution she established and led, Bethune revealed aspects of a simple constructive ecclesiology that took seriously eschatology as the theological framework for her evangelistic educational ministry.

When introduced to the study of evangelism, the ministries of these women offer examples for faithful theology and practices of evangelism within the contemporary church. Their ministries addressed persistent obstacles related to evangelism such as the implications of racism, anti-intellectualism, and lack of theological reflection. These obstacles continue to carry implications for evangelistic theology and practice in the contemporary church. The retelling of the history of these selected women in evangelism retrieves women's religious history, specifically in the study of evangelism, while also providing an opportunity for a constructive practical theology of evangelism. By focusing on these women and their relationship to church and society, we discover that faithful and effective evangelism is often the result of a dynamic relationship between formation in Christian faith, theological influences, and practices. Their examples offer possibilities for a constructive practical theology of evangelism that not only reunites verbal proclamation with the gospel's implications for social holiness within the reign of God, but examples of Christian discipleship embodied in individuals and communities of faith.

1

⟫ DOROTHY RIPLEY ⟪

*Going from city to city, from one nation to another, [I have] discovered the
iniquity that lurks under the various masks of professing godliness.*[1]

Dorothy Ripley (1767–1831) devoted her adult life to spreading the
Christian gospel. Her efforts included a constellation of practices
from the more familiar publication and itinerant preaching to social
and—more remarkable—political action. As a result of what she
described as a divine commission (Ripley did not hold membership in
a particular denomination), she understood that God called her to
leave her homeland of England to preach the gospel, particularly
among enslaved Africans and slave owners.[2] Ripley's vocation ultimately directed her evangelistic efforts toward political action against
slavery and racial oppression. Ripley's evangelistic ministry in the
United States during the early decades of the nineteenth century,

[1] D. Ripley, *The Extraordinary Conversion, and Religious Experience of Dorothy
Ripley, with Her First Voyage and Travels in America* (New York: G&R Waite, 1810),
23. The passage continues, ". . . each different denomination thinking themselves the
most sincere: but Alas! When I seek for pious souls redeemed from the maxims and
fashions of the present day, I almost seek in vain, and ask if there are any who live now
as Jesus Christ taught his followers in the days of his flesh, both by his example and
precept?"

[2] Ripley's ministry and travels were incredibly bold. While many Quaker women
made similar journeys, her persistence in crossing the Atlantic numerous times, coupled with her vocation and commitment to preach—specifically addressing the sinful
nature of slavery—set her apart.

prior to the 1833 organization of the American Anti-Slavery Society, was remarkable if not outstanding.[3]

Ripley crossed the Atlantic at least eight times to pursue her itinerant ministry in the United States. Her call to preach is consistent with traditional notions of evangelism. She broke ground in 1806 as the first woman to preach in the U.S. Hall of Representatives, one of only two women ever given that honor.[4] Despite such recognition, Ripley was reluctant to call her activity preaching, perhaps because her ministry faced consistent opposition.[5] In addition to the resistance in the United States, Ripley had difficulty answering her call in England. After her early itinerant ministry in the United States, she preached an evangelistic tour in 1818 in England, accompanying Lorenzo Dow, a well-known American itinerant and open-air preacher, an endeavor during which they were both imprisoned.[6]

---

[3] Ripley's ministry among slaves and slave owners substantially predates the American Anti-Slavery Society, which convened in December 1833, and the Anti-Slavery Convention of American Women, which held three annual sessions from 1837 to 1839. See I. Brown, "'Am I not a Woman and a Sister?' The Anti-Slavery Convention of American Women, 1837–1839," in *Abolitionism and Issues of Race and Gender*, ed. J. McKivigan (New York: Garland, 1999), 185.

[4] Brekus, *Strangers and Pilgrims*, 18. Harriet Livermore preached to Congress four times: the first time was in January 1827.

[5] "On first day an appointment was made for me by J. E. who acquainted the public, that D. Ripley, from England, a Gospel minister, would preach; at three in the afternoon, the Gospel of our Lord Jesus Christ. I did not approve of the word preach, because I never prepared any thing for the purpose, as I have seen Episcopalians, Methodists, Baptists, Presbyterians and some other ministers, which I have been much astonished at: for I pray, and give my heart tongue for God to inspire and speak by" (D. Ripley, *The Bank of Faith and Works United* [Philadelphia: J. H. Cunningham, 1819], 197). This resonates with Wesley's advice to women in the early British Methodist movement, suggesting, for example, some caution in not preparing remarks, taking a text, and strategic use of prayer. See P. W. Chilcote, *She Offered Them Christ: The Legacy of Women Preachers in Early Methodism* (Nashville: Abingdon, 1993).

[6] William Clowes, *The Journals of William Clowes* (London: Hallam & Holliday, 1844), 191. Lorenzo Dow (1777–1834), an American pioneer preacher and evangelist, was converted in 1791 and began to preach in 1794, receiving a license to preach from Bishop Francis Asbury in 1798. He preached widely and visited prisons, itinerating not only in the United States but also in Ireland and England. He met Dorothy Ripley and Hugh Bourne, one of the founders of Primitive Methodism in Great Britain, at an open-air meeting near Nottingham. J. Wilkinson and R. Stockham, "Lorenzo Dow," in *The Encyclopedia of World Methodism*, ed. N. Harmon (Nashville: United Methodist Publishing House, 1974), 1:711–12. Dow printed over seventy editions of twenty different works between 1800 and 1835, transforming himself through strategic marketing from a simple preacher to a well-known figure. Brekus, *Strangers and Pilgrims*, 257.

While verbal proclamation of the gospel remained her primary focus, Ripley's evangelistic ministry to enslaved Africans and slave owners in the United States addressed not only the spiritual implications of the sinful system, but also the more provocative social and economic implications.[7] For example, in *An Account of Rose Butler* (1819), Ripley narrated with some detail Butler's last hours prior to her execution by hanging, including her repentance and coming to faith. Butler, a nineteen-year-old slave, was executed for the attempted arson of her mistress's home. While the individual spiritual component of Ripley's narrative is significant, she added further dimension by shifting the focus of *An Account of Rose Butler* to the systemic implications of Christian salvation with an evangelistically motivated biblical and theological argument against capital punishment. In *An Account of Rose Butler*, as in the whole of her evangelistic ministry, Ripley not only preached repentance and forgiveness of sins for the salvation of individuals, acknowledging the implications of sin within social systems, she labored alongside the marginalized through a range of ministry practices from compassionate presence to political action.

Ripley left numerous sources describing her evangelistic ministry, including two substantial volumes narrating her religious and travel experiences—*The Extraordinary Conversion, and Religious Experience of Dorothy Ripley* (1810) and *The Bank of Faith and Works United* (1819).[8] Writing and publishing spiritual autobiographies was a relatively common occurrence among late eighteenth- and nineteenth-century Wesleyan and Quaker preaching women, the religious groups with whom Ripley most closely affiliated.[9] Ripley explained that the aim of

---

[7] Ripley's vocation to evangelistic ministry resonates with that of Freeborn Garrettson (1752–1827). Upon his conversion to American Methodism, Garrettson freed the slaves he owned before commencing his new vocation as an itinerant preacher and antislavery advocate. See *The Experience and Travels of Mr. Freeborn Garrettson, Minister of the Methodist Episcopal Church in North America* (Philadelphia: Parry Hall, 1791).

[8] For example, see D. Ripley, ed., *Letters, Addressed to Dorothy Ripley from several Africans and Indians on Subjects of Christian Experience & C* (Chester, U.K.: J. Hemingway, 1807); and Ripley, *An Account of Rose Butler, Aged Nineteen Years, Whose Execution I Attended in the Potter's Field* (New York: John C. Totten, 1819). *Letters* is a collection of correspondence, some later included in the above-mentioned volumes, which represent the various constituencies with whom Ripley ministered.

[9] See Susie C. Stanley, *Holy Boldness: Women Preachers' Autobiographies and the Sanctified Self* (Knoxville: University of Tennessee Press, 2002), xxx–xxxv, 26, 158, 204; see also Brekus, *Strangers and Pilgrims*, 173, 257–58. See also Ripley, *The Extraordinary Conversion*, 115: "[W]hat a weighty thing it is to preach the Gospel of our Lord Jesus Christ, and to publish an experience of faith. . . ."

her writing was evangelistic: "My only motive for printing those travels, is to disseminate the Gospel of our Lord Jesus Christ, and do good among the indigent, where my lot is cast by the Providence of God; as He teaches His children Mercy in all their ways."[10] While written for evangelistic purposes, the published accounts also provided a form of credential for her ministry: "For three months past I have been heavily afflicted in my spirit, believing God requires me to preach repentance to the Africans in the Cities of America, and that it will be necessary for me to print my conversion and life of faith, before I engage in any work for them here."[11] In addition, the texts produced small profits that supplied needed support during her later travels: "I have been also enabled to pay my own expenses many times, at Inns, by printing, where a door of entrance is not found among the various professing Christians of this day."[12] These writings not only give insight into Ripley's theological foundations, but they also offer a contemporaneous reflection of and an apologetic for her provocative evangelistic ministry.[13]

Ripley's ministry, framed by a Wesleyan emphasis on universal atonement, focused upon offering individuals salvation in Jesus Christ, a salvation that was available to all. Her ministry addressed a profound spiritual and social disconnect that separated the conversion of individuals (and peoples) from their condition.[14] For Ripley, the salvation of individuals could not ignore the social implications of salvation from those sins. For example, in 1802 at the commencement of her first United States tour, Ripley felt called to meet with President Thomas Jefferson to request his consent for her ministry among enslaved Africans and slave owners. During this interview she inquired into his sinful slaveholding practices. For Ripley, salvation was not merely a personal episode accompanied by a predictable set of occasional pious practices; she would refer to those who embraced such a minimalist faith as "profess'd Christians," implying their faith was Christian in name only.[15] Rather, salvation was a spiritual dynamic

---

[10] Ripley, *The Bank of Faith*, 3.

[11] Ripley, *The Extraordinary Conversion*, 115.

[12] Ripley, *The Bank of Faith*, 4.

[13] See P. Fredriksen, "Paul and Augustine: Conversion Narratives, Orthodox Traditions, and the Retrospective Self," *JTS* 37 (1986): 3–34.

[14] See D. Strong, "A Real Christian Is an Abolitionist: Conversion and Antislavery Activism in Early American Methodism," in *Conversion in the Wesleyan Tradition*, eds. K. Collins and J. Tyson (Nashville: Abingdon, 2001), 69–82.

[15] Ripley, *The Bank of Faith*, 16. Ripley's lengthy autobiographical poem recorded

with direct implications for every aspect of a follower's life. Thus, her evangelistic ministry among enslaved Africans, slave owners, Native Americans,[16] the imprisoned, infirm, and dying consisted of visitation

---

that, in addition to Africans, she ministered to those in "prison," "the hospital sick," "poor-house," among "the rich," "the deists," and "profess'd Christians," "hypocrites," and "backsliders." Ripley often mentioned "deists" and "profess'd Christians" in the same statement, if not equating them, then at least acknowledging similarities. Ripley did not, therefore, seem to use the term *deist* to refer explicitedly to the set of beliefs prominent in the seventeenth and eighteenth centuries, particularly in England, which could include any or all of the following as described by Samuel Johnson in his (1755) *Dictionary*: (1) belief in a supreme being that lacked intellect and will, (2) belief in a God, but without providential compassion for the world, (3) belief in a God, but without a promise of afterlife, (4) belief in a God, but rejection of other doctrines. See A. Wood, "Deism," in *The Encyclopedia of Religion*, ed. M. Eliade (New York: Macmillan, 1987), 4:262–64. According to Brekus, deism added to the unsettled religious landscape of the early nineteenth century, particularly in light of its popularity among the nation's elite, such as Jefferson and Franklin (*Strangers and Pilgrims*, 122).

[16] While this study focuses on Ripley's ministry among enslaved Africans and their owners, she intentionally expanded the scope of her ministry during her second and subsequent journeys. In addition to visiting prisons and almshouses, Ripley took a particular interest in several groups of Native Americans, particularly those near Oneida, New York. In the preface to *Letters*, Ripley stated she received "a new commission to cross the ocean again, and to call the Indians to repentance, and to testify to them that they were of Jeroboam's house" (iv).

In June 1805 Calvin Young, an innkeeper in Vernon, New York, accompanied Ripley to Oneida Castle "to see the Indians of the Six Nations, and particularly Skanandoa, the oldest Chief, who was a great favorite of his" (Ripley, *The Bank of Faith*, 75). Chief John Skanandoa was present for the Treaty of Canandaiuga in 1794, a "Land Treaty with Six Nations," during which he signed as one of the Oneida's representatives. The Oneida people expressed appreciation generally for the Quaker presence and help (M. H. Bacon, *Mothers of Feminism: The Story of Quaker Women in America* [San Francisco: Harper, 1986], 79). This engagement marked the beginning of the New York Yearly Meeting's cultivation of "peace and friendship" with the Native Americans (H. Barbour et al., eds., *Quaker Crosscurrents: Three Hundred Years of Friends in the New York Yearly Meetings* [Syracuse, N.Y.: Syracuse University Press, 1995], 96). The 1794 Philadelphia Yearly Meeting applauded their members' support of the Native Americans in their area during the previous year. Ripley claimed that many of the Native Americans with whom she interacted did not profess the Christian faith. Though the Quakers hoped the Native Americans would become Christian, they were less concerned with their Christianization than were missionaries sent by other denominations. The Quakers focused their efforts on equipping the Native Americans with skills to address the growing economic implications of their encroaching European neighbors. The Quakers taught European methods of agriculture and weaving, supplied animals and tools, and provided a loan to construct a saw mill (Barbour et al., *Quaker Crosscurrents*, 97). By 1810 the New York Yearly Meeting was beginning to advocate for the "pagan" faction of the Oneida on questions of land ownership.

and preaching, bold endeavors for women of the time, as well as a set of multifaceted practices of compassion and reconciliation that promoted social and economic justice through political action as part of a comprehensive Christian witness.

Formation and Commission

Dorothy Ripley "was born of religious parents" in Whitby, Yorkshire, England, on April 24, 1767.[17] Ripley's autobiography provides a detailed and lengthy account of her coming to faith and the religious experiences that culminated in her divine commission to evangelistic ministry.[18] *The Extraordinary Conversion* both interprets her past in light of her ministry and demonstrates that her formation and commission largely conformed to the expectations of the communities of faith from which she received that formation.[19] This section distills major themes of her formation in faith and her commission in order to theologically frame subsequent reflection upon her evangelistic ministry. The two most significant aspects of Ripley's faith formation were her father's influence and example, and the substantial grief and spiritual anxiety she sustained as a result of multiple losses suffered in adolescence and young adulthood.

Ripley greatly admired her father, Methodist preacher William Ripley (1739–1784), a man known for his hospitality to strangers and his compassion for the poor and outcast. William Ripley played at least two significant and related roles in Dorothy's formation and commission. First, he emerged as the subject of his daughter's hagiog-

---

[17] Ripley claimed April 24, 1767, as her date of birth in *The Extraordinary Conversion*, 7. See also P. W. Chilcote, *John Wesley and the Women Preachers of Early Methodism* (Metuchen, N.J.: Scarecrow, 1991), 276.

[18] According to S. Stanley's survey of literature in autobiographical studies, some scholars argue that autobiographies are largely fabricated and therefore fictional in character. Although attentive to the complexities of this argument, Stanley nuances her own position, acknowledging that "autobiographical theory and historical analysis overlap" (*Holy Boldness*, 24). For further discussion of the complexities of autobiography, particularly its subjectivity as self-interpretation, and reflection/response to culture and social performance, see D. Bjorklund, *Interpreting the Self: Two Hundred Years of American Autobiography* (Chicago: University of Chicago Press, 1998).

[19] Fredriksen, "Paul and Augustine," 33. While Stanley argues for the overlapping of autobiographical theory and historical analysis, Fredriksen and Gaventa both disagree, acknowledging the distinctions between autobiography and history. See Fredriksen, "Paul and Augustine," 34, and B. R. Gaventa, *From Darkness to Light: Aspects of Conversion in the New Testament* (Philadelphia: Fortress, 1986), 6–7, 146–47.

raphy. In the spirit of the early Christian tradition, Ripley wrote the life of her father as a virtuous example for imitation, particularly her own.[20] Second, Ripley's description of her father and his ministry serves as a hermeneutical key for understanding her coming to faith and acceptance of what she described as a divine commission to evangelistic ministry among the racially oppressed in America. Thus, William Ripley became a lens through which his daughter reinterpreted her own past (formation in faith) in light of her present (evangelistic ministry).[21]

Himself a religious outcast, William Ripley had been exiled from his home at nineteen by the Lord of Ingleby Manor for listening to John Wesley's preachers. But exile did not weaken William's faith; he built Whitby's first large Methodist meeting house, which he led for twenty years.[22] He also accompanied John Wesley on preaching tours in 1772 and 1784, pursuing the latter tour despite his wife's objections due to his ill health.[23] In correspondence with William Ripley, John Wesley expressed fondness for him; and after William's death, Wesley declared that he was "for many years a burning and a shining light."[24]

Ripley described her father as a virtuous example, the most like Jesus Christ she ever saw. She remembered her father rising every morning at four to read the Scriptures through once each year and instructing all his children in this practice. She claimed not to remember one day in which "my Father omitted calling his children, and

[20] See R. Wilken, *Remembering the Christian Past* (Grand Rapids: Eerdmans, 1995), 122, 127, 131–32. According to Wilken, "Of the several paths that lead to virtue, the broadest and the most obliging is the way of imitation. By observing the lives of holy men and women and imitating their deeds, we become virtuous" (121). Ripley's description of her father's ministry and his influence upon her commission and evangelistic ministry exemplifies Wilken's description of the rise of Christian hagiography by the early fourth century and its two characteristic features: (1) imitation as the path to virtue, and (2) subjects with whom the author was acquainted (127, 131–32). Westerhoff names "Role Models" as an important component, among many, for catechesis, which for him follows evangelism and evangelization. J. Westerhoff, "Evangelism, Evangelization, and Catechesis," *Interpretation* 48 (1994): 164.

[21] See A. Segal, *Paul the Convert: The Apostolate and Apostasy of Saul the Pharisee* (New Haven: Yale University Press, 1990), 296, and Gaventa, *From Darkness to Light*, 7.

[22] Ripley, *The Extraordinary Conversion*, 12.

[23] S. Rogal, "Ripley, William," in *A Biographical Dictionary of 18th-Century Methodism* (Lewiston, Md.: Edwin Mellen, 1997), 6:106–7.

[24] Rogal, "Ripley, William." See also John Wesley's journal entry on June 13, 1786, in *The Journal of the Rev. John Wesley, A.M.*, ed. N. Curnock (1916; repr., London: Epworth, 1938), 7:287.

servants together to worship in spirit, the Creator of the Universe."[25]
Her father led family devotions three times each day, "which appeared
to be done in the fear and love of God; love being his peculiar characteristic, whereby he was well known."[26] Such practices of family
devotion among Nonconformists in the late eighteenth and early
nineteenth centuries helped form and maintain serious Christian
belief and habits.[27]

In this deeply spiritual environment, Ripley's father encouraged
her vocation to a Christian preaching ministry, an unusual recommendation from parents, even within Methodist families of the time.
Although late eighteenth-century gender constructs allowed for the
audibility of single women's religious voices within the ecclesiastic as
well as the biological family,[28] the practice of female preaching was
unusual.[29] Deeply grieved by her father's death in 1784, Ripley
acknowledged his significant role in cultivating her emerging vocation as a preacher: "In my eighteenth year I had a severe trial to pass
through, which was the death of a pious father, who offered me to
God before I was born, to be a preacher of righteousness: and who
trained me up in the 'Fear of the Lord,' for his Kingdom."[30] In her
second volume, *The Bank of Faith and Works United*, Ripley included a
lengthy poem she composed that narrated her life and ministry. The
first stanzas of "A Hymn from my Nativity" describe her father and
his influence upon her vocation:

[25] Ripley, *The Extraordinary Conversion*, 13.

[26] Ripley, *The Extraordinary Conversion*, 13.

[27] L. Davidoff and C. Hall, *Family Fortunes: Men and Women of the Middle Class 1780–1850* (London: Hutchinson Education, 1987; repr., London: Routledge, 2002), 108. See also 107–48, for further discussion of the significance of family prayers within middle-class households and their role in the family's hierarchical structure.

[28] According to Davidoff and Hall, "That [religious] voice [for women] was primarily defined as being within the family, the audience of a married woman was her
own husband, children and servants; that of unmarried women their brothers,
nephews and fathers together with the family of the church" (*Family Fortunes*, 117–18).

[29] Z. Taft, *Biographical Sketches of the Lives and Public Ministry of Various Holy Women*, vols. 1 and 2 (London: Kershaw, Baynes & Son, 1826).

[30] Ripley, *The Extraordinary Conversion*, 12. According to Davidoff and Hall, "[T]heir female duties could only be overridden if there was certainty that they had been 'called.' The human sanction of the clerical father, husband or brother was usually necessary before the 'call' could be verified" (*Family Fortunes*, 125).

Before I was born, my father was priest,
And built to Christ Jesus, a house for the least,
To worship Jehovah, the True Living God,
Who gave us His favour, and Shed forth His Blood.
. . . .
My father gave me to his Gracious God,
From sin for to save, through His precious Blood,
Design'd me a preacher, before I was born,
And set me a teacher, to blow David's horn.[31]

However, it would be several years before Ripley would live into her vocation, beginning to preach at the age of twenty-four.

After her father's death, Ripley recollected the influence of his life and example upon her ministry: "Believing it his duty, he fed the hungry, clothed the naked, and so increased his treasure above, winning many souls to God by the merchandise of wisdom."[32] Following his example of religious devotion and care for the poor, her evangelistic ministry was inspired by Matthew 25:31-46, not sundering care for bodies and souls, but rather integrating preaching with ministry practices of presence and compassion. Ripley would, as her father had, find herself in a form of exile seemingly as a result of her faith commitments.

Eighteenth-century English women, faced with hardships such as illness, childbirth, and loveless marriages (contracted for financial and social security within a patriarchal society), often immersed themselves in intense religious devotion.[33] Interdependent dynamics of religious experience and emotional crisis repeatedly punctuated Ripley's formation in faith.[34] Shortly after her elder brother's death in 1782, which created intense spiritual anxiety, she emerged from the trauma and testified, "A living union was established with God, my heavenly Father." At this time Ripley prayed, asking for assurance of

[31] Ripley, *The Bank of Faith*, 7.

[32] Ripley, *The Extraordinary Conversion*, 13. Her father's care for the marginalized constituted another set of habits influential to Ripley's ministry. See Wilken, *Remembering the Christian Past*, 135.

[33] S. Gill, *Women and the Church of England: From the Eighteenth Century to the Present* (London: SPCK, 1994), 65. Gill explains that religion provided an essential comfort and distraction from social injustices inflicted upon women, who then pursued "a spirituality of almost masochistic self-martyrdom."

[34] While emotional or ecstatic experiences are not the only characteristics of conversion, according to Segal the conflict that facilitates an individual's conversion can come from anxiety related to doubt and stress (*Paul the Convert*, 292).

her salvation: "[I]lluminate my soul with the divine light that has dawned already upon it; and deign to be my Shepherd and leader through this rugged path, which I shall be led into for the proving of my faith, and perfecting me in the knowledge of those graces, which are the fruits of thy Spirit."[35] Ripley's reference to illumination echoed the Quaker emphasis on "inner light."[36] Her theological understandings, shaped by Wesleyan and Quaker themes, were often demonstrated in the descriptions of her many mystical visions.[37]

The unfolding of Ripley's commission and developing spiritual formation occurred in the midst of not just significant bereavement but other personal crises as well. After the deaths of her brother and beloved father, at the age of twenty-one Ripley suffered yet more tragedy: her family home was devastated by an earthquake: "[M]y mother lost all the property which she had, by a shock in the ground, which rent the foundation of the houses where we lived."[38] Whitby, a small port on the North Sea, sits perched along steep cliffs that line a relatively narrow river inlet. Based on Ripley's description of her father's Methodist meeting house and the small vicinity of the village in the late eighteenth century, her family's home at the time was most likely located on the south cliff, the steeper and more precarious setting of the older village below the ancient abbey and parish church. In retrospect, Ripley recorded her reflections in her spiritual autobiography, narrating this trauma as a cause for the deepening of her Christian faith: "Strong in the faith of Jesus Christ I appeared, having a hope of immortality, through the Redeemer's merit: so, that I bid adieu to all finite things, that is, I determined to take my Maker for my husband, and seek to build up a spiritual house for him hence-

[35] Ripley, *The Extraordinary Conversion*, 11.

[36] Interestingly, Wesley also referred to light in relation to faith in his sermon "Scripture Way of Salvation" (1765). See John Wesley, Sermon 43, "The Scripture Way of Salvation," in *Sermons II*, ed. A. Outler, vol. 2 of *The Bicentennial Edition of the Works of John Wesley* (Nashville: Abingdon, 1976), 152–69. See also R. Heitzenrater, *Wesley and the People Called Methodists* (Nashville: Abingdon, 1995), 220. Heitzenrater provides a comprehensive commentary on Wesley's *via salutis*. Many of the components are discussed in the pages that follow and in a section included in chap. 3.

[37] Although Stanley claims in the introduction to her study of Wesleyan/Holiness women's autobiographies that "visions did not play a major role in the spiritual lives of later Wesleyan/Holiness women," her study highlights several women for whom mystical visions did contribute significantly to their spiritual journey and vocation in a way similar to Ripley's. Unfortunately, Ripley's autobiography falls outside the bounds of Stanley's study (*Holy Boldness*, xxxii).

[38] Ripley, *The Extraordinary Conversion*, 15.

forward."[39] The losses of these years transformed her identity and focused her purpose.[40]

Ripley's commitment to faith in Christ and a life devoted to Christian practices of singleness and simplicity endured throughout her ministry. In light of gender constructs of the time, when women's dependence upon male relatives was expected and even necessary for survival, Ripley's losses, particularly her father's death and the destruction of her family home, contributed considerably to a sense of instability and chaos.[41] Her remarks, therefore, seem to demonstrate a shift from the typical single female's dependence upon her parents, particularly her father, to dependence upon God, her heavenly Father. This shift parallels the increased intensity in subsequent years of Ripley's mystical visions, visions that were not unusual among eighteenth-century Methodists.[42] These visions led to her commission to evangelistic ministry, which, while characterized by a single-minded dependence upon the divine, also grew into a profound autonomy from ecclesiastical structures.

Prior to accepting her commission to evangelistic ministry, Ripley suffered further bereavement and a life-threatening illness. Ripley's sister Mary died of consumption in 1788 after a three-year illness, which resulted in Ripley's subsequent illness and brush with death: "I was seized with a consumption, and brought nigh to the point of death by too great fatigue, having sat up with my dear sister Mary

[39] Ripley, *The Extraordinary Conversion*, 15–16.

[40] According to Segal, early studies acknowledge age, specifically youth, and pre-conversion feelings of unworthiness and self-doubt as indicative of the conversion process (*Paul the Convert*, 286–87). While Ripley does not fit neatly into the categories identified by Segal and Gaventa, her formation in faith seems most closely related to Gaventa's understanding of conversion as transformation. According to Gaventa (*From Darkness to Light*, 11), "a transformation involves a new perception, a re-cognition, of the past." Gaventa goes on to describe transformation in relation to Paul, "a more complex relationship between the believer's past and present . . . [in which] the past is not rejected but reinterpreted; it takes on a different meaning because of a new set of circumstances" (149).

[41] According to Davidoff and Hall, "If a man's ability to support and order his family and household lay at the heart of masculinity, then a woman's femininity was best expressed in her dependence. Dependence was at the core of the evangelical Christian view of womanhood, and the new female subject, constructed in real religious terms, was the godly wife and mother" (*Family Fortunes*, 114).

[42] D. W. Bebbington, *Evangelicalism in Modern Britain: A History from the 1730s to the 1980s* (London: Unwin Hyman, 1989), 38. Although John Wesley turned away from mysticism after 1736, Charles Wesley remained intrigued throughout his life. Some evangelicals were drawn to the mystical through William Law's later writings.

every other night, for some weeks previously to her departure out of this mutable state." In her spiritual autobiography, Ripley narrated this brush with death in the context of her vocation: "[D]eath tried his utmost power over me, to strike with awe my mind, knowing the Lord had chosen me to bear the joyful tidings of salvation to poor sinners."[43] Ripley explained that mystical visions calmed her anxiety and gave her hope for both her future evangelistic ministry and her heavenly reward. She heard God cry, "I am thy life! I am thy strength! I will restore. Arise and preach salvation unto fallen man beyond the seas, where poor Ethiopia's chains of darkness shall fall off."[44] Female preachers often claimed to receive their commissions encountering the divine in dreams, visions, and voices.[45] Ripley stated that she kept this emerging vocation to herself for seven years as she prepared to depart for the New World.

In the meantime, her bereavement was compounded in 1796 by the loss of another sibling after an acute illness of only one week—Ann was nineteen years old.[46] The depth of Ripley's grief now combined with doubt and anxiety for her own spiritual journey. As she grasped for divine comfort, Ripley experienced God's presence: "Astonished at this new salvation! . . . In silence, now I saw Jehovah by his Spirit, lay a new foundation of righteousness, and joy, and peace, which was my new Heaven, where the Father, Son, and Holy Ghost, were to dwell in perfect unison forever."[47] Ripley's description of this mystical vision seems to represent a second distinct work of faith demonstrating perhaps a learned interpretation of her experience conforming the narrative of her formation in faith to the Wesleyan tradition:[48] "On 28th, 2nd month, 1797, entering my room

---

[43] Ripley, *The Extraordinary Conversion*, 16. According to *Webster's New World Medical Dictionary* (2d ed., s.v. "consumption"), consumption is an older term used to describe the wasting away of the body, particularly from tuberculosis. A person suffering from tuberculosis seemed consumed by the disease.

[44] Ripley, *The Extraordinary Conversion*, 17.

[45] Brekus, *Strangers and Pilgrims*, 182. According to Brekus, while men's vocations to preach were often subtle, white women tended to receive their divine commissions to preach in dreams, and African American women more often encountered the divine in visions (183–85). For discussion of women's visions during eighteenth-century revivals see pp. 23, 41, 54, and 65, and for a discussion of women's visions during nineteenth-century revivals see pp. 145, 206, and 288.

[46] Ripley, *The Extraordinary Conversion*, 18.

[47] Ripley, *The Extraordinary Conversion*, 19.

[48] John Wesley, a strong influence upon Ripley's father, would most likely describe such an experience as one of entire sanctification related to Christian per-

to worship God, the power of God felled me to the earth, where I lay
as covered with his glorious Majesty, beholding as through his Spirit
the riches of his Kingdom 'Which God hath prepared for them that
love him' (I Cor. 2:9)."[49]

During the unfolding of this subsequent religious experience,
Ripley recounted attending the local Quaker meetings. Seeking the
comfort of Christian worship, and despite her father's Methodist leadership, she requested membership in the Society of Friends. However,
the meeting denied her request, possibly because of her "enthusiastic"
spirituality, characterized by dramatic mystical visions. While such
mystical visions were common among eighteenth-century English
Methodists, the Society of Friends only began to accept such evangelical influences in the mid-nineteenth century, before which they
maintained a form of quietism.[50] Ripley inquired, "If they could tell
me why they did not receive me?" But Quaker representatives replied,
"We cannot tell."[51] Such rejection did not, however, prevent Ripley
from accepting her divine commission. Against the background of her
deep grief and loss, the reluctance of the Society of Friends to accept
her seems to have contributed to her growing sense of autonomy from
ecclesiastical structures and to her continued dependence upon God
for her vocational direction.

In the immediate aftermath of the Whitby Quaker Meeting's
denial, Ripley narrated another vision, one that commissioned her
to an independent itinerant ministry: "In this situation, the Lord
commanded me to 'Go ten thousand miles,' to 'Provide neither gold
nor silver, neither two coats, neither shoes, nor yet a staff' (Matt.

---

fection. See Wesley, "Scripture Way of Salvation," *Sermons*, 153–69; and John
Wesley's compiled work on the topic, "A Plain Account of Christian Perfection," in
The Works of John Wesley (1872; repr., Grand Rapids: Zondervan, 1958–1959),
11:366–446. However, Ripley continued to seek God's pardon and peace in response
to her subsequent feelings of shortcoming, doubt, etc.

[49] Ripley, *The Extraordinary Conversion*, 19.

[50] See Bebbington, *Evangelicalism in Modern Britain*, 38, 71, 155–56. Another
possible reason for the denial may relate to the collective practice of discernment,
though mystical, of seeking the inner light through the guidance of the Holy Spirit.
Women, in particular, who experienced such discernment individually, confronted
the precarious situation of losing or not attaining the support of their meeting. See
S. M. Stuard, "Women's Witnessing: A New Departure," in *Witnesses for Change:
Quaker Women over Three Centuries*, eds. E. P. Brown and S. M. Stuard (New
Brunswick, N.J.: Rutgers University Press, 1989), 12.

[51] Ripley, *The Extraordinary Conversion*, 21. Ripley was most likely not alone in
this exclusion.

10:9-10)."[52] Directed by Jesus' ministry and teaching, Ripley remained faithful to this latter stipulation of her vocation, never permitting a collection to be taken on her behalf, thereby maintaining her dependence upon God.

Ripley's evangelistic ministry of preaching and compassion commenced after she received the following ultimate commission to ministry:

> Ethiopia's, or Africa's children, by oppressors were brought to till the ground for many of the American planters: therefore was I led thither by the unsearchable wisdom of their Creator, and mine, to exhort them with tears to 'Stretch out their hand, unto the Lord' (cf. Ps. 68:31) that they might find redress from a gracious God whose compassion fails not to any of the children of men.[53]

In 1801 Ripley finally stepped forward into this divine commission, departing from her home in Whitby to minister for the first time among enslaved Africans and slave owners in the United States: "[A]nd it sufficeth me to believe that [God] will soon cause the oppressors to cease their oppression; and reward with peace such who travail in Spirit for the spread of the gospel of our Lord Jesus Christ."[54] Forged through substantial suffering and loss, and influenced by her father's example, Ripley's formation in faith led to an evangelistic ministry that reached beyond merely itinerant verbal proclamation to a vision for addressing spiritual and physical oppression in the United States.

Neither Methodist nor Quaker?

Ripley boldly asserted her Christian faith, and despite her affinities with Methodists and Quakers, she was nearly as bold in her declarations that she maintained membership in no particular denomina-

---

[52] Ripley, *The Extraordinary Conversion*, 21. She received support for room, board, and passage only through the generosity of others.

[53] Ripley, *The Extraordinary Conversion*.

[54] Ripley, *The Extraordinary Conversion*, 37. Ripley remained steadfast to her unfolding commission to a remarkable evangelistic ministry among the marginalized in America. According to Segal, "One important aspect of the study of cognitive dissonance is the finding that the strength of the new belief structure will be directly proportional to the difficulty or strength of the conversion experience. The stronger and more difficult the conversion experience, the stronger and more difficult it will be to dissuade the beliefs held" (*Paul the Convert*, 298–99).

tional tradition. Although she connected with communities of faith, individuals, and families on her journeys, and despite the growing prominence of women's religious associations during the early decades of the nineteenth century,[55] Ripley's itinerant evangelistic ministry remained largely singular. In both her narrative volumes she made such a declaration at the outset. In *The Extraordinary Conversion*, she stated, "Should any make the enquiry, of what persuasion I am, they will find that I believe in Jesus Christ the true God. . . . But I am a member with no professing people."[56] Likewise in *The Bank of Faith and Works United*, she said, "As I am not a member of any community, no society can answer for my irregular conduct; neither do I wish to apologize to the world for my procedure; as I believe the Lord is my Shepherd, and Bishop of my soul."[57] But as she persisted in her itinerant evangelistic ministry, the lack of endorsement made more challenging an already difficult struggle for credibility.

Ripley attempted unsuccessfully on more than one occasion prior to her departure to the United States to secure membership and thus a certificate of endorsement from the Quaker meeting in Whitby.[58] Lacking such a credential, Ripley was frustrated and even persecuted in her evangelistic endeavors. However, according to her, this at no point hindered the effectiveness of her ministry since she understood her commission to be divinely given. Although the Methodists in the United States generally accepted Ripley's evangelistic ministry, including her preaching, she politely declined any formal affiliation,

[55] See N. Cott, *The Bonds of Womanhood: "Woman's Sphere" in New England, 1780–1835*, 2d ed. (New Haven: Yale University Press, 1997), 132–33. According to Cott, "This flowering of women's associational activities was part of the revival movement of the early nineteenth century in which Protestants tried to counteract religious indifference, rationalism, and Catholicism and to create an enduring and moral social order" (133). However, Cott also points out that while clergy contributed to the rhetoric of women's moral and religious responsibilities, their support for women's preaching and religious leadership remained largely theoretical (146–48, 157). See also Brekus, *Strangers and Pilgrims*, 125–31.

[56] Ripley, *The Extraordinary Conversion*, 4.

[57] Ripley, *The Bank of Faith*, 4.

[58] For example, Ripley, *The Bank of Faith*, 20, 26, 28, 32–34, 37–38, 41, 44, 53, 56, 71; see also Ripley, *The Extraordinary Conversion*, 33, 53, 98. While there remains much room for further study of women and conversion, particularly related to crises and/or trauma, an interesting contemporary study examines women and deconversion. See J. Jacobs, "The Economy of Love in Religious Commitment: The Deconversion of Women from Nontraditional Religious Movements," *Journal for the Scientific Study of Religion* 23 (1984): 155–71.

thereby maintaining openness to the Society of Friends.[59] Upon returning from her first voyage to the United States, Ripley visited Quaker acquaintances, who greeted her with disappointment: "We are glad to see thee, to bring tidings of thyself. Dost thou still attend Friends' meetings, and continue to believe with us? For news was sent from Ann Thomson that thou hadst left Friends, and gone amongst the Methodists." To this Ripley replied, "I trust I shall never leave them. . . . I have no intention of joining the Methodists, but I believe it my duty to appoint meetings with them when I can have liberty to follow the leadings of the Spirit, it being the infallible Guide of my life."[60] She later admitted, "I had told the people, that I was not a member of any Society, although I professed with the Friends, to be a Quaker in sentiment."[61]

Ripley did not leave a clear explanation for her allegiance to the Society of Friends rather than remaining with the Methodists, to whom her father had adhered.[62] On one issue important to Ripley— slavery—Methodists and Quakers held strong and similar positions. From 1743, John Wesley demonstrated his opposition to slavery through a statement, included in the General Rules for the United Societies, in which he prohibited "the buying or selling the bodies and souls of men, women, and children, with an intention to enslave them."[63] Wesley recorded in his journal that he had read a book by

[59] Ripley, *The Extraordinary Conversion*, 117–18.

[60] Ripley, *The Extraordinary Conversion*, 151–52.

[61] Ripley, *The Bank of Faith*, 61. According to Stuard, women who felt empowered to lead ministry efforts and reform outside the Quaker meeting faced painful choices: "The Quaker meeting had supplied women a supportive environment for hearing a call to witness, but if that witnessing led a woman out of meeting, the group whose presence had been so significant for the calling no longer served for support. For that reason many leaders among women may be called only Quaker-related because they ceased, for their own or their meetings' reasons, being members of the Society of Friends" ("Women's Witnessing," 21).

[62] A significantly higher number of single as compared with married women participated in English Methodist religious societies during the eighteenth century. While male membership within religious societies may have contributed to a "settling down," for single women, participation in Methodist religious societies was an assertion of independence distinct from the responsibilities of marriage and family. See G. Malmgreen, "Domestic Discords: Women and the Family in East Cheshire Methodism, 1750–1839," in *Disciplines of Faith: Studies in Religion, Politics and Patriarchy*, ed. J. Obelkevich et al. (London: Routledge/Kegan Paul, 1987), 55–70.

[63] John Wesley, quoted in D. Mathews, *Slavery and Methodism: A Chapter in American Morality 1780–1845* (Princeton: Princeton University Press, 1965; repr., Westport, Conn.: Greenwood Press, 1978), 5–6.

Anthony Benezet, "an honest [American] Quaker, on that execrable sum of all villanies [*sic*], commonly called the Slave-trade."[64] Wesley also wrote on the subject in 1774, *Thoughts Upon Slavery*, outlining his opposition to the practice, and the last letter Wesley penned was to British antislavery leader William Wilberforce, expressing his support: "O be not weary of well doing! Go on, in the name of God and in the power of His might, till even American slavery (the vilest that ever saw the sun) shall vanish away before it."[65] Early American Methodism also opposed slavery.[66] Francis Asbury led the emerging denomination to take a strong position against slavery at the historic "Christmas Conference" in 1784, which included its denouncement that slavery was "contrary to the golden law of God . . . and the inalienable rights of mankind."[67] In similar fashion, the founder of the Society of Friends, George Fox, adamantly opposed slavery. By 1830 Quakers shared this stance throughout the movement in England and the United States, the latter in large part due to the efforts of John Woolman.[68]

---

[64] John Wesley, quoted in L. Purifoy, "The Methodist Anti-Slavery Tradition, 1784–1844," in *Abolitionism and American Religion*, ed. J. McKivigan (New York: Garland, 1999), 27.

[65] John Wesley to William Wilberforce, February 24, 1791, *The Letters of the Rev. John Wesley, A.M.*, ed. J. Telford (London: Epworth, 1931), 8:265. However, some scholars critique Wesley's relatively minimal attention to the cause, and the foundation of his argument in natural philosophy rather than Scripture.

[66] According to Strong, "For [Freeborn] Garrettson (like Wesley before him), a real Christian was one who was converted to Christ; and, since conversion necessarily implied disengagement from the sin of slavery, then, according to Garrettson, a real Christian was also an abolitionist. Many other Methodists in the revolutionary period, steeped in the democratic idiom of the day, linked the Wesleyan understanding of conversion directly to their commitment to abolition." However, this position eroded: "A number of historians have offered explanations for the abandonment of abolitionist standards among antebellum American Methodists. They note that the rise of sectionalism and the desire to expand the church in the South caused denominational leaders to surrender the church's antislavery principles" ("A Real Christian Is an Abolitionist," 72).

[67] See Purifoy, "The Methodist Anti-Slavery Tradition, 1784–1844," 27ff. Additional requirements were adopted by the 1784 conference: all members were required to free their slaves within twelve months or a prescribed period, and pastors were to keep a record of slaveholding members to enforce the requirement. In 1780 and 1783, respectively, traveling pastors and local pastors were forbidden to own slaves. Methodist Episcopal Church, *Minutes of the Annual Conference (1780)*, 12, and (1783), 18. Mathews's appendix in *Slavery and Methodism*, 293–303, includes "Methodist Rules Concerning Slavery from 1789–1844."

[68] For examples of antislavery positions among Quakers, see J. W. Frost, ed., *The*

While Ripley's antislavery views were in step with both Quakers and Methodists, the ambiguity of her denominational affiliation may relate to the issue of female preaching. Quaker women preached as early as the seventeenth century when public expression was broadly denied to women outside the royal family.[69] But the situation of women preachers in Methodism, a renewal movement within the Church of England, was not so progressive in Ripley's time. From the early years of John Wesley's renewal movement in Britain, women were granted numerous ministry opportunities as class leader, steward, and visitor of the sick. In the later years of Wesley's leadership, women with vocations to preach that were accompanied by ministries of fruit were permitted and even encouraged by Wesley. Although Wesley at no point sanctioned female preaching categorically, he was open to specific cases that followed the qualifications of call and fruits. As the movement matured into the second half of the eighteenth century, Wesley cultivated a growing number of Methodist women for leadership, including preachers.[70] However, following his death in 1791, controversy erupted around a number of volatile issues, includ-

---

Quaker Origins of Antislavery (Norwood, Pa.: Norwood Editions, 1980), an instructive collection of primary sources dating from George Fox's *Gospel Family-Order* (1676) to the Philadelphia Yearly Meeting *Minutes* (1796). For early British Methodist antislavery responses, see J. Wesley, *Thoughts Upon Slavery* (London: R. Hawes, 1774) and "Letter to William Wilberforce" (February 24, 1791), *Letters of Wesley*. In the United States, see E. Clark, ed., *The Journal and Letters of Francis Asbury* (London: Epworth, 1958), 1:25, 441; and F. Garrettson, *A Dialogue Between Do-Justice and Professing Christian* (Wilmington, Del.: Peter Brynberg, 1805). For a discussion of slavery and Methodism in America, see Mathews, *Slavery and Methodism*.

[69] See Stuard, "Women's Witnessing," 3. Margaret Fell (1614–1702), wife of Quaker founder George Fox (1624–1691), and Fox both argued for women's full equality within the community of faith. Fell wrote *Women's Speaking Justified*, most likely published in 1666; Early in his ministry, Fox wrote *Concerning Sons and Daughters, and Prophetesses Speaking and Prophesying in the Law and the Gospel*. See chapter 2 for further discussion of women and slavery among the Society of Friends in nineteenth-century America and implications for evangelism.

[70] E. D. Graham is a helpful resource in this area. In addition to "Chosen by God: The Female Itinerants of Early Primitive Methodism" (Ph.D. diss., University of Birmingham, 1987) see also idem, "Chosen by God: A List of the Female Travelling [*sic*] Preachers of Early Primitive Methodism," *Wesley Historical Society* (North Lodge, UK: Bankhead, 1989); idem, "Women Local Preachers," in *Workaday Preachers: The Story of Methodist Local Preaching*, eds. Geoffrey Milburn and Margaret Batty (Petersborough, UK: Methodist Publishing House, 1995); and a revision of the latter, idem, "Methodist Women Local Preachers," *Wesley Historical Society Proceedings* (New Zealand), 68 (1999).

ing female preaching, as Wesley's successors struggled to assume the movement's leadership. The 1803 English Wesleyan Methodist Conference formally terminated female preaching (a suspension that lasted for approximately a century), resulting in the voluntary and forced exile of women committed to fulfilling their preaching vocations.[71] The situation was only a little better in American Methodist denominations. With the strongest resistance in the South, occasionally clergy and congregations in the North advocated for and extended hospitality to particular female preachers in the early decades of the nineteenth century.[72]

Although, as mentioned above, Ripley claimed that Methodists expressed openness to her preaching ministry, she most likely experienced forms of opposition. While some submitted in silence during this period, many women called to preach found their way to the Society of Friends and Methodist-related traditions such as the Bible Christians and Primitive Methodists.[73] Between 1700 and 1800 there were over one thousand women ministers active in the transatlantic Quaker community.[74] Additionally, during the eighteenth century at least forty-two Quaker women from America visited Quaker meetings in England.[75]

Ripley's allegiance to the Quakers, who broadly welcomed her preaching gift, would persist, though she never turned her back on her Methodist heritage. She seemed to settle on autonomy: "I am a member with no professing people, neither is any answerable for my conduct, should I differ in sentiment from others—Why I am not joined to any sect is, because the Lord hath led me forth by his spirit, to subject my will."[76]

Theological Frame

Despite her autonomy, Ripley's theological foundations were strongly influenced by Wesleyan themes. Most likely as a result of her father's example and teaching, Ripley's understanding of conversion resonated

[71] D. Valenze, *Prophetic Sons and Daughters: Female Preaching and Popular Religion in Industrial England* (Princeton: Princeton University Press, 1985), 55, 91–93.

[72] Brekus, *Strangers and Pilgrims*, 132–34.

[73] Chilcote, *John Wesley and the Women Preachers*, 232–37; see also Taft, *Biographical Sketches*.

[74] See Stanley, *Holy Boldness*, 51.

[75] See Brekus, *Strangers and Pilgrims*, 75–76.

[76] Ripley, *The Extraordinary Conversion*, 4.

with the teachings of John Wesley. Framed by an Arminian emphasis upon universal atonement, Ripley understood her ministry as a faithful response to her commission, which grew largely from Wesleyan doctrinal foundations of justification and sanctification.

Conversion for Wesley consisted namely of two doctrines: *justification*, what God does *for* persons, which includes an Arminian emphasis upon universal atonement and assurance of one's salvation; and *sanctification*, what God does *in* persons, with its implications for holy living that included faithful Christian practices (an antidote to nominal Christianity).[77] Upon meeting Bishops Francis Asbury and Richard Whatcoat at the Methodist Episcopal Conference in Baltimore in 1802, Ripley testified to both her justification and sanctification:[78]

> Being left alone with the two Methodist Bishops, a solemn awe covered my mind while we remained silent for the space of five minutes, and then Bishop Asbury, asked me those important questions, "Were you ever justified?" replying Yes, he said, "Are you justified now?" to which I again said Yes, then he simply enquired, "Were you ever sanctified?" answering as before Yes, he brought the matter closer, by adding "Are you sanctified now?" Being called upon to make this confession in the presence of God, and in the midst of two good judges of Israel, I said as follows. My body is the temple of the Living God, which sufficed the good old veterans, almost worn out in the vineyard of our Lord.[79]

[77] See Wesley, "Scripture Way of Salvation," 153–69. While Wesley identified himself as an Arminian, according to Maddox his reading of Arminius was limited. Wesley's "Arminianism" was less related to Calvinist distinctions than to an English tradition "that affirmed a role for human co-operation in salvation." R. Maddox, *Responsible Grace: John Wesley's Practical Theology* (Nashville: Kingswood, 1994), 90. See also Jones, *The Evangelistic Love of God and Neighbor*, 41–42. According to Jones, "One of the crucial dimensions of this view of God's gracious activity is that it has been and is being offered to every human being," (41).

[78] According to Heitzenrater, "For Wesley, justification and sanctification were both necessary parts of the daily drama of salvation. And the exercise of 'faith working through love' meant not simply love of God but also love of neighbor, works of piety and also works of mercy. And just as Wesley would point out to the Calvinists that faith itself is made possible by grace, so also he would stress that these works are made possible by grace. Wesleyan theology is a thoroughgoing theology of grace" (*Wesley and the People*, 320). See also chap. 3 for further discussion of the Wesleyan doctrines of justification and sanctification. See also Maddox, *Responsible Grace*, 157–90.

[79] Ripley, *The Extraordinary Conversion*, 118. Asbury continued the interview, asking Ripley, "'I suppose you travel without money?' feeling thankful to my bountiful

   This doctrinal foundation informed her evangelistic theology and practice: "Before the Lord sent me forth to preach the gospel he testified by his Spirit, that he would keep me unto the day of redemption: and gave me faith to believe that I should stand firm in Jesus Christ a new creature, being clothed upon with his imparted righteousness, 'The saints pure white linnen [*sic*]' (cf. Rev. 15:6)."[80] Here, Ripley acknowledged that sanctification through Christ's righteousness preceded her vocation to preach and was foundational to her evangelistic ministry.

Universal Atonement

The Wesleyan emphasis upon an Arminian theme of universal atonement guided Ripley's multifaceted evangelistic ministry.[81] Wesley's ministry and teaching generally opposed Calvinist emphases following the Synod of Dort, emphases that included predestination and irresistible grace. He taught instead that Christians can choose to participate in determining their eternal fate. While one cannot *earn* salvation through good works, since salvation by faith alone or justification precedes sanctification and holy living, one can *choose* to receive salvation, which is then demonstrated in good works that are the fruits of one's salvation.[82] For Wesley, universal atonement (as opposed to a Calvinist emphasis upon limited atonement) emerged as a formative theological foundation that framed the renewal movement he led within the Church of England.[83]

   The distinctive practices of the early Methodist movement included field preaching, lay leadership including women, and small groups for ministry among those responding to the preaching, including marginalized individuals such as laborers, imprisoned, and the

---

Father, I answered, No, I never am without money." Whatcoat then volunteered that they held "all things common here!" (119).

   [80] Ripley, *The Extraordinary Conversion*, 24.

   [81] See Heitzenrater, *Wesley and the People*, for an introduction to Jacob Arminius (including the Synod of Dort), 11–12, 268, and Arminianism, 11–12, 17–19, 240–42 related to Wesleyan/Methodist traditions.

   [82] See D. W. Bebbington, "Holiness in the Evangelical Tradition," in *Holiness Past and Present*, ed. S. Barton (London: T&T Clark, 2003), 299–301, 305–8; see also 302–5 for a discussion of Reformed (or Calvinist) Holiness in comparison.

   [83] Maddox, *Responsible Grace*, 87. For a discussion of Wesley's doctrinal emphases particularly related to Wesley's anthropology and understanding of restoring grace, see 65–90, and the universality of grace, 87–90.

infirm. These practices led to a number of missional efforts that advocated for social and economic justice, such as abolition. Such activism, both for the spiritual conversion and physical plight of all persons, was more apparent among the Methodists than other eighteenth-century participants in British evangelicalism.[84] Although English Wesleyan Methodists would not establish a foreign mission society until 1813, Wesley's—and Ripley's—evangelistic aims coincided with the late eighteenth century's increased emphasis upon the gospel mandate of the Great Commission in Matthew 28.[85]

The doctrine of free choice guided Ripley's evangelistic ministry, offering salvation to all: "Yea and the excellent God, will delight himself with the least of his saints, who love him through choice, and not of necessity."[86] Ripley's own choice to repent and receive God's forgiveness grounded her ministry in such a way that the love of God could not be limited:

> It is my choice to serve the eternal I AM, because he is infinitely good, and gracious, full of wisdom, and full of compassion to all nations without respect of persons, if I believe "Jesus Christ tasted death for every man" (cf. Heb. 2:9) and surely I must believe this, if I believe he died at all; or died for me the chief of sinners. Did men consider that the very name and nature of God is love! love to all the fallen race, this would prove an incitement to them to return to the great and glorious Parent.[87]

Just as Christ died for her, Ripley understood that God's goodness, grace, wisdom, and compassion were extended "to all nations,"

---

[84] Bebbington, *Evangelicalism in Modern Britain*, 41, 52. For Bebbington's study, Quakers were not included among the evangelical Dissent. Bebbington supports the claims that Wesley's "beliefs in religious tolerance, freewill and antislavery have rightly been identified as Enlightenment affinities" (52).

[85] Bebbington, *Evangelicalism in Modern Britain*, 40–42. The Great Commission was not given any "expository comment in the Geneva Bible that was widely used among English-speaking Protestants of the seventeenth century" 40–41. Cotton Mather notes the "scandal" of this omission in the early eighteenth century, though William Carey seems to make the stronger case for the continued binding of the text upon Christian disciples in his *An Enquiry into the Obligation of Christians to Use Means for the Conversion of the Heathen*, published in 1792. According to Bebbington, "The new breed of Evangelicals practiced what they preached" (*Evangelicalism in Modern Britain*, 41). For additional discussion on the history of interpretation related to Matthew 28, see also D. Bosch, "The Structure of Mission: An Exposition of Matt. 28:16-21," in *Exploring Church Growth*, ed. W. Shenk (Grand Rapids: Eerdmans, 1983).

[86] Ripley, *The Extraordinary Conversion*, 24.

[87] Ripley, *The Extraordinary Conversion*, 24

thus supporting her ministry that reached to slaves and slave owners: "The Spirit of the Lord groaned in me for the redemption of master and servants, which are all equal in his sight, and I do earnestly intreat [*sic*] the God of all grace to follow them each with his convicting love . . . that [they may be] clothed upon with the covering of Jesus Christ's righteousness, who cancels the debt of every enormous sinner that sincerely repents."[88]

Despite the accessibility of salvation for all, Ripley decried the nominal acceptance of Christianity by many. In her opinion, this tepid faith demonstrated continuing evidence of human depravity:

> If I mourn at all, it is on account of the depravity of the world, which appears more wicked than ever. . . . Going from city to city, from one nation to another, [I have] discovered the iniquity that lurks under the various masks of professing godliness . . . but Alas! when I seek for pious souls redeemed from the maxims and fashions of the present day, I almost seek in vain, and ask if there are any who live now as Jesus Christ taught his followers in the days of his flesh, both by his example and precept?[89]

Ripley recognized the need to cultivate this life of faith in herself and others after the "example and precept" of Jesus Christ because such a life would facilitate the blessings of salvation and avoid the dangers of nominal Christianity.

This theological framework and the teaching and example of Jesus Christ for faithful practices of love to God and neighbor structured Ripley's ministry: "If we are desirous to know the true God, and to have his divine favor, we must attend to his precepts, and strive to imitate the pattern of living faith, which is an example for rich and poor to conform their lives unto—then we shall believe with our hearts unto righteousness, and shew forth his love to the children of

---

[88] Ripley, *The Extraordinary Conversion*, 26; 88. This statement provides another example of the interdependence of Ripley's faith with her evangelistic ministry. Jones echoes this dynamic: "It is instructive, however, that in [William] Abraham's discussion of the moral aspect of initiation, no mention is made of how Christians themselves have the responsibility of being active participants in the evangelistic process. While different persons will have different gifts and thus play different roles in the process, all Christians are expected to share their faith verbally with others" (*Evangelistic Love*, 74).

[89] Ripley, *The Extraordinary Conversion*, 23. Ripley seemed to resonate with Jones's claims: "Discipleship involves conversion, a new moral orientation, the reception of spiritual gifts, and the practice of spiritual disciplines" (*Evangelistic Love*, 72).

men without partiality."[90] Ripley pointed to Jesus as the example to which faithful Christian disciples should aspire, particularly those who suffer or benefit from the sinful system of slavery:

> [A]ll the stubborn who are in nature unlike Jesus Christ, who was meek and lowly in heart. I mourn; I sigh; and water my pillow night by night, while I pass along this desert land, where thousands are toiling to support luxury and haughtiness of spirit. . . . [L]et it suffice me then that my labours shall not be in vain, and let me also remember how many years of sorrow my Lord and Saviour Jesus Christ endured before he opened his Gospel-mission, and proclaimed liberty to the captive souls. O that my faith may increase for this purpose! That my love to the indigent may not be suppressed; neither, a weariness in the spirit or in the flesh impede the work of salvation, that is even now compleating [sic] by the eternal Spirit, who is working in me and many others, whom he appointeth to work in this land for the redemption of his creatures.[91]

In this passage Ripley contrasted the example of Jesus Christ with the plight of oppressed slaves exploited for economic benefit by their owners. Ripley then characterized salvation by referring to Jesus' example, specifically his "Gospel-mission" in which he proclaimed "liberty to captive souls," an allusion to the biblical concept of jubilee.[92] Finally, Ripley grounded her evangelistic ministry—inviting others to receive salvation—in her own religious experience.

[90] Ripley, *The Extraordinary Conversion*, 4. For Jones, to evangelize is to love: "To evangelize non-Christian persons without loving them fully is not to evangelize them well. To love non-Christian persons without evangelizing them is not to love them well. Loving God well means loving one's non-Christian neighbor evangelistically and evangelizing one's non-Christian neighbor lovingly" (*Evangelistic Love*, 21).

[91] Ripley, *The Extraordinary Conversion*, 81. While Ripley did not employ the language of kingdom or reign of God as in recent studies in evangelism, her reference to Jesus' "Gospel-mission" evokes similar imagery. William Abraham's use of this concept and imagery is among the most helpful for understanding a theologically astute evangelism: "Evangelism should be housed very firmly within the dynamic rule of God on earth" (*The Logic of Evangelism*, 18). Abraham nuances his position: "By restoring the inner logic of God's action as it embraces past, present, and future, we can build on their insights without embracing their costly errors. God's reign has begun; he has come in Jesus to bring judgment and liberation; he comes repeatedly in history in salvation and discipline; his rule is within reach of both individuals and nations; we can now enter into its penultimate inauguration as we strive toward its full and final consummation" (34).

[92] For a discussion of the theological and ethical implications of the jubilee, see J. H. Yoder, *The Politics of Jesus: Vicit Agnus Noster* (Grand Rapids: Eerdmans, 1972), 64–77. For implications of the jubilee to evangelism specifically, see Arias and Johnson, *The Great Commission*, 56–77.

Ripley regularly called upon the teaching and example of Jesus Christ to inform her ministry: "My earnest supplications are treasured up in Heaven for them, and I know my labour was not in vain in the Lord, in behalf of individuals, who will praise God and the Lamb with me, in the Kingdom of Glory, when Jesus Christ shall say, 'I was sick, and ye visited me; I was in prison, and ye came unto me.' "[91] Ripley referred to Matthew 25:31-46, echoing her father's ministry, a ministry characterized by Christ-like compassion for the outcast. Practices of compassion, after the example of Jesus Christ, took on evangelistic import in Ripley's ministry for the redemption of sin, both individual and systemic: "We were made to love each other; not despise: to help and succour one another; not to defraud and neglect in time of distress, poverty, sickness, temptation, or any calamity, which follow all in this mutable state, through the curse that remains in the world."[92]

Economic Implications

A multidimensional understanding of salvation guided Ripley's evangelistic ministry, an understanding that refused to separate conversion from social and material condition. This led her to take seriously the economic implications of the teaching and example of Jesus Christ. While her sensitivities and commitments adhered to those of other evangelicals in the nineteenth century,[93] she often set a bold and provocative standard.

As mentioned earlier, Ripley understood her divine commission to require simplicity of life similar to John Wesley's. Although Wesley accepted collections, he did so on behalf of the poor, setting a vigorous

[91] Ripley, *The Bank of Faith*, 61. Interestingly, Ripley and other women in this study turn to the example of Jesus Christ rather than the apostle Paul to inform their evangelistic ministries.

[92] Ripley, *The Bank of Faith*, 201. Consistent in her echo of Wesleyan doctrinal themes, particularly related to sanctification, Ripley also resonated with Wesley's concept of a "real Christian" (*The Extraordinary Conversion*, 26).

[93] For helpful historical analysis of benevolence in England and the British Isles, see K. Heasman, *Evangelicals in Action: An Appraisal of Their Social Work in the Victorian Era* (London: Geoffrey Bles, 1962), and F. K. Prochaska, *Women and Philanthropy in Nineteenth-Century England* (New York: Oxford University Press, 1980); in America, see L. Ginzberg, *Women and the Work of Benevolence: Morality, Politics, and Class in the Nineteenth-Century United States* (New Haven Yale University Press, 1990), and A. F. Scott, *Natural Allies: Women's Associations in American History* (Urbana: University of Illinois Press, 1991).

example for the Methodist connexion to care for the whole needs of its constituents. Affluent by birth, and financially successful through stipends and publishing royalties, Wesley shared his wealth with others, accomplishing his goal of dying with minimal, if any, resources.[94] Ripley not only professed simplicity, but strove to embody her message: "The easiest way to live, and die, is to possess little in time, and much in eternity."[95] Although a difficult path, Ripley committed herself in faithful expectation that God would provide for her passage and needs.[96] Indeed, she considered her reliance on God to be a spiritual discipline: "When I am convinced it is right for me to move from one place to another, I do not say, Lord, how shall I get there, having no money? but in Faith, I believe I shall reach there; and so a way always opens for me to pass along, that I may faithfully fulfill the Lord's appointments."[97] Such obedience to God enabled her to persist in witnessing to faithful Christian practices that included wealth-sharing.[98]

Ripley understood the economic implications of the Christian gospel and its inevitable connection to an evangelistic witness.[99] A significant component of Ripley's evangelistic ministry—her antislavery work—is highlighted in her criticism of the accumulation of wealth:

> Perhaps there was never greater need to testify of the power of God than in this day; because the people require as it were, signs and wonders, to convince them that Jesus Christ has verily died for the

[94] For further discussion, see Heitzenrater, *Wesley and the People*; T. Jennings, *Good News to the Poor: John Wesley's Evangelical Economics* (Nashville: Abingdon, 1990); M. D. Meeks, ed., *Portion of the Poor* (Nashville: Kingswood Books, 1995); and R. Heitzenrater, ed., *The Poor and the People Called Methodists* (Nashville: Kingswood Books, 2002).

[95] Ripley, ed., *Letters*, 50. In a letter to William Ripley, Wesley wrote, "If you increase in substance, you are in great danger of decreasing in grace. . . . To prevent worldly-mindedness be as much employed in the work of God as you possibly can." See John Wesley's letter to William Ripley from Westminster, November 13, 1777, *Letters of Wesley*, 287–88.

[96] Ripley, *The Bank of Faith*, 35. According to Brekus, "By the late eighteenth century, the Quakers [in America] had matured from a radical sect into a prosperous, middle-class, and politically powerful denomination, resulting in their ability to extend hospitality to itinerant ministers such as Ripley" (*Strangers and Pilgrims*, 76).

[97] Ripley, *The Bank of Faith*, 145.

[98] Ripley, *The Bank of Faith*, 45.

[99] Ripley, ed., *Letters*, v: "I have been unjustly censured in this quarter of the world for preaching the gospel of our Lord Jesus Christ for hire. I deny the charge, having never suffered a public collection to be made in any religious meeting I have held in England. Trusting to the rich beneficence of my inward Teacher, his everlasting love hath not left me once destitute of silver."

sins of all nations, to restore them to the favour and image of their
Maker. Why there is so little piety amongst professing christians
[*sic*] I know not, except that their hearts dwell too much upon their
earthly treasure, which they are striving to increase contrary to the
express command of Jesus Christ.[100]

She confidently named the sinful economic implications of slavery that
emerged, in her opinion, through nominal Christianity. For Ripley,
some of the most egregious aspects of nominal Christianity were
demonstrated by the exploitation of slaves by owners. She was painfully
mindful of the economic underpinnings of the system of slavery:

> We returned back this day, and I felt satisfied in my mind that I had
> a peaceable residence to come to, where those friends have freed all
> their slaves, which I think will prove a blessing to their dear chil-
> dren, and I hope the Lord will bestow on them his riches, which are
> unspeakable, and that tranquility which is the result of obedience
> and a compensation for surrendering up that which Jehovah calls
> for at our hands, even contrary to our present interest as we suppose
> for a season. How hard is it to lay aside our interest for the good of
> others, yet how noble in the eyes of God it appears, and how much
> is it like the blessed Redeemer.[101]

Ripley employed biblical imagery, including Jesus' example, in her
theological response to the evils of slavery. She directly connected
obedience to Jesus with the faithful practices of those owners who
freed their slaves. For Ripley, Christian discipleship included practices
shaped not only by the implications of individual sins, but by an
understanding of the systemic implications of those sins.

Within the context of slavery enabled by nominal Christianity,
Ripley pursued her vocation to an evangelistic ministry that reached
beyond the familiar practice of preaching to a more complex witness.
Her ministries were not only of compassion but also of social and

[100] Ripley, *The Extraordinary Conversion*, 3–4.

[101] Ripley, *The Extraordinary Conversion*, 88. See also Ripley's evangelistic conversation with another family of slave owners: "I ventured to inquire of my friend
how many slaves he owned, but he said, 'I do not know the number,' answering, it is
a pity thou shouldst be a possessor of slaves. He appeared pleased at my freedom, and
was willing that I should take liberty in addressing him, bearing with me patiently,
while I endeavored to shew the injustice and base consequences that attended slavery.
I parted with this family in peace, desiring in my mind that they, and their children
might be brought to the knowledge of the true God, which will teach them to deny
themselves of the pomp, and vanity of this world" (110–11).

political action that addressed the socioeconomic implications of systemic sin:

> I hope that my life will speak this to honor the name of Jesus which is despised through deistical principles spread abroad every where, and by the conduct of fruitless professors who dishonor the Lord and prevent many thousands coming at the Truth; for they stumble by reason of not knowing the way, looking at others for an example who perhaps have an appearance of Truth, yet destitute of the power of godliness.[102]

Without a Christian community to endorse her, Ripley claimed her autonomy and prophetic voice, depending upon divine support and guidance. Influenced by both Quaker and Wesleyan faith commitments, her theological emphases, framed by universal atonement, seemed to resonate strongly with Wesleyan themes. Ripley grounded her evangelistic ministry in her own faith and salvation. Her ministry, structured after the example and teaching of Jesus Christ, took seriously the gospel mandate to love one another and did not neglect the economic implications of that mandate. The final section focuses upon Ripley's evangelistic ministry in the United States, particularly among the enslaved and their owners. Her example provides a significant contribution to the contemporary discourse on evangelistic theology and practice that in its desire to increase church membership often stops short of a faithful, comprehensive embodiment of the gospel.

Evangelistic Ministry

From the age of twelve, Ripley described an unfolding divine commission to minister among enslaved Africans in America. Although her vocation expanded to address the spiritual and physical well-being of additional constituencies, Ripley maintained this focus throughout her ministry despite growing danger for antislavery supporters. As previously mentioned, Ripley practiced her evangelistic ministry prior to the organization of the American Anti-Slavery Society in 1833. By the 1830s, speaking publicly against slavery in the American South had grown nearly impossible, often provoking imprisonment and even violence.[103] In spite of such danger, Ripley, most often traveling

---

[102] Ripley, *The Extraordinary Conversion*, 89.

[103] P. Harvey, "The Christian Doctrine of Slavery," in *Religions of the U.S. in Practice*, ed. C. McDannell, Princeton Readings in Religions 1 (Princeton: Princeton University Press, 2001), 466. According to Harvey, by the 1820s attempted and exe-

alone, relied upon divine authority for her ministry. She witnessed to the contradiction between the violent oppression of slavery and the message of the gospel, identifying the fundamental disconnect of spiritual conversion from the actual living conditions of individuals and communities.[104]

Faithful to her theological roots—that is, God's love and salvation available to all after the example of Jesus Christ—Ripley's ministry addressed both the powerful and powerless. Although her evangelistic travels in the United States commenced with her efforts to gain an audience with President Jefferson, the following section first briefly examines the precarious social and theological background of enslaved Africans and their owners.[105]

Ripley's commitment to evangelistic political action, while remarkably courageous, seems characteristic of British Evangelicalism of the time. Though not innovative in its contributions to the antislavery movement, Evangelicalism demonstrated a persistent dedication that strongly influenced public opinion.[106] The British slave trade was abolished in 1807 and dismantled formally in 1833 as a result of

---

cuted slave revolts resulted in substantial limits upon free speech in the American South.

[104] Ripley's bold evangelistic ministry exemplified Cott's claim: "Yet religious identity also allowed women to assert themselves, both in private and in public ways. It enabled them to rely on an authority beyond the world of men and provided a crucial support to those who stepped beyond accepted bounds—reformers, for example" (*Bonds of Womanhood*, 140).

[105] Ripley's evangelistic ministry also exemplified Lesslie Newbigin's claim: "But [the church] must also recognize that its own ethical perceptions are limited and blurred by its own sinful self-interest. In preaching Christ it will certainly make clear (perhaps more effectively by example than by word) that conversion will have ethical implications. But it must also be ready to be surprised by the fresh insights of the converts into the ethical implications of the gospel and must expect to have to revise and correct its own patterns of obedience" (*The Open Secret: An Introduction to the Theology of Mission*, rev. ed. [Grand Rapids: Eerdmans, 1995], 139). See also Abraham: "This is not just a matter of getting the word out to all who will listen, using any means of communication that comes to hand. It is a matter of the power of the living God, unveiling himself to the minds and hearts of the listener as the gospel is taught and made known" (*The Logic of Evangelism*, 60).

[106] See Bebbington, *Evangelicalism in Modern Britain*. According to Bebbington, "Evangelicalism cannot be given all the credit for the humanitarian victory over slavery, but it must be accorded a large share" (72). "[E]vangelicals were committed to a negative policy of reform. Their proposals were regularly for the elimination of what was wrong, not for the achievement of some alternative goal. Their campaigns were often explicitly 'anti', as in the anti-slavery and the anti-Contagious Diseases Acts movements" (135).

converging antislavery momentum. While Quakers led among Christians in antislavery reform through financial support and leadership, other Evangelicals, such as Methodists, followed.[107] The founders of Amer-ican Methodism, Asbury and Coke, held firmly to the British antislavery position. Although the arguments that provoked strong support for the later abolitionist movement were biblical and theological,   the movement emerged largely as a fruit of the Enlightenment.[108] Ironically, Enlightenment themes such as Social Darwinism and Scottish commonsense realism produced the epistemological constructs that created the notions of race that supported the practice of slavery in the first place, particularly in the American South.[109] Ripley's evangelistic ministry, though inflected by Enlightenment principles, remained grounded in biblical and theological foundations.

From the late seventeenth century, European slave owners generally accepted the notion that the conversion and baptism of slaves led to their emancipation.[110] In response to this conflict of interest for

[107] Bebbington, *Evangelicalism in Modern Britain*, 71.

[108] See Bebbington, *Evangelicalism in Modern Britain*, 71–72. "Such charitable work [e.g., Strangers' Friends Societies] can hardly be attributed to the Enlightenment. It was the spontaneous expression of a Christian movement. Yet it was entirely in harmony with the spirit of an age that set benevolence among its highest values. On the other hand, the greatest example of Evangelical humanitarianism, the anti-slavery campaign, was undoubtedly the fruit of the Enlightenment. Antislavery was not intrinsic to Evangelicalism: some of the stoutest defenders of slavery in the American South were preachers of the gospel" (71).

[109] See Harvey, "The Christian Doctrine of Slavery," 467, 468. According to Harvey, "They [moral philosophers] relied on the common-sense realist notion of conscience, the innate sense in all humans of what is right and good. Common-sense realists were spread throughout the nation, and certainly many were antislavery. In fact, abolitionists often made oblique reference to common-sense realist arguments, insisting that slavery violated the moral conscience of man. Yet southerners particularly came to rely on moral philosophy and common-sense realism to provide an intellectual foundation for the proslavery argument" (468). For further discussion of the influence of the Enlightenment and natural law upon categories of race and slavery, see K. Tiainen-Anttila, *The Problem of Humanity: The Blacks in the European Enlightenment* (Helsinki: Finnish Historical Society, 1994).

[110] J. Van Horne, "Impediments to the Christianization and Education of Blacks in Colonial America: The Case of the Associates of Dr. Bray," *Historical Magazine of the Protestant Episcopal Church* 50 (1981): 247. According to Van Horne, "This belief itself undoubtedly arose from the understanding that Christians could not legally be enslaved. . . . This distinction on the basis of religious belief posed a dilemma for devout slaveholders in the American colonies. Their Christian duty enjoined them to convert their slaves, but in so doing they would be making their slaves Christian and, therefore, incapable of being held in bondage."

slave owners in the American South, a series of laws was enacted—initially in Maryland (1664), New York (1665), and Virginia (1667)—to protect the property rights of slave owners whose enslaved Africans were Christianized.[111] Biblical rationales were added to these efforts in order to conform social policy to public sentiment. They followed along the line of an early plea for the Christianizing of slaves. This document, published in London (1702), attempted to soothe the fears of slave owners by claiming that sharing the Christian faith with slaves offered them a spiritual salvation separate from the slave's current social oppression.[112] While Christian baptism of slaves was a difficult issue for slave owners, the practice was never unlawful in the American colonies.[113]

The example and teaching of Christ, along with the theological foundation of universal atonement and comprehensive understanding of sin and its implications, directed Ripley's evangelistic ministry among the enslaved in profound ways. She most often focused upon those without access to the gospel of Jesus Christ: "I have gone into many of their little huts, which are clean and neat; but my spirit hath been bowed down on their account, feeling a secret wish that they might be taught to believe that there is a God who sees and knows all things which are done by them in time." Ripley encountered African women taught by their slave owners that "there is neither Heaven nor hell, God or devil." The oppression of women bought and held "for no better purpose than to gratify the passions of vile white men" distressed Ripley. She argued that these women have "no power to resist, for soul and body are not theirs but their master's, who can buy as many as he pleases, and compel them, if it is by threatening to starve them, which has been done frequently." Ripley, alongside others concerned for the salvation of the enslaved, taught many the Christian Scriptures "to inform them how to live in the fear of God, and to teach others whom they have in their care of how they should conduct themselves towards God, their great Creator." Ripley exhorted many of African descent to faith claiming that although some did not

---

[111] Van Horne, "Impediments," 248–49. According to Van Horne, "The fact that colonial assemblies deemed legislation necessary and that Englishmen drafted acts of Parliament to the same effect reveals the pervasiveness and tenacity of the belief that Christians could not be enslaved" (251).

[112] See A. Hill, "After Baptizatus: or, The Negro turn'd Christian" (London, 1702), in *American Religion: Literary Sources & Documents*, ed. D. Turley (Mountfield, U.K.: Helm Information, 1998), 1:276–77.

[113] Van Horne, "Impediments," 254.

respond, others did saying they knew there was a God, "and I gave credit thereunto, believing their sins convicted them at this moment, as they wept."[114]

Risking her life at times by proclaiming the gospel's message of salvation for whole persons, and confronting the systemic and complex dynamics of racial and gender oppression that separated the conversion of slaves from their condition, Ripley committed herself and her ministry to "the cause for the rights of the African nation." She prayed, "Good and gracious God, I beseech thee to give those blessed privileges of nature back again to this race, which a country has unjustly taken from them."[115]

During her travels, Ripley witnessed the violent oppression by slave owners upon the enslaved, leading her to name their sinful behavior: "My feelings have been pained exceedingly from the cruel treatment of one of the slave-holders, who has lashed his slaves himself till they had scarcely any skin left on them, and that by his severity they have died soon after."[116] Such ravages were compounded for Ripley by the lack of justice for what she considered criminal acts: "[Y]et he himself hath escaped punishment of men thus far."[117] Seemingly disillusioned with these injustices, Ripley exclaimed, "It appears marvelous to me that the judgments of the Lord do not pursue such with unlimited vigour in this life; but he hath reserved them for his vengeance to be exercised in the world to come."[118] Ripley did not shy from calling slave owners to Christian faith as well as to faithful practices: "O that all would learn to fear him whose judgments are

[114] Ripley, *The Extraordinary Conversion*, 121: "My spirit was humbled on their account, and has long sought relief for them by drawing nigh to God in secret, and I could not help agonizing with him in behalf of such who are in the Southern States prohibited from hearing the sound of the Gospel of Jesus Christ"; 87–88, 74, 82, 92.

[115] Ripley, *The Extraordinary Conversion*, 88.

[116] Ripley, *The Extraordinary Conversion*, 86. Ripley was warned of the danger to her life if she traveled throughout the South: "I was much pleased with some who were blessed with a discerning spirit, and saw how the Lord had been dealing with me from a child, signifying also, that go where I would the Shepherd of Israel would condescend to accompany me from one place to another, yet one testified, by reason of my feeling so much for the oppressed Africans, my life would be in great danger, if I went to the southward" (67).

[117] Ripley, *The Extraordinary Conversion*, 86. Slave owners were not prosecuted for violent assault committed against their slaves. See M. Tushnet, *Slave Law in the American South: State v. Mann in History and Literature* (Lawrence: University Press of Kansas, 2003), esp. 17–18.

[118] Ripley, *The Extraordinary Conversion*, 86.

so tremendous, that I tremble for every oppressor! for every one who deals hardly to any of God's creatures: knowing it will be repaid back again by him who has a love for everything which he has made."[119]

Ripley ministered both to slave holders and to their children: "Many young Baptists were present when I supplicated the throne of mercy, and they also were melted into tears, and wept much that they were born in a land of oppression; fearing the blood of their fathers would be on their heads, as their parents were slave holders." Realizing the significance of the young people's repentance of their complicity in the sins of slavery, Ripley made the most of their openness: "They all vowed in my presence that when they came to inherit their property of slaves, that they would free them, that they might free themselves from the curse of their fathers, or as they expressed it, 'Their blood which was upon their father's heads.'"[120] Thus, Ripley strategically addressed the children of slaveholders, facilitating both their salvation and eventual liberty of the slaves they would inherit, so that at least in some future time the system of slavery might be broken.

A Presidential Interview

Ripley embarked upon her initial itinerant evangelistic tour to proclaim the gospel to all Americans—particularly enslaved Africans and their owners—with confidence and hope for the salvation of souls and bodies captive to the systemic sin of slavery.[121] She departed on her first voyage to the United States from Bristol on February 13, 1802, on the brig *Triton*, sailed by Captain Gilbert Howland, a Quaker.[122]

---

[119] Ripley, *The Extraordinary Conversion*, 87.

[120] Ripley, *The Extraordinary Conversion*, 76. However, not all encounters were quite so clearly redemptive. For example, Ripley accepted the hospitality of a slaveholder: "We had an elegant supper: but the thoughts of their possessing a vast number of slaves embittered our sumptuous feast, nevertheless, God appointed this rich slave-holder to conduct a poor worm [Ripley] to the city where she wished to worship him in spirit with his people. . . . The sister to the person who gave me the invitation had yielded up all her slaves from a sense of duty, and had united with the Quakers about two years ago" (110).

[121] Again, Ripley's evangelistic ministry generally illustrated Newbigin's claim: "The church can only represent the righteousness of God in history in the way that Jesus did. It is enabled to do this by being constantly reincorporated into Jesus' saving action through baptism and the Eucharist and through the preaching and hearing of the Word, which explains these and applies their meaning to the actual situation" (*The Open Secret*, 111).

[122] Ripley, *The Extraordinary Conversion*, 41.

After a "rugged" crossing, the ship arrived in the New World at Rhode Island, April 1. Despite advice to the contrary from ministers and elders of a Philadelphia Quaker meeting, Ripley immediately turned her journey toward Washington, D.C.

Ripley planned to obtain an appointment with the president of the United States, "for the Lord required me to go on to Washington City that very day to have an interview with the President, so I told them it would have been pleasant to me if I could have taken their advice, but I must obey God and not man."[123] Ripley tenaciously claimed that the meeting with the president was a specific part of her evangelistic vocation, "according to my faith from this weighty testimony that awed my mind all the way previous to my visit."[124] Ripley did not adhere to the confining gender expectations of the time, moving intentionally and often alone within the public and private spheres. This may have been the result of her perception of an equality of spirit received through conversion that superseded the social and biological with spiritual attributes for the purpose of sharing the Christian gospel.[125]

Though frequently dissuaded, Ripley received assistance from many along her journey. One woman opposed Ripley's endeavor on the basis that she was "such an insignificant person": the woman believed the task should instead be pursued instead by "honorable women." This was most likely an allusion to Ripley's simplicity and lower social status. In her critic's opinion a more "respectable" woman, if a woman at all, should be trusted with such an important task. Ripley claimed, however, that this woman, who initially discouraged her, later "was so obliging as to let her black man accompany me, lending us her chaise."[126] The irony of the woman's offer did not seem lost on Ripley.

Ripley arrived in Washington just before dark on May 4 with a letter of recommendation, which she delivered immediately. In the process, Ripley came upon a gathering of the nation's leaders, the most helpful of which were secretary of state James Madison, whose wife,

---

[123] Ripley: "During the time of the yearly meeting, I staid with Ann Mifflin, who was a sympathizing sister to me [particularly on the issue of slavery]. . . . [M]any of the ministers and elders sat a little with me at the close of the meeting . . . which was very acceptable to me, although I could not take their advice. . ." (*The Extraordinary Conversion*, 62).

[124] Ripley, *The Extraordinary Conversion*, 66.

[125] See Brekus, *Strangers and Pilgrims*, 146–54.

[126] Ripley, *The Extraordinary Conversion*, 63.

Dolly, extended Ripley an invitation for lodging, and General Dearborn, secretary of war. Dearborn offered to accompany Ripley to see the president, "so that the Lord was gracious to me in preparing the way thus far." Ripley visited the president the following morning with several others, including Dearborn. Vice President Aaron Burr made the introductions, after which President Jefferson received all in his sitting room, and according to Ripley, "listened to my tale of wo [*sic*]!"[127]

Ripley recounted her words to the president: "[M]y concern was at present, for the distressed Africans, that I felt disposed to lay aside my own ease and happiness, to put forth an effort to promote their's if possible." She then revealed the purpose for her visit, "[I] wish to have thy approbation before I move one step in the business, understanding thou art a slave holder." Ripley revealed the agenda for her comprehensive evangelistic ministry without too sharply confronting the president's complicity in slavery. At this the president bowed his head, and replied, "You have my approbation, and I wish you success: but I am afraid you will find it an arduous task to undertake." Ripley repeated, "Then I have thy approbation." At this the president "rose and performed the same ceremony over, repeating nearly the same sentence he had already done, with this addition, 'I do not think they are the same race; for their mental powers are not equal to the Indians.'" Ripley countered: "God had made all nations of one blood."[128]

Receiving his consent for her evangelistic ministry among the enslaved and their slave holders, Ripley expressed to the president particular concern for women of African descent, "on account of their exposed situations to the vile passions of men." She did not leave the president's company without inquiring directly into his ownership of slaves: "He informed me, that some time since he had three hundred, but the number was decreased." Ripley determined that it was "a seasonable time to signify how my nature was shocked to hear of the souls and bodies of men being exposed to sale like the brute creation,

---

[127] Ripley, *The Extraordinary Conversion*, 64.

[128] Ripley, *The Extraordinary Conversion*. Her counter was not necessarily the most informed rationale for the contemporary discourse, but a prophetic witness considering the context and circumstances. Her response is most likely informed by Paul's assertion in Galatians 3:28 that there are neither male nor female in Jesus Christ, a claim prevalent among nineteenth-century female preachers. See Brekus, *Strangers and Pilgrims*, 119.

and I implored his pity and commiseration." Ripley reported that following the dialogue "we parted in peace."[129]

Ripley's exchange with President Jefferson demonstrated the central aim—and exceeding courage—of her evangelistic ministry. Ripley addressed nominal Christianity and its implications for faithful practices within sinful social systems that refused to acknowledge the relationship between conversion and the subsequent condition of individuals and communities. Although she persistently referred to the ultimate dismantling of slavery, Ripley knew that God would accomplish this task in divine time. It is not apparent that Ripley expected her conversation with the president, or her subsequent ministry efforts, to cause that dismantling in her lifetime. In her mind, the effectiveness of her evangelistic ministry was to be determined instead by her faithfulness to God's commission for her life.

Following Ripley's provocative evangelistic witness to President Jefferson, doors to power opened for her. Jefferson permitted her to preach to Congress in the Hall of Representatives. On a subsequent tour, in January 1806, Ripley addressed Maryland legislators and the U.S. Congress.[130] In both cases she highlighted the significance of wisdom for the nation's leaders. In Annapolis, Ripley advised her audience to look to Moses, the prophets, and Jesus Christ to inform their faith and leadership: "I said a talent of great light is in the possession of some, while others are intrusted [*sic*] with a talent of gold, to occupy faithfully to the Glory of God, being no more than stewards over his goods: therefore I commanded them seriously to consider that those things were not their own."[131] With President Jefferson and other significant figures present in the U.S. Congress, Ripley claimed that "it was Wisdom that adorned my mind and through the condescension of so noble a mistress, I was empowered to speak to the honour of God, and not regard the appearance of any man, high or low."[132] Though she worked largely through conversation, itinerant preaching, and publication, compassionate presence and service among the disenfranchised and the bold step of approaching Jefferson directly led to further political action with the aim of revising social policies.

---

[129] Ripley, *The Extraordinary Conversion*, 64; 65; 65; 65.

[130] Ripley, *The Bank of Faith*, 2d ed. (1822), n.p.; quoted in Taft, *Biographical Sketches*, 235–36.

[131] Ripley, *The Bank of Faith*, 235. Ripley dated the address in the evening, January 6, 1806, with Tobias E. Stansbury, the Speaker of the House, offering her the chair.

[132] Ripley, *The Bank of Faith*, 237.

'I was in prison, and ye came unto me'

On Ripley's subsequent evangelistic journeys in the United States she expanded her ministry to include other constituencies. While committed to preaching, she had a deep compassion for those who suffered not only from spiritual brokenness, but from marginalization: "I have traveled thirty thousand miles and thus afforded me an opportunity to comfort the prisoners, instruct the poor in their solitary life, and lead the sick to the Physician of souls, whose healing power I have seen extended to several who are now adoring the richness of his merit in the kingdom of glory."[133] Ripley sprinkled her two narrative volumes with testimonies of her presence and conversation with the imprisoned, infirm, and dying, noting her care for the physical and spiritual needs in life and death, including presiding at a number of funerals. While Ripley's interview with President Jefferson, and subsequent preaching occasions in congressional venues, demonstrate her willingness to engage in the political arena, her evangelistic ministry among the imprisoned, specifically with Rose Butler, reveals further facets of the social and political dimensions of her vocation. The example and teaching of Jesus Christ and an universal offering of atonement continued to frame Ripley's ministry.

Ripley devoted a significant amount of time ministering to the imprisoned, leading worship, proclaiming the gospel, and engaging in conversation with those she encountered. Although she did not seem to focus her time upon prison reform as some Quaker women did,[134] her ministry among the imprisoned themselves resonated with efforts among the Society of Friends and Methodists of her time. For example, "The fifth first day [Sunday] I had three meetings. [The first] in the morning, at ten, I went to the State Prison of New York . . . when I passed through the midst of three hundred and fifty prisoners, who were assembled together in a neat place of worship."[135] Ripley

---

[133] Ripley, *Letters*, v.

[134] See Bacon, *Mothers of Feminism*, 79, 138–44. According to Bacon, though men participated, Quaker women had been active in prison ministry since Elizabeth Hooten protested the poor conditions of prisons to the king in 1655. Ripley's prison ministry seems reminiscent of the work of the Society for Alleviating the Miseries of the Public Prisons founded in Philadelphia in 1787. While Elizabeth Fry began her prison reform work among women and their children after a visit to Newgate Prison, London, in 1813, that then inspired other similar projects, such as Mary Waln Wistar's Female Prison Association of Friends in Philadelphia in 1823. Ripley does not mention these efforts, nor does she seem to participate in similar prison reform efforts.

[135] Ripley: "O! the sympathy of my heart, to many bright Englishmen, who were

described her evangelistic work that morning, demonstrating its interdependence upon her own faith journey: "My earnest supplications are treasured up in Heaven for them, and I know my labour was not in vain in the Lord, in behalf of individuals, who will praise God and the Lamb with me, in the Kingdom of Glory, when Jesus Christ shall say, 'I was sick, and ye visited me; I was in prison, and ye came unto me.' "[136]

Ripley's ministry to the imprisoned was distinctive for more than her compassion to souls and bodies. In her collection of *Letters, Addressed to Dorothy Ripley from several Africans and Indians on Subjects of Christian Experience*, she acknowledged criticism of her evangelistic ministry by a prisoner and her openness to receive accountability. The criticism reached Ripley by letter from a prison in the "City of Washington," dated "6th April 1806" and signed by Philip Williams, who wrote, "[Y]our short visit to us prisoners, in this jail today, has made an impression [of grateful sensibility] on my mind which will never be erased." Williams identified Ripley's courage, describing her as "undaunted, undismayed by loathsome dungeons, and the appearance of their wretched inhabitants, you seek good in the midst of evil. . . . [Y]ou display an unparalleled example of feminine virtue and heroism, by an endeavor to snatch your fellow-beings from the very verge of endless ruin." In the context of his appreciation for Ripley's ministry, he offered the following criticism: "You told the black women 'that if they had been good girls, it was not likely they would have been there.' Granted, it is not likely; still it is not impossible that they might have been there, though as spotless as the virgin Mary." In a bold move on his part, Williams reminded her that Jesus, though perfect, was convicted and executed as a felon. Williams argued, "Whenever prisoners are addressed, their feelings should be spared; at least by one of your benevolent and charitable nature. The possibility of their being innocent ought in my opinion to be always admitted."[137] Ripley did not provide an explicit response to Williams's criticism, though her inclusion of his letter in this collection demonstrates receptivity to his feedback.

As previously mentioned, Ripley's ministry among the imprisoned did not address prison reform. However, later she did advocate

---

there residenced, unknown to their friends, or families: but God sees them, and I hope will assuage their grief, and heal their souls of the malady of sin" (Ripley, *The Bank of Faith*, 60).

[136] Ripley, *The Bank of Faith*, 61.

[137] Ripley, *Letters*, 33; 33–34; 38; 39.

strongly against capital punishment in her publication, *An Account of the Death of Rose Butler*. In *An Account of Rose Butler*, Ripley narrated in detail the hours leading up to Butler's execution by hanging. Butler, a nineteen-year-old slave in New York, was sentenced to death for setting fire two years earlier to her mistress's house. The crime of arson in the first degree, or knowingly setting fire to a dwelling place at night when inhabited, was until 1862 punishable by death for any perpetrator.[138] Although Ripley's evangelistic ministry of presence and compassion in Butler's last hours is instructive, her overall purpose was not merely to attest to Butler's repentance and conversion, but to build a theological case against capital punishment, a case that unfolded in the last half of the text. Underlying Butler's circumstances was the dual legal status of slaves in New York:[139] as a slave, Butler was considered the property of her owner and, therefore, denied civil rights; added to this was her subjection to criminal law, which granted slaves personhood that included accountability to such laws enforced with harsh forms of punishment.

An Account of Rose Butler, along with much of Ripley's evangelistic ministry, preached universal access to repentance and forgiveness of sins to enable the salvation of individuals, as well as witnessing to the unfolding embodiment of that salvation in social implications. Ripley began her narrative, "The Lord strengthened me to go a mile to Bridewell, on the 8th, to visit a young woman, who was under sentence of death for setting fire to the house where her mistress lived."[140] Although intent on securing Butler's salvation, she heard Butler confess faith in Jesus Christ and receive assurance of the forgiveness of her sins; Ripley also persisted in advocating for the young woman's humane treatment, including the care of a doctor:

---

[138] J. Edmonds, *Statutes at Large of the State of New York* (Albany, N.Y.: Weare C. Little, Law Bookseller, 1863), 2:676, 678, 686–87. The punishment for arson in the second, third, and fourth degrees was imprisonment of one to ten years. From 1815 the punishment for arson of an insured property was life imprisonment (*Laws of the State of New York* [Albany: Websters and Skinners, 1815], 3:17). The original arson law in New York (1778–1797) specified that any convicted of the crime "shall be hanged by the neck until he, she or they shall be dead" (*Laws of the State of New York* [New York: Thomas Greenleaf, 1797], 2:74).

[139] See A. Fede, *People without Rights: An Interpretation of the Fundamentals of the Law of Slavery in the United States South* (New York: Garland, 1992), 3. According to Fede, "[T]he slave had a dual legal status that was consistent with and epitomized the oppression of slavery."

[140] Ripley, *An Account of Rose Butler*, 3.

I agreed with her to pray all the last night at home, if she would in prison; and the Lord removed the guilt from her soul during the night season: for she said, "I have sat up most of the night, and I felt lighter, and my burthen go off at twelve o'clock. I fell into a doze when I lay down at day-break; and I thought I heard beautiful singing this morning."

She has been very sick, and attended by a doctor, but she told my friend Eames and me, thus—"I believe it was nothing but my burthen of sins that was the cause of my sickness; but I did not know what was the matter with me!"[141]

Despite the treatment that prompted Rose's anger, she claimed she was able to forgive her mistress: "I forgive everyone, and hate nobody." Ripley asked, "[A]rt thou willing to die?" to which Butler replied, "Yes." Ripley asked Butler, "Dost thou think it is just for thee to be hung [*sic*]?" Butler replied, "Yes, but I do not think that I was so much to blame as them who put me up to it; for I was young and ignorant: but never mind, Justice will find them out as well as me someday." Ripley explained that many had visited Butler: "[Y]et there appeared a want of faith in some; for [Butler] named one minister who said, 'You are sure to go to hell;' which grieved [Butler] so much, that she said to [Ripley], 'I do not think he is fit to preach; for he is not a gospel minister.'"[142]

Finally, Ripley accompanied Butler on the day of her death: "We were at Bridewell more than seven hours, during which time I prayed thrice; and ministers of various professions enquired into her state, and prayed also with her that God would be gracious to her soul. Four coloured preachers were there, who sung and prayed with great solidity, being much affected." Ripley facilitated additional accommodations for Butler: the delay of her binding, ensuring the ropes were not too tight, the provision of two enclosed coaches (instead of open carts) for transport to the gallows so that additional friends and ministers might accompany her, and the attention of a doctor who supplied medication, cold water, and fruit for Butler's comfort as far as possible:[143]

The sheriff untied the ribbons of Rose's shroud, to tie below her feet decently; and I made an effort to assist him. He then put the halter on the hook, and pulled her cap over her face; and I took my last farewell by saying, Rose, pray, "Lord receive my spirit," and I

[141] Ripley, *An Account of Rose Butler*, 3.
[142] Ripley, *An Account of Rose Butler*, 3–5.
[143] Ripley, *An Account of Rose Butler*, 5–7.

will do the same for thee. She answered me meekly, "I will" without shedding one tear; with all the patience, or resignation of a fortified Christian.[144]

Fulfilling her promise, Ripley continued to pray until she felt Butler's "soul was gone." Attempting unsuccessfully to preach to the estimated more than ten thousand witnesses, Ripley "felt it impossible to reach the multitude on all sides, that were warded off by the soldiers, or horsemen and officers."[145] Ripley remained with Butler's body until it was laid to rest:

> Jesus, my merciful Master, bid me stay till Rose was taken down; and put into her coffin, and grave; so I paid that respect to her lifeless clay; and as she was not counted worthy of burial service, after the manner of the day, I committed her body to the ground, by supplication, in faith and hope, that God would raise it at the last, in case they would let it lay undisturbed; but should even the medical men separate her flesh from her bones, (according to my expectation) I signified the Lord would find her, out at the last, when the Trumpet shall sound, and the dead hear His voice.[146]

Ripley explained that some were offended that Butler had received such accommodations, and they damned Ripley, calling her an "Old Quaker b——." Ripley concluded that "Satan was very angry that he had lost his prey." She closed the account of Butler's last hours with a poem expressing compassion for the young woman, "Composed for Rose Butler, aged nineteen years whom I attended to the gallows, when she was executed in the Potter's Field, on the 8th of the 7th mo. for setting fire to her mistress' dwelling house."[147]

Ripley's experience with Butler, informed by her visits to other imprisoned persons, led her to append to the narrative account of Butler's last hours a passionate essay against capital punishment. Ripley's initial argument focused on the limits that such a punishment, often hastily executed, placed upon the accused for reform as well as salvation. Thus, Ripley's goal for social reform was evangelistic: "[N]umbers of subjects and citizens, hurried into eternity in the very bloom of life, with all their sins and imperfections on their heads; and cut off at once from all power of reformation; from all possibility

---

[144] Ripley, *An Account of Rose Butler*, 8.
[145] Ripley, *An Account of Rose Butler*, 8.
[146] Ripley, *An Account of Rose Butler*, 8–9.
[147] Ripley, *An Account of Rose Butler*, 9, 12ff.

of making amends to the *state* they have injured, to the *friends* they have distressed, and the *God* they have daringly offended."[148] Ripley included addresses from other authors to build her case. She then turned to biblical texts, beginning with the story of Cain, demonstrating the lack of precedent for the punishment of death. She discussed the complexities of "the Laws of Moses," and the superseding example of Jesus Christ:[149]

> It might have been expected that, among a people professing the mild and tolerating religion of Christianity, no one would be found to advocate a practice so contrary to its principles as the depriving of a fellow creature of his life. . . . [Jesus'] whole life is represented to have been a Pattern of meekness, gentleness, love and forbearance. "Lord, said Peter, how oft shall my brother sin against me, and I forgive him? until seven times? Jesus saith unto him, I say not unto thee, until seven times, but until seventy times seven."[150]

Ripley also entertained the question of whether or not capital punishment served as a deterrent, and concluded negatively: "To inspire him with a horror of murder, you commit one before his eyes, and you commit it with indifference, with preparation in cold blood, and with the forms of law."[151] Ripley closed the pamphlet with the following plea:

> O my God! hasten; O! hasten the day when violence shall be done away, and righteousness fill the earth. I am determined, as an individual, however, to put forth an effort to contribute to alleviate the sorrows of the abject; let others do as they please: and I hope when my short life is run, millions of the fair sex will try to excel me in my sphere of action, to enlarge the territories of Zion; and impede the progress of sin, and lay waste the kingdom of Satan in the hearts of unbelievers in all Nations.[152]

---

[148] Ripley, *An Account of Rose Butler*, 17.

[149] Ripley: "When we attend a little to the case of Cain, who murdered his brother Abel, as recorded in the fourth chapter of Genesis, we shall find, notwithstanding the cruel and aggravating circumstances attending it, that the punishment of death was not inflicted upon the murderer" (*An Account of Rose Butler*, 19–20). See also 20: "The institutions of Moses were made to regulate a people peculiarly situated, and for very special purposes. They were never intended to serve as a code of Laws for the rest of mankind."

[150] Ripley, *An Account of Rose Butler*, 21.

[151] Ripley, *An Account of Rose Butler*, 27.

[152] Ripley, *An Account of Rose Butler*, 34.

Ripley's multifaceted evangelistic ministry theologically framed by universal atonement reached out to the multitudes: "While in America persons of all distinctions partook of my gospel labour from the President of the United States to the meanest slave, . . . prisons, hospitals, and the houses appointed for the poor, so that thousands rejoiced in my sympathy, . . . feeling love and good will to all nations."[153] By integrating verbal proclamation—itinerant preaching and publication—with practices of compassion—visitation and efforts to influence social systems to recognize racial and economic injustice—Dorothy Ripley embodied the gospel of Jesus Christ.

> *[W]e shall believe with our hearts unto righteousness, and shew forth his love . . . without partiality.*[154]

---

[153] Ripley, *Letters*, 55. Ripley died on December 23, 1831, while ministering in the United States, and is buried in Mecklenburgh, Virginia. P. W. Chilcote, *Her Own Story: Autobiographical Portraits of Early Methodist Women* (Nashville: Kingswood Books, 2001), 131.

[154] Ripley, *The Extraordinary Conversion*, 4.

Sarah Moore Grimké *Angelina Grimké Weld*

Library of Congress

2

ᨆ SARAH AND ANGELINA GRIMKÉ ᨆ

"The woman who prays in sincerity for the regeneration of this guilty world, will accompany her prayers by her labors."[1]

Sarah Moore Grimké (1792–1873) and her younger sister Angelina Emily Grimké Weld (1805–1879) are well known for their pioneering work for abolition and woman's rights. Offering a complex and textured understanding of sin, they also make an important contribution to evangelistic theology and practice. Their efforts extended beyond verbal proclamation to include faithful responses to the systemic sins of racial and gender discrimination.

The Grimkés are well known as the only southern white women to become leading abolitionists. Also advocates for women's rights, both their writings remain pertinent to contemporary feminist conversations.[2] Foundational to their leadership for antislavery and feminist

---

[1] S. Grimké, *Letters on the Equality of the Sexes and Other Essays*, ed. E. A. Bartlett (New Haven: Yale University Press, 1988), 53.

[2] G. Lerner, *The Grimké Sisters from South Carolina: Pioneers for Women's Rights and Abolition* (Chapel Hill: University of North Carolina Press, 2004), xviii. Lerner's biography, recently reprinted, remains the definitive biographical resource for Angelina and Sarah Grimké. For additional background, see K. Du Pre Lumpkin, *The Emancipation of Angelina Grimké* (Chapel Hill: University of North Carolina Press, 1974); and B. G. Hersh, *The Slavery of Sex: Feminist Abolitionists in America* (Urbana: University of Illinois, 1978). See also C. Birney, *The Grimké Sisters: Sarah and Angelina Grimké, The First Women Advocates of Abolition and Woman's Rights* (Boston: Lee & Sheppard, 1885), 229. For understanding the language of feminism see S. Jones, *Feminist Theory and Christian Theology: Cartographies of Grace* (Minneapolis: Fortress, 2000), 14. The term *feminist*, according to Jones, refers to "a

reforms was their commitment to a vital Christian faith.[3] In response
to their conversions, the Grimké sisters developed a significant ministry through publication and public speaking that included a distinctive evangelistic component within the context of the Second Great
Awakening. Encouraged by Charles Grandison Finney (1792–1875)
and one of his prominent followers, Theodore Dwight Weld
(1803–1895), whom Angelina would later marry, the Grimkés understood that Christian faith required repentance of sins, not merely personal and spiritual, but sins with social implications—such as slavery.

The Grimké sisters, born in Charleston, South Carolina, to a
slave-owning family, received baptism as infants in the Protestant
Episcopal Church. Though thirteen years separated the sisters, both
experienced evangelical conversions in adolescence facilitated by
Presbyterian clergy.[4] The Grimkés' evangelistic theology and practices responded to the inconsistencies of their social formation as
white Christian women in the South. A growing maturity of faith,
alongside disillusionment as a result of encounters among local
churches with largely lukewarm responses to the sins of slavery, led
both to engage the Society of Friends while still living with their fam-

---

special interest in the lives of women, their stories, their hopes, their flourishing and
failures, and their multilayered experiences of oppression. . . . It is a theology that
articulates the Christian message in language and actions that seek to liberate women
and all persons, a goal that Christian feminists believe cannot be disentangled from
the central truth of the Christian faith as a whole."

[3] Though previous biographical and other surveys have largely not dealt ade-
quately with these components, attention to religious and confessional influences
upon female abolitionists is beginning to emerge. For example, see A. Speicher, *The
Religious World of Antislavery Women: Spirituality in the Lives of Five Abolitionist
Lecturers* (Syracuse, N.Y.: Syracuse University Press, 2000), 4–10; D. McCants,
"Evangelicalism and Nineteenth-Century Women's Rights: A Case Study of Angelina
E. Grimké," *Perspectives in Religious Studies* 14 (1987): 39–57.

[4] The Grimkés' historical context was strongly influenced by evangelicalism,
which subsequently contributed to the shape of their evangelistic theology and practices. While evangelicalism cannot be reduced to "a static, monolithic structure of
belief," according to Heyrman, the late eighteenth-century possibilities for marginalized groups such as "the poor, the young, the female, the black" gave way during the
early nineteenth century. "Women usually predominated, but after about 1800 they
were an increasingly silent majority. African Americans began to join biracial
churches in larger numbers in the wake of the Revolution, but as whites pushed them
to the margins of fellowship, black members organized to conduct their worship
apart." See C. L. Heyrman, *Southern Cross: The Beginnings of the Bible Belt* (New York:
Alfred A. Knopf, 1997), 254–55. The early themes of evangelicalism most likely
attracted the Grimké sisters. However, their probable encounter with later themes
most likely contributed to an eventual departure to the Society of Friends.

ily in South Carolina. Their maturing Christian faith contributed to a strong opposition to slavery, both eliciting resistance from their family and local churches. Separately the Grimké sisters each made the difficult choice in young adulthood to leave their home and family traveling north to adhere to the Society of Friends. The emerging American Anti-Slavery Society, with Weld among the leadership, enlisted the Grimkés' participation. The Grimkés participated in the American Anti-Slavery Society, attending the New York gathering in 1836. The American Anti-Slavery Society, founded in December 1833, sponsored the Anti-Slavery Convention of American Women, which held three annual sessions from 1837 to 1839; the Grimkés attended each.[5] By then already beginning to write and speak publicly, the Grimkés significantly shaped the movement from the mid-1830s. They remained active until 1839, after which Angelina and Weld, with Sarah, established a household together. Sarah joined the family to care for Angelina, who suffered chronic illness throughout her adult life. The Grimké sisters learned later they had nephews of African-American descent whom they embraced as family.[6]

Although their active public life was brief, the Grimkés contributed profoundly not only to antislavery and feminist reforms, but upon recovery of a constructive evangelistic theology and practice. While numerous primary sources related to the Grimkés remain accessible for study, a close reading of two essays focus this discussion: Angelina Grimké's *Appeal to Christian Women of the South* (1836) and Sarah Grimké's *Letters on the Equality of the Sexes* (1838). Angelina's *Appeal* inaugurated the Grimkés' public ministry, evoking an invitation for Angelina to attend the 1836 American Anti-Slavery Convention. Sarah's *Letters* was the first known American-authored and fully developed feminist argument, published a decade before the first woman's rights gathering in Seneca Falls, New York, in 1848. In these essays, the Grimké sisters outline an evangelistic theology that

---

[5] I. Brown, " 'Am I not a Woman and a Sister?' The Anti-Slavery Convention of American Women, 1837–1839," in *Abolitionism and Issues of Race and Gender*, ed. J. McKivigan (New York: Garland, 1999), 185. The abolitionist movement was inaugurated by William Lloyd Garrison's publication of the periodical *Liberator* in January 1831. According to Speicher, the Grimkés did not attend the 1839 gathering (*Religious World of Antislavery Women*, 100).

[6] With Weld, the Grimké sisters established an integrated school in New Jersey followed by another more progressive project in New York. The sisters, even after Angelina's marriage to Weld, resided together most of their lives. They continued to advocate for civil rights as well as woman's suffrage, Angelina in particular, until their deaths.

confronted not only the injustices of racism embodied in the institution of slavery, but the disenfranchisement of women—including slave-owning Christian women's complicity in sinful social structures. From their discovery of the antislavery cause, the Grimkés subsequently discovered the women's cause.[7] Similar to the other women in this study, the Grimkés' evangelistic theology and practice refused to separate conversion from condition, particularly for enslaved African Americans and women. For the Grimkés, a textured understanding of sin emerged as the definitive framework for their evangelistic theology and practice.

While contemporary evangelistic theology often construes sin in Western juridical terms, namely as prideful independence that separates one from God, and conversion as merely a personal dramatic experience realizing one's dependence upon God with assurance of a distant salvation—the Grimkés offer nuance. For the Grimkés, sin, particularly of many southern white women, even those professing an evangelical conversion to Christianity, included a lack of self rather than an excess of pride. With conversion the sinner becomes divinely empowered. Such empowerment evokes a response in faith to use her God-given talents. The Grimkés, therefore, advocated such empowerment of self and use of talents for a vital life of faith through prayer, Bible study, and other intellectual cultivation not only for women, but all disenfranchised.

Formation in Faith

Sarah was born on November 26, 1792, the second daughter and sixth of fourteen children to John and Mary Grimké, respected and affluent members of Charleston society with impressive ancestry.[8] Sarah and

---

[7] P. Japp, "Esther or Isaiah?: The Abolitionist-Feminist Rhetoric of Angelina Grimké," *Quarterly Journal of Speech* 71 (1985): 335.

[8] Lerner, *The Grimké Sisters*, 11–12. John Faucheraud Grimké studied law in England; fought in the Revolutionary Army; served in the South Carolina House of Representatives, including as a delegate to the state ratifying convention of the Constitution; and later became a judge, rising to a position equivalent to that of chief justice. Mary Smith Grimké's ancestors were also revered leaders and heroes in Charleston and South Carolina history, including two colonial governors and a speaker of the Commons House Assembly. Her father was among the wealthiest in the state. For a thorough biographical treatment of the Grimké family, including Sarah and Angelina, their parents, and descendants, see M. Perry, *Lift Up Thy Voice: The Grimké Family's Journey from Slaveholders to Civil Rights Leaders* (New York: Viking, 2001).

Angelina, the youngest of the Grimké siblings born February 20, 1805, resided in their family's permanent home in Charleston on Front Street. For a few months during most years the family temporarily resided on a large plantation "up-country" near Bellemont, approximately two hundred miles from Charleston in the northwest portion of the state.[9] Life in a southern slaveholding household revolved around a social order defined by gender and race. Though enslaved women lacked the freedom and access to basic privileges possessed by women of slave-owning families, both remained captive to a broad, but shared, spectrum of gender expectations.[10] Within southern society, churches maintained such gender conventions, preaching a distinct message of station and calling by gender in both households and communities.[11] This hierarchical social structure, threaded with Christian themes and endorsed by Christian institutions, framed the Grimké sisters' formation in faith. Both were disillusioned because the sinful system of slavery was inconsistent with their later experience of an evangelical Christianity. For Sarah, in particular, the inaccessibility of education for women added to this disillusionment.

At least two incidents demonstrate such inconsistencies. First, as youth, attending worship services with their family at St. Phillip's Episcopal Church in Charleston, Sarah and Angelina with other young women of affluent families often occupied their Sunday afternoons teaching the Bible to enslaved children. However, as Sarah discovered, the young teachers were not permitted to teach pupils to read. Sarah pursued this and related questions, demonstrating an early evangelistic imperative. Although the catechesis and baptism of slaves were both socially and religiously acceptable, this acceptance was preceded by a long and uneasy history. Early opposition arose to the catechesis of slaves as a result of a widely shared belief that Christian baptism must lead to their emancipation.[12] As mentioned in chapter 1,

[9] A. G. Weld, "Testimony of Angelina Grimké Weld," in *American Slavery As It Is: Testimony of a Thousand Witnesses*, ed. T. D. Weld (1839; repr., Salem, N.H.: Ayer, 1991), 53. There is some discrepancy in the historical literature with regard to the identity of the actual editor and compiler of this text. While the title page of the volume designates Timothy Dwight Weld as the compiler and editor, other works take Theodore Dwight Weld to be the compiler and editor.

[10] E. Fox-Genovese, *Within the Plantation Household: Black and White Women of the Old South* (Chapel Hill: University of North Carolina Press, 1988), 194. Fox-Genovese offers a detailed and insightful discussion of the implications of gender within southern social and family structures.

[11] Fox-Genovese, *Within the Plantation Household*, 196.

[12] J. Van Horne, "Impediments to the Christianization and Education of Blacks

while the Christian baptism of slaves was a difficult issue for slave owners, this practice was never unlawful in the American colonies. However, by comparison, slave literacy most alarmed slave owners and supporters of the slave system. Both South Carolina (1740) and Georgia (1755) passed legislation prohibiting teaching slaves to read and write. Other states followed these precedents in the years leading up to the Civil War further restricting laws on slave literacy, but not prohibiting slave conversion.[13] Sarah recollected her inability to accept such seemingly inconsistent truths, which with her own desire for education strongly influenced the Grimkés' later ministry. Sarah persisted in teaching Hetty to read, a young slave girl within the Grimké household.

> My great desire in this matter would not be totally suppressed, and I took an almost malicious satisfaction in teaching my little waiting-maid at night, when she was supposed to be occupied in combing and brushing my long locks. The light was put out, the keyhole screened, and flat on our stomachs, before the fire, with the spelling-book under our eyes, we defied the laws of South Carolina.[14]

However, the bold dissidents were discovered, resulting in Hetty narrowly escaping punishment by whipping and Sarah summoned before her father to receive a fierce lecture.[15]

The second confrontation with inconsistencies of the Grimkés' context related to a strong desire for learning, also on the part of Sarah. Prior to Angelina's birth, among her siblings Sarah preferred the company of Thomas, her elder brother by six years. With their father's approval, Thomas shared with Sarah his lessons in mathematics, geography, world history, Greek, natural science, and botany.[16]

---

in Colonial America: The Case of the Associates of Dr. Bray," *Historical Magazine of the Protestant Episcopal Church* 50 (1981): 247.

[13] Van Horne, "Impediments," 254–55. For example, see Louisiana (1830), Alabama (1832), and Arkansas (1847).

[14] Sarah Grimké's Diary, 1827, Theodore Dwight Weld Collection, William L. Clements Library, the University of Michigan, Ann Arbor, Michigan (hereafter cited as Weld MSS), quoted in Lerner, *The Grimké Sisters*, 18. According to Lerner, this was the one act of open defiance Sarah recorded in all the years of her childhood.

[15] Lerner, *The Grimké Sisters*, 18. See also Perry, *Lift Up Thy Voice*, 2.

[16] Lerner, *The Grimké Sisters*, 14. According to Lerner, "Sarah acquired 'different branches of polite education for ladies' at one of the numerous institutions provided for the daughters of wealthy Charleston. Typically, this would be needlework, white on white, stitchery and cross stitch, and if one were good at that, fancywork, beadwork, silk on velvet, colors. Reading, writing, enough arithmetic for managing a home, a little French were the essentials. Drawing was taught from printed patterns

Sarah voraciously consumed the materials, eager to learn. She asked permission to study Latin with Thomas, but Judge Grimké disapproved.[17] Despite her interest and motivation, Sarah, and later Angelina, with their sisters, were limited to a "polite education for ladies" suitable to their gender and class. Women were considered unable to receive education because of fragile physical and/or mental capacity in comparison with men; their minds were basically considered not worth cultivating.[18] While the Grimké sisters received more education than women of lower social status, even their lessons were limited to elementary instruction.[19] Only a small number gained introductory access to a subset of those subjects approved by Judge Grimké, such as natural history, geography, and basic mathematics; beyond these, a woman's learning relied upon independent reading.[20] However, Judge Grimké did admire Sarah's ability and lively interest in education, the study of law in particular. According to a later account by a personal friend of the Grimké sisters, Judge Grimké declared that if Sarah had only been a boy, she would have made the greatest jurist in the country.[21]

Although the Grimké daughters received a good education for women of the period, at age twelve with the departure of her brother

---

and, as the grand accomplishment, came the sketching of a vase with flowers from model. A little singing, sufficient piano to accompany the voice, gave a young lady an acquaintance with music. The most important thing to learn was manners, the proper way for a young lady to comport herself in company. It was a curriculum offering a little of everything and not very much of anything, designed not to tax excessively the gentle female mind" (13–14).

[17] G. Lerner, *The Feminist Thought of Sarah Grimké* (New York: Oxford University Press, 1998), 6. See also Perry, *Lift Up Thy Voice*, 1–2.

[18] N. Cott, *The Bonds of Womanhood: "Women's Sphere" in New England, 1780–1835*, 2d ed. (New Haven: Yale University Press, 1977), 101, 106. Both Sarah and Angelina argue for the significance of intellectual cultivation among women as well as enslaved women and men in their evangelistic theology and practice. While the limitations imposed by gender expectations clearly contribute to the social dynamics they encounter, the Grimkés' advocacy for "the life of the mind" resonates with Mark Noll's proposal in *The Scandal of the Evangelical Mind* (Grand Rapids: Eerdmans, 1994). Ironically, Noll acknowledges the role of revivalism in the eclipse of the evangelical mind in American Protestantism, specifically Finney's leadership and emphases. See Cott, 59–64. The Grimkés seem to offer a nuance if not an alternative to Noll's thesis.

[19] J. C. Spruill, *Women's Life and Work in the Southern Colonies* (1972; repr., New York: W. W. Norton, 1998), 206.

[20] Spruill, *Women's Life and Work*, 207.

[21] See Birney, *The Grimké Sisters*, 229.

Thomas for Yale,[22] Sarah was dramatically confronted by the lack of formal educational opportunities afforded to women.[23] She expressed in a letter later in life bitter feelings related to the oppressive limitations inflicted upon women: "With me learning was a passion. . . . Had I received the education I craved and been bred to the profession of law, I might have been a useful member of society, and instead of myself and my property being taken care of, I might have been a protector of the helpless."[24] The frustration of Sarah's remark fueled her desire not only for education, but also usefulness, contributing to the evangelistic theology and practice she would share with her sister.[25]

Following such disappointments, Angelina's birth temporarily averted Sarah's resigned acceptance. Almost thirteen, Sarah pleaded with her parents to allow her to assume the role of godmother, to which they agreed. Sarah fulfilled the role of Angelina's primary caregiver with little "Nina" referring to Sarah, much to her delight, as "Mother" for decades to follow, establishing the foundation of their lifelong friendship.[26]

The following narrates Sarah's and then Angelina's spiritual and moral awakenings. Their journeys into adulthood demonstrate additional acknowledgment of the inconsistencies of their social and religious contexts. The Grimké sisters, separately in adolescence and together as adults, responded to these inconsistencies with a provocative evangelistic ministry.

At the age of sixteen, Sarah entered society and for a time was absorbed by the "gaities and vanities" of social life.[27] This participation in the social expectations of her southern society reveals the

[22] Thomas Grimké graduated from Yale in 1807, a devout follower of Thomas Dwight, then president of the college and advocate of educational reform and critic of deism. See Perry, *Lift Up Thy Voice*, 24, 28–30.

[23] According to Cott, "The improvement of women's higher education in the half-century after the Revolution was an uphill battle. The best-educated women in those years were self-taught, or tutored at home by teachers or relatives, although institutions offering secondary education for girls began to be founded" (*The Bonds of Womanhood*, 112).

[24] Sarah Grimké to Harriot Hunt, December 31, 1852, Weld MSS, quoted in Lerner, *The Feminist Thought of Sarah Grimké*, 6.

[25] The argument for the education of women (as well as men) was based upon social usefulness. However, in the case of women's education this usefulness remained largely in the domestic sphere as daughters, wives, and mothers. Interestingly, despite this initial focus within the domestic sphere, education led women to look beyond and even subvert such expectations. See Cott, *The Bonds of Womanhood*, 108, 125.

[26] Lerner, *The Feminist Thought of Sarah Grimké*, 7.

[27] Lerner, *The Grimké Sisters*, 24.

complicity of affluent "ladies" to the structure of class and race, placing them within a social hierarchy not only above enslaved persons, but above those women not able to afford servants.[28] However, as she later recounted, this did not last for Sarah.

> Often during this period have I returned home, sick of the frivolous beings I had been with, mortified at my own folly, and weary of the ball-room and its gilded toys. Night after night, as I glittered now in this gay scene, now in that, my soul has been disturbed by the query "Where are the talents committed to thy charge?"[29]

This latter image, stewardship of one's talents as an essential component of one's faithful Christian discipleship, framed the theological foundation of the Grimkés' evangelistic theology and practice. Sarah and later Angelina challenged constraints of race and gender through evangelical conversions, facilitated by Presbyterian clergy, followed by affiliation with the Society of Friends and their participation in the antislavery movement.

As a single woman at twenty-four years of age, Sarah experienced an evangelical conversion. Through the revival preaching of the Rev. Henry Kollock, a well-known Presbyterian minister of the time, Sarah repented of sins and received conversion.[30] Although plagued with guilt for her propensity to backsliding, Sarah's conversion led her to abstain from most of the worldly and social practices popular in her time, such as novels, parties, and dancing.[31] In place of these less wholesome practices she read religious books, attended prayer meetings, and visited almshouses and the poor.[32]

---

[28] Fox-Genovese, *Within the Plantation Household*, 196–98. According to Fox-Genovese, "the most prestigious models promoted the ideals of the southern lady and gentleman or cavalier. . . . [T]hese public roles carried serious responsibilities for the expression and reinforcement of social order. In innumerable subtle and overt ways, slavery as a social system marked southern gender conventions. . . . The emphasis on leisure and civility identified social classes freed from the labor afforded by slaves" (196–97).

[29] Lerner, *The Grimké Sisters*, 25.

[30] Lerner, *The Grimké Sisters*, 29–30.

[31] According to A. F. Segal, "Psychologically, conversion becomes the solution to unbearable guilt and sin, which is in keeping with the traditional Lutheran view of Paul's conversion" (*Paul the Convert: The Apostolate and Apostasy of Saul the Pharisee* [New Haven: Yale University Press, 1990], 287). While this assertion is made in the context of simplistic and disputed findings regarding gradual versus crisis conversions, Sarah's and later Angelina's theological reflection substantially nuance traditional assumptions of sin and conversion specifically related to pride.

[32] Lerner, *The Grimké Sisters*, 30. According to D. G. Mathews, "the Evangelical

Sarah's conversion occurred within an emerging Evangelicalism in the southern United States during the late eighteenth and early nineteenth centuries. Southern Evangelicalism expanded from its early British influence upon Episcopalians into numerous traditions in the United States, such as Methodist, Baptist, and Presbyterian.[33] Evangelicalism's characteristics included an emphasis upon a personal relationship with Jesus Christ facilitated by the Holy Spirit and initiated through a conversion experience, sometimes dramatic, which then led to a life of religious devotion marked by intentional practices.[34] By 1792, the year of Sarah's birth, Evangelicals accounted for the majority of professing Christians, demonstrating their broad acceptance following disestablishment that dated from 1778 in South Carolina.[35] In southern states, parallel with other locations, women outnumbered men in the churches almost two to one, though men outnumbered women in the general population.[36]

As a result of Sarah's lingering sense of guilt unresolved through her conversion experience and related to remaining inconsistencies of her social context and religious commitments, she interpreted her father's falling seriously ill as a result of her sinfulness.[37] She, there-

call to come out of the world, a call to create new social distinctions on the basis of religious commitments, was clear and unmistakable" (*Religion in the Old South* [Chicago: University of Chicago Press, 1977], 20).

[33] See Heyrman, *Southern Cross*, for an interesting and provocative study of Evangelicalism in the South.

[34] See Mathews, *Religion in the Old South*. Although Evangelicalism seems initially focused upon the individual (i.e., conversion), it was also strongly oriented toward that individual's initiation and participation in a community of faith. In addition to the eradication of unwholesome practices such as dancing, horse racing, or ostentatious dress following one's ego-shattering repentance of sin, one's subsequent life of holiness was then characterized by a new identity (35, 37). See also McCants, "Evangelicalism and Nineteenth-Century Women's Rights," 41, 42.

[35] Mathews, *Religion in the Old South*, 47. "In 1776 and 1777 North Carolina and Georgia guaranteed by constitutional provision that no person would be required by law to support a particular church. South Carolina tried through a 'general assessment' to provide state support for all Christian denominations in 1778, but by 1790 had given up the idea for complete disestablishment" (56). Heyrman's study focuses upon Methodist, Baptist, and Presbyterian Evangelicalism in the South. She concludes that membership in these denominations among the white and black southern population age sixteen and over in 1790 was 18.1 percent and adherence, 46.6 percent (*Southern Cross*, 264–65).

[36] Mathews, *Religion in the Old South*, 47. Southern women outnumbered men in the churches 65:35, while men outnumbered women in the general population 51.5:48.5.

[37] Lerner, *The Grimké Sisters*, 30.

fore, committed herself to his care and faithful practices of Christian devotion. Doctors in Charleston advised a consultation with a highly respected surgeon in Philadelphia. The Grimké family chose Sarah from among the children to accompany Judge Grimké on the journey.[38] After two months Judge Grimké was still very ill. The doctor, a Quaker, helped Sarah find accommodation in a Quaker lodging in Long Branch, a resort area in New Jersey. Alone and distant from family and friends, Sarah nursed and tended to her father as he quietly suffered, never leaving their chambers, and finally dying in his sleep. Sarah described these months: "We lived in the constant sacrifice of selfishness . . . and became friends indeed. I may say that our attachment became strengthened day by day. I regard this as the greatest blessing next to my conversion that I have ever received from God."[39] Sarah's dutiful care of her father, followed by her encounter with Quakers, helped to resolve her lingering guilt.

After her father's death, Sarah continued to interact with Quakers, staying with a family in Philadelphia before embarking on the journey home to Charleston. Sarah met an additional group of Quakers that included Israel Morris, a Philadelphia merchant and member of a respected and prosperous Quaker family.[40] Morris introduced her to the principles of Quaker beliefs, inviting further correspondence and giving Sarah a copy of the autobiography of John Woolman (1720–1772), a Quaker minister known for preaching in the South against the sin of slavery.[41] Through words and living testimony, Woolman significantly inspired the Grimkés' evangelistic ministry: "Conduct is more convincing than language."[42]

[38] Lerner, *The Grimké Sisters*, 30.

[39] Sarah Grimké's Diary, Weld MSS, quoted in Lerner, *The Grimké Sisters*, 32–33. As noted in Segal's survey, "The conflict in the case of conversion . . . could come from doubt, stress, consciousness of incoherent or wrong beliefs, the perception of hypocrisy or contradiction" (*Paul the Convert*, 292).

[40] Lerner, *The Grimké Sisters*, 36; Lerner, *The Feminist Thought of Sarah Grimké*, 8.

[41] Lerner, *The Grimké Sisters*, 36. Woolman not only preached Quaker principles, but attempted as far as possible to live them out, namely as an abolitionist and pacifist. His autobiography was published posthumously in 1774. See J. Woolman, *The Works of John Woolman*, ed. W. Beardslee (1774; repr., New York: Garrett, 1970).

[42] Lerner, *The Grimké Sisters*, 40. J. Woolman also referred to faithful and responsible economy of talents, a biblical image that informed the Grimkés' evangelistic theology and practice. "Our Duty and Interest is inseparably united, and when we neglect or misuse our Talents, we necessarily depart from the heavenly Fellowship, and are in the Way to the greatest of Evils" ("Some Considerations on the Keeping of Negroes Recommended to Professors of Christianity of every

Through correspondence Morris encouraged Sarah to join the Society of Friends. Sarah began to worship at a meeting-house in Charleston.[43] However, her family and friends strongly disparaged such a move.[44] Feeling called to the Quaker ministry, Sarah seemed frozen by fear to act upon her inner voice. With the guidance of Morris's correspondence and an increasing courage, Sarah decided to leave Charleston to travel north and become a Quaker minister.[45] Accompanied by her widowed sister Anna Frost and Anna's daughter, Sarah departed, sailing to Philadelphia in May 1821. Although Sarah left under the pretense of a temporary trip for health reasons, she would return only to visit.

In 1823, the Arch Street Meeting of the Society of Friends accepted Sarah as a member. During the early 1820s, Lucretia Mott held membership in the same Quaker meeting and served as a respected minister. Catherine Morris, also single, actively served as a Quaker elder, frequently traveling to offer leadership. Despite the

---

Denomination" [1754], 22, in *The Quaker Origins of Antislavery*, ed. J. W. Frost [Norwood, Pa.: Norwood Editions, 1980], 138–66). Woolman also published "Considerations on Keeping Negroes: Part Second" (1762).

[43] According to Mathews, Quakers were less concerned with increasing their membership, while the membership remained loyal to shared faith commitments such as antislavery (*Religion in the Old South*, 77). For an institutional history, see also S. Weeks, *Southern Quakers and Slavery: A Study in Institutional History* (Baltimore: The Johns Hopkins University Press, 1896).

[44] According to Mathews, "religious dissent was looked upon not as a mere difference of opinion, but as a challenge to authority and therefore a disruption of community" (*Religion in the Old South*, 5). Although religious affiliation in the colonial South was relatively diverse, Anglicans, later Protestant Episcopalians, were the most numerous with less stringent expectations, namely a conversion experience or retreat from worldliness. According to Heyrman, "they drew assurance from frequent allusions to the divine origin of a social hierarchy that set rich over poor, men over women, and white over black" (*Southern Cross*, 11). Heyrman continues, "But it was more than their impulse to honor or conciliate the better sort that made many ordinary southerners so wary of evangelicals. Indeed, what many feared more deeply were the ways in which evangelical moral codes and ritual practices estranged their converts from the community of their peers, neighborhood networks of yeoman and tenant farming families. . . . As the paths of evangelicals diverged from those of their neighbors and friends, friction often resulted" (18–19). "In sum, what held the center of lay concern, what aroused their sharpest fears, were the ways in which Baptists and Methodists [with other groups such as Quakers] struck at those hierarchies that lent stability to their daily lives: the deference of youth to age; the submission of children to parents and women to men; the loyalties of individuals to family and kin above any other group; and the rule of reserve over emotion within each person" (26).

[45] Lerner, *The Feminist Thought of Sarah Grimké*, 9.

precedent and example of these women, Sarah struggled with her call to ministry, receiving little support and sometimes discouragement from her community of faith. Living on a modest income from her inheritance, from 1823 to 1829 Sarah resided among a conservative group of Quakers in which Israel Morris and his family participated.[46] After the death of his wife, Morris later proposed marriage to Sarah. Although apparently affectionate toward Morris, Sarah struggled with an eventual denial, possibly opting for a life of greater independence.[47]

During this period Angelina grew into an assertive, confident, and independent young woman. At the age of thirteen she refused to be confirmed in her family church of St. Phillips.[48] Presumably, Angelina did not feel ready to make such a commitment, perhaps because of a lack of religious experience.[49] Precipitated by a series of deaths during 1824–1825, she prayed in the winter of 1825–1826 for God to make her "a true christian [*sic*]."[50] Angelina, moved by the newly called Presbyterian minister, the Rev. William McDowell, experienced conversion and joined his congregation in 1826.[51] Angelina actively participated in her local congregation, teaching a Sunday school class that grew to 150 children. Efforts by her previous community of faith,

[46] Lerner, *The Feminist Thought of Sarah Grimké*, 10. This was a contentious time for the Society of Friends in Philadelphia, which eventually led to the estrangement of the Hicksite group. According to Lerner, "There is no telling how her life would have developed, if she had been free to mingle with the liberal Hicksite Quakers, at least one of whom, Lucretia Mott, was closer to her in antislavery sympathies and incipient feminist thought than any of the group of people with whom she then lived."

[47] During the seventeen years in which Sarah participated in this Quaker meeting she consistently expressed disappointment and ultimately departed from the Society of Friends. For additional insight with regard to Sarah's spiritual turning point see Speicher, *The Religious World of Antislavery Women*, 13–21.

[48] Birney, *The Grimké Sisters*, 40. Angelina declared she could not agree with the pledge stated in the prayer book. "If, with my feelings and views as they now are, I should go through that form, it would be acting a lie. I cannot do it."

[49] There is not an apparent source of contention for her refusal in the Confirmation Liturgy. See "Liturgy for Confirmation," *Book of Common Prayer* (1784). According to Speicher, Angelina later explained that she had "determined never to join any Church until . . . [she] had real, heart-felt piety" and claimed to have "passed near 19 years in entire indifference as to my eternal welfare"; this may explain at least in part her refusal (*The Religious World of Antislavery Women*, 21).

[50] A. Grimké, "Narrative of Religious Experience," 1–3, Papers, quoted in McCants, "Evangelicalism and Nineteenth-Century Women's Rights," 43.

[51] Speicher, *The Religious World of Antislavery Women*, 22–23. For Angelina, the description of her conversion experience seemed to resonate with what Segal describes in his survey as "decision-making" based on cognitive psychology; see *Paul the Convert*, 295.

St. Phillips, to facilitate her return failed.

> I could not conscientiously belong to any church which exalted itself
> above all others and excluded ministers of other denominations from
> its pulpit—the principle of liberality is what especially endears the
> Presbyterian Church to me . . . I have lately succeeded in establish-
> ing a female prayer-meeting among Baptists, Methodists, Congrega-
> tionalists and Presbyterians—we assemble on the first Monday of
> every Month in the afternoon (about twenty attend). It is a sweet
> meeting to many hearts.[52]

McDowell, Angelina's Presbyterian minister, originally from the
North, relocated to Charleston for the milder climate in 1823. His
strong reservations against slavery evoked Angelina's high regard. He
encouraged Angelina to hold daily prayer-meetings for the family's
slaves. Although initially met with opposition from her mother, eventually Angelina's mother, sisters, and slaves, including those of other
families, attended.[53] Angelina pushed McDowell on the issue of slavery, questioning the morality of a system of bondage by professing
Christians over other professing Christians. McDowell agreed with
Angelina on the immorality of the system, but advised her to pursue
the issue through patient prayer.[54] Dissatisfied with this response,
Angelina urged McDowell to preach on the immorality of slavery, to
which he declined.[55] Angelina, still dissatisfied and incredibly persis-

[52] Lerner, *The Grimké Sisters*, 48–49. While the Methodists recognized official
rules constituting a seeming antislavery position among its constituency from 1743,
the Presbyterians in the United States passed a similar rule in 1815. See Mathews,
Slavery and Methodism, 32, 293–303. Mathews refers to A. T. McGill, *American
Slavery as viewed and acted on by the Presbyterian Church in the United States of America*
(Philadelphia: 1865).

[53] Lerner, *The Grimké Sisters*, 49. See also McCants, "Evangelicalism and
Nineteenth-Century Women's Rights," 44.

[54] Lerner, *The Grimké Sisters*, 49.

[55] According to Mathews, the response to Angelina was indicative of a trend that
occurred with the shift of generations from preachers concerned with antislavery to
more youthful acceptance. "In 1818 the Presbyterian General Assembly declared
slavery a moral dilemma, but discouraged emancipationists by calling their activities
socially disruptive" (*Religion in the Old South*, 75). See also Heyrman, *Southern Cross*,
26: "Misgivings widely shared by southern whites focused on the prominence of
young men and of women of every age in Baptist and Methodist churches, the priz-
ing of religious fellowship over the family, the rejection of prevailing ideals of masculinity, and the demand for introspection and self revelation. Indeed, for all those
reasons, many lay people were more disposed to locate early Baptists and Methodists
on the radical fringe, along with such other despised groups as the Quakers and
Shakers, than in the respectable mainstream of Protestant Christianity."

tent, attended the elders' meeting of her local Presbyterian congregation, all slaveholders, and suggested they should compose a statement against slavery.[56] They too politely declined.

Angelina, growing disillusioned with the local Presbyterian congregation, questioned more than a perceived apathy with regard to slavery. Her theological formation began to depart from traditional Calvinist teachings to embrace Arminian themes. She recorded that some fellow church members "heard me with suspicion advocate the Doctrine of Universal Grace, Perfection and some tho't I was going to turn Methodist. My Pastor also desired a conversation with me and found I was no longer the zealous promoter of Presbyterianism."[57] Angelina eagerly received Sarah's Quaker teaching, during her sister's visit in the winter of 1827.[58] "I regarded Baptism and the Sacrament to say no more at least [as] quite unnecessary."[59] By the spring, Angelina, discontented with the Presbyterian Church, acted on a call to join the Quaker meeting in Charleston.[60] However, this community of faith was also disappointing, consisting of only two elderly men.[61] Later that year after Angelina's Presbyterian congregation brought charges against her for neglecting public worship, the Lord's Supper, and the

[56] Birney, *The Grimké Sisters*, 70–71.

[57] A. Grimké, autobiographical manuscript, 1828, quoted in Speicher, *The Religious World of Antislavery Women*, 23. See also McCants, "Evangelicalism and Nineteenth-Century Women's Rights," 45.

[58] Birney, *The Grimké Sisters*, 71. According to McCants, "She might have turned to Methodism, but did not. To her mind only Quaker understanding of the doctrine [of perfection] was scriptural" ("Evangelicalism and Nineteenth-Century Women's Rights," 45).

[59] Grimké, autobiographical manuscript, 1828, quoted in Speicher, *The Religious World of Antislavery Women*, 23.

[60] Birney, *The Grimké Sisters*, 72–73. According to Heyrman, by the 1830s Evangelicalism in the South had begun to internalize much of the social hierarchy valued by southern culture and therefore minimizing previously held religious and social commitments. "Southern whites came to speak the language of Canaan as evangelicals learned to speak with a southern accent" (*Southern Cross*, 27).

[61] Quakers in Charleston possessed a difficult past. When Quakers Mary Peisley of Ireland and Catherine Payton of England arrived in Charleston in 1753, they found a very small languishing Quaker community that had dwindled so substantially in membership they no longer held meetings. Sadly, the reformation effort of these British Quaker visitors was not warmly received and did not seem effective. See R. Larson, *Daughters of Light: Quaker Women Preaching and Prophesying in the Colonies and Abroad, 1700–1755* (New York: Alfred A. Knopf, 1999), 206–7. According to Speicher, Angelina attempted an intervention to reconcile the two feuding members of the Charleston Quaker meeting. In response, one of the disgruntled men called Angelina "a busy body about other men's business" (*The Religious World of Antislavery Women*, 25).

means of grace, they promptly sent notice of her expulsion.[62] Angelina's expulsion demonstrated early nineteenth-century Evangelicalism's strict accountability among individuals within authoritative communities of faith. For approximately a year, Angelina struggled to reconcile the inconsistencies of slavery and faithful Christian discipleship in the place of her birth. In November 1829, with her mother's consent, Angelina left Charleston to move north, joining Sarah.[63] Together the Grimké sisters continued to challenge the constraints of race and gender through their participation in the antislavery movement. Within this context they composed an evangelistic theology informed by a deep-textured understanding of sin.

Evangelism and Antislavery Reform

The revivalism and social reform of Charles G. Finney and Theodore Dwight Weld within the context of the Second Great Awakening provides a background upon which to view the Grimkés' commitments, namely woman's education and ministry as well as the doctrinal emphasis of slavery as sin. The Grimkés' emphasis upon a holistic understanding of salvation, and therefore evangelism as not spiritual alone, grows from the Second Great Awakening generally, and the antislavery movement more specifically. Weld was among the organizers of the 1836 American Anti-Slavery gathering. Weld, a young revivalist converted by Finney, was inspired by Finney's support of William Lloyd Garrison's American Anti-Slavery Society and focused his efforts on abolition reform. The unprecedented move to train antislavery agents for the purpose of converting individuals to aboli-

---

[62] Birney, *The Grimké Sisters*, 82–84.

[63] Lerner, *The Feminist Thought of Sarah Grimké*, 11. Angelina, following Sarah, experienced strong opposition to her conversion and subsequent religious commitments. According to Segal, "One important aspect of the study of cognitive dissonance is the finding that the strength of the new belief structure will be directly proportional to the difficulty or strength of the conversion experience. The stronger and more difficult the conversion experience, the stronger and more difficult it will be to dissuade the beliefs held" (*Paul the Convert*, 298–99). As Fredriksen and Gaventa acknowledge, the convert narrates their past through their present reaffirming current commitments. Thus, the Grimkés' mention of their conversion experiences illumine subsequent decisions not historically, but rather through an apologetic lens. See P. Fredriksen, "Paul and Augustine: Conversion Narratives, Orthodox Traditions, and the Retrospective Self," *JTS* 37 (1986): 33–34; and B. R. Gaventa, *From Darkness to Light: Aspects of Conversion in the New Testament* (Philadelphia: Fortress, 1986), 6–7, 146–47.

tion followed the American Anti-Slavery Society's decision in spring 1836 to abandon pamphlet distribution as its major strategy. Instead, the organization decided in favor of increasing the number of anti-slavery agents to seventy, which according to the gospels was the number Jesus sent to engage in evangelistic ministry.[64]

The Grimké sisters spent the summer of 1836 separately with friends in New Jersey. Angelina composed a pamphlet, entitled *Appeal to Christian Women of the South*, for the purpose of engaging southern white women in the antislavery cause.[65] Without Sarah's input, Angelina sent the material to Elizur Wright, secretary of the American Anti-Slavery Society.[66] Sarah attempted to dissuade Angelina from such activities during the previous year to avoid the disapproval of their Quaker meeting.[67] The reply was swift and enthusiastic, communicating Wright's intention to publish the pamphlet and his desire for Angelina to lead parlor meetings among women in New York for the purpose of enlisting them in the antislavery cause.[68]

Sarah attempted to persuade Angelina to decline the invitation, but Angelina was firm in her decision to accept. Sarah, after much discussion, finally agreed to accompany Angelina to New York despite the opposition such a move would arouse from their Quaker meeting in Philadelphia. The Grimkés embarked on a momentous journey that would bring their vocations into conversation with the stirring currents of revivalism and social reform. The Grimké sisters accepted invitations to participate in the American Anti-Slavery Society gathering in New York held in November 1836, becoming the first southern women to serve as agents within the movement.[69]

[64] G. Barnes and D. Dumond, eds., *Letters of Theodore Dwight Weld, Angelina Grimké Weld, and Sarah Grimké 1822–1844* (New York: D. Appleton-Century, 1934), x.

[65] McCants, "Evangelicalism and Nineteenth-Century Women's Rights," 47.

[66] Lerner, *The Feminist Thought of Sarah Grimké*, 12–13. Angelina had previously written a letter supporting Garrison in 1835, which he reprinted in the periodical he edited, the *Liberator*. S. H. Lindley, *"You Have Stept Out of Your Place": A History of Women and Religion in America* (Louisville, Ky.: Westminster/John Knox, 1996), 108.

[67] See Speicher, *The Religious World of Antislavery Women*, 27. A possible reason for their eventual estrangement from the Quaker meeting, according to McCants: "Angelina, for example, was quick to distinguish it from the doctrine by which Quakers recognized female ministers. Quakers recognized women as ministers on the ground of spiritual gifts: the gift to preach. Angelina [and Sarah] Grimké stood on broader grounds: the ground of humanity or moral right" ("Evangelicalism and Nineteenth-Century Women's Rights," 56).

[68] Lerner, *The Feminist Thought of Sarah Grimké*, 13; Speicher, *The Religious World of Antislavery Women*, 28.

[69] Lerner, *The Feminist Thought of Sarah Grimké*, 13–14.

This was a daring move on the part of all. The American Anti-Slavery Society divided in 1840 over the question of women's participation.[70] Beginning in January 1837, the Grimkés began speaking publicly for the American Anti-Slavery Society, addressing approximately eighty-eight meetings in sixty-seven towns, totaling 40,500 individuals during this initial five-month tour.[71]

Weld, although generally less recognized than other nineteenth-century abolitionists such as Garrison, was a significant force behind the movement. Weld came to leadership within the American Anti-Slavery Society as a result of Finney's revival preaching. While a student at Hamilton College, Weld expressed skepticism with regard to the revivals, although from a long line of clergymen, his father a Congregationalist minister. In the winter of 1825, at Utica, Weld's aunt managed to persuade her nephew to attend the morning service. " 'When we came to the pew door,' he said later, she 'motioned me to go in and followed with several ladies, and shut me in.' " When Finney rose to speak, Weld attempted to escape, but was foiled by his aunt leaning forward in prayer blocking his way. Finney preached on "One Sinner Destroyeth Much Good." Weld was decisively converted, became the leader of Finney's Holy Band of revivalists, and joined the abolitionist movement.[72] Weld was described as an evangelist, "eloquent as an angel, and powerful as thunder."[73]

---

[70] Women were welcomed as full members of the American National Anti-Slavery Society while the American and Foreign Anti-Slavery Society split off and disallowed the full participation of women. See B. Zink-Sawyer, *From Preachers to Suffragists: Woman's Rights and Religious Conviction in the Lives of Three Nineteenth-Century American Clergywomen* (Louisville, Ky.: Westminster/John Knox, 2003), 16. According to Zink-Sawyer, "Several women had followed in the dangerous footsteps of the Grimké sisters and had earned reputations—positive ones for the quality of their presentations and negative ones for their audacity in transgressing gender roles—for their speeches before 'promiscuous,' that is, mixed-gender audiences."

[71] Lerner, *The Grimké Sisters*, 227. The Massachusetts lecture tour concluded abruptly as a result of illness suffered by Angelina. In February 1838, Angelina addressed the Legislative Committee of Massachusetts. In March, the Grimkés presented a lecture series at the Odeon in Boston. See also McCants, "Evangelicalism and Nineteenth-Century Women's Rights," 47, 53; according to McCants, "A few weeks later [Angelina] attracted capacity audiences of 3,000 for six lectures on abolition at one of Boston's largest and most central halls, an unprecedented event in that city" (53).

[72] N. Hardesty, *Women Called to Witness: Evangelical Feminism in the Nineteenth Century* (Nashville: Abingdon, 1984), 27–28; Barnes and Dumond, *Weld Grimké Letters*, xxi.

[73] Barnes and Dumond, *Weld Grimké Letters*, xviii.

Charles Finney "emerged as the best-known revivalist in the United States" following the generation of Frances Asbury.[74] A lawyer in Adams, New York, Finney experienced a religious conversion in 1821, received ordination in the Presbyterian Church in 1823, began preaching the next year, and in 1825 a revival in Rochester introduced him to the nation.[75] More than any other individual of his day he effectively integrated evangelical religion and social reform,[76] along with his support of women's public prayer and preaching, provoking substantial opposition. Finney's theology modified the dominant Calvinism of his day.[77] He asserted that individuals did have the ability to choose to receive God's salvation, emphasizing the human (in addition to the divine role) in conversion.[78] Therefore, Finney's theology relied heavily upon Arminianism, perhaps even more so than John Wesley, since Wesley emphasized God's prevenient grace followed by humanity's gracious response to this divine role.[79] Finney never allowed other interests to supersede evangelism but emphasized the relationship of conversion to practices of reform such as benevolence, abolition, coeducation, temperance, and peace.[80] By the mid-

[74] M. Noll, *A History of Christianity in the United States and Canada* (Grand Rapids: Eerdmans, 1992), 174.

[75] E. B. Holifield, *Theology in America: Christian Thought from the Age of the Puritans to the Civil War* (New Haven: Yale University Press, 2003), 361–62.

[76] Noll, *A History of Christianity*, 174.

[77] According to Holifield, "Finney did not abandon everything Calvinist." His thoughts related to the will and election did not conform to traditional Calvinism, neither to an Arminian doctrine in the Methodist sense. However, Finney and the Oberlin school left Calvinism with their emphasis upon perfectionism, which led to benevolence, making Oberlin the center of many Christian reform movements (*Theology in America*, 366–67).

[78] According to Noll, "The theology of the Second Great Awakening also differed from the earlier revival tradition. Stressing God's sovereignty in all things, Edwards and Whitfield had emphasized the inability of sinful people to save themselves. The theology of leading revivalists in the nineteenth century, both North and South, suggested that God had bestowed on all people the ability to come to Christ. This shift in perspective was related to the larger political and intellectual developments . . . but it also arose from a widespread desire for a theology of action that could encourage and justify the expanding revivals of Christianity" (*A History of Christianity*, 170).

[79] Noll, *A History of Christianity*, 177, 181, 235. See also Melvin Dieter, ed., *The 19th-Century Holiness Movement*, Great Holiness Classics 4 (Kansas City: Beach Hill, 1998), 182.

[80] Noll, *A History of Christianity*, 174. Finney supported coeducation while at Oberlin College by accepting Antoinette Brown Blackwell as a student in 1847, the first college in the country to matriculate a female student (176). Admittedly, Finney

1830s, Finney was mentoring a substantial number of young reformers, such as Weld, interested in Christianity's role in renewing society through the conversion of individuals and their faithful responses.[81]

Finney is remembered for employing strategic techniques, at the time referred to as "new measures," to receive those wrestling with the process of repentance and conversion in revival meetings. Often called "protracted meetings," the nightly gatherings could persist for several weeks. These techniques demonstrated Finney's confidence that conversion could be facilitated and not left entirely to God's timing, unlike his revivalist predecessors.[82] In his advice to converts Finney explained:

> Sinners ought to be made to feel that they have *something* to do, and that is *to repent*; that it is something which *no other* being can do for them, neither God nor man, and something which *they can* do, and do *now*. Religion is something to *do*, not something to *wait for*. And they must do it now or they are in danger of eternal death.[83]

Finney's mature theology, in place by his faculty appointment in 1835 to the newly formed Oberlin College, consisted of three components: "(1) a commitment to 'new measures' in revivalism, (2) a commitment to moral reform, and (3) a belief in a second, more mature stage of Christian life."[84]

---

also "formalized ties between conservative theology and industrial wealth that still characterize evangelical culture" (174–75). Despite Finney's support of coeducation and women's roles in the revival, emphasis upon individualism and immediacy eventually undermined Christian intellectualism (Noll, *The Scandal of the Evangelical Mind*, 61). "The problem with revivalism for the life of the mind, however, lay precisely in its antitraditionalism" (63). Throughout Christian tradition in the midst of "heroic missionary efforts and practical aid for the downtrodden," each generation "encouraged serious contemplation of God" and "promoted serious learning as an offering to the Lord" (44).

[81] Noll, *A History of Christianity*, 176.

[82] Noll, *A History of Christianity*, 176.

[83] C. G. Finney, *Lectures on Revivals of Religion*, ed. W. McLoughlin (Cambridge: Belknap, 1960), 207. All italics in quotataions are original unless otherwise noted.

[84] Noll, *A History of Christianity*, 235. The latter component was developed by various professors at Oberlin, such as Asa Mahan, using such terms as "holiness" and "Christian perfection." Previous to joining the Oberlin College faculty, Finney preached itinerantly until 1832, when he accepted a pastorate at Second Free Presbyterian Church in New York City because of health reasons. Finney later served as president of the college from 1851 to 1866, and pastor of the First Congregational Church in town from 1867 to 1872. He remained active until shortly before his death in 1875. Finney's academic appointment occurred even though he had never attended a college or a seminary. He later published *Skeletons of a Course of Theological Lectures*

Finney encouraged women as well as men to speak in mixed meetings.[85] Weld followed Finney's example in cultivating opportunities for women to speak and pray publicly in revival meetings.[86] Thus, the Grimkés joined the abolitionist movement as a response in faith to pursue their own Christian discipleship, which in turn created opportunities for the conversion of others. Angelina Grimké wrote, "I am persuaded that woman is not to be as she has been, a mere secondhand agent in the regeneration of the fallen world, but the acknowledged equal and coworker with man in this glorious work."[87] Weld met Angelina and Sarah Grimké at the agents' convention in November 1836. Theodore and Angelina married on May 14, 1838.[88]

The driving doctrine behind the anti-slavery movement was an affirmation of slavery as sinful.[89] This belief was described in the pamphlet *The Bible Against Slavery*, authored by Weld, which emerged from the Finney revivals.[90] The American Anti-Slavery Society also employed religious language, such as repentance and conversion, and even protracted

---

in 1840 and in 1846–1847 *Lectures on Systematic Theology*, which became the foundation of the Oberlin theology. See Holifield, *Theology in America*, 362.

[85] C. A. Brekus: "Experimenting with new forms of revivalism, a small number of Presbyterian and Congregationalist clergymen began to imitate lower-class evangelicals by allowing women to pray aloud, testify, and exhort. Charles Finney, the most influential, created a storm of controversy by encouraging women as well as men to testify in 'promiscuous' prayer meetings" (*Strangers and Pilgrims: Female Preaching in America 1740–1845* [Chapel Hill: University of North Carolina Press, 1998], 276).

[86] Brekus: "Theodore Weld remembered, he often heard people debating about women's right to pray publicly, but he could not find 'one in ten who believed it was unscriptural. They grieved and said perhaps, and that they didn't know, and they were opposed to it, and that it [was] not best; but yet the practice of female praying in promiscuous meetings grew every day'" (*Strangers and Pilgrims*, 276).

[87] Angelina Grimké to Jane Smith, August 10, 1837, quoted in Hardesty, *Women Called to Witness*, 43.

[88] Barnes and Dumond, *Weld Grimké Letters*, xxiv.

[89] According to Mathews, "[Southern] Evangelicals could never successfully identify slaveholding as sin itself. The importance of this omission is evident when we remember the Evangelical emphasis upon the necessity of a conviction of sin, which then led a person into psychic confusion, from which he was saved by conversion and reintegrated into society through the church. Words which called slavery a moral evil, and even defined it as sinful could by implication make slaveholding a sin. But the words were belied by a persistent reluctance to excommunicate slaveholders who knelt in prayer with their slaves" (*Religion in the Old South*, 74).

[90] Barnes and Dumond, *Weld Grimké Letters*, xii. See also T. D. Weld, *The Bible Against Slavery: An Inquiry into the Patriarchal and Mosaic Systems on the Subject of Human Rights*, 3d ed. (New York: American Anti-Slavery Society, 1838).

revival meetings. This could seem an artificial exploitation of popular traditional evangelistic practices of the time for conversion to a subordinate cause in comparison to the salvation of persons to the Christian faith. However, Weld, Finney, and the Grimké sisters understood the repentance of sins, particularly the sin of slavery, as constitutive to a meaningful Christian conversion and faith.[91]

The sin of slavery became "the standard to which the abolitionist is to rally." The extinction of sin, specifically slavery, became the focus of conversion. Weld's antislavery meetings usually extended over eight successive evenings, sometimes stretching to as many as twenty.[92] At the conclusion of each meeting, converts to abolition were called upon to stand—usually resulting in the whole audience rising to their feet.[93] Thus, individuals were not converted to an abstract notion of belief or goodness, but rather to a concrete Christian life characterized by faithful practices.[94] In addition to the protracted meeting of the revivalists was the reform lecture, considered a corollary to evangelism by Finney's followers.[95] In the reform lecture, women, including Sarah and Angelina Grimké, obtained an opening to this public ministry of Christian evangelism and social reform.[96] Many of the antislavery

---

[91] This notion resonates with W. J. Abraham's claim that "attempts to articulate the morphology of conversion have turned much of the theology of evangelism, which this language fosters, into an introspective anthropocentrism that neglects the richer tapestry of Christian theology and encourages the development of a narrow and inadequate piety" (*The Logic of Evangelism* [Grand Rapids: Eerdmans, 1989], 122).

[92] Barnes and Dumond, *Weld Grimké Letters*, xviii. In form and spirit they were very similar to Finney's protracted meetings of the Second Great Awakening.

[93] Barnes and Dumond, *Weld Grimké Letters*, xviii. According to Barnes and Dumond, "Usually the whole audience would rise, not only the restless reformers but the sober business and professional men of the community. He [Weld] was especially powerful with the lawyers. . . . [M]any others later prominent in national politics were converted by his preaching."

[94] G. Barnes, *The Anti-Slavery Impulse, 1830–44* (New York: D. Appleton-Century, 1933; repr., New York: Harcourt, Brace & World, Harbinger Book, 1964), 104–6, paraphrased in Hardesty, *Women Called to Witness*, 84. According to Noll, Theodore Weld and Frances Willard, the late nineteenth-century temperance reformer and advocate for women's ecclesiastic rights and suffrage, "attempted in their efforts to remake the character of America according to a largely religious vision" (*A History of Christianity*, 303).

[95] Hardesty, *Women Called to Witness*, 84.

[96] According to Hardesty, "As a result, at least in part, of Finney's revivals, women in nineteenth-century America began to fill new roles as pastors, preachers, evangelists, exhorters, and lecturers. Their goal was to win souls, to usher in the Millennium, to institute the kingdom of God on earth. Their critics said allowing women to assume

agents worked previously as missionary agents for other campaigns such as tract, temperance, and Bible societies.[97]

In the more recent ecclesiastical climate the conversion of souls can be estranged from responses of sustained Christian practices or at least compartmentalized as separate entities as indicated by the use of language—evangelism and social reform. However, for these revivalists influenced by and connected to Finney and Weld, conversion and one's faithful response were impossible to separate. Finney wrote to Weld in July 1836:

> How can we save our country and affect the speedy abolition of slavery? This is my answer. What say you to it? The subject is now before the publick [*sic*] mind. It is upon the conscience of every man, so that now every new convert will be an abolitionist of course. Now if abolition can be made an append[a]ge of a general revival of religion all is well. I fear no other form of carrying this question will save our country or the liberty or soul of the slave.[98]

Finney expressed his fear that the country would be consumed by a violent polemic, namely civil war, on the issue of slavery. Finney argued that if the public focused on the question of abolition primarily, rather than the salvation of individuals to the Christian faith, violence would ensue. Therefore, he insisted that "the public[k] mind can be engrossed with the subject of salvation [making] abolition an appendage, just as we made temperance an appendage of the revival in Rochester."[99] Finney, with Weld, maintained the primacy of individual

---

these new roles would change the structure of society. They were right" (*Women Called to Witness*, 85).

[97] Hardesty, *Women Called to Witness*, 100. Similarly perhaps for Leslie Newbigin, "There is no knowledge of God apart from the love of God, and there is no love of God apart from the love of the neighbor, 'He who does not love does not know God' (I John 4:8; cf. 3:14-24)" (*The Open Secret: An Introduction to the Theology of Mission*, rev. ed. [Grand Rapids: Eerdmans, 1995], 97). In an earlier remark, Newbigin explains, "Over and over again it has been urged that all this 'social service' deflects the attention of missions from the primary business of evangelism. New agencies have been formed, vowing to avoid all this entanglement in secular affairs and to concentrate entirely on the preaching of the gospel. But again and again the simple logic of the gospel itself has drawn them irresistibly into some work of education, healing the sick, feeding the hungry, helping the helpless" (92).

[98] Charles Finney to Theodore Weld from Oberlin, Ohio, July 21, 1836, in Barnes and Dumond, *Weld Grimké Letters*, 318–19.

[99] Barnes and Dumond, *Weld Grimké Letters*, 319. According to Timothy Smith, "Finney, for example, inspired many an abolitionist. But he never thought himself primarily a reformer. . . . Though always an abolitionist, he believed his first work was

salvation and conversion to the Christian faith. However, their evangelistic theology and practice focused upon individual salvation through the repentance of sins (specifically slavery) and conversion (namely abolition), maintaining the connection between faith and practice. Finney was not satisfied with the expectation that merely personal conversions within protracted meetings would dismantle social ills.[100] Rather, Finney preached a "whole" Christian gospel, individual salvation, and social reform.[101] Upon this foundation, Finney and others during the Second Great Awakening led the church to repentance of individual sins and conversion while not separating these from the subsequent implications for redeeming sinful lives and structures.[102] The Grimkés built upon this foundation, carrying the implications for the redemption of sins related to racism and sexism even further.

Finney provided further detail to his argument in his *Lectures on Revivals of Religion*. He delivered the lectures at the Chatham Street Theatre leased by Lewis Tappan for Finney while serving as the pastor of the Second Free Presbyterian Church in New York City.[103] According to Finney, "All preaching should be *practical*. The proper end of all doctrine is practical. Any thing brought forward as doctrine, which cannot be made use of as practical, is not preaching the gospel."

---

to save souls not free slaves" (*Revivalism and Social Reform in Mid-Nineteenth-Century America* [New York: Abingdon, 1957], 149–50).

[100] According to Noll, "In the long view of history, the Civil War can be seen as the last chapter in the Christian story of the Second Great Awakening. In the North, one of the reforms inspired by the revival was abolition, the drive to abolish slavery. Not all abolitionists were revivalist Protestants by any means, but many of them were. One of the most effective antislavery agents, for example, was Theodore Dwight Weld (1803-1895), a convert under revivalist Charles G. Finney who worked throughout the 1830s and 1840s with equal fervor to convert sinners and end slavery" (*A History of Christianity*, 314).

[101] Hardesty, *Women Called to Witness*, 87, 99.

[102] Smith, *Revivalism and Social Reform*, 108, see also 145, 158. According to Smith, "Finney's perfectionism flourished widely despite considerable criticism. Like other aspects of the Oberlin platform—revivalism and humanitarian reform—it was fitted to the temper of the times. A synthesis of the Quaker, Pietist, Methodist, and Puritan traditions of personal holiness [sanctification] was at work in American religion" (108).

[103] Hardesty, *Women Called to Witness*, 31. The theatre was outfitted as a chapel with seating for two thousand people. In his famous *Lectures on the Revivals of Religion*, Finney articulated a theology and methodology for revivals that still serve as a resource for many in the contemporary church. Finney served the Second Free Presbyterian Church from 1832 to 1836, when he became a Congregationalist and began pastoring New York's Sixth Free Church, also known as Broadway Tabernacle.

The organic wholeness of Finney's doctrine of practicality resulted in a sharp indictment of the church:

> The church is mighty orthodox in *notions*, but very heretical in practice, but the time must come when the church will be just as vigilant in guarding orthodoxy in practice as orthodoxy in doctrine, and just as prompt to turn out heretics in practice as heretics that corrupt the doctrines of the gospel. In fact, it is vastly more important.[104]

Finney seemed to avoid the deep waters of works of righteousness with his focus on personal conversion, while at the same time not succumbing to an antinomian shunning of good works by grounding them in holiness.

Against this background the Grimkés constructed a comprehensive evangelistic theology and practice integrating a complex understanding of sin and conversion with faithful responses—namely repentance of the sins of racism and sexism accompanied by conversion, which included abolition and gender rights.[105] Following their active public reform efforts, Sarah and Angelina, with husband Theodore Weld, compiled *American Slavery As It Is: A Testimony of a Thousand Witnesses* (1839); Sarah and Angelina contributed personal testimonies.[106] Sarah, calculating the incongruence, formulated the following rationale for her departure from South Carolina. "As I left my native state on account of slavery, and deserted the home of my fathers to escape the sound of the lash and the shrieks of tortured victims, I would gladly bury in oblivion the recollection of those scenes with which I have been familiar."[107]

The Grimké sisters' testimony demonstrated for them the inseparability of conversion from faithful Christian practices, particularly antislavery reform and the accessibility of women to education (so that all might faithfully employ their God-given talents). In her initial

---

[104] Finney, *Lectures on Revivals of Religion*, 198, 401.

[105] Later in life both Sarah and Angelina would venture further into Christian sectarianism, Sarah embracing Spiritualism and Angelina participating in the Millerite movement. Speicher, *The Religious World of Antislavery Women*, 62–66, 133–38. By request Sarah compiled examples of racial prejudice demonstrated within the Society of Friends (see p. 102).

[106] Theodore Weld, *American Slavery As It Is: Testimony of a Thousand Witnesses* (1839; repr. Salem, N.H.: Ayer, 1991). This material served as a resource for the later composition of *Uncle Tom's Cabin*, written by Harriet Beecher Stowe and published in 1852.

[107] S. Grimké, "Narrative and Testimony of Sarah M. Grimké," in Weld, *American Slavery As It Is*, 22.

submission to the compiled volume of testimonies, Sarah described the brutality inflicted on a young slave woman by a professing Christian woman.

> A handsome mulatto woman, about 18 or 20 years of age, whose independent spirit could not brook the degradation of slavery, was in the habit of running away: for this offence she had been repeatedly sent by her master and mistress to be whipped by the keeper of the Charleston work-house. This had been done with such inhuman severity, as to lacerate her back in a most shocking manner; a finger could not be laid between the cuts.[108]

The young woman continued to attempt escape, according to Sarah, "the love of liberty was too strong to be annihilated by torture." Again she was brutally whipped and a heavy iron collar with three long prongs was placed around her neck. In addition to this severe and painful punishment, the young woman's front tooth was extracted, serving as a mark of identification in the event of a subsequent escape.[109]

> Her sufferings at this time were agonizing; she could lie in no position but on her back, which was sore from scourgings, as I can testify, from personal inspection, and her only place of rest was on the floor, on a blanket. These outrages were committed in a family where the mistress daily read the scriptures, and assembled her children for family worship.[110]

Sarah saw the young woman in this condition and was unable to reconcile such rancorous violence on the part of the mistress with her appearance of Christian piety and faithfulness.

> She was accounted, and was really, so far as alms-giving was concerned, a charitable woman, and tender hearted to the poor; and yet this suffering slave, who was the seamstress of the family, was continually in her presence, sitting in her chamber to sew, or engaged in her other household work, with her lacerated and bleeding back, her mutilated mouth, and heavy iron collar, without, so far as appeared, exciting any feelings of compassion.[111]

---

[108] Grimké, "Narrative and Testimony of Sarah M. Grimké," in Weld, *American Slavery As It Is*, 22.

[109] Grimké, "Narrative and Testimony of Sarah M. Grimké," 22. See also Lerner, *The Grimké Sisters*, 37.

[110] Grimké, "Narrative and Testimony of Sarah M. Grimké," 22.

[111] Grimké, "Narrative and Testimony of Sarah M. Grimké," 22.

In her testimonies, Angelina echoed Sarah's horror to the cruelty of slavery, specifically practiced by professing Christians.

> I will first introduce the reader to a woman of the highest respectability—one who was foremost in every benevolent enterprise, and stood for many years, I may say, at the *head* of the fashionable elite of the city of Charleston, and afterwards at the head of the moral and religious female society there. It was after she had made a profession of religion, and retired from the fashionable world, that I knew her; therefore I will present her in her religious character.[112]

The weight of both Sarah and Angelina's detailed accounts is magnified by the violence perpetrated by Christian women and men of social standing. During the time it was often assumed that with affluence attended the additional characteristic of moral capacity. Angelina continued:

> After the 'revival' in Charleston, in 1825, she opened her house to social prayer-meetings. The room in which they were held in the evening, and where the voice of prayer was heard around the family altar, and where she herself retired for private devotion thrice each day, was the very place in which, when her slaves were to be whipped with the cowhide, they were taken to receive the infliction; and the wail of the sufferer would be heard, where, perhaps only a few hours previous, rose the voices of prayer and praise.[113]

The Grimké sisters would not allow themselves to rest in silent resignation, but pursued a treacherous path calling for the repentance and reconciliation of such sinful inconsistencies through an evangelistic ministry.[114]

[112] Weld, "Testimony of Angelina Grimké Weld," in Weld, *American Slavery As It Is*, 53.

[113] Weld, "Testimony of Angelina Grimké Weld," 53. See also L. Ceplair, ed., *The Public Years of Sarah and Angelina Grimké: Selected Writings 1835–1839* (New York: Columbia University Press, 1989), 340–41.

[114] The Grimkés' evangelistic ministry resonates with Brad Kallenberg's assertion, "Our notion of evangelism must be broadened so that we insist on embodying the story in the web of relationships that constitutes our identity" (*Live to Tell: Evangelism for a Postmodern Age* [Grand Rapids: Brazos, 2002], 8). This takes on some urgency in light of continued reluctance among contemporary evangelicals to consider the implications of race for their often enthusiastic, but truncated, evangelistic practices. The following is from J. Stott's (previously cited; see n. 20 to the introduction) description of the International Congress on World Evangelization held in Lausanne, Switzerland, July 16–24, 1974. A groundbreaking gathering in many ways, the excerpt demonstrates a relatively recent expression of such reluctance. "Thirdly,

Evangelistic Theology and Practice

Sarah and Angelina Grimké's inability to reconcile the inconsistencies of their understanding of Christian faith and discipleship with the social landscape of their context led them to compose a bold evangelistic theology.[115] Through their participation in the American Anti-Slavery Society, the Grimkés assembled an evangelistic theology that refused to separate conversion from condition—particularly for enslaved African Americans and women. This led to a provocative understanding of sin not merely as pride, but also as lack of self.

During their brief careers as agents for the American Anti-Slavery Society from 1836 to 1839, the Grimké sisters wrote copiously for the movement. As mentioned earlier, Angelina Grimké wrote *Appeal to Christian Women of the South* (1836) while summering in New Jersey. The response to this essay was emphatic, resulting in Angelina's invitation to attend the American Anti-Slavery Society's Agents' Convention. Sarah Grimké later wrote *Letters on the Equality of the Sexes* (1838), the first American-authored fully developed women's rights argument, ten years before the first women's rights convention in Seneca Falls, New York. Sarah wrote this essay, which appeared in a series of published pieces in the *New England Spectator* and the *Liberator* in 1837 and 1838, ultimately as a response to controversy ignited by a pastoral letter circulated by Congregational clergy.[116] The

---

Lausanne emphasized the need to take culture seriously. The relation of culture to evangelism was a major topic of debate. Although there is still hesitation among us about contemporary references to black theology, African theology, etc. . ." ("The Significance of Lausanne," *International Review of Mission* 64 [1975]: 290–91). According to McCants, the purpose of *Appeal* "was to preach personal and national salvation" ("Evangelicalism and Nineteenth-Century Women's Rights," 52; see also 51 for related themes).

[115] Although the Grimkés struggled to find communities of faith within which to live in accountable relationship, their persistence in working to reconcile the inconsistencies of their Christian faith with the social landscape is echoed by Kallenberg. "In Paul's first letter to Timothy, he urges him to do the work of an evangelist. Significantly, one way Timothy is to discharge this responsibility is by caring for the quality of life within the local body—because the fit between church's corporate life and its message is crucial to getting the message through" (*Live to Tell*, 49–50).

[116] Speicher, *The Religious World of Antislavery Women*, 110–11, 113; Lerner, *The Feminist Thought of Sarah Grimké*, 5. According to Lerner, "The Congregational clergy, which had long sought to silence antislavery speakers in the churches, on July 28, 1837, issued a 'Pastoral Letter of the General Association of Massachusetts to the Congregational Churches under their care' which warned all churches against females 'who so far forget themselves as to itinerate in the character of public lecturers and teachers' and exhorted women to 'their appropriate duties' as stated in the

essays demonstrate the development of the Grimkés' evangelistic theology that emerged from Angelina's antislavery argument (1836) and its development into Sarah's women's rights argument (1838) empowering women to use their gifts in Christian service.

Angelina Grimké's "Appeal to the Christian Women of the South"

Angelina Grimké spent almost half of the entire length of her essay offering a comprehensive biblical argument against slavery. The Grimkés' abolitionist position is clearly documented in their published tracts demonstrating the biblical foundations. Angelina surveyed both Old and New Testament texts to outline her biblical argument, beginning with Genesis and highlighting Jesus' teaching.[117] Upon this biblical foundation, Angelina appealed to women from her sense of Christian duty.

Angelina stated her evangelistic motive in addressing women on the subject of slavery: "It is because I feel a deep and tender interest in your present and eternal welfare that I am willing thus publicly to address you." She continued, "I do not believe the time has yet come when *Christian women* 'will not endure sound doctrine,' even on the subject of Slavery, if it is spoken to them in tenderness and love, therefore I now address you." With Finney and Weld, Angelina declared slavery sinful and therefore contrary to the efficacy of conversion and an impediment to Christian faithfulness. "It will be, and that very soon, clearly perceived and fully acknowledged by all the virtuous and the candid, that in *principle* it is as sinful to hold a human being in bondage who has been born in Carolina, as one who has been born in Africa."[118]

New Testament. This attack on the only two women then publicly lecturing in New England [Sarah and Angelina Grimké], which was read from the pulpits in many churches and widely distributed, was part of an ongoing struggle within the New England churches over the issue of slavery and abolition and aimed, in its veiled attack on William Lloyd Garrison, to split the more conservative abolitionists from Garrison" (19). *The Pastoral Letter* was published in response to the Grimkés' 1837 lecture tour. Interestingly, the Grimkés were invited and intended to speak only to groups of women. However, men, often critics rather than supporters, also attended the gatherings, ironically creating the very dynamic they then vehemently opposed (Speicher, *The Religious World of Antislavery Women*, 109–22).

[117] Sarah proposed seven arguments against slavery—five biblical, the remaining two based on natural rights. See Speicher, *The Religious World of Antislavery Women*, 90–91.

[118] A. Grimké, "Appeal to Christian Women of the South," *The Anti-Slavery Examiner* 1 (1836): 1–2. Although Angelina referred to the Bible as her "ultimate appeal in all matters of faith and practice," she made a brief reference to the

Angelina then shifted to the role of Christian women. "But perhaps you will be ready to query, why appeal to *women* on this subject?
We do not make the laws which perpetuate slavery. *No* legislative
power is vested in *us*; *we* can do nothing to over throw the system,
even if we wished to do so." Angelina expanded upon the implications
of her evangelistic motive. "To this I reply, I know you do not make
the laws, but I also know that *you are the wives and mothers, the sisters
and daughters of those who do*; and if you really suppose *you* can do nothing to overthrow slavery, you are greatly mistaken."[119] Here Angelina
began to reveal an underlying thread of women's empowerment or
feminism that Sarah would later expand in *Letters on the Equality of the
Sexes*. Angelina penned a letter during the same summer she composed her *Appeal* in which she further supported the evangelistic ministry of women. "A woman was the only earthly parent of the Prince
of Peace. . . . To a woman too, he first appeared after his resurrection.
. . . If then the Prince of Peace has conferd [*sic*] such high and special
tokens of regard upon woman, ought she not to aid in spreading far
and wide those principles?"[120] Angelina also alluded to the southern
white woman's role, though qualified, within the domestic context.
Southern Evangelical Christians reluctant to pursue antislavery
reform often argued for slavery's domestic character as an extension
of the family household.[121] With the elevation of the home in the
nineteenth century, southern Evangelicals, among others, elaborated
upon the possibly expanded role of women within domesticity.[122] For
Angelina, the powerlessness of southern Christian women was an
inadequate response to the sin of slavery in their midst.

Angelina outlined instructions in four areas for women to subvert
the sinful system in which they lived: "1st. You can read on this sub-

---

founding fathers, "this self evident truth that all men are created equal, and that they
have certain unalienable right liberty" (3, 25). Angelina demonstrated the inconsistencies related to the foundation of the nation and its oppressive practices such as
slavery.

[119] A. Grimké, "Appeal to Christian Women of the South," 16.

[120] Angelina Grimké to L. Dodge [and Olive Branch Circle], July 14, 1836,
Theodore Weld papers, Library of Congress, quoted in Speicher, *The Religious World
of Antislavery Women*, 114. With the other women in this study (with the possible
exception of Julia Foote), the Grimkés referred to Jesus' example and ministry to support their arguments and shape their ministries, while often alluding to and undermining Pauline critiques.

[121] Mathews, *Religion in the Old South*, 100.

[122] Cott, "The ideology of domesticity may seem to be contradicted functionally
and abstractly by feminism, but historically—as they emerged in the United States—
the latter depended on the former" (*The Bonds of Womanhood*, 9).

ject. 2d. You can pray over this subject. 3d. You can speak on this subject. 4th. You can act on this subject." Angelina promptly addressed placing reading prior to praying, "I have not placed reading before praying because I regard it more important, but because, in order to pray aright, we must understand what we are praying for; it is only then we can 'pray with the understanding and the spirit also.'" Angelina encouraged women to "Read then on the subject of slavery. Search the Scriptures daily, whether the things I have told you are true."[123] Angelina previewed the theme of empowerment through intellectual cultivation that Sarah would later elaborate. "Judge for yourselves whether *he* [Jesus] *sanctioned* such a system of oppression and crime."[124]

The second practice Angelina named, "Pray over this subject," although seemingly passive, actually pointed to a comprehensive revivalism in the spirit of Finney and Weld.

> When you have entered into your closets, and shut the doors, then pray to your father, who seeth in secret, that he would open your eyes to see whether slavery is *sinful*, and if it is, that he would enable you to bear a faithful, open and unshrinking testimony against it, and to do whatsoever your hands find to do, leaving the consequences entirely to him, who still says to us whenever we try to reason away duty from the fear of consequences, "*What is that to thee, follow thou me.*"[125]

Similarly, the third instruction, "Speak on this subject" also pointed to a more comprehensive set of practices, such as communication through "the tongue, the pen, and the press, that truth is principally propagated . . . to your relatives, your friends, your acquaintances on the subject of slavery."[126] Angelina continued, expanding a seeming

---

[123] A. Grimké, "Appeal to Christian Women of the South," 16–17. According to Cott, "By 1840, however, almost all women in New England could read and write, women's literacy having approximately doubled since 1780" (*The Bonds of Womanhood*, 15; see also 100, 103). Literacy rates generally were lower in the South. Among Christian women within households with the means to own slaves, a more substantial literacy would have existed. Many young affluent women received education in their homes, often alongside (usually limited) instruction in female academies. See Mathews, *Religion in the Old South*, 81–135.

[124] A. Grimké, "Appeal to Christian Women of the South," 17.

[125] A. Grimké, "Appeal to Christian Women of the South," 17.

[126] A. Grimké, "Appeal to Christian Women of the South," 17. Angelina softened her appeal to women with regard to speaking, omitting a call to public speaking. According to Brekus, "Eventually, of course, Sarah and Angelina Grimké helped create a more sexually egalitarian culture, but during the 1830s and 1840s, they caused

evangelistic focus upon verbal proclamation to include ministries of compassion.

> If you are served by the slaves of others, try to ameliorate their condition as much as possible. . . . Discountenance *all* cruelty to them, all starvation, all corporal chastisement. . . . If possible, see that they are comfortably and *seasonably* fed, whether in the house or the field; it is unreasonable and cruel to expect slaves to wait for their breakfast until eleven o'clock, when they rise at five or six. Do all you can, to induce their owners to clothe them well, and to allow them many little indulgences which would contribute to their comfort.[127]

Angelina's emerging evangelistic theology of empowerment included educational opportunities for slaves and women for the purpose of pursuing faithful and holy Christian lives. "Above all, try to persuade your husband, father, brothers and sons, that *slavery is a crime against God and man*, and that it is a great sin to keep *human beings* in such abject ignorance; to deny them the privilege of learning to read and write."[128]

Discussing at great length the fourth instruction, "Act on this subject," Angelina wove a robust antislavery and emerging feminist perspective into her evangelistic theology. "Some of you *own* slaves yourselves. If you believe slavery is *sinful*, set them at liberty, 'undo the heavy burdens and let the oppressed go free.' If they wish to remain with you, pay them wages, if not let them leave you." Both Angelina and Sarah included threads of intellectual cultivation in this rich tapestry. "Should they [one's slaves] remain teach them . . . they have minds and those minds, *ought to be improved*. So precious a talent as intellect, never was given to be wrapt in a napkin and buried in the earth."[129] Angelina's allusion to the gospel parable of the talents admonished the dominant white southern culture for their disobedience to Christ's teaching that called for faithful stewardship of the "tal-

---

such a furor that any woman who spoke in public, even a theological conservative, seemed inherently dangerous. Ironically, the Grimkés had hoped to convince the American public to allow women into the pulpit, but instead, they inadvertently strengthened the prejudices against female preaching. They could never have foreseen how their battle for female equality would generate a conservative backlash against biblical as well as equalitarian feminists (Brekus, *Strangers and Pilgrims*, 281).

[127] Grimké, "Appeal to Christian Women of the South," 17–18. Angelina commented on the language of "*seasonably* fed," explaining that slaves who begin their labors early in the morning require their first nourishment of the day before 11 a.m.

[128] Grimké, "Appeal to Christian Women of the South," 18.

[129] Grimké, "Appeal to Christian Women of the South," 18.

ent" or gifts bestowed to them in Christ.[130] Angelina then nuanced her argument to include all, presumably implying the inclusion of her audience of all, including white southern, women in addition to slaves.

> It is the *duty* of all, as far as they can, to improve their own mental faculties, because we are commanded to love God with *all our minds*, as well as with all our hearts, and we commit a great sin, if we *forbid or prevent* that cultivation of the mind in others, which would enable them to perform this duty. Teach your servants then to read &c, and encourage them to believe it is their *duty* to learn, if it were only that they might read the Bible.[131]

As illustrated earlier, the practice of teaching a slave to read was illegal in many southern states. Nonetheless, Angelina valiantly rebutted opposing arguments. For Angelina these laws *"ought to be no barrier* in the way of your duty, and I appeal to the Bible to prove this position."* For one of many biblical allusions used to support her rebuttal, Angelina looked to the apostles Peter and John.

> When the rulers of the Jews, "not to speak at all, nor teach in the name of Jesus," what did they say? "Whether it be right in the sight of God, to hearken unto you more than unto God, judge ye." And what did they do? "They spake the word of God with boldness, and with great power gave the Apostles witness of the *resurrection* of the Lord Jesus"; although *this* was the very doctrine, for the preaching of which, they had just been cast into prison, and further threatened.[132]

Angelina countered the argument "if we do free our slaves, they will be taken up and sold, therefore there will be no use in doing it" with the following: "Peter and John might just as well have said, we will not

---

[130] Other female preachers and social reformers, particularly those interested in suffrage, throughout the nineteenth century do not seem to reference this parable, nor pursue a similar interpretation as the Grimkés. See Zink-Sawyer, *From Preachers to Suffragists*. Zink-Sawyer provides an index of biblical passages employed by women in their advocacy of women's ecclesiastic and political rights. However, the Grimkés' exegesis and biblical interpretation of the parable of the talents is consistent with southern Evangelicalism's early emphasis and Finney's doctrinal and revivalistic emphasis upon the converted individual's response of faith characterized by a life of holiness and disciplined practices.

[131] Grimké, "Appeal to Christian Women of the South," 18. Interestingly, according to Heyrman, the Evangelicalism that informed the Grimkés? evangelistic theology and practice, at least in part, perceived intellectual cultivation, specifically "unenlightened learning," as a threat (*Southern Cross*, 3–4, 6, 8).

[132] Grimké, "Appeal to Christian Women of the South," 19.

preach the gospel, for if we do, we shall be taken up and put in prison, therefore there will be no use in our preaching."[133] Angelina boldly called southern Christian women to accept the duty of their faith to witness to the resurrection of Jesus Christ, and thus embody the gospel message through their words and in their lives.

Angelina's clarity on the question of slavery and the Christian's faithful evangelistic response rang clearly. She witnessed the violent oppression of slavery upon her housemates and neighbors, recognized and identified the inconsistency of such a system with the Christian faith, and received excommunication for her refusal to submit in silent prayer. Aware of the consequences of suffering for such actions, Angelina proclaimed, "If Prophets and Apostles, Martyrs, and Reformers had not been willing to suffer for the truth's sake, where would the world have been now? If they had said, we cannot speak the truth, we cannot do what we believe is right, because the *laws of our country or public opinion are against us*, where would our holy religion have been now?" Angelina juxtaposed obedience to God as "the doctrine of the Bible" with obedience to "man." "You must take it up on *Christian* ground, and fight against it with Christian weapons, whilst your feet are shod with the preparation of the gospel of peace."[134]

Indicative of their public ministry, Sarah and Angelina's focus upon the sin of slavery led them to uncover the related sin of woman's disenfranchisement. Both Grimké sisters textured their evangelistic theology and practice with the empowerment of woman.

> *Women* as well as men were to be living stones in the temple of grace, and therefore *their* heads were consecrated by the descent of the Holy Ghost as well as those of men. Were *women* recognized as fellow laborers in the gospel field? They were! Paul says in his epistle to the Philippians, "help those *women* who labored with me, in the gospel;" Phil. iv, 3.[135]

Angelina reiterated the theme of empowerment in the context of "religious duty," an allusion to the believers' responsibility to pursue good

[133] A. Grimké, "Appeal to Christian Women of the South," 19.

[134] A. Grimké, "Appeal to Christian Women of the South," 20; 26. Admittedly this last statement is a mixed metaphor?weapons to prepare the gospel of peace. Sarah Grimké committed to pacifism later in life.

[135] A. Grimké, "Appeal to Christian Women of the South," 22. Angelina's treatment of women's empowerment particularly in the South spoke directly to the intricate gender conventions of that society which at all levels placed women in subordinate roles to men. See Fox-Genovese, *Within the Plantation Household*, 195.

works, through her encouragement of southern women to read scripture, and pray on the question of slavery. Angelina claimed, "This is all *they* [northern women] can do for you, *you* must work out your own deliverance with fear and trembling, and with the direction and blessing of God, *you can do it.*"[136] For Angelina, with Finney and Weld, antislavery reform remained an inseparable appendage of Christian salvation through faith alone. Angelina passionately petitioned:

> Are there no Shiphrahs, no Puahs among you, who will dare in Christian firmness and Christian meekness, to refuse to obey the *wicked laws* which require *woman to enslave, to degrade and to brutalize woman*? Are there no Miriams, who would rejoice to lead out the captive daughters of the Southern States to liberty and light? Are there no Huldahs there who will dare to *speak the truth* concerning the sins of the people and those judgments, which it requires no prophet's eye to see, must follow if repentance is not speedily sought? Is there no Esther among you who will plead for the poor devoted slave?[137]

Angelina's antislavery argument provided an evangelistic witness to the Christian gospel, which included redemption for southern white women complicit within a sinful system. Angelina's essay previewed several themes Sarah later elaborated on, constructing an argument both for the abolition of slavery and the empowerment of women within an evangelistic theology.

Sarah Grimké's "Letters on the Equality of the Sexes"

Angelina and Sarah Grimké composed an evangelistic theology that empowered women to respond to God's salvation in Jesus Christ. The Grimkés' nuanced conception of sin not merely as pride (with related juridical implications), but also as lack of self, offered insight and further alternatives to reigning themes of repentance and conversion.[138]

---

[136] A. Grimké, "Appeal to Christian Women of the South," 24. This is not to say that northern Christians, and women in particular, could not also be largely apathetic to the evils of slavery and racial prejudice in their own forms of complicity.

[137] A. Grimké, "Appeal to Christian Women of the South," 25.

[138] For example, see Susan Juster's study of more than two hundred accounts of early nineteenth-century religious conversions: "'In a Different Voice': Male and Female Narratives of Religious Conversion in Post-Revolutionary America," *American Quarterly* 41 (1989): 40–43, cited in Speicher, *The Religious World of Antislavery Women*, 75.

Sarah's perception of a woman not fulfilling her potential "as an immortal being" created in the image of God grounded her contribution to an evangelistic theology.

> When I view woman as an immortal being, traveling through this world to that city whose builder and maker is God,—when I contemplate her in all the sublimity of her spiritual existence, bearing the image and superscription of Jehovah, emanating from Him and partaking of his nature, and destined, if she fulfils her duty, to dwell with him through the endless ages of eternity,—I mourn that she has lived so far below her privileges and her obligations, as a rational and accountable creature; and I ardently long to behold her occupying that sphere in which I believe her Creator designed her to move.[139]

For Sarah, through faithful Christian discipleship women could realize God's potential for them. In her *Letters on the Equality of the Sexes*, Sarah outlined an evangelistic theology for women that included: (1) woman's reading and interpreting scripture (preferably in its original languages), (2) an acknowledgment of woman's equality with man, thereby claiming her evangelistic ministry, (3) the oppression of woman, particularly white affluent women, had resulted in her "vacuity of mind" necessitating her intellectual cultivation, (4) through (white affluent) woman's salvation and holiness she may confess to her complicity in the sins of racism, (5) which lead her to respond in ministry to the spiritual and material welfare of others, namely slaves. Therefore, for the Grimkés the proclamation and embodiment of the gospel, particularly for and among the disenfranchised, included acknowledgment of self, good use/stewardship of "talents," and intellectual cultivation toward a more textured understanding and experience of sin and salvation.

Sarah began her argument in *Letters on the Equality of the Sexes* persuading women to work toward the extinction of sin by receiving empowerment through their reading of Scripture.

---

[139] S. Grimké, *Letters on the Equality of the Sexes and Other Essays*, ed. Elizabeth Ann Bartlett (New Haven: Yale University Press, 1988), 67–68. Sarah, building on Angelina's previous arguments for the empowerment of women, offered glimpses of insights later expanded by Valerie Saving's groundbreaking thesis regarding woman's particular experience in theology, specifically sin. Serene Jones has composed a careful harmony of feminist theory and Christian theology that addresses woman's experience of justification and sanctification, among other theological issues, illuminating the Grimkés' early reflections (*Feminist Theory and Christian Theology*, 55–68, 110–11).

My present object is to show, that, as woman is charged with all the sin that exists in the world, it is her solemn duty to labor for its extinction; and that this she can never do effectually and extensively, until her mind is disenthralled of those shackles which have been riveted upon her by a *"corrupt public opinion, and a perverted interpretation of the holy Scriptures."*[140]

Sarah's remark that woman was "charged with all the sin that exists in the world" is an allusion to woman's complicity with Eve in the fall. Sarah understood woman to possess responsibility for working toward the extinction of sin in the world in part because of her high moral nature, a perspective largely consistent with nineteenth-century gender constructs. While the ideological shift in gender expectations from the eighteenth to the nineteenth century is one of the most important in American history, scholars have not yet fully explained how woman's complicity in the fall became woman's innate virtue.[141] Sarah argued, though, that for women to capably pursue this endeavor they must reclaim biblical foundations for the reinterpretation of those gender constructs that also limit woman's potential for participation in the reign of God.

Sarah emphasized the need for women to read scripture in the original languages for the purpose of interpreting the biblical texts for themselves, rather than relying upon male clergy and other ecclesiastical leaders to interpret for them.

King James's translators certainly were not inspired. I therefore claim the original as my standard, *believing that to have been inspired,* and I also claim to judge for myself what is the meaning of the inspired writers, because I believe it to be the solemn duty of every individual to search the Scriptures for themselves, with the aid of the Holy Spirit, and not be governed by the views of any man, or set of men.[142]

[140] Grimké, *Letters on the Equality of the Sexes and Other Essays,* 96.

[141] According to Brekus, the shift in gender expectations from the eighteenth to the nineteenth century is "one of the most important ideological transformations in American history" (*Strangers and Pilgrims,* 146). "Unlike the Puritan clergymen of New England, or the Separates of the first Great Awakening, or the Founding Fathers of the American Revolution, nineteenth century ministers believed that women were as virtuous, if not *more* virtuous, than men" (146). Brekus goes on to acknowledge that "historians still have not fully explained why there was such a remarkable shift in attitudes toward women in the late eighteenth and early nineteenth centuries. How did the sinful, lustful Eve become the pure and passionless Mary?" (147).

[142] S. Grimké, *Letters on the Equality of the Sexes and Other Essays,* 32. According

Sarah's argument encouraged women to read and interpret scripture utilizing the radical individualism of Enlightenment ideology in response to a selective application to the rights and social constructs attributed to women and people of African descent. In her strategy to empower women, Sarah interpreted the creation and fall narratives in Genesis:

> In all this sublime description of the creation of man, (which is a generic term including man and woman), there is not one particle of difference intimated as existing between them. They were both made in the image of God; dominion was given to both over every other creature, but not over each other. Created in perfect equality, they were expected to exercise the vicegerence intrusted to them by their Maker, in harmony and love.[143]

Sarah continued her interpretation of the Genesis fall narrative describing Eve's infraction and Adam's subsequent sharing in the same sin, though "not through the instrumentality of a supernatural agent, but through that of his equal." The eighteenth-century "one-sex" model of gender that perceived women as similar physically to men although weaker and incomplete, meant that for women to preach they must overcome the limitations of their gender. In contrast, the nineteenth-century "two-sex" model of gender perceived women as different from men, and their femininity included an innate virtue that could allow women to preach as women.[144]

> Had Adam tenderly reproved his wife, and endeavored to lead her to repentance instead of sharing in her guilt, I should be much more ready to accord to man that superiority which he claims. . . . [I]t appears to me that to say the least, there was as much weakness

---

to Lerner, in her introduction to *The Feminist Thought of Sarah Grimké*, 22–24, Sarah had read Locke, Jefferson, and other founding fathers—thus she was acquainted with the rights ideology of the Enlightenment. According to Bartlett the intellectual and social context of Sarah's feminism was not only (1) liberal politics/enlightenment but also (2) romanticism and (3) utopic socialists. Additional social roots of Sarah's thought included (1) deprivation of status among middle-class women, (2) cult of domesticity, (3) and other social reform movements such as health reform, temperance, antislavery, or generally "moral reform" (see Bartlett, introduction to *Letters on the Equality of the Sexes*, 6–13).

[143] S. Grimké, *Letters on the Equality of the Sexes and Other Essays*, 32.

[144] S. Grimké, *Letters on the Equality of the Sexes and Other Essays*, 33. See Brekus, *Strangers and Pilgrims*, 14–15.

exhibited by Adam as by Eve. They both fell from innocence, and consequently from happiness, *but not from equality.*[145]

Woman's equality with man in the fall, then, held woman responsible with man for sins in the world. "The Lord Jesus defines the duties of his followers in his Sermon on the Mount. He lays down grand principles by which they should be governed, without any reference to sex or condition."[146] For Sarah, woman's empowerment required their acknowledgment of complicity in the sins of racism. However, for women to address sins of racism, their repentance required more texture.

Sarah vehemently argued against the Congregationalist clergy's patronizing claim that, "We appreciate the *unostentatious* prayers and efforts of woman in advancing the cause of religion at home and abroad, in leading religious inquirers TO THE PASTOR for instruction." Sarah's rebuttal began with the *ostentatious* efforts of "Anna the prophetess, (or preacher,) who departed not from the temple, but served God with fasting and prayers night and day and spake of Christ to all them that looked for redemption in Israel." Sarah then audaciously turned to the apostle Paul. "The apostle Paul encourages women to be ostentatious in their efforts to spread the gospel."[147] Sarah was clearly unconvinced by the position that women should lead religious inquirers to pastor's for instruction.

> The Lord Jesus says,—"Come unto me and learn of me" [Matt 11.29]. He points his followers to no man; and when woman is made the favored instrument of rousing a sinner to his lost and helpless condition, she has no right to substitute any teacher for Christ; all she has to do is, to turn the contrite inquirer to the

---

[145] S. Grimké, *Letters on the Equality of the Sexes*, 33. According to Gerda Lerner, the interpretation that Adam and Eve both fell from innocence, but not from equality was "an interpretation made before her by Isotta Nogarola (1418–1466), Rachel Speght (1600?–?), and Aemilia Lanyer (1569–1645), among others" (*The Feminist Thought of Sarah Grimké*, 23).

[146] S. Grimké, *Letters on the Equality of the Sexes*, 38. Sarah continued, "I follow him through all his precepts, and find him giving the same directions to women as to men, never even referring to the distinction now so strenuously insisted upon between masculine and feminine virtues: this is one of the anti-christian 'traditions of men' which are taught instead of the 'commandments of God.' Men and women were CREATED EQUAL; they are both moral and accountable beings, and whatever is right for man to do, is *right* for woman." Sarah, although here arguing against gender social constructs, also at times claimed to support them. S. Grimké, "Sisters of Charity," in *Letters on the Equality of the Sexes*, 162–63.

[147] S. Grimké, *Letters on the Equality of the Sexes*, 39–40.

"Lamb of God which taketh away the sins of the world" [John 1.29].
More souls have probably been lost by going down to Egypt for
help, and by trusting in man in the early stages of religious experience, than by any other error. . . . The business of men and women,
who are ORDAINED OF GOD to preach the unsearchable riches
of Christ to a lost and perishing world, is to lead souls to Christ, and
not to Pastors for instruction.[148]

Despite severe limitations upon woman's ecclesiastic rights, Sarah
bravely proposed woman's role with man's to serve as evangelistic
ministers of Christ.

The cornerstone of Sarah's evangelistic theology, specifically
addressed to women, was the conviction of their unfaithful stewardship of the talents granted them by God. "God created us equal;—he
created us free agents;—he is our Lawgiver, our King and our Judge,
and to him alone is woman bound to be in subjection, and to him
alone is she accountable for the use of those talents with which her
Heavenly Father has entrusted her."[149] For Sarah, woman, like man,
must accept accountability for her duty to utilize faithfully the talents
and gifts entrusted to her by God.

The woman who goes forth, clad in the panoply of God, to stem the
tide of iniquity and misery, which she beholds rolling through our
land, goes not forth to her labor of love as a female. She goes as the
dignified messenger of Jehovah, and all she does and says must be
done and said irrespective of sex. She is in duty bound to communicate with all, who are able and willing to aid her in saving her fellow creatures, both men and women, from that destruction which
awaits them.[150]

For Sarah, a woman's response to God in Jesus Christ and subsequent participation in evangelistic ministry as "the dignified messenger of Jehovah" superseded social constructions of gender. Gender
constructs of the time, still inseparable from social constructs of race
and class, impeded opportunities for women, defining women as

[148] S. Grimké, *Letters on the Equality of the Sexes*, 40.

[149] S. Grimké, *Letters on the Equality of the Sexes*, 34

[150] S. Grimké, *Letters on the Equality of the Sexes*, 43. Church was the arena for
women during the nineteenth century. During the Second Great Awakening the ratio
of female to male converts was three to two. Clergy called on women to use their
unique moral natures to reform the world. To prepare and sustain this mission the
women were formed in prayer groups, missionary societies, and moral reform societies. See the introduction by Bartlett, 13.

weaker physically, emotionally, and intellectually. Women, specifically affluent women of considerable social status, were often forbidden from serving their neighbors when those in need were of inferior social status. Many considered such interaction as potentially dangerous, for it was perceived that it could tarnish one's perceived purity.

> So far from woman losing any thing of the purity of her mind, by visiting the wretched victims of vice in their miserable abodes, by talking with them, or of them, she becomes more and more elevated and refined in her feelings and views. While laboring to cleanse the minds of others from the malaria of moral pollution, her own heart becomes purified, and her soul rises to nearer communion with her God.[151]

Sarah linked the conversion of individuals, specifically women, to their response in faith to serve their neighbors in need despite social perceptions.

Sarah urged women, particularly white affluent women, not to remain content in their comfortable domestic settings. "Fashionable women regard themselves, and are regarded by men, as pretty toys or as mere instruments of pleasure."[152] Indeed, affluent women's complicity in the sins of racism extended to the implications of their many comforts and even the ideal of "lady," a concept intimately connected to the gender and racial presuppositions of the time.[153] Sarah based her argument in the faithful Christian disciple's responsibility to appropriately steward one's gifts and the Christian woman's obligation to dismantle socially constructed barriers of class and race.

> Shall woman shrink from duty in this exigency, and retiring within her own domestic circle, delight herself in the abundance of her own selfish enjoyments? Shall she rejoice in her home, her husband, her children, and forget her brethren and sisters in bondage, who know not what it is to call a spot of earth their own, whose husbands and wives are torn from them by relentless tyrants, and whose children are snatched from their arms by their unfeeling task-masters? . . . Did God give her those blessings to steel her heart to the sufferings of her fellow creatures? . . . Ah no! for every such blessing, God demands a grateful heart; and woman must be recreant to

---

[151] S. Grimké, *Letters on the Equality of the Sexes*, 43.

[152] S. Grimké, *Letters on the Equality of the Sexes*, 56–57.

[153] See Fox-Genovese, *Within the Plantation Household*, 198–203, 212–16, for further detailed discussion. According to Fox-Genovese, "Southern ladies took their religious responsibilities seriously, but they were more likely to weave them into their ideals of rank than to draw upon them for criticism of their society" (232).

her duty, if she can quietly sit down in the enjoyments of her own domestic circle, and not exert herself to procure the same happiness for others.[154]

Sarah countered the opposing argument that "woman has a mighty weapon in secret prayer," agreeing that woman does possess this gift "*in common with man.*" She then claimed, "but the woman who prays in sincerity for the regeneration of this guilty world, will accompany her prayers by her labors." According to Sarah women plagued by "vacuity of mind," "heartlessness," and "frivolity" "have been called from such pursuits by the voice of the Lord Jesus, inviting their weary and heavy laden souls to come unto Him and learn of Him, that they may find something worthy of their immortal spirit, and their intellectual powers." Then these women "may learn the high and holy purposes of their creation, and consecrate themselves unto the service of God; and not, as is now the case, to the pleasure of man."[155]

In the service of God, rather than man, woman may respond in faithfulness practicing good stewardship of her gifts, particularly that of intellect. Sarah implored women to read scripture in its original languages, naming "vacuity of mind," "heartlessness," and "frivolity" as sinful distractions from a life of faithful Christian discipleship. Sarah quoted Adam Clarke's observation. "Woman has been invidiously defined, *an animal of dress.* How long will they permit themselves to be thus degraded?" Sarah responded, "Could [Christian women in the Roman Empire] have had their minds occupied by the foolish vanity of ornamental apparel? No! Christianity struck at the root of all sin." In comparison, "now if we look at Christendom, there is scarcely a vestige of that religion, which the Redeemer of men came to promulgate."[156] Sarah realized that although woman had been severely criticized for her interest in fashion, this was a symptom of woman's oppression. According to Sarah, in modern times the "universal dissemination of knowledge in all Protestant communities" and woman's participation "in the great moral enterprises of the day" such

---

[154] S. Grimké, *Letters on the Equality of the Sexes*, 53; 57.

[155] S. Grimké, *Letters on the Equality of the Sexes*, 57.

[156] S. Grimké, *Letters on the Equality of the Sexes*, 68–69. Sarah demonstrated her point with an illustration, "Many a woman will ply her needle with ceaseless industry, to obtain money to forward a favorite benevolent scheme, while at the same time she will expend on useless articles of dress, more than treble the sum which she procures by the employment of her needle, and which she might throw into the Lord's treasury, and leave herself leisure to cultivate her mind, and to mingle among the poor and the afflicted more than she can possibly do now" (70).

as moral reform, temperance, and antislavery have elevated her char-acter.[157] Sarah claimed God had commanded woman "not to be con-formed to this world, but to be transformed by the renewing of her mind, that she may know what is the good and acceptable and perfect will of God."[158]

With Finney, for both Sarah and Angelina, Christian faith should not remain an individual piety. The Grimké sisters insisted that Christians could not remain faithful without confession of their com-plicity in the sins of slavery. Sarah described the oppression of white women through lack of educational opportunities, subservience to men, and subsequent sins of "vacuity of mind," "heartlessness," and "frivolity." Alongside these descriptions, Sarah carefully acknowledged the plight of female slaves, while not equating the circumstances of female slaves with that of white women, but rather naming the more complex and severe oppression from which female slaves suffered.

> The virtue of female slaves is wholly at the mercy of irresponsible tyrants, and women are bought and sold in our slave markets, to gratify the brutal lust of those who bear the name of Christians. In our slave States, if amid all her degradation and ignorance, a woman desires to preserve her virtue unsullied, she is either bribed or whipped into compliance, or if she dares resist her seducer, her life by the laws of some of the slave States may be, and has actually been sacrificed to the fury of disappointed passion.[159]

Sarah referred to a statement quoted from the *Circular of the Kentucky Union*, "That such a state of society should exist in a Christian nation, claiming to be the most enlightened upon earth, without calling forth any *particular attention* to its existence, though ever before our eyes and *in our* families, is a moral phenomenon at once unaccountable and disgraceful."[160] Sarah clearly distinguished between the oppression of

[157] S. Grimké, *Letters on the Equality of the Sexes*, 69–70. Sarah quoted: "The sim-ple cobbler of Agawam, who wrote in Massachusetts as early as 1647, speaking of women, says 'It is no marvel they wear drailes on the hinder part of their heads, hav-ing nothing, as it seems, in the fore part, but a few squirrels' brains to help them frisk from one fashion to another'" (69).

[158] S. Grimké, *Letters on the Equality of the Sexes*, 71. This reference is to Romans 12:1-2.

[159] S. Grimké, *Letters on the Equality of the Sexes*, 59. According to Lerner, Sarah constructed social theory based on comparing two systems of oppression, but did not equate white women's position with that of the enslaved African American, particu-larly women (*The Feminist Thought of Sarah Grimké*, 24).

[160] S. Grimké, *Letters on the Equality of the Sexes*, 60.

white women and that of enslaved African women, calling white women to accountability for the complicity of their silence.

> In the daily habit of seeing the virtue of her enslaved sister sacrificed without hesitancy or remorse, she looks upon the crimes of seduction and illicit intercourse without horror. . . . Can any American woman look at these scenes of shocking licentiousness and cruelty, and fold her hands in apathy and say, "I have nothing to do with slavery"? *She cannot and be guiltless.*[161]

The Grimké sisters passionately advocated against slavery as an appendage of their own salvation by faith and that of others. The Grimkés were among the boldest to proclaim the connection between slavery and racial discrimination, understanding the deep roots of racism and identifying education as a means to alleviate this social evil.

Sarah authored a resolution that passed at the 1838 Women's Anti-Slavery Convention describing "the duty of abolitionists to identify themselves with these oppressed Americans, by sitting with them in places of worship, by appearing with them in our streets, by giving them our countenance in steam-boats and stages, by visiting them at their homes and encouraging them to visit us, receiving them as we do our white fellow citizens."[162] Sarah characterized the Grimkés' evangelistic ministry with one of its biblical foundations in this supplication to her readers, "How little do we comprehend that simple truth, 'By this shall all men know that ye are my disciples, if ye *have love one to another*" [John 13:25].[163]

Sarah and Angelina Grimké proclaimed the Christian gospel in their words, written and uttered, and in their lives as a response to

---

[161] S. Grimké, *Letters on the Equality of the Sexes*, 60–61.

[162] *Proceedings of the Anti-Slavery Convention* (1838), 8, quoted in Speicher, *The Religious World of Antislavery Women*, 100. Jones also acknowledges the varied implications of repentance and conversion, namely that at times grace is costly, such as in the case of the moneychangers and tax collectors like Zaccheus. At other times grace fulfills physical, mental, and spiritual longings. "In each of these cases, God's grace came through words and deeds that met the person's deepest needs and offered that person salvation" (S. Jones, *The Evangelistic Love of God and Neighbor: A Theology of Witness and Discipleship* [Nashville: Abingdon, 2003], 45–47).

[163] S. Grimké, *Letters on the Equality of the Sexes*, 62. Sarah extended her argument to include pacifism, "With the precepts and example of a crucified Redeemer, who, in that sublime precept, 'Resist not evil,' has interdicted to his disciples all war and all violence, and taught us that the spirit of retaliation for injuries, whether in the camp, or at the fire-side, is wholly at variance with the peaceful religion he came to promulgate."

their own conversions. The Grimkés' Christian faith was not limited to antislavery reform, but it did necessitate an extension beyond personal piety to its embodiment in lives of faithfulness and compassion. Through the Grimkés' participation in the antislavery movement they composed an evangelistic theology that refused to separate an individual's conversion from social and material condition. This led the Grimkés to a provocative understanding of sin not merely as pride, but also as lack of self. For the Grimkés the proclamation and embodiment of the gospel, particularly among the disenfranchised, included acknowledgment of self and faithful stewardship of one's talents—particularly intellect—toward a more textured understanding of sin and its relationship to the sinful structures of racial and gender discrimination.

> *I am persuaded that woman is not to be as she has been, a mere secondhand agent in the regeneration of the fallen world, but the acknowledged equal and coworker with man in this glorious work.*[164]

---

[164] Angelina Grimké to Jane Smith, August 10, 1837, quoted in Hardesty, *Women Called to Witness*, 43.

Julia A. J. Foote. Used by permission of the Robert W. Woodruff Library of the Atlanta University Center

3

~~JULIA A. J. FOOTE~~

How many at the present day profess great spirituality, and even holiness, and yet are deluded by a spirit of error, which leads them to say to the poor and the colored ones among them, "Stand back a little—I am holier than thou."[1]

Julia A. J. Foote's (1823–1901) evangelistic ministry assumed that with Christian faith persons could experience a *real change*.[2] As a result of her receipt of entire sanctification and such a real change, Foote answered a call to evangelistic ministry that included her advocacy of women's ecclesiastic rights and racial reconciliation. Foote, the first woman in the African Methodist Episcopal Zion Church to receive ordination as deacon in 1895 and the second woman to receive ordination as elder in 1899,[3] is well known among nineteenth-century

[1] J. Foote, "A Brand Plucked from the Fire: An Autobiographical Sketch by Mrs. Julia A. J. Foote" (Cleveland: W. F. Schneider, 1879), reprinted in W. Andrews, ed., *Sisters of the Spirit: Three Black Women's Autobiographies of the Nineteenth Century* (Bloomington: Indiana University Press, 1986), 167.

[2] The concept of real change is used by John Wesley in his sermon, "Scripture Way of Salvation." According to Wesley, "And at the same time that we are justified, yea, in that very moment, sanctification begins. In that instant we are 'born again', 'born from above', 'born of the Spirit'. There is a real as well as a relative change" ("The Scripture Way of Salvation," Sermon 43 in *Sermons* II, ed. A. Outler, *The Bicentennial Edition of the Works of John Wesley* (Nashville: Abingdon, 1976), 2:152–69, specifically 158. While Foote does not explicitly use these terms, her understanding of the doctrine of entire sanctification is consistent with Wesley's, as demonstrated later in the chapter.

[3] B. Collier-Thomas, *Daughters of Thunder: Black Women Preachers and Their*

African-American holiness preachers. Her autobiography "A Brand Plucked from the Fire," published in 1879, numbers among the few primary sources from nineteenth-century African-American women available for study.[4] In her autobiography, Foote described her evangelistic ministry, which extended beyond traditional notions of evangelism as verbal proclamation through publication and itinerant preaching, the latter stretching for more than fifty years.[5]

Traumatic experiences often rooted in racism, which punctuated her childhood and youth, informed Foote's faith and subsequent evangelistic ministry.[6] For example, Foote described the ill-treatment of her family in a local congregation and her first school teacher's execution by hanging for the murder of a young woman. Later, while residing with a white family, Foote was falsely accused of a small infraction, whipped, and subsequently contemplated suicide. In the face of such traumatic experiences, she described herself in childhood as one seeking spiritual direction, learning to pray and read the Bible, in spite of limited educational opportunities.

Foote's conversion unfolded similar to other African-American women preachers of the time in dramatic visions finally culminating in a much-desired experience of "full" or entire sanctification.[7] Her religious experiences in many ways fulfilled expectations of holiness

---

Sermons, 1850–1979 (San Francisco: Jossey Bass, 1998), 59. Collier-Thomas claims Foote was ordained deacon in 1895, with a reference to the *Minutes of the New York Conference*, 21, 31. Andrews names May 20, 1894, and cites Julia A. J. Foote, "A Brand Plucked from the Fire." See Andrews, *Sisters of the Spirit*, 10. Albert Raboteau does not distinguish between Foote's ordinations as deacon and elder. According to Raboteau, "The first black denomination to ordain a black woman was the African Methodist Episcopal Zion Church, which ordained Julia Foote in 1895" (*African-American Religion* [Oxford: Oxford University Press, 1999], 45).

[4] For further discussion of the role of spiritual autobiography in lending credibility to the evangelistic ministries of preaching women see S. Stanley, *Holy Boldness: Women Preachers' Autobiographies and the Sanctified Self* (Knoxville: University of Tennessee Press, 2002), xxx–xxxv, 26, 158, 204; and C. Brekus, *Strangers and Pilgrims: Female Preaching in America 1740–1845* (Chapel Hill: University of North Carolina Press, 1998), 173, 257–58.

[5] Collier-Thomas, *Daughters of Thunder*, 4, 59. Two of Foote's sermons are included in this volume, "A 'Threshing' Sermon" (Detroit, 1851), 64–65, and "Christian Perfection" (published in the Star of Zion, 1894), 66–68.

[6] For a thorough and helpful discussion of autobiography in America, see D. Bjorklund, *Interpreting the Self: Two Hundred Years of American Autobiography* (Chicago: University of Chicago Press, 1998).

[7] For an accessible description of the doctrine of sanctification from a Wesleyan/Holiness perspective, see Stanley, *Holy Boldness*, 1–17, 53–54.

communities, including loss of self and rebirth in Christ. Foote's experiences seemed also to contribute to a counteridentity formation, taking the perceived frailty of her human and feminine weakness and witnessing to its transformation into substantial strength for the purpose of sharing the gospel.[8] Christian faith often provided an empowering influence in the lives of African Americans, particularly women. Such spiritual interaction conferred a sense of personhood not accessible in other social realms.[9]

Foote seemed to be the only early African-American woman preacher to directly refer to Christian perfection, language that describes an experience of entire sanctification.[10] Her interpretation of her experience of entire sanctification was firmly located within Wesleyan/holiness tradition and was informed by both John Wesley and Phoebe Palmer (1807–1884), a prominent nineteenth-century holiness figure. Foote's theological imagination led her to understand entire sanctification as real change—"rooted and grounded in love."[11] Foote's experience resulted in her vocation to lead others to receive this religious experience.[12] However, such an experience for Foote and

[8] See Andrews, *Sisters of the Spirit*, 4, 14; Brekus, *Strangers and Pilgrims*, 180–81 and Stanley, *Holy Boldness*, 82–83, 94. See also K. R. Connor, *Conversions and Visions in the Writings of African-American Women* (Knoxville: University of Tennessee Press, 1994). Connor's cultural study identifies the significance of religion, specifically conversion and call to preach among African-American women's writings. According to Connor, this "recurrent pattern of emphasis on and concern with identity formation" among African-American women was born out of what W. E. B. Dubois described as the "double consciousness" of being an African-American woman. "In such a confrontation, all aspects of one's being and relationship to reality are called into question: race, gender, social status, intellectual and cultural background, and finally spiritual orientation" (Connor, *Conversions and Visions*, 2).

[9] According to Katherine Bassard, "within these private encounters with Spirit . . . African American women often experienced a conferral of personhood denied by larger social constructions of African American and female subjectivity" (*Spiritual Interrogations: Culture, Gender, and Community in Early African American Women's Writing* [Princeton: Princeton University Press, 1999], 3).

[10] Collier-Thomas, *Daughters of Thunder*, 59.

[11] See Foote, "A Brand Plucked from the Fire," 187, 163.

[12] The Wesleyan concept of real change in Foote's understanding of conversion resonates with Brad Kallenberg's claim, "the phenomenon of conversion can also be described from the human side. Behaviors change, associations change, directions change. In fact, the term conversion very simply means 'change.'" Kallenberg offers further clarification: "Simply put, when viewed through a postcritical lens, conversion can be understood as entailing the change of one's social identity, the acquisition of a new conceptual language, and the shifting of one's paradigm" (*Live to Tell: Evangelism for a Postmodern Age* [Grand Rapids: Brazos, 2002], 31, 32).

those with whom she ministered reached beyond merely individual implications. Foote included the following statement in the brief preface to her autobiography: "Those who are fully in the truth cannot possess a prejudiced or sectarian spirit."[13] While Foote's evangelistic ministry included itinerant preaching and ordinary practices of prayer and visitation, her experience of entire sanctification led her to additional implications resulting in her embrace of women's ecclesiastic rights and racial reconciliation.[14]

Formation in Faith

Born in Schenectady, New York, in 1823, Foote was her mother's fourth child. Although her father was born free, as a child he was stolen and enslaved.[15] Her mother, born a slave, suffered physical abuse. Her father also endured many hardships, including persistent exposure to severe weather. Her father eventually bought his freedom, then the freedom of his wife and first child. Foote described the vivid memory of her parents narrating how they were led to religion. After a nearly fatal accident one night on the way home from a dance, in which Foote's mother with an infant in her arms almost drowned, her parents decided, "We'll go to no more dances." According to Foote, they kept their word and soon after "made a public profession of religion and united with the M[ethodist] E[piscopal] Church."[16]

---

[13] Foote, "A Brand Plucked from the Fire," 163.

[14] Bassard addresses similar themes for different aims in her study: "The sense of a dialogue between metadiscursive realms—between different 'worlds,' we might say—for the purpose of both self-empowerment and communal political engagement informs" her text (*Spiritual Interrogations*, 4).

[15] Although the slave trade ceased in 1808, marked by celebrations among African-American congregations, slavery persisted. While slavery in the North is described as "milder" than its southern agrarian counterpart, it still "bore all the legal, economic, social, and racial markings of a slave system" (*Spiritual Interrogations*, 12). New York was the first state to pass a law in 1817 for the total abolition of slavery. This occurred gradually, with July 27, 1827, marking the end of slavery in New York (A. Zilversmit, *The First Emancipation: The Abolition of Slavery in the North* [Chicago: University of Chicago Press, 1967], 208–14).

[16] Foote, "A Brand Plucked from the Fire," 166–67. By 1787, African Americans constituted 15 percent of Methodist membership; by 1800 this increased to 20 percent, numbering 13,500, leading the General Conference to allow bishops to ordain local deacons of "African brethren," though the added stipulations resulted in this gesture never being fully realized. In 1816, the Methodist Episcopal Church had grown to 42,500 African-American and 172,000 Euro-American members. Despite the preaching of the gospel and affirmations of faith in Christ, this faith did not nec-

Similar to her parents, Foote's religious experiences seemed to respond, even protest, the traumas—most often rooted in racism—that punctuated her childhood.

The Methodist Episcopal Church was established in 1784 with antislavery commitments, largely as a result of the leadership of John Wesley and Frances Asbury. However, these commitments eroded during subsequent decades. Despite her parents' membership in the ME congregation they experienced racial prejudice. According to Foote, "They were not treated as Christian believers, but as poor lepers. They were obliged to occupy certain seats in one corner of the gallery, and dared not come down to partake of the Holy Communion until the last white communicant had left the table."[17] Thus, at an early age Foote understood the deep wounds of racism not only within society, but also the church.

> One day my mother and another colored sister waited until all the white people had, as they thought, been served, when they started for the communion table. Just as they reached the lower door, two of the poorer class of white folks arose to go to the table. At this, a mother in Israel caught hold of my mother's dress and said to her, "Don't you know better than to go to the table when white folks are there?" Ah! she did know better than to do such a thing purposely. This was one of the fruits of slavery.[18]

Foote explained the theological inconsistency of her mother's painful encounter. "Although professing to love the same God, members of the same church, and expecting to find the same heaven at last, they could not partake of the Lord's Supper until the lowest of the whites had been served." Foote, outraged by this fundamental

---

essarily include the challenging of sinful structures. See D. Mathews, *Slavery and Methodism: A Chapter in American Morality 1780–1845* (Princeton: Princeton University Press, 1965; repr., Westport, Conn.: Greenwood Press, 1978), 63, 25. Tensions continued to build on the issue of slavery and its implications for church polity in the Methodist Episcopal Church leading to the departure of Orange Scott and the Wesleyan Methodist Connexion in 1842 and the division of the Methodist Episcopal Church and Methodist Episcopal Church, South in 1844. See F. Norwood, *The Story of American Methodism: A History of the United Methodists and Their Relations* (Nashville: Abingdon, 1974), 197–210.

[17] Foote, "A Brand Plucked from the Fire," 167. Such practices of separate seating and receipt of the sacrament were common throughout the ME Church, north and south, during the early and middle nineteenth century. See Mathews, *Slavery and Methodism*, 66.

[18] Foote, "A Brand Plucked from the Fire," 167.

inconsistency in Christian doctrine and practice, conversion and condition, later voiced a call to accountability. "How many at the present day profess great spirituality, and even holiness, and yet are deluded by a spirit of error, which leads them to say to the poor and the colored ones among them, 'Stand back a little—I am holier than thou.'" Foote demonstrated, not only the way in which such prejudice undermines the vitality and integrity of Christian experience among the dominant culture, but also the possibility of debilitating effects for the faith journeys of the disenfranchised. "My parents continued to attend to the ordinances of God as instructed, but knew little of the power of Christ to save; for their spiritual guides were as blind as those they led."[19] According to Foote's account, her parents remained active in church communities. Foote remained affiliated to congregations even during her itinerant travels. She did not abandon the importance of the worshiping community, although she would be excommunicated from at least one.

Foote's earliest "distinct religious impression" occurred at eight years of age. During a "big meeting" at the church in which her parents held membership, two ministers called at their home. "One had long gray hair and beard, such as I had never seen before. He came to me, placed his hand on my head, and asked me if I prayed." Although Foote answered in the affirmative, she was so frightened she fell down on her knees in front of the minister and prayed the only prayer she knew: "Now I lay me down to sleep." To which he responded by lifting her up and saying, "You must be a good girl and pray." He then prayed for her "long and loud." She recounted, "I trembled with fear, and cried as though my heart would break, for I thought he was the Lord, and I must die." After the ministers departed, Foote's mother talked with her "about my soul more than she ever had before, and told me that this preacher was a good man, but not the Lord; and that, if I were a good girl, and said my prayers, I would go to heaven. This gave me great comfort."[20] Although she continued to pray that simple

[19] Foote, "A Brand Plucked from the Fire," 167.

[20] Foote, "A Brand Plucked from the Fire," 169. Foote's process of conversion seems characteristic of nineteenth-century Evangelicalism with conviction of sin and assurance of salvation. Foote's conversion also resonates with Wesleyan themes, specifically the emphasis upon salvation available to all or universal atonement. While one cannot earn salvation through good works, salvation by faith alone or justification precedes sanctification and holy living. See D. W. Bebbington, "Holiness in the Evangelical Tradition," in *Holiness Past and Present*, ed. S. Barton (London: T&T Clark, 2003), 299–301, 305–8; see also 302–5 for a discussion of Reformed (or Calvinist) holiness in comparison.

prayer, shortly thereafter Foote stated, "A white woman, who came to our house to sew, taught me the Lord's prayer. . . . It has always seemed to me that I was converted at this time."[21] While Foote invoked the language of conversion to describe this incident, her coming to a vital faith and experience of entire sanctification would unfold in subsequent, more dramatic chapters. Additionally, the practice of prayer would assume a significant place in Foote's evangelistic ministry as she grew into adulthood.

Foote's father led family worship each Sunday morning, in which she took great delight. From these encounters, Foote claimed she began to have a desire to learn to read the Bible. None of her family could read, with the exception of some limited ability on the part of her father. Although Foote stated her father would have gladly educated his children, "there were no schools where colored children were allowed." Thus, at hearing her father read aloud one day, she asked that he teach her the letters of the alphabet. "The children of the present time, taught at five years of age, can not realize my joy at being able to say the entire alphabet when I was nine years old." Following her conversion experience in adolescence she recounted, "I studied the Bible at every spare moment, that I might be able to read it with a better understanding." Foote was ecstatic at the gift of a new Bible from her minister. "Had he given me a thousand dollars, I should not have cared for it as I did for this Bible." Although she felt the need for an education more than ever, she claimed "the dear Holy Spirit helped me by quickening my mental faculties."[22] In this way Foote's conversion and the learning it inspired contributed to a counterformation to the oppression of racism.

Throughout her autobiography, Foote repeatedly mentioned the importance of receiving an education. Literacy for enslaved and free African Americans represented proximity to or attainment of freedom, both spiritual and physical.[23] While Christian education was the earliest organized effort to address the plight of the enslaved, these efforts could succumb to the confining expectations of slave owners.[24]

---

[21] Foote, "A Brand Plucked from the Fire," 169.

[22] Foote, "A Brand Plucked from the Fire," 170, 182.

[23] Raboteau, *African-American Religion*, 67.

[24] C. Foster and F. Smith with G. Shockley, *Black Religious Experience: Conversations on Double Consciousness and the Work of Grant Shockley* (Nashville: Abingdon, 2003), 35. American Methodism's early commitment to the education of African Americans was demonstrated in a statement included in the 1785 General Conference Journal, " 'What can be done in order to instruct poor children, white

Although denominations and missionary organizations expressed concern for the Christian education of enslaved African Americans, laws prohibiting gatherings for instruction in reading and writing confounded the fulfillment of good intentions. Following the Emancipation Proclamation in 1863 and the conclusion of the Civil War in 1865, Sunday schools were largely neglected, particularly in the South, though some resources went into establishing denominational colleges for African Americans.[25]

At the age of ten, Foote was sent to live in a rural area with a white family named Prime.[26] Residing with the Prime family from 1833 to 1836 seemed to provide the necessary circumstances to facilitate her pursuit of a simple education.[27] Sadly, this would be thwarted by a traumatic set of events.

> Our teacher's name was John Van Paten. He was keeping company with a young lady, who repeated to him a remark made by a lady friend of hers, to the effect that John Van Paten was not very smart, and she didn't see why this young lady should wish to marry him. He became very angry, and, armed with a shotgun, proceeded to the lady's house, and shot her dead.[28]

Van Paten, the teacher, promptly turned himself into the authorities. After the funeral the bereaved husband visited the former teacher in prison and prayed for his conversion until his prayers were answered.

> Finally the day came for the condemned to be publicly hung [*sic*] (they did not plead emotional insanity in those days). Everybody went to the execution, and I with the rest. Such a sight! Never shall I forget the execution of my first school-teacher. On the scaffold he made a speech, which I cannot remember, only that he said he was happy, and ready to die. . . . The remembrance of this scene left such an impression upon my mind that I could not sleep for many a night. As soon as I fell into a doze, I could see my teacher's head tumbling about the room as fast as it could go; I would waken with a scream, and could not be quieted until some one came and staid [*sic*] with me.[29]

---

and black, to read?' . . . 'Let us labor, as the heart of one man, to establish Sunday Schools, in or near the place of public worship'" (37).

[25] Foster, Smith, and Shockley, *Black Religious Experience*, 39, 40.

[26] Foote, "A Brand Plucked from the Fire," 171.

[27] According to Collier-Thomas, Foote attended a small integrated school while living with this family from 1833 to 1836 (*Daughters of Thunder*, 57).

[28] Foote, "A Brand Plucked from the Fire," 173–74.

[29] Foote, "A Brand Plucked from the Fire," 173–74.

A tragic situation, which clearly haunted Foote, had long-term implications, inhibiting Foote's educational pursuits. Although a devastating experience in her youth, the ministry of prayer and presence pursued by the bereaved husband that led to reconciliation and the convicted teacher's conversion seemed to make an impression upon Foote.

Foote endured yet another traumatic experience with more intimate ramifications. After a false accusation while residing with the Primes that resulted in a whipping, Foote contemplated suicide. Despite her parents' assistance in finding resolution for the situation, Foote's spiritual journey stalled. She left the Primes' household at twelve years of age. "The experience of that last year made me quite a hardened sinner. I did not pray very often, and, when I did, something seemed to say to me, 'That good man, with the white hair, don't like you any more.' "[30] Foote's statement seemed to represent growing doubt regarding her faith triggered by racism. She moved home to help with household tasks and tend to the four younger children while her mother worked. She then moved with her family to Albany, New York, in 1836, and began attending an African Methodist Church.[31]

> My father and mother both joined the church, and went regularly
> to all the services, taking all the children with them. This was the
> first time in my life that I was able to understand, with any degree
> of intelligence, what religion was. The minister frequently visited
> our house, singing, praying, and talking with us all.[32]

In this context, surrounded by family, Foote's Christian discipleship received cultivation in a nurturing community of faith despite the distractions of social life.[33]

---

[30] Foote, "A Brand Plucked from the Fire," 176.

[31] Collier-Thomas, *Daughters of Thunder*, 57. The congregation her parents attended may have been affiliated with the African Methodist Episcopal Church, founded by Richard Allen and Daniel Coker in 1816. This separation from the Methodist Episcopal Church responded to similar racial discrimination experienced by Foote and her parents. Both Allen and Coker were ordained by Frances Asbury. An additional motivation for Allen's establishing the denomination was to reclaim Wesleyan roots. See Norwood, *The Story of American Methodism*, 170–71.

[32] Foote, "A Brand Plucked from the Fire," 177.

[33] According to Raboteau, "The independent church movement among African Americans gave black Christians the freedom to control their own churches, but many worshiped within churches led by white ministers or priests in denominations that had few, if any, black clergy. Sometimes this situation led to conflict, sometimes to mutual understanding and respect" (*African-American Religion*, 45). While Foote's

During this time, Foote reflected upon her difficulty in resisting the temptation of social life, such as parties and the theatre. "The pomps and vanities of the world began to engross my attention as they never had before." Despite her mother's punishments and "a faint desire to serve the Lord," Foote claimed, "Thus I bartered the things of the kingdom for the fooleries of the world."[34]

> Yet I did not entirely forget God. I went to church, and said my prayers, though not so often as I had done. I thank my heavenly Father that he did not quite leave me to my own self-destruction, but followed me, sometimes embittering my pleasures and thwarting my schemes of worldly happiness, and most graciously preserving me from following the full bent of my inclination.[35]

Eventually, Foote received a dramatic religious experience with significant spiritual implications, a recurrent theme particularly in the writings of African-American women preachers.[36] While dancing, she felt a heavy hand upon her arm pulling her down to the floor. While the crowd assumed her ill, she tried to explain she was not ill, but that it was wrong for her to dance. "Such loud, mocking laughter as greeted my answer, methinks is not often heard this side the gates of torment." Ashamed, Foote responded to their urgings and attempted once more to dance, "but I had taken only a few steps, when I was seized with a smothering sensation, and felt the same heavy grasp upon my arm, and in my ears a voice kept saying, 'Repent! Repent!'" Foote immediately left the floor. "The company gathered around me, but not with mocking laughter as before; an invisible presence seemed to fill the place. The dance broke up—all leaving very quietly. Thus was I again 'plucked as a brand from the burning.' Had I persisted in

---

family attended a mixed congregation, they had experienced racial prejudice demonstrated in separate seating and receipt of the sacrament.

[34] Foote, "A Brand Plucked from the Fire," 177–78.

[35] Foote, "A Brand Plucked from the Fire," 177–78.

[36] See E. Reis, "African American Vision Stories," in *Religions of the United States in Practice*, ed. Colleen McDannell (Princeton: Princeton University Press, 2001), 426–29ff. As mentioned in chap. 1, although Stanley claims, "Visions did not play a major role in the spiritual lives of later Wesleyan/Holiness women, but several . . . did describe mystical visions," she describes some women's "call [to ministry] came in a vision," such as Julia Foote (*Holy Boldness*, xxxii, 102). In Brekus's analysis of women preachers in America, she emphasizes the distinction of white women often called to preach in dreams from "black female preachers [who] insisted . . . they had seen heavenly visions or heard angelic voices while they were fully awake and conscious," such as Julia Foote (*Strangers and Pilgrims*, 183).

dancing, I believe God would have smitten me dead on the spot." Foote concludes this chapter of her autobiography with the dramatic portrayal and several admonitions. She addresses the reader with a series of questions, concluding with the statement, "The Holy Spirit whispers to your inmost soul, to come out from among the wicked and be separate." Following biblical references she then firmly states, "Put away your idols, and give God the whole heart."[37]

Foote claims, "I was converted when fifteen years old. It was on a Sunday evening at a quarterly meeting."[38] She explains, "Yes, I have been serious before, but I could never sing the new song until now."[39] Although Foote had previously professed Christian faith, her belief had lacked a mature depth characteristic of Wesleyan doctrinal emphases related to justification, including a meaningful grasp of original sin and assurance of forgiveness. That evening the minister preached from Revelation 14:3, "And they sung as it were a new song before the throne." Foote describes the scene, "As the minister dwelt with great force and power on the first clause of the text, I beheld my lost condition as I never had done before." After falling unconscious to the floor, Foote was carried home, and several remained with her through the night singing and praying. After crying, "Lord, have mercy on me, a poor sinner!" a ray of light flashed across her eyes, accompanied by distant singing that became more distinct. When she caught the words, "This is the new song—redeemed, redeemed!" she arose from her bed where she had been for twenty hours and began to sing the new song.[40]

With this renewed assurance of her salvation, Foote rejoiced "in the new song" and God's work of justification for her. In the months that followed, Foote experienced uninterrupted peace and joy. However, when injured in an accident involving her younger brother

[37] Foote, "A Brand Plucked from the Fire," 178–79.

[38] Foote, "A Brand Plucked from the Fire," 180. Quarterly meetings in the Methodist tradition gathered clergy and laypersons from a geographic region to worship and address issues of polity. See L. Ruth, *A Little Heaven Below: Worship at Early Methodist Quarterly Meetings* (Nashville: Kingswood Books, 2000).

[39] Foote, "A Brand Plucked from the Fire," 181. According to Susan Lindley, though "conversion might occur in a dramatic moment, often during a revival meeting but sometimes alone, and it might be accompanied by a visionary experience . . . the preliminary stages could last for weeks, months, or even years," as in the case of Jarena Lee, a free African-American woman born in 1783 (*"You Have Stept Out of Your Place": A History of Women and Religion in America* [Louisville, Ky.: Westminster/John Knox, 1996], 179–80).

[40] Foote, "A Brand Plucked from the Fire," 180.

at play with other children, resulting in her losing sight in one eye, she claimed it left her angry and with many doubts related to her faith. "The more my besetting sin troubled me, the more anxious I became for an education. I believed that, if I were educated, God could make me understand what I needed." In spite of Foote's desire for a deeper theological understanding of her faith, her preacher, class leader, and parents claimed that Foote needed nothing since "all Christians had these inward troubles to contend with, and were never free from them until death."[41] However, she had heard of the doctrine of entire sanctification that could bring freedom from sins, such as her anger, and she wished to learn more.[42]

Theological Influences

Foote's formation in faith culminated with a much desired experience of entire sanctification as a distinct and second work of the Holy Spirit. As previously mentioned, while her religious experiences reflected in her spiritual narrative in many ways fulfilled expectations of holiness communities, Foote's experiences also seemed to contribute to a counteridentity formation. The prevalence of holiness themes of the time gave shape to her depiction of her evangelistic ministry, which had broad implications including Christian practices of reconciliation.

[41] Foote, "A Brand Plucked from the Fire," 182–84. Classes were based on geographic divisions of ten to twelve members in early Methodism, initially instituted in 1742 to assist with collecting payments for a building debt. The class leader accepted responsibility for the financial burden of the group with regard to the initial building debt, but in making weekly rounds discovered additional needs for spiritual nurture. Thus, John Wesley appointed leaders of the classes—"those to whom I could most confide"—and attempted to meet with them weekly (quoted in R. Heitzenrater, *Wesley and the People Called Methodists* [Nashville: Abingdon, 1995], 118–19). The role of class leader continued in American Methodism (see Norwood, *The Story of American Methodism*, 129–32). For women's roles as class leaders in American Methodism, see also J. M. Schmidt, *Grace Sufficient: A History of Women in American Methodism 1760–1939* (Nashville: Abingdon, 1999), 27, 54, 55, 63–65, 293–94. For a more detailed historical account of the role, see D. L. Watson, *Class Leaders: Recovering a Tradition* (Nashville: Discipleship Resources, 1991).

[42] Interestingly, Kallenberg claims it is not the job of the evangelist to translate confusing terms (*Live to Tell*, 51). Foote, while eager for education and theological knowledge and a passionate advocate for entire sanctification following her experience, does not provide a lengthy or in-depth explanation of the doctrine. For Kallenberg, reductionism and simplicity of language undermines the fullness of the terms. "Righteousness has been reduced to equality, agape has paled to fraternity, sin has been replaced with maladjustment, and salvation has become mere civility" (52).

Foote's Christian identity as described in her spiritual autobiography was shaped in profound ways that reached beyond, though remained consistent with, general expectations within holiness communities.

After her accident in which she was blinded in one eye, she was plagued with anger, impatience, and doubts, all seemingly inconsistent with Foote's expectations of Christian faithfulness and that of the holiness community generally.

> I continued to live in an up-and-down way for more than a year, when there came to our church an old man and his wife, who, when speaking in meeting, told of the trouble they once had had in trying to overcome their temper, subdue their pride, etc. But they took all to Jesus, believing his blood could wash them clean and sanctify them wholly to himself; and, oh! the peace, the sweet peace, they had enjoyed ever since. Their words thrilled me through and through.[43]

Although Foote told her parents, minister, and class leader she wanted to be sanctified, they told her "sanctification was for the aged and persons about to die, and not for one like [her]." Disobeying her mother, Foote visited "these old saints" who told her that entire sanctification was for the young as well as the old. After another meeting in which many biblical passages were explained, and further waiting upon the Lord, Foote's "large desire was granted, through faith in [her] precious Savior. The glory of God seemed almost to prostrate [her] to the floor. There was, indeed, a weight of glory resting upon [her]. [She] sang with all [her] heart." Foote explained that she "no longer hoped for glory, but had the full assurance of it." Her constant prayer had been answered, that strengthened by the Holy Spirit she might be "rooted and grounded in love . . . [and] able to comprehend with all saints what is the length, and breadth, and height, and depth, and to know the love of Christ which passeth knowledge, and be filled with all the fullness of God."[44]

[43] Foote, "A Brand Plucked from the Fire," 185. Although Foote's account seems to connect her anger to the accident that resulted in partial blindness, according to Jean Humez, conversion for African-American women resulted in an emotional transformation in which the women learned to "face and control the debilitating repressed anger and fear provoked by living with white racism" ("'My Spirit Eye': Some Functions of Spiritual and Visionary Experience in the Lives of Five Black Women Preachers, 1810–1880," in *Women and the Structure of Society: Selected Research from the Fifth Berkshire Conference on the History of Women*, eds. B. Harris and J. McNamara [Durham, N.C.: Duke University Press, 1984], 134).

[44] Foote, "A Brand Plucked from the Fire," 185–87. The passages to which Foote referred include John 17; 1 Thess 4:3, 5:23; 1 Cor 6:9-12; Heb 2:11.

Foote shared her experience of entire sanctification with her parents and friends, thus beginning her evangelistic ministry in earnest. "I at once began to read to them out of my Bible, and to many others, thinking, in my simplicity, that they would believe and receive the same blessing at once. To the glory of God, some did believe and were saved, but many were too wise to be taught by a child—too good to be made better." Her message was not always eagerly received. "From this time, many, who had been my warmest friends, and seemed to think me a Christian, turned against me, saying I did not know what I was talking about—that there was no such thing as sanctification and holiness in this life—and that the devil had deluded me into self-righteousness." Foote claimed, "Many of them fought holiness with more zeal and vigor than they did sin." Despite resistance, Foote remained at peace and joyful in her "new religion," as her pastor called it. In response to hearing several biblical passages on the subject read to him, Foote's pastor replied, "They are all well enough; but you must remember that you are too young to read and dictate to persons older than yourself, and many in the church are dissatisfied with the way you are talking and acting." This did not discourage Foote, who claimed "though my gifts were but small, I could not be shaken by what man might think or say."[45]

Foote's experience of entire sanctification granted her an empowered sense of self in relationship to God with implications for her relationships with others.[46] As an African-American woman, Foote encountered emotionally, and sometimes physically, brutal traumas that influenced her identity formation in complex ways.[47] Although Foote's account connected her anger to the accident that resulted in partial blindness, conversion for African-American women often resulted in an emotional transformation in which the women learned to confront repressed anger and other emotions related to their experiences of oppression.[48] In a social system that oppressed African-American women, religious conversion often brought increased

---

[45] Foote, "A Brand Plucked from the Fire," 188–89. The biblical passages included Pss 66:16, 32:1; Rom 6:14; Ezek 34.

[46] Connor, *Conversions and Visions*, 4–5. Though Foote's conversion included a turning away from sin, which runs contrary to Connor's argument, Foote's conversion does resonate with Connor's assertion that conversion for nineteenth-century African-American women represents a "moving beyond roles that are products of certain social expectations to a more stable and conscious level of identity" (4).

[47] Connor, *Conversions and Visions*, 2.

[48] Humez, "'My Spirit Eye,'" 134.

confidence, self-esteem, and dignity as a result of God's acceptance.[49] This is not to conclude that Christian institutions, even those striving for gender and racial justice, did not retain some prejudice within their structures. Foote, among others, would not necessarily be wholly saved from continued experiences of racism and disenfranchisement. However, for Foote, at least in part and related to her depiction of her evangelistic ministry, her experience of entire sanctification seemed to grant her a vocation directly from God and a boldness to address such sins as sexism and racism even within ecclesial structures.

After Foote's experience of entire sanctification at the age of sixteen, she married at eighteen.[50] The young man was familiar to Foote from when she frequented "places of amusement." She "had formed quite an attachment" for George Foote, who "professed faith in Christ and united with the same church." She struggled with his offer of marriage as he was not "sanctified," although open to seek it. Within days of their marriage, they departed for Boston. She claimed her experience of entire sanctification brought a new confidence. "Once, the thought of leaving my father's house, to go among strangers, would have been terrible, but now I rejoiced."[51] The marriage seemed to endure, though Foote's husband most often worked at a distance. He later dissented from her strong advocacy of entire sanctification. Initially, because of the distance of his work they lived separately, but this arrangement persisted until his death. The separation did not seem to be without estrangement, most likely due in part to Foote's enthusiasm for the doctrine of entire sanctification.[52]

Holiness in the Wesleyan Tradition: From Wesley to Palmer

Foote's interpretation of her experience of entire sanctification is informed both by John Wesley and Phoebe Palmer, definitive figures within the Wesleyan/holiness traditions. The holiness movement appeared on the American Protestant landscape in the mid-nineteenth century, emphasizing the possibility of attaining Christian perfection in this life. Doctrinal themes of holiness were largely rooted in Wesley's theological writings, as many Methodists and related traditions

---

[49] See Lindley, *"You Have Stept Out of Your Place,"* 180.
[50] Andrews, introduction to *Sisters of the Spirit*, 9.
[51] Foote, "A Brand Plucked from the Fire," 190–91.
[52] Foote, "A Brand Plucked from the Fire," see chaps. 12, 13, 15, and 24.

attempted to reclaim Wesleyan foundations. Palmer emerged as a prominent figure in the nineteenth-century holiness movement, initially leading weekly prayer meetings followed by international preaching and numerous publications including a periodical series.

Foote's experience and teaching of entire sanctification are perhaps the most firmly grounded in the Wesleyan tradition of nineteenth-century African-American woman preachers.[53] Foote's doctrine of entire sanctification is consistent with Wesley's teachings, while also exhibiting affinity with the nineteenth-century holiness movement, particularly the teachings of her contemporary Palmer. Both Wesley and Palmer acknowledge the opportunity to receive sanctification "now." Although clearly within the Wesleyan tradition, Palmer's altar theology stretched Wesley's framework further. Palmer claimed the omnipotence of God to make one holy "by laying all on the altar," thus shifting from a more passive human role to an active one.[54] The following sections offer brief surveys of both Wesley and Palmer regarding the doctrine of entire sanctification.

John Wesley

Foote referred to "Wesley's perfect love," related to the doctrine of entire sanctification or Christian perfection, in one of only two of her extant sermons.[55] In one of his most often preached sermons and the most comprehensive example of his mature theological reflection, "The Scripture Way of Salvation" (1765), Wesley provided an outline of his understanding of salvation or *via salutis*.[56] For Wesley, faith alone was essential for salvation: "The end is, in one word, salvation: the means to attain it, faith."[57] Justification described the imputation

---

[53] D. Strong, "The Doctrine of Christian Perfection Among Nineteenth Century African American Preaching Women" (unpublished paper, n.d.), 19.

[54] Lindley, *"You Have Stept Out of Your Place,"* 119. Lindley quotes this language from Charles White, a biographer of Palmer, in *The Beauty of Holiness: Phoebe Palmer as Theologian, Revivalist, Feminist, and Humanitarian* (Grand Rapids: Francis Asbury, Zondervan, 1986), 23.

[55] J. Foote, "Christian Perfection," in Collier-Thomas, *Daughters of Thunder*, 66–68, specifically 68.

[56] Wesley, "The Scripture Way of Salvation," 153–69. See also Heitzenrater, *Wesley and the People Called Methodists*, 220. See Heitzenrater for a comprehensive commentary on Wesley's *via/ordo salutis*. Many of the components are discussed in the pages that follow.

[57] Wesley, "The Scripture Way of Salvation," 156.

of God's righteousness through Jesus Christ to repentant individuals for the forgiveness of sins or what God does for us, namely pardon.[58]

> Justification is another word for pardon. It is the forgiveness of all our sins, and (what is necessarily implied therein) our acceptance with God. The price whereby this hath been procured for us (commonly termed the 'meritorious cause' of our justification) is the blood and righteousness of Christ, or (to express it a little more clearly) all that Christ hath done and suffered for us till 'he poured out his soul for the transgressors.' The immediate effects of justification are, the peace of God, a 'peace that passeth all understanding', and a 'rejoicing in *hope* of the glory of God', 'with *joy* unspeakable and full of glory'.[59]

Foote most likely experienced justification throughout the series of events in her childhood and youth—beginning with the pastoral visit at age five, followed by the dramatic dancing experience, and what Foote named as her conversion at the Sunday evening quarterly meeting at age fifteen. Through justification a person receives assurance of God's forgiveness, which for Wesley could occur repeatedly.

Wesley described sanctification as beginning at the time of justification. Sanctification is the imparted righteousness of Christ through the Holy Spirit in persons or what God does in us. This imparted righteousness through sanctifying grace results in a real change in persons.[60] According to Wesley, "And at the same time that we are justified, yea, in that very moment, *sanctification* begins. In that instant we are 'born again', 'born from above', 'born of the Spirit'. There is a *real* as well as a *relative* change."[61]

The language of sanctification is closely related to holiness in Scripture. In sanctification persons are made holy through the presence of the Holy Spirit that empowers individuals to respond to God's grace with practices of love for God and neighbor. Wesley continued:

> We are inwardly renewed by the power of God. We feel the 'love of God shed abroad in our heart by the Holy Ghost which is given unto us', producing love to all mankind, and more especially to the children of God; expelling the love of the world, the love of pleasure, of

---

[58] Heitzenrater, *Wesley and the People Called Methodists*, 104.

[59] Wesley, "The Scripture Way of Salvation," 157–58.

[60] Wesley, "The Scripture Way of Salvation," 158. See also Heitzenrater, *Wesley and the People Called Methodists*, 104.

[61] Wesley, "The Scripture Way of Salvation," 158.

ease, of honour, of money; together with pride, anger, self-will, and every other evil temper—in a word, changing the 'earthly, sensual, devilish' mind into 'the mind which was in Christ Jesus'.[62]

After the injury that left her partially blinded, Foote longed to possess these characteristics of a real change as a result of entire sanctification. Upon receipt, Foote rejoiced, "I am crucified with Christ: nevertheless, I live; yet not I, but Christ liveth in me" [Gal 2:20]. She explained, "I had been afraid to tell my mother I was praying for sanctification, but when the 'old man' [Rom 6:6] was cast out of my heart, and perfect love took possession, I lost all fear."[63]

Wesley claimed sanctification could occur instantaneously in the context of an event, resulting in a person's receipt of entire sanctification or Christian perfection,[64] such as Foote and Palmer described. According to Wesley, "God is both able and willing to sanctify us *now*."[65] However, Wesley, and later Foote, realized the difficulty of such language and, therefore, seemed to most often refer to sanctification as a process. "How naturally do those who experience such a change imagine that all sin is gone!"[66] In his latest published remarks on the topic, Wesley clarified terms. "By perfection I mean the humble, gentle, patient love of God, and our neighbour, ruling our tempers, words, and actions."[67] Although entire sanctification or Christian perfection was possible, Wesley offered the disclaimer that such events were rare. "But it is seldom long before they are undeceived, finding sin was only suspended, not destroyed."[68] Foote resonated with

[62] Wesley, "The Scripture Way of Salvation," 158.

[63] Foote, "A Brand Plucked from the Fire," 187.

[64] Wesley at times referred to entire sanctification as Christian perfection, for example in his "A Plain Account of Christian Perfection: as believed and taught by the Reverend Mr. John Wesley, from the year 1725, to the year 1777," a rather controversial aspect of Wesley's language related to sanctification. This essay consists of material compiled over Wesley's life and ministry on the subject. Though the publication date, or last revision, is dated 1777, the final remarks are designated January 27, 1767. This is the only material dated following the publication of "The Scripture Way of Salvation" (1765), and in its extreme brevity does not add any further contribution, but repeats main points. See also Heitzenrater, *Wesley and the People Called Methodists*, 48, 106–7.

[65] Wesley, "The Scripture Way of Salvation," 168. In the conclusion of her autobiography Foote explained, "according to God's promise, he is able to perform, and will do it now—doeth it now." Foote, "A Brand Plucked from the Fire," 234.

[66] Wesley, "The Scripture Way of Salvation," 158.

[67] Wesley, "A Plain Account of Christian Perfection," 63.

[68] Wesley, "The Scripture Way of Salvation," 159.

Wesley's qualification regarding Christian perfection, offering her own near the end of her autobiography: "Do not misunderstand me. I am not teaching absolute perfection, for that belongs to God alone. Nor do I mean a state of angelic or Adamic perfection, but Christian perfection—an extinction of every temper contrary to love."[69]

For Wesley, recognizing the danger of backsliding, faith is not often sustained without participation in good works. Salvation is by faith alone with such good works facilitated by the Holy Spirit as a response to God's work of salvation in persons. This creates, through a process if not an event, a real change in persons.

> From the time of our being 'born again' the gradual work of sanctification takes place. We are enabled 'by the Spirit' to 'mortify the deeds of the body', of our evil nature. And as we are more and more dead to sin, we are more and more alive to God. We go on from grace to grace, while we are careful to 'abstain from all appearance of evil', and are 'zealous of good works', 'as we have opportunity doing good to all men'; while we walk in all his ordinances blameless, therein worshipping him in spirit and in truth; while we take up our cross and deny ourselves every pleasure that does not lead us to God.[70]

Wesley energetically argued faith as the constitutive requirement for salvation related to both doctrines of justification and sanctification. However, Wesley considered good works a significant aspect of one's faith. "God does undoubtedly command us both to repent and to bring forth fruits meet for repentance. . . . But they are not necessary in the *same sense* with faith, nor in the *same degree*; for those fruits are only necessary *conditionally*, if there be time and opportunity for them." Wesley emphasized that Christian practices or good works are merely *means* of receiving God's grace and not *ends*, thus avoiding the danger of works righteousness. For Wesley, works of piety and mercy, "these the fruits meet for repentance . . . are necessary to full sanctification. This is the way wherein God hath appointed his children to wait for complete salvation."[71] Thus, Foote's understanding of entire sanctification grounded in Wesleyan foundations led her to pursue an evangelistic ministry framed by such an understanding of holiness leading to practices of good works. As the minister explained to Foote immediately prior to her conversion, "My child, it is not the altar nor

---

[69] Foote, "A Brand Plucked from the Fire," 232.
[70] Wesley, "The Scripture Way of Salvation," 160.
[71] Wesley, "The Scripture Way of Salvation," 162–63, 166.

the minister that saves souls, but faith in the Lord Jesus Christ, who died for all men."[72]

Phoebe Palmer

An important figure contributing to understandings of sanctification in the Wesleyan tradition is Phoebe Palmer, an internationally recognized nineteenth-century holiness preacher and author. Palmer suffered deep bereavement as a result of the deaths of her first three children in infancy. Plagued with guilt and painfully grieved, she feared her earthly love for her children eclipsed her love for God and Christian duty.[73] A Methodist laywoman, Palmer contributed significantly to the holiness movement, developing the "Tuesday Meetings for the Promotion of Holiness" with her sister beginning in 1836. Palmer later experienced entire sanctification on July 26, 1837. She encouraged work among the poor through the New York Female Missionary Society that later established the Five Points House of Industry in 1854. She began preaching at summer camp meetings in the 1840s and preached widely, including in Canada and Great Britain, from 1857 to 1859. In addition to writing a defense of women's preaching, *Promise of the Father* (1859), Palmer wrote *The Way to Holiness* (1843) and edited the widely subscribed journal *Guide to Holiness* (1864–1901).[74]

During Foote's young adulthood Palmer began to teach on the doctrine of entire sanctification. Although firmly within the Wesleyan tradition, Palmer's doctrine offers distinctive emphases from John Wesley's teaching in that she claimed "a shorter way."[75] Wesley's understanding of assurance depended upon a passive receiving on the part of the believer. According to Wesley, "It is thus that we wait for entire sanctification."[76] In comparison, Palmer advocated a more pragmatic understanding and active response.[77] Foote's experience of

---

[72] Foote, "A Brand Plucked from the Fire," 181.

[73] Lindley, *"You Have Stept Out of Your Place,"* 118.

[74] Lindley, *"You Have Stept Out of Your Place,"* 118–20. See Schmidt, *Grace Sufficient*, 133–44. For a helpful biography of Palmer, see White, *The Beauty of Holiness*.

[75] Phoebe Palmer, *The Way of Holiness, with Notes by the Way; Being a Narrative of Experience Resulting from A Determination to Be a Bible Christian* (New York: Piercy & Reed, 1843), 5–10. Quoted in R. Richey, K. Rowe, and J. M. Schmidt, eds., *The Methodist Experience in America* (Nashville: Abingdon, 2000), 2:263.

[76] Wesley, "The Scripture Way of Salvation," 160.

[77] Diane Leclerc, "The Spirit's Cry in the Soul," in *"Heart Religion" in the*

entire sanctification seemed more closely to resemble Wesley's teaching, "while waiting on the Lord, my large desire was granted,"[78] while Foote's preaching incorporated Palmer's emphasis upon immediacy, as demonstrated below.

Palmer promoted this nuanced Wesleyan doctrine of entire sanctification in her spiritual autobiography, *The Way of Holiness* (1843), selling one hundred thousand copies.[79] "On looking at the requirements of the word of God, she beheld the command, 'Be ye holy.' She then began to say in her heart, 'Whatever my former deficiencies may have been, God requires that I should *now* be holy. Whether *convicted*, or otherwise, *duty is plain*. God requires *present* holiness.' "[80] Foote, with Palmer, emphasized God's command, "Be ye therefore perfect."[81] Although confident that God required holiness, and offered the means to receive it, Palmer had previously not considered knowledge of these truths sufficient. However, upon reflection she claimed the simple truth: "Knowledge is conviction."[82] This laid a foundation for Palmer's altar theology, yet she was still faced with another difficulty.

> She had been accustomed to look at the blessing of holiness as such a high attainment, that her general habit of soul inclined her to think it almost beyond her reach. This erroneous impression rather influenced her to rest the matter thus:—"I will let every high state of grace in name alone, and seek only to be *fully conformed to the will of God, as recorded in his written word*. My chief endeavors shall be centered in the aim to be an humble *Bible Christian*."[83]

Thus, Palmer strove to live not by the opinions of others, but taking the Bible "as the rule of life." Although aware of "past

---

Methodist Tradition and Related Movements, ed. R. Steele, Pietist and Wesleyan Studies 12 (Lanham, Md.: Scarecrow Press, 2001), 189.

[78] Foote, "A Brand Plucked from the Fire," 186.

[79] Stanley, *Holy Boldness*, 3. Leclerc argues that reading Palmer's *The Way of Holiness* as "an exact replica of [Palmer's] actual experience" overlooks important rhetorical nuances of her theology contained in her letters and diaries, since the text was "written for popular consumption and therefore gives structure and offers formulas so that the reader may also take specific steps to attain a similar experience" ("The Spirit's Cry in the Soul," 188–89).

[80] Palmer, *The Way of Holiness*, quoted in Richey et al., *The Methodist Experience*, 264.

[81] Foote, "Christian Perfection," 66.

[82] Palmer, *The Way of Holiness*, quoted in Richey et al., *The Methodist Experience*, 264.

[83] Palmer, *The Way of Holiness*, quoted in Richey et al., *The Methodist Experience*, 264.

unfaithfulness," with humility she was enabled, "through grace, to resolve, with firmness of purpose, that entire devotion of heart and life to God should be the absorbing subject of the succeeding pilgrimage of life."[84]

Palmer's "shorter way" required a subsequent step to claim the faithfulness of God, quoting 1 Thessalonians 5:24, "Faithful is he who hath called you, who also *will* do it."

> And now realizing that she was engaged in a transaction eternal in its consequences, she here, in the strength, and as in the presence of the Father, Son, and Holy Spirit, and those spirits that minister to the heirs of salvation, said, "O, Lord, I now call heaven and earth to witness that I *now lay body, soul, and spirit, with all these redeemed powers, upon thine altar, to be for ever* thine! 'Tis done! Thou hast promised to receive me! Thou canst not be unfaithful! *Thou dost receive me now!* From this time henceforth I *am thine—wholly thine!*"[85]

Despite the temptation of "the enemy" to inflict doubt, "'Tis but the work of your own understanding—the effort of your own will," the spirit of the Lord presented the truth to Palmer, "Do not your perceptions of right—even your *own understanding*—assure you that it is a matter of *thanksgiving to God* that you have been thus enabled to present your all to him?" "Yes," responded her whole heart, "it has been all the work of the Spirit." Palmer continued, "HOLINESS, SANCTIFICATION, *perfect love*, were now no longer so incomprehensible, or indefinite in nature or bearing, in relation to the individual experience of the Lord's redeemed ones."[86]

Foote's experience and preaching of entire sanctification, including its urgency, share emphases with Palmer, while Foote seemed to align herself more closely with Wesley's doctrinal teaching. Historical scholarship focusing upon Foote notes the impact of the 1830s and 1840s holiness movements, often with Methodist connections, in New York and Ohio, upon her understanding of the doctrine of entire sanctification. However, later in life Foote seemed to embrace earlier themes. For example, in her sermon "Christian Perfection," pub-

---

[84] Palmer, *The Way of Holiness*, quoted in Richey et al., *The Methodist Experience*, 265.

[85] Palmer, *The Way of Holiness*, quoted in Richey et al., *The Methodist Experience*, 266.

[86] Palmer, *The Way of Holiness*, quoted in Richey et al., *The Methodist Experience*, 266–67; small caps in the original.

lished in 1894, after claiming biblical foundations, including both the Old and the New Testament for her belief in perfection, Foote claimed Wesley and Luther as precedents.[87]

Evangelistic Ministry

Foote's receipt of entire sanctification led her to embark upon evangelistic ministry. Foote's experience of a real change resulted in her vocation to lead others to receive this religious experience. However, such an experience for Foote, and those with whom she ministered, reached beyond merely individual implications.[88] While Foote's evangelistic ministry consisted of itinerant preaching and publication alongside ordinary practices of prayer and visitation, her ministry reached beyond these to address social implications. Foote's evangelistic ministry reached even further than Palmer, an internationally known evangelist. While Palmer advocated for women's right to preach and ministered with the poor, she did not endorse women's ordination or racial reconciliation as Foote did.[89]

At first glance, Foote's evangelistic ministry may seem traditional, constrained to verbal proclamation. For example, in addition to her later vocation to preach, Foote's writing and publication of her autobiography contributed to her evangelistic ministry. In her preface to the autobiography, Foote stated:

> My object has been to testify more extensively to the sufficiency of the blood of Jesus Christ to save from all sin. Many have not the means of purchasing large and expensive works on this important Bible theme.
>
> Those who are fully in the truth cannot possess a prejudiced or sectarian spirit. As they hold fellowship with Christ, they cannot reject those whom he has received, nor receive those whom he

---

[87] Foote, "Christian Perfection," 66–68. According to Collier-Thomas, in this sermon Foote distanced herself from the perfectionism of the Burned Over District and Oneida Perfectionists. See *Daughters of Thunder*, 62.

[88] Foote's Christian faith and ministry, specifically her experience of entire sanctification, with other African-American Christian women in the nineteenth century, took seriously the material and this-worldly dimensions of life. See Connor, *Conversions and Visions*, 19.

[89] See T. L. Smith, *Revivalism and Social Reform in Mid-Nineteenth-Century America* (New York: Abingdon, 1957). Although Palmer encouraged ministry among the poor, she did not advocate for abolition of slavery.

rejects, but all are brought into a blessed harmony with God and each other.

[. . .] My earnest desire is that many—especially my own race—may be led to believe and enter into rest; "For we which have believed do enter into rest" [Heb 4:3]—sweet soul rest.[90]

The autobiography as a whole demonstrates evangelistic themes and purpose, with many of the chapters concluding with an explicit evangelistic message, soliciting a faith commitment.[91] According to Foote throughout her autobiography, contemporaries repeatedly referred to her as an evangelist, but most often in the limited connotation of the term—itinerant preacher.[92] However, for Foote, a real change in persons included implications beyond the personal and spiritual.[93] The following explores the ordinary and extraordinary facets of Foote's evangelistic ministry from prayer and visitation to ecclesiastic rights for women and racial reconciliation.

Prayer and Visitation

Foote recognized the substantial power of prayer for Christians and their ministries from an early age. First, with regard to her own salvation journey, Foote took seriously the practice of prayer as an essential component of her Christian discipleship. Later in childhood, Foote responded eagerly to the request of a dying man to pray for him.[94] Throughout her ministry as an adult, she continued to offer prayer and presence to the dying and their loved ones as they prepared for the next stage of their journeys.

One example of Foote's ministry with the dying and their families occurred shortly after her arrival in Boston. Foote's evangelistic ministry in such situations was framed by her theological emphasis upon entire sanctification. When the health of a dear friend, Mrs. Simpson, rapidly declined, Foote remained with her. Despite previously suffer-

[90] Foote, "A Brand Plucked from the Fire," 163.

[91] Foote, "A Brand Plucked from the Fire," 168, 170, 172, 174, 179, 223, 226, 227.

[92] Foote, "A Brand Plucked from the Fire," 164.

[93] Kallenberg's claims continue to resonate with Foote's evangelistic ministry and understanding of conversion. For example, "First, conversion involves a change in social identity. Second, in large measure, this new social identity is accomplished by the acquisition of new language skills. Finally, conversion is constituted by a paradigm shift that results in bringing the world into focus in a whole new way" (*Live to Tell*, 46).

[94] Foote, "A Brand Plucked from the Fire," 169, 171.

ing "great pain," Simpson persevered, having received entire sanctification so that she exhibited "such calmness, patience and resignation through suffering" as Foote had never witnessed. Simpson's husband, not yet a recipient of entire sanctification, was called, embraced, and exhorted by his wife "to receive God in all his fullness."[95]

> There, in the death-chamber, in the stillness of night, we prayed for that pious and exemplary man, that he might present his body a living sacrifice. He was deeply moved upon by the Holy Spirit, so that he cried aloud for deliverance; but almost on the instant began to doubt, and left the room. His wife requested me to read and talk to her about Jesus, which I did, and she was filled with heavenly joy.[96]

After sleeping and some release from pain, though very weak, for several days Simpson talked to all who came to see her of "salvation free and full." On the morning of her death:

> She was peaceful and serene, with a heavenly smile upon her countenance. She asked me to pray, which I did with streaming eyes and quivering voice. She then asked us to sing the hymn,
> "Oh, for a thousand tongues to sing, My great Redeemer's praise."
> She sang with us in a much stronger voice than she had used for many days. As we sang the last verse, she raised herself up in bed, clapped her hands and cried: "He sets the prisoner free! Glory! glory! I am free! They have come for me!"[97]

Simpson's mother inquired of her, "Who had come?"—to which she replied, "Don't you see the chariot and horses?" Simpson dropped back to her pillow into eternal rest. Foote most likely assisted with arrangements and preparations of the body for burial, in addition to ministering to and facilitating the evangelistic ministry of Mrs. Simpson. Foote's ministry of prayer, presence, and song offered an evangelistic message of hope, not only to Simpson in her transition, but also to her husband, mother, and visitors. "Thus did another sanctified saint enter into eternal life. Though her period of sanctification was short, it was full of precious fruit."[98]

---

[95] Foote, "A Brand Plucked from the Fire," 194.
[96] Foote, "A Brand Plucked from the Fire," 194.
[97] Foote, "A Brand Plucked from the Fire," 195.
[98] Foote, "A Brand Plucked from the Fire," 195.

Women, limited to roles deemed appropriate by gender constructs of the time, often pursued domestic visitation in their Christian vocations.[99] Visitation provided a consistent and respectable means of contact with potential and believing Christians. Foote's arrival in Boston and developing friendship with "Mam" Riley and her daughters facilitated Foote's evangelistic ministry of visitation that emerged from her experience of entire sanctification. Riley's eldest daughter received entire sanctification leading to the shared ministry of Foote and this newly sanctified sister in the gospel.

> God wonderfully honored the faith of this young saint in her ceaseless labor for others. We attended meetings and visited from house to house, together, almost constantly, when she was able to go out. Glory to God! the church became much aroused; some plunged into the ocean of perfect love, and came forth testifying to the power of the blood.[100]

For Foote, and countless other women, domestic visitation remained the primary means for fulfilling one's Christian vocation, particularly evangelistic ministries. "Having no children, I had a good deal of leisure after my husband's departure, so I visited many of the poor and forsaken ones, reading and talking to them of Jesus, the Saviour."[101]

Visitation could be extemporaneous, as demonstrated by this reference in Foote's autobiography, or more organized through the training and organization of women in most nineteenth-century American mainline Protestant denominations. During such extemporaneous visitation, Foote found a long-lost brother.

> One day I was directed by the Spirit to visit the Marine Hospital. In passing through one of the wards I heard myself called by my maiden name. Going to the cot from whence the voice came, I

---

[99] For example, in the Methodist Episcopal Church in March 1868 the Ladies' and Pastors' Christian Union was organized to structure women's evangelistic visitation among the disenfranchised. See Schmidt, *Grace Sufficient*, 152–54.

[100] Foote, "A Brand Plucked from the Fire," 193. According to Collier-Thomas (*Daughters of Thunder*, 57), in Boston, Foote joined the African Methodist Episcopal Zion congregation pastored by Rev. Jehiel C. Beman, a leading antislavery speaker and president of the Massachusetts Temperance Society of Colored People. Beman joined the New York Conference in 1830 and was appointed to Boston as the congregation's first pastor in 1838. See also W. Walls, *The African Methodist Episcopal Zion Church: Reality of the Black Church* (Charlotte, N.C.: AME Zion Publishing House, 1974), 148.

[101] Foote, "A Brand Plucked from the Fire," 198.

beheld what seemed to me a human skeleton. As I looked I began to see our family likeness, and recognized my eldest brother, who left home many years before, when I was quite young. Not hearing from him, we had mourned him as dead. With a feeble voice, he told me of his roving and seafaring life; "and now sister," he said, "I am dying."[102]

Urging her brother to pray despite his reluctance and fear of death, she encouraged him "to believe that Jesus died for all." Praying for her brother and staying with him as much as possible, Foote compassionately ministered to him until arriving one morning not to find him, learning he had died during the night.[103]

Whether visiting in homes, hospitals, or other institutions, such practices opened numerous possibilities for care and nurture of whole persons. Foote's evangelistic ministry as portrayed in her autobiography focused upon the salvation of individuals, but that did not ignore or perceive as separate one's physical/material well-being. She expressed deep concern for ecclesiastic and social reform, including moral and temperance, for which her evangelistic ministries inspired by her experience of entire sanctification carried implications.

"Lord, I cannot go!": Preaching and Women's Ecclesiastic Rights

Foote's preaching ministry, while seemingly representative of a traditional notion of evangelism, emerged from a subsequent religious experience following her receipt of entire sanctification. Similar to earlier religious experiences, her call to preach was consistent with a continuing counteridentity formation.[104] "For months I had been

---

[102] Foote, "A Brand Plucked from the Fire," 198.

[103] Foote, "A Brand Plucked from the Fire," 198.

[104] For some women influenced by the Holiness movement, conversion was followed not only by a second distinct work of sanctification, but a call to preach. Many of these women report an initial reluctance similar to Foote's (Lindley, *"You Have Stept Out of Your Place,"* 180–81). According to N. Hardesty, L. S. Dayton, and D. Dayton, six factors contribute to the receptivity of women's leadership among Holiness groups: "(1) a theology centered in experience (conversion and sanctification as a second work of grace); (2) biblical authority along with subjective interpretation of Scripture in line with experience; (3) an emphasis on the work of the Holy Spirit; (4) freedom to be experimental; (5) a reformist or revolutionary outlook that questioned the status quo; and (6) a tendency to form sects with organizational flexibility and that recognized a need for the gifts and leadership women offered" ("Women in the Holiness Movement: Feminism in the Evangelical Tradition," in *Women of Spirit,* ed. R. Ruether and E. McLaughlin [New York: Simon & Schuster,

moved upon to exhort and pray with the people, in my visits from house to house; and in meetings my whole soul seemed drawn out for the salvation of souls." Initially Foote was reluctant to pursue the practice of preaching. She even admitted, "I had always been opposed to the preaching of women, and had spoken against it, though, I acknowledge, without foundation. This rose before me like a mountain, and when I thought of the difficulties they had to encounter, both from professors and non-professors, I shrank back and cried, 'Lord, I cannot go!'" As God's calling became more and more profound, she questioned her fitness for the role. "I thought it could not be that I was called to preach—I, so weak and ignorant. Still, I knew all things were possible with God, even to confounding the wise by the foolish things of this earth. Yet in me there was a shrinking." Foote took her doubts and fears to God in prayer, "When, what seemed to be an angel, made his appearance. In his hand was a scroll, on which were these words: 'Thee Have I chosen to preach my Gospel without delay.' The moment my eyes saw it, it appeared to be printed on my heart." Instantly, the angel was gone and Foote described herself in agony crying out, "'Lord, I cannot do it!' It was eleven o'clock in the morning, yet everything grew dark as night. The darkness was so great that I feared to stir."[105]

Following this dramatic religious experience, Foote's appetite failed and she was unable to sleep. "I seemed as one tormented. I prayed, but felt no better." Even though a close friend and sister in Christ encouraged Foote to follow this call to preach, she was unable to comply. "One of them seemed to understand my case at once, and advised me to do as God had bid me, or I would never be happy here or hereafter. But it seemed too hard—I could not give up and obey." Foote eventually submitted to God's call to preach following another encounter with the angel, which came with these words on his breast: "You are lost unless you obey God's righteous commands," to which she concluded, "I saw the writing, and that was enough."[106]

1979], 241–48). See also D. Dayton, ed., *Holiness Tracts Defending the Ministry of Women, "The Higher Christian Life"; Sources for the Study of Holiness, Pentecostal and Keswick Movements* (New York: Garland, 1985).

[105] Foote, "A Brand Plucked from the Fire," 200–201. According to Reis, "Nineteenth century African American conversion narratives frequently included the story of a supernatural vision of either an angel or Christ" ("African American Vision Stories," 427).

[106] Foote, "A Brand Plucked from the Fire," 201.

Nearly two months from the time I first saw the angel, I said that I would do anything or go anywhere for God, if it were made plain to me. He took me at my word, and sent the angel again with this message: "You have I chosen to go in my name and warn the people of their sins." I bowed my head and said, "I will go, Lord."[107]

Foote's reluctance to accept her call was understandable in light of the fervent opposition expressed toward women's public speaking. For example, the Grimké sisters seem to have actually worsened the climate against women preachers beginning in the 1840s.[108] This danger was compounded for Foote and other African-American women preachers by racial prejudice.

Strong opposition to women's preaching and ordination pervaded much of the nineteenth-century church in the United States. However, within the holiness movement a number of women found space for a prophetic, if not a priestly, ministry.[109] Yet, even with this theological foundation, support remained limited, as with Foote's own family and pastor. In the face of such opposition, Foote's extensive apologetics for her decision demonstrated her understanding of the divine nature of her calling.

Then God the Father said to me: "You are now prepared, and must go where I have commanded you." I replied, "If I go, they will not believe me." Christ then appeared to write something with a golden pen and golden ink, upon golden paper. Then he rolled it up, and said to me: "Put this in your bosom, and, wherever you go, show it, and they will know that I have sent you to proclaim salvation to all."[110]

When visiting with friends and recounting her experience, Foote described herself reaching for this letter of authority to show them. "But I soon found, as my friends told me, it was in my heart, and was

---

[107] Foote, "A Brand Plucked from the Fire," 202.

[108] Brekus, *Strangers and Pilgrims*, 281. "Ironically, the Grimkés had hoped to convince the American public to allow women into the pulpit, but instead, they inadvertently strengthened the prejudices against female preaching."

[109] For example, Phoebe Palmer supported woman's preaching in public to mixed audiences, but did not advocate woman's ordination or sacramental ministry (see Lindley, *"You Have Stept Out of Your Place,"* 122). Thus, Palmer supported woman's prophetic ministry, but not priestly ministries. Foote would come to support not only woman's public speaking or prophetic ministry, but also the church's recognition of woman's ordination and therefore priestly ministry.

[110] Foote, "A Brand Plucked from the Fire," 203.

to be shown in my life, instead of in my hand."[111] Foote's reflexive gesture demonstrates the tendency among African-American women preachers, even more so than white women, to look not merely to an internal source of commission, but to the authority of God from outside herself to justify her preaching ministry.[112]

Alongside evangelistic practices of prayer and visitation, Foote preached, leading meetings in homes and church halls. While in Philadelphia, Foote became acquainted with three women also called to public ministry. They, too, had encountered substantial opposition, most often from ministers. Foote suggested that together they "procure a place and hold a series of meetings."[113] Foote described some apprehension, considering a woman had not conducted a meeting there, yet in the end all were generally pleased with the proposal. The meetings continued eleven nights. "The room was crowded every night—some coming to receive good, others to criticise (sic), sneer, and say hard things against us. . . . These meetings were a time of refreshing from the presence of the Lord. Many were converted, and a few stepped into the fountain of cleansing [entire sanctification]."[114] Foote labored in many places during her ministry as she traveled throughout Pennsylvania, New York, Ohio, and beyond.[115] In addition, Foote accepted a pressing invitation from Rev. (later Bishop) Daniel Payne of the AME Church to minister in Baltimore.[116]

---

[111] Foote, "A Brand Plucked from the Fire," 203.

[112] Brekus, *Strangers and Pilgrims*, 182–83.

[113] Foote, "A Brand Plucked from the Fire," 210–11. According to Bassard (Spiritual Interrogations, 107), "Black women called to preach in pre-Emancipation America could not wait for those who had power . . . to 'relinquish the floor' to them."

[114] Foote, "A Brand Plucked from the Fire," 211. Foote continued, saying, "We closed with a love-feast, which caused such a stir among the ministers and many of the church-members, that we could not imagine what the end would be. They seemed to think we had well nigh committed the unpardonable sin."

[115] Foote, "A Brand Plucked from the Fire," 212, 215, 216, 217, 218, 219, 220, 221, 222, 224, including Philadelphia, Flatbush, Binghamton, Ithaca, Rochester, Albany, Bethlehem, Pittsburgh, Cincinnati, New York, Burlington, Trenton, Princeton, Rahway, Brunswick, Newark, Columbus, Chillicothe, Zainesville, Cleveland, and Washington, DC. Although Foote did not mention the Underground Railroad, a study cross-referencing her preaching venues with significant points may uncover some overlap and perhaps further connections. For a detailed though dated treatment, including analysis of maps and routes, see W. H. Siebert, *The Underground Railroad from Slavery to Freedom* (New York: Macmillan, 1898).

[116] Foote, "A Brand Plucked from the Fire," 219–20. Payne became bishop in 1841. Daniel Payne is also well known for his educational contributions. Forced to leave Charleston, South Carolina, in 1835 because of his efforts to educate African

"From this time [beginning to preach] the opposition to my life-work commenced." For example, despite the desire by some of her worshiping congregation for her to preach in the church hall, many were anxious, so Foote was invited to preach in a member's home. The minister was displeased with this development. "He appointed a committee to wait upon the brother and sister who had opened their doors to me, to tell them they must not allow any more meetings of that kind, and that they must abide by the rules of the church, making them believe they would be excommunicated if they disobeyed him." Foote then held meetings in her home. However, the church members in attendance were told that if they continued they would be punished. Subsequently, Foote too was threatened with excommunication. She was asked to submit to the rules of the discipline, to which she answered, "Not if the discipline prohibits me from doing what God has bidden me to do; I fear God more than man." Shortly after this exchange, Foote received notice that she was no longer a member of the church because she had violated the rules of the denomination's discipline by preaching. Foote replied that she considered herself "a member of the Conference, and should do so until they said [she] was not."[117] Although she appealed to the annual conference, her request was overlooked. "My letter was slightingly noticed, and then thrown under the table. Why should they notice it? It was only the grievance of a woman, and there was no justice meted out to women in those days. Even ministers of Christ did not feel that women had any rights which they were bound to respect."[118]

Foote relied upon God's work of entire sanctification creating a real change in her, and God's explicit call to preach and minister toward the salvation of others. She tended not to focus upon changing denominational structures, which as social constructions often contributed to her disenfranchisement.[119] As a result of such opposition Foote took up the cause of ecclesiastic rights for women. Initially, she was strongly opposed to women's preaching. However, informed

---

Americans, Payne served as president of Wilberforce University, the only African-American Methodist college founded before the Civil War, dating back to 1844. See Norwood, *The Story of American Methodism*, 219–20.

[117] Foote, "A Brand Plucked from the Fire," 205–7. This is a claim that if supported by the annual conference would imply a similar authority and membership as ordination, which she later received.

[118] Foote, "A Brand Plucked from the Fire," 207.

[119] See Bassard for further discussion of intertextuality as self-revisionism in *Spiritual Interrogations*, 95.

by her understanding of entire sanctification, Foote's perspective shifted. Thus, Foote's efforts for women's ecclesiastic rights emerged from her theological framework and assumed the evangelistic imperative that characterized her ministry practices.

> I could not believe that it was a short-lived impulse of spasmodic influence that impelled me to preach. I read that on the day of Pentecost was the Scripture fulfilled as found in Joel ii. 28, 29; and it certainly will not be denied that women as well as men were at that time filled with the Holy Ghost, because it is expressly stated that women were among those who continued in prayer and supplication, waiting for the fulfillment of the promise. Women and men are classed together, and if the power to preach the Gospel is short-lived and spasmodic in the case of women, it must be equally so in that of men; and if women have lost the gift of prophecy, so have men.[120]

Based on these biblical texts, and numerous others, Foote, with other nineteenth-century women preachers and missionaries, argued for the ministry of women alongside men. "If it be necessary to prove one's right to preach the Gospel, I ask of my brethren to show me their credentials, or I can not believe in the propriety of their ministry."[121] Foote's biblical foundation for the preaching ministry of women echoes the arguments of others before and since the nineteenth century.

> But the Bible puts an end to this strife when it says: "There is neither male nor female in Christ Jesus" [Gal 3:28]. Philip had four daughters that prophesied, or preached. Paul called Priscilla, as well as Aquila, his "helper," or, as in the Greek, his "fellow-laborer." Rom. xv. 3; 2 Cor. viii. 23; Phil. ii. 5; 1 Thess. iii. 2. The same word, which, in our common translation, is now rendered a "servant of the church," in speaking of Phebe (Rom. xix. 1.), is rendered "minister" when applied to Tychicus. Eph. vi. 21. When Paul said, "Help those

---

[120] Foote, "A Brand Plucked from the Fire," 208. The biblical passage Joel 2:28-29 was often used by nineteenth-century African-American women preachers and missionaries "to combat opposition from whites and men to their preaching, these lines were meant to create space in divine will to refute nineteenth century gender and racial ideologies that suggested they should not and could not preach" (C. Haywood, "Prophesying Daughters: Nineteenth Century Black Religious Women, the Bible, and Black Literary History," in *African Americans and the Bible: Sacred Texts and Social Textures*, ed. V. Wimbush [New York: Continuum, 2000], 355).

[121] Foote, "A Brand Plucked from the Fire," 209.

women who labor with me in the Gospel," he certainly meant that they did more than pour out tea. In the eleventh chapter of First Corinthians Paul gives directions, to men and women, how they should appear when they prophesy or pray in public assemblies; and he defines prophesying to be speaking to edification, exhortation and comfort.[122]

Although both Foote's mother and father initially expressed opposition to her preaching vocation, both individually gave explicit approval. Foote's mother offered her blessing first.

> As my mother embraced me [after an absence of six years], she exclaimed: "So you are a preacher, are you?" I replied: "So they say." "Well, Julia," said she, "when I first heard that you were a preacher, I said that I would rather hear you were dead." These words, coming so unexpectedly from my mother, filled me with anguish. Was I to meet opposition here, too? But my mother, with streaming eyes, continued: "My dear daughter, it is all past now. I have heard from those who have attended your meetings what the Lord has done for you, and I am satisfied."[123]

Foote's father later expressed approval to his daughter on his deathbed. "Just before leaving us for the better world, he called each of his children that were present to his bedside, exhorting them to live here in such a manner that they might meet him in heaven. To me he said: 'My dear daughter, be faithful to your heavenly calling, and fear not to preach full [entire] salvation.' "[124]

The African Methodist Episcopal Church refused to authorize the preaching of women, first, in a proposal presented in Nathan Ward's petition to make such licenses available to women in 1844,

[122] Foote, "A Brand Plucked from the Fire." Foote relied heavily on New Testament epistles for her defense of woman's preaching, including Paul, while other women in this study tended to rely upon the example of Jesus Christ. Foote's evangelistic ministry seems to resonate with George Hunsberger's claim that while Paul's freedom from the law led him to the affirmation in Gal 3:28, "he also believed a variation on that language: 'In Christ there is both Jew and Greek, there is both slave and free, there is both male and female.' That is to say, Paul's affirmation of the essential oneness across lines of race, culture, class and gender depended upon his affirmation of the integrity of the varieties of culture and heritage" ("Is there Biblical Warrant for Evangelism?" *Interpretation* 48 [1994]: 139).

[123] Foote, "A Brand Plucked from the Fire," 212. Foote's mother most likely offered her blessing in 1844.

[124] Foote, "A Brand Plucked from the Fire," 218. Foote's father died in May 1849.

then echoed in the Daughters of Zion petitions proposed and defeated in 1848 as well as in 1852.[125] Foote and other women continued their preaching ministries.[126] "Though opposed, I went forth laboring for God, and he owned and blessed my labors, and has done so wherever I have been until this day. And while I walk obediently, I know he will, though hell may rage and vent its spite."[127] For example, two references to Foote preaching at camp meetings appear in the

---

[125] See Foote, "A Brand Plucked from the Fire," 244 n 14. J. Dodson, "Nineteenth Century A.M.E. Preaching Women," in *Women in New Worlds*, ed. H. Thomas and R. S. Keller, Historical Perspectives on the Wesleyan Tradition 1 (Nashville: Abingdon, 1981), 280–81.

[126] D. Payne's *History of the African Methodist Episcopal Church* (1891) and C. S. Smith's *A History of the African Methodist Episcopal Church* (1922). Jarena Lee (1783–1850) was most likely the first female preacher in the African Methodist Episcopal Church, experiencing a call to preach and responding to that call beginning in the 1810s and 1820s. See Schmidt, *Grace Sufficient*, 98, 100–104. According to Andrews, "Early in 1845 [Foote] began to travel in upstate New York, preaching from various Methodist pulpits, often in company with or invited by ministers of the African Methodist Episcopal Church" (*Sisters of the Spirit*, 10). According to Foote's account, Payne invited her to minister in the Baltimore area (219–20) prior to a seeming change of heart resulting in the defeat of the petitions. This shift in support coincides with the AME Church's efforts in the mid-1830s toward increased respectability (see Brekus, *Strangers and Pilgrims*, 295–96). Although the Daughters of Zion petitions for preaching licenses to General Conference were refused, in 1868 the AME Church's General Conference allowed an official if subordinate female office of stewardess; in 1884 women were granted preaching licenses, followed by the office of deaconess in 1900. The AME Church did not grant full ordination to women until the middle of the twentieth century. See Lindley, *"You Have Stept Out of Your Place,"* 181; see also Dodson, "Nineteenth Century AME Preaching Women," 285–87. The duties of the stewardess included "looking after females of the church; going into sick-rooms and attending to such duties among the females as might be imprudent for a man to perform," such as preparing women for baptism, caring for female mourners as well as assisting with the Lord's Supper and love-feast, and preparing the parsonage. See Bishop H. M. Turner, *The Genius and Theory of Methodist Polity, or The Machinery of Methodism. Practically Illustrated Through a Series of Questions and Answers* (Philadelphia: Publication Department, AME Church, 1885), 165–68.

[127] Foote, "A Brand Plucked from the Fire," 209. "In April, 1851, we visited Chillicothe, and had some glorious meetings there. Great crowds attended every night, and the altar was crowded with anxious inquirers. Some of the deacons of the white people's Baptist church invited me to preach in their church, but I declined to do so, on account of the opposition of the pastor, who was very much set against women's preaching. He said so much against it, and against the members who wished me to preach, that they called a church meeting, and I heard that they finally dismissed him" (221).

unpublished journal of D. S. Warner, the founder of the Church of God (Anderson, Indiana) after he was expelled from a small German pietist sect in 1878 following his experience of entire sanctification.[128] In 1884, the AME General Conference passed resolutions reluctantly allowing women to receive preaching licenses, but limiting women's preaching ministry to evangelistic work, namely itinerant preaching rather than appointed to specific local churches. This qualified action prohibited woman's ordination, which was made explicit in 1884.[129]

According to historians, Foote's activities following the publication of her autobiography are largely unknown. After serving as a missionary for the African Methodist Episcopal Zion Church,[130] Foote was the first woman ordained deacon in that denomination.[131] Shortly before her death, which occurred November 22, 1900, Foote was ordained elder, the second woman to receive this official role in the AMEZ denomination.[132]

Signs of Racial Reconciliation

From the outset of her autobiography, Foote acknowledged not only the sins of racism within Christian communities, but its inconsistency

---

[128] Stanley, *Holy Boldness*, 220 n 21. Foote preached at two camp meetings, one in Marion, Indiana, in 1878 and the other in Churubasko, Michigan, in 1879. The journal includes entries from 1872 to 1879. Quoted in Stanley, D. S. Warner, "Journal of D. S. Warner" (unpublished manuscript), 345, 380.

[129] Dodson, "Nineteenth Century AME Preaching Women," 287–88.

[130] The African Methodist Episcopal Zion Church was established in 1821, but dates back to developments in the 1780s and the John Street Church in New York City. The denomination's development at one time endorsed a principle of full democracy for both male and female members (Norwood, *The Story of American Methodism*, 172–74).

[131] Collier-Thomas, *Daughters of Thunder*, 59. Collier-Thomas claims Foote was ordained deacon in 1895, with a reference to the *Minutes of the New York Conference*, 21, 31. Andrews names May 20, 1894, and cites J. A. J. Foote, "A Brand Plucked from the Fire" (Cleveland: the author, 1879). See Andrews, *Sisters of the Spirit*, 10.

[132] Andrews, *Sisters of the Spirit*, 10. In her analysis that includes the writings of Jarena Lee, another African Methodist female itinerant preacher, Bassard asserts that Lee's preaching in the face of denominational opposition did not seek to "dismantle community but to effect communal change." Additionally, the acceptance of Lee's preaching by Richard Allen, similar to Foote's ordination, "is not to be read as 'co-optation' or an embrace of the status quo . . . but seeks to create a heterophonous base for community, one that, ultimately, will do away with the need for hegemonic practices within the boundaries of collective subjectivity" (Bassard, *Spiritual Interrogations*, 107).

with Christian doctrine—namely a real change in persons created through entire sanctification—and her desire to work toward racial reconciliation in Christian faithfulness.[133] In addition to the pain of racism experienced by her parents, Foote was affected by racism as a child.[134] In her autobiography, Foote described numerous occasions during her itinerant ministry in which racism was cruelly present. On her travels prior to the AME General Conference in Pittsburgh, most likely held in 1844, Foote recounted, "There was but one passenger in the stage besides myself. He gave his name as White, seemed very uneasy, and, at each stopping place, he would say: 'I am afraid the public will take me for an abolitionist to-day;' thus showing his dark, slave-holding principles."[135] Before arriving at the General Conference, while sailing on a "canal packet" she entered the women's cabin the first evening, after departing at 6 a.m. that morning, to find an empty bed upon which to sleep.

> In a short time a man came into the cabin, saying that the berths in the gentleman's cabin were all occupied, and he was going to sleep

[133] Stanley discusses the tendency of the "empowered self" to "defy racism," in *Holy Boldness*, 96–99; see also 190–94 for a brief survey of racism and efforts against it in the ministries of women included in Stanley's study. When holiness evangelist Amanda Berry Smith (1837–1915) received sanctification, she claimed also to lose her fear of white persons. See Hardesty, *Women Called to Witness*, 51–52. Foote's evangelistic ministry resonates with Scott Jones's later claim, "The reign of God is best understood as that state where all of God's creatures are fully loved" (*The Evangelistic Love of God and Neighbor: A Theology of Witness and Discipleship* [Nashville: Abingdon, 2003], 47).

[134] Foote, "A Brand Plucked from the Fire," 184. For example, in her youth while she yearned for education another school experience was thwarted. "Mrs. Phileos and Miss Crandall met with great indignity from a pro-slavery mob in Canterbury, Conn., because they dared to teach colored children to read. If they went out to walk, they were followed by a rabble of men and boys, who hooted at them, and threw rotten eggs and other missiles at them, endangering their lives and frightening them terribly." According to Andrews, "Prudence Crandall opened a female boarding school in Canterbury, Connecticut, in the fall of 1832 but closed it soon thereafter as a result of community resistance to the fact that she had admitted one black pupil. In February 1833 she opened a school for black girls, which was forcibly closed in late May by an act of the state legislature making any such school as hers illegal. Much litigation ensued over the school's right to exist. During this time the school was the target of attempted arson and other destructive assaults which effectively prevented it from opening again" (Andrews, *Sisters of the Spirit*, 243 n 4). See A. T. Child Jr., "Prudence Crandall and the Canterbury Experiment," *Bulletin of the Friends Historical Association* 22 (1933): 35–55.

[135] Foote, "A Brand Plucked from the Fire," 215.

in the ladies' cabin. Then he pointed to me and said: "That nigger has no business here. My family are [*sic*] coming on board the boat at Utica, and they shall not come where a nigger is." They called the captain, and he ordered me to get up; but I did not stir, thinking it best not to leave the bed except by force. Finally they left me, and the man found lodging among the seamen, swearing vengeance on the "niggers."[136]

In the early 1850s, while traveling to Cleveland, despite the arrangements of "one of the brethren" to reserve passage and pay her fare, Foote was not permitted to leave until four days after the intended departure. "At the time a colored person was not allowed to ride in the stage if any white passenger objected to it. There were objections made for three mornings, but, on the fourth, the stage called for us, and we had safe journey to Cleveland."[137]

Despite the consistent obstacles of racism to her evangelistic ministry, Foote persevered, encouraging signs of racial reconciliation. Occasionally Foote received invitations to preach from white congregations. Foote declined one invitation from a Methodist congregation that, "did not want the colored people to attend the meeting." Foote concluded: "I would not agree to any such arrangement, and, therefore, I did not speak for them. Prejudice had closed the door of their sanctuary against the colored people of the place, virtually saying: 'The Gospel shall not be free to all.' Our benign Master and Saviour said: 'Go, preach my Gospel to all'" [Mark 16:15]. While visiting Zanesville, Ohio, Foote labored for "white and colored people."[138]

> The white Methodists opened their house for the admission of colored people for the first time. Hundreds were turned away at each meeting, unable to get in; and, although the house was so crowded, perfect order prevailed. We also held meetings on the other side of the river. God the Holy Ghost was powerfully manifest in all these meetings. I was the recipient of many mercies, and passed through various exercises.[139]

[136] Foote, "A Brand Plucked from the Fire," 215.

[137] Foote, "A Brand Plucked from the Fire," 224.

[138] Foote, "A Brand Plucked from the Fire," 221, 222. In addition to receiving an invitation to preach from "some of the deacons of the white people's Baptist church" near Chillicothe, "white Methodists invited me to speak for them." Mark 16:15: "Go into all the world and preach the gospel to the whole creation" (RSV), John Wesley's most often preached text.

[139] Foote, "A Brand Plucked from the Fire," 222. Following these events in Zanesville, Ohio, Foote traveled to Detroit, Michigan. "One day, quite an influential

Foote's evangelistic ministry, which emerged from her experience of entire sanctification, took seriously, as evidence of a real change in persons, Christian practices that worked toward racial reconciliation. These practices, as manifestations of Christian faith, then shaped relationships within and among communities.[140]

In addition to advocating for racial reconciliation, a significant Christian practice in Foote's evangelistic vocation, she also encouraged other practices of reconciliation and justice. For example, following the tragic narrative of her teacher's criminal act of murder and the bereaved husband's subsequent forgiveness and evangelistic ministry with the teacher prior to his hanging, Foote closed that chapter of her autobiography:

> Never since that day have I heard of a person being hung, but a shudder runs through my whole frame, and a trembling seizes me. Oh, what a barbarous thing is the taking of human life, even though it be 'a life for a life,' as many believe God commands [Exod 21:23]. That was the old dispensation. Jesus said: 'A new commandment I give unto you, that ye love one another' [John 13:34]. Again: 'Resist not evil; but whosoever shall smite thee on the right cheek, turn to him the other also' [Matt. 5:39]. Living as we do in the Gospel dispensation, may God help us to follow the precepts and example of Him, who, when he was reviled, reviled not again, and in the agony of death prayed: 'Father, forgive them, for they know not what they do" [Luke 23:34].[141]

Foote concluded the paragraph with the following pivotal statement: "Christian men, vote as you pray, that the legalized traffic in ardent spirits may be abolished, and God grant that capital punishment may

---

man in the community, though a sinner, called on me and appeared deeply concerned about his soul's welfare. He urged me to speak from Micah iv. 13: 'Arise and thresh, O daughter of Zion,' etc. I took his desire to the Lord, and was permitted to speak from that passage." A sermon text seems to follow this excerpt from Foote's autobiography. The sermon, entitled "A 'Threshing' Sermon" (1851), is also available in Collier-Thomas, *Daughters of Thunder*, 57–68, with another sermon, "Christian Perfection" (1894), both of which offer insight regarding Foote's doctrinal understanding of sanctification.

140 Bassard argues that the spiritual events, of direct divine revelation, and social embodiments of resistance among African-American women, such as Jarena Lee, "produced layers of narrative that work against the intent of the traditional Anglo-Christian morphology of conversion" (*Spiritual Interrogations*, 103).

141 Foote, "A Brand Plucked from the Fire," 174.

be banished from our land."[142] Thus, according to Foote, entire sanctification is the key to abolishing not only the individual's captivity to sin, but also sinful social constructs of intemperance and capital punishment. "O Prejudice! thou cruel monster! wilt thou ever cease to exist? Not until all shall know the Lord, and holiness shall be written upon the bells of the horses—upon all things in earth as well as in heaven. Glory to the Lamb, whose right it is to reign!"[143] For Foote, these practices of social reform were intimately connected to one's faith, particularly one's conversion and receipt of entire sanctification, so that her evangelistic preaching may not be isolated from such practices. Early in her autobiography, Foote admonished her readers, "Put away your idols, and give God the whole heart."[144] Then, in the penultimate chapter, entitled "Love not the World," Foote expanded upon the implications of her doctrine of entire sanctification. "If we be of God and have the love of the Father in our hearts, we are not of the world, because whatsoever is of the world is not of God. We must be one or the other."[145] Offering accountability to the Christian community she sharply stated:

> As we look at the professing Christians of to-day, the question arises, Are they not all conformed to the maxims and fashions of this world, even many of those who profess to have been sanctified? But they say the transforming and renewing here [Rom. xii.2] spoken of means, as it says, the mind, not the clothing. But, if the mind be renewed, it must affect the clothing. It is by the Word of God we are to be judged, not by our opinion of the Word.[146]

[142] Foote, "A Brand Plucked from the Fire," 174. With temperance and advocacy against capital punishment, Foote also assisted in establishing a moral reform society. "Monday evening I went with some of the sisters of the church, where there was a meeting for the purpose of forming a moral reform society" (213).

[143] Foote, "A Brand Plucked from the Fire," 218. This statement concludes yet another account of racial prejudice suffered by Foote on her journeys. "I spent one Sunday in Poughkeepsie, working for Jesus. I then went to New York, where I took the boat for Boston. We were detained some hours by one of the shafts breaking. I took a very severe cold by being compelled to sit on deck all night, in the cold, damp air—prejudice not permitting one of my color to enter the cabin except in the capacity of a servant."

[144] Foote, "A Brand Plucked from the Fire," 179.

[145] Foote, "A Brand Plucked from the Fire," 230.

[146] Foote, "A Brand Plucked from the Fire," 230. Foote referred to 1 Tim 2:9-10; 1 Pet 3:3-5. She then focused on the priestly office specifically, "But it is a lamentable fact that too many priests' lips speak vanity. Many profess to teach, but few are able to feed the lambs, while the sheep are dying for lack of nourishment and the true knowledge of salvation" (231).

With Wesley, Foote's doctrine of entire sanctification and her evangelistic ministry could not exclude the manifestation of faith in changed lives of holiness. Foote's evangelistic ministry seemed focused upon verbal proclamation through preaching and publication. However, her receipt of entire sanctification and that of others created a real change, which while abolishing the root of sin, resulted in fruits characterized by love and reconciliation. Through ordinary Christian practices such as prayer and visitation, pressing needs were addressed, reaching individuals with the gospel and reshaping lives of holiness. For Foote, the doctrine of entire sanctification led to a reordering of sinful social structures, resulting in racial reconciliation as well as ecclesiastic rights for women.

All are brought into a blessed harmony with God and each other.[147]

---

[147] Foote, "A Brand Plucked from the Fire," 163.

Chapter 4

⤜Frances E. Willard⤛

Men preach a creed; women will declare a life.[1]

Frances E. Willard's (1839–1898) ministry vocation led her to facilitate women's evangelistic ministry within the National Woman's Christian Temperance Union (NWCTU), encouraging aspects of a woman's church.[2] One of the most influential women of her time and one of the few women honored in the U.S. Capitol's Statuary Hall,[3] Willard was a committed member of the Methodist Episcopal Church. Willard's Christian faith, informed by the Wesleyan theme of holiness, grounded her roles as educator and reformer. Invited to serve as the president of the newly founded Evanston College for Ladies in 1871, Willard was the first woman in America to confer a college degree.[4] But it was her work with the NWCTU that reflected

---

[1] F. Willard, *Woman in the Pulpit* (1889; repr., Washington, DC: Zenger, 1978), 47.

[2] The WCTU, based mostly in small-town congregations, claimed the largest number of participants of nineteenth-century women's organizations. L. D. Ginzberg, *Women and the Work of Benevolence: Morality, Politics, and Class in the Nineteenth-Century United States* (New Haven: Yale University Press, 1990), 204. By 1879, Wittenmeyer, then president, and Willard, corresponding secretary, during a cross-country tour "created or encouraged" one thousand local unions and petitions to Congress. A. F. Scott, *Natural Allies: Women's Associations in American History* (Urbana: University of Illinois Press, 1991), 96.

[3] N. Hardesty, *Women Called to Witness: Evangelical Feminism in the Nineteenth Century* (Knoxville, Univerity of Tennessee Press, 1999), 2.

[4] Hardesty, *Women Called to Witness*, 4–5. C. Gifford, ed., *Writing Out My Heart: Selections from the Journal of Frances E. Willard, 1855–96* (Urbana: University of Illinois Press, 1995), 6. See also F. Willard, *Glimpses of Fifty Years: The Autobiography*

her greatest influence. Elected president of the NWCTU in 1879, Willard served in that role, challenging and leading the organization, until her death almost two decades later.

The NWCTU organized following the Woman's Crusade against liquor dealers. Started in Ohio during the winter of 1873–1874, the crusade quickly spread to neighboring states, then across the country, and finally linked with other movements across the world.[5] Recognizing the systemic implications of intemperance, Willard strategically expanded the NWCTU's horizons to address a wide range of issues affecting women—suffrage, poverty, ecclesiastic rights, marriage, and labor. Willard guided the growth of the NWCTU from a small, precarious organization with a simple focus of temperance to the largest women's organization in the nation with a complex agenda of social reform.[6]

In her journal and autobiography, Willard narrated the way her Christian faith shaped her practices of reform.[7] Willard struggled throughout her faith journey, often lacking assurance of her salvation. This struggle led her actively to seek such assurance through "doing good," resulting in her focus on education and reform. Willard's international travels encouraged her desire to do good. During her travels she witnessed the relationship of educational opportunities and economic resources (or lack thereof) to women's opportunities (or

---

of an American Woman (Chicago: Woman's Temperance Publication Association, 1889), 198–225.

[5] By April 1874 over one thousand saloons had been closed, and beer production in at least one state was estimated at one-third less. B. L. Epstein, *The Politics of Domesticity: Women, Evangelism, and Temperance in Nineteenth-Century America* (Middletown, Conn.: Wesleyan University Press, 1981), 100. See also C. Gifford, "'The Woman's Cause Is Man's'? Frances Willard and the Social Gospel," in *Gender and the Social Gospel*, ed. W. D. Edwards and C. D. Gifford (Urbana: University of Illinois Press, 2003), 26. The World's Woman's Christian Temperance Union was organized in 1884.

[6] Gifford, *Writing Out My Heart*, 7. According to Epstein (*The Politics of Domesticity*, 125), the attitude of the WCTU differentiated it from the numerous other social reforms of the time; "in every aspect of its work, it kept uppermost its concern for women, framed in terms of its own understanding of women's interests."

[7] Willard's journal of fifty volumes, forty-nine of which were discovered more than half a century after her death, has been transcribed by Carolyn DeSwarte Gifford and is available with other primary sources on microfilm in The Temperance and Prohibition Papers. Gifford, the leading scholar on Frances Willard, selected and edited excerpts of Willard's journal published as *Writing Out My Heart*. Willard compiled an autobiography of approximately seven hundred pages at the request of the NWCTU entitled *Glimpses of Fifty Years*.

oppression). Blocked from leadership in the academy and frustrated by a seemingly unanswerable call to ordained ministry, Willard channeled her Christian vocation into the trajectory of the NWCTU. Prior to her election as president in 1879, Willard experienced what she would refer to as a "conversion" to women's suffrage, linking her faith to participation in causes beyond temperance reform.[8]

Within the NWCTU Willard engaged in and facilitated women's evangelistic ministries. While advocating for women's suffrage and ecclesiastic rights within the Methodist Episcopal Church (MEC), Willard implemented ecclesiological elements in the programs of the NWCTU. In her text *Woman in the Pulpit*, Willard argued for the ordination of women and suggested that, if the current disenfranchisement persisted, women should consider ordaining themselves, effectively proposing a women's church.[9] Willard's proposal did not materialize, as some had feared and others hoped, through a massive exodus of female church members from mainline Protestant and evangelical denominations. However, the NWCTU did provide women with Christian vocations to preach and other ministry roles with evangelistic training and practice. Thus, through the NWCTU's "Evangelistic Work Department," Willard encouraged the reclamation of the church's mission described in biblical texts, following in particular the example of Jesus Christ.[10]

[8] Willard, *Glimpses of Fifty Years*, 351. Hardesty, *Women Called to Witness*, 6. See also B. Zink-Sawyer, *From Preachers to Suffragists: Women's Rights and Religious Conviction in the Lives of Three Nineteenth-Century American Clergywomen* (Louisville, Ky.: Westminster John Knox, 2003), 4–6, 171–216. Zink-Sawyer focuses her study on three individuals (Antoinette Brown Blackwell, Olympia Brown, and Anna Howard Shaw) who share Willard's vocation to preach and support suffrage.

[9] Willard, *Woman in the Pulpit*, 56. See also N. Garner, "The Woman's Christian Temperance Union: A Woman's Branch of American Protestantism," in *Re-forming the Center: American Protestantism, 1900 to the Present*, ed. D. Jacobsen and W. Trollinger (Grand Rapids: Eerdmans, 1998), esp. 271–83.

[10] The emphases of Willard's evangelistic ministry resonate with the significance given to the role of Christian communities for effective and faithful evangelistic practices in the contemporary academic study of evangelism. According to Brad Kallenberg, "We can at least provisionally conclude that faithfulness in evangelism must simultaneously attend to both the group and the individual" (*Live to Tell: Evangelism for a Postmodern Age* [Grand Rapids: Brazos Press, 2002], 21, 47–64). See also D. L. Guder and L. Barret, eds. *Missional Church: A Vision for the Sending of the Church in North America* (Grand Rapids: Eerdmans, 1988), 5, 110–268; W. J. Abraham, *The Logic of Evangelism* (Grand Rapids: Eerdmans, 1989), 57, 92–184; and S. J. Jones, *The Evangelistic Love of God and Neighbor: A Theology of Witness and Discipleship* (Nashville: Abingdon, 2003), 17, 71, 139–58.

Formation in Faith

Frances Elizabeth Caroline Willard was born September 28, 1839, to Josiah Flint Willard and Mary Thompson Hill Willard, in Churchville, New York, fourteen miles west of Rochester. The fourth of five children, Frances was one of but three to survive to adulthood.[11] Raised in an attentive Christian home, Willard narrated her faith formation reflecting expectations of the time for conversion and later holiness. In 1841 the Willard family moved from New York to Oberlin, Ohio, where Josiah planned to prepare for the ministry.[12] In 1846 the family moved to a farm outside of Janesville, Wisconsin, where Willard resided with her family until 1858, when she and her younger sister, Mary, enrolled in North Western Female College in Evanston, Illinois.[13] Shortly following their matriculation, Willard's older brother, Oliver, enrolled in Garrett Biblical Institute, also in Evanston, to train for the Methodist ministry.[14] The Willard family

[11] Willard, *Glimpses of Fifty Years*, 1–2. According to Hardesty, "Two Willards served as early presidents of Harvard University. One of them, Samuel, as pastor of Old South Church in Boston, opposed the burning of witches. Her [Willard's] mother, Mary Thompson Hill (1805–1892), was born in Danville, Vermont. Josiah Flint Willard (1805–1868) was born in Wheelock, Vermont. Both families migrated from Vermont to New York's Genesee Valley when the children were about ten. Mary and Josiah were married on 3 November 1831. Both had been successful teachers. Josiah managed a local store" (*Women Called to Witness*, 2).

[12] Hardesty, *Women Called to Witness*, 3. According to Hardesty, "Oberlin [Collegiate Institute] was the first college to admit both men and women, so Mary and her sister Sarah Hill would take classes too. . . . The Willards wanted to associate with Oberlin because of its stand on abolition, in which both firmly believed. Their cellar in Oberlin became a haven for travelers on the Underground Railroad, and Frances learned to read from The Slave's Friend, an abolitionist magazine for children." Although very young, Frances remembered hearing Finney preach while her family attended the First Congregational Church in Oberlin.

[13] According to Gifford, "After small beginnings as early as the second decade of the nineteenth century, Methodist educational institutions had proliferated by the 1830s, 40s, and 50s. Among these were a number of female seminaries (the equivalent of high schools). Methodist activity in higher education reflected an increasing national interest in universal education with both public and private school systems developing in the middle decades of the century." C. Gifford, "'My Own Methodist Hive': Frances Willard's Faith as Disclosed in Her Journal, 1855–1870," in *Spirituality and Social Responsibility: Vocational Vision of Women in the United Methodist Tradition*, ed. R. S. Keller (Nashville: Abingdon, 1993), 85. For a helpful analysis of the female seminary movement and its emphases, see L. Sweet, "The Female Seminary Movement and Woman's Mission in Antebellum America," *Journal of Church History* 54 (1985): 41–55.

[14] Gifford, *Writing Out My Heart*, 5.

had become active in the MEC during the 1850s and attended an ME congregation in Evanston after the parents moved there to join their children.[15]

Willard struggled throughout her formation in faith, often lacking assurance of her salvation. In her lengthy autobiography, commissioned by the NWCTU, Willard made comparatively brief references to the events leading up to and including her own public profession of faith. Perhaps reflective of her own precarious faith journey she included a plea for teachers to take seriously their responsibility for the Christian formation of their pupils. According to Willard, only one of her teachers, Mrs. W. P. Jones, "ever spoke to me on spiritual things."[16] Willard described a visit with Mrs. Jones, during which Mrs. Jones inquired if she might pray for Willard.

> I told her I would be very glad to have her, whereupon we knelt down beside my bed and with her arm around me she prayed earnestly that I might be led to see the light and do the right. I am sure that every school-girl if approached as wisely and sincerely as I was by that good and noble woman, would respond as gratefully as I did. Teachers lose very much when they fail to utilize the good-will they have enlisted for the good of the cause to which they are devoted.[17]

Willard's recollection closed with a reference to the important, but rarely noted, evangelistic role of teachers. This idea of an evangelistic component to the teaching role most likely shaped her vocation as she narrated her faith journey later in life.[18]

Relying heavily on the account (written twenty-five years after the events described) of Professor William P. Jones Jr. (1831–1886), founder of North Western Female College and advocate of women's higher education,[19] Willard provided a picture of herself as a student grappling with questions of faith. In one of Professor Jones's classes, the reading for the day was Wayland's *Moral Science*. Finding himself without a text, Jones borrowed Willard's. He recounted that the book opened itself at the beginning of the chapter on "Virtue," and on the

[15] Gifford, *Writing Out My Heart*, 8.

[16] Willard, *Glimpses of Fifty Years*, 119.

[17] Willard, *Glimpses of Fifty Years*, 119.

[18] See P. Fredriksen, "Paul and Augustine: Conversion Narratives, Orthodox Traditions, and the Retrospective Self," *Journal of Theological Studies* 37 (1986): 33.

[19] Willard, *Glimpses of Fifty Years*, 21 n 21. Professor W. P. Jones was principal of North Western Female College from 1855 to 1862.

opposite page the following memorandum was written in Willard's hand: "When I began this study, I could not say whether there was a God or no—and if there was, whether He cared for me or not. Now, thanks to President Wayland and my faithful instructors, I can say from my heart I believe that there is a God, and that He is my Father."[20] This epiphany did not resolve Willard's larger quest for a vital Christian faith, but seemed to reflect her difficulty in understanding her religious experiences and accepting her questions.

Willard graduated from North Western Female College in June 1859, but was "unable to bear my examinations, read my essay, & graduate regularly" due to a life-threatening case of typhoid fever. She remarked in her journal that there was no "Valedictory," since she was too ill to give the address.[21] During her illness, Willard experienced a crisis of faith that echoed the struggle recorded in Jones's story. Willard recounted an episode during her illness in which she heard the doctor say that "the crisis would soon arrive." While the doctor undoubtedly referred to a medical crisis, a spiritual crisis also ensued:

> My whole soul was intent, as two voices seemed to speak within me, one of them saying, "My child, give me thy heart. I called thee long by joy, I call thee now by chastisement; but I have called thee always and only because I love thee with an everlasting love." The other said, "Surely you who are so resolute and strong will not break down now because of physical feebleness. You are a reasoner, and never yet were you convinced of the reasonableness of Christianity. Hold out now and you will feel when you get well just as you used to feel."[22]

Willard narrated a seemingly lengthy struggle, which finally relented, yet left her unable to feel an assurance of her salvation. "But at last, solemnly, and with my whole heart, I said, not in spoken words, but in the deeper language of consciousness, 'If God lets me get well I'll try to be a Christian girl.' But this resolve did not bring peace. 'You must at once declare this resolution,' said the inward voice." Willard called to her mother and said, "Mother, I wish to tell you that if God lets me get well I'll try to be a Christian girl." Willard's mother took her hand, knelt beside the bed, and wept and prayed.[23]

---

[20] Willard, *Glimpses of Fifty Years*, 122.

[21] Gifford, *Writing Out My Heart*, 44–45. According to Gifford, "[N]o one gave her speech, 'Horizons,' which she had written before her illness."

[22] Willard, *Glimpses of Fifty Years*, 622.

[23] Willard, *Glimpses of Fifty Years*, 622–23.

Willard's lack of assurance of her salvation led her actively to seek such assurance through doing good. The next month, on July 23, 1859, Willard wrote in her journal, "I shall be twenty years old in September & I have as yet, been of no use in the world." Her crisis of faith, likely triggered by the dangerous illness, was fueled by an inability to reconcile her intellectual pursuits with her spiritual desire for Christian faith. "Ever since I was sick, I have thought much of Religion. I wish that I stood in right relations to God. I wish I could practically apply the intellectual belief I have in Christ. I wish I could trust in him whom I have not seen, as I trust even in my friends on the earth who are tangible to me." Willard struggled with "feeling" her sinful condition, "I see it, I acknowledge it, intellectually, but I don't *feel* it." Despite her anxiety, she persevered. "But I shall not give it up. . . . For Christ's sake, I ask Thee, O Lord, to spare me until then. Divest me of all false pride, let me *feel* as I see, how glorious a thing it is to be at peace with Him by whom I was created, by whom I am preserved. Let me truly repent, and help me to please Thee, and to be useful in the world, I ask it very humbly and sincerely, *only* for Christ's sake."[24] Willard's need "to be useful in the world" seemed to drive her vocational trajectory and lasting contributions.

Later that year the First MEC in Evanston hosted revival services. Having recovered slowly through the late summer and autumn, Willard described these meetings as "my first public opportunity of declaring my new allegiance."[25] Willard attended a Sunday morning lecture given by Randolph Sinks Foster (1820–1903), president of Northwestern University from 1857 to 1860, and later bishop in the MEC. Foster lectured on Proverbs 23:7, "As a man thinketh in his heart, so is he." According to Willard, "Dr. F. demonstrated with sufficient certainty, that any one may know by his thoughts—by carefully analyzing them, & ascertaining what his habitual trains of thought are,—just what he is himself, & may from them predict what he will be." As a result, Willard devoted much time reflecting in her journal, evaluating her potential Christian faithfulness and character. Although Willard largely concluded with a negative self-evaluation, she added, "Since my recent illness, it is just to say that I have thought most of God. Underlying all my ideas & wishes, has been the idea that Christ would love & pardon me, if I rightly asked him,—the wish that

---

[24] Gifford, *Writing Out My Heart*, 45, 47.

[25] Willard, *Glimpses of Fifty Years*, 623. All italics in quotations are original unless otherwise noted.

I were reconciled to God, and doing good in the world. As yet, I have no light, but, I will not, if God will help me, be wearied in striving."[26]

With the encouragement and guidance of Christian mentors, Willard continued to reflect upon her faith while participating in individual and communal Christian practices—attending worship, reading biblical texts, and engaging in prayer. During a worship service, Willard witnessed "several went forward to the Altar for prayers. I shall go when I feel impressed with a desire, a need, a necessity to go. I shall not go before."[27]

On December 13, 1859, Willard attended worship to hear Bishop Matthew Simpson (1811–1884) preach. "His sermon was—as I think—the most movingly practical of any I have ever heard."[28] Simpson "told us that it was idle in an unconverted person to wait for feeling before he attempted to become better. He said you might as well tell a frozen person to feel warm as a frozen heart to melt. First the sinner must commence to do what his reason taught him was best, and in the act of striving for the right, feeling would come."[29] Rather than receiving faith, Willard seemed to decide to embark actively upon the life of faith.[30] She recorded Simpson's words in her journal: "My dear friends, you have thought it a little thing to sin publicly, and it is just and right that you *publicly* declare by your actions if not by your words that you intend to stop sinning;—that you intend with Christ's help to be reconciled to God."[31] Willard responded eagerly yet with hesitation to Simpson's invitation.

---

[26] Gifford, *Writing Out My Heart*, 48.

[27] Gifford, *Writing Out My Heart*, 53; journal entry, December 12, 1859.

[28] Gifford, *Writing Out My Heart*, 53. Bishop Matthew Simpson was elected to the episcopacy in 1852, after which he served as the acting president of Garrett Biblical Institute from 1859 to 1863. According to Gifford, "A powerful speaker and an opponent of slavery, he was active on behalf of the Union at the national level in the Civil War years. During Abraham Lincoln's presidency Simpson was able to persuade him to appoint several prominent Methodists to posts within the administration. Simpson preached Lincoln's funeral sermon in 1865" (36 n 24).

[29] Gifford, *Writing Out My Heart*, 53. Simpson's argument took after the example of John Wesley and his opposition to Quietism in the Fetter Lane Society. See Heitzenrater, Wesley and the People Called Methodists, 106.

[30] See A. F. Segal, *Paul the Convert: The Apostolate and Apostasy of Saul the Pharisee* (New Haven: Yale University Press, 1990), 295.

[31] Gifford, *Writing Out My Heart*, 53–54. Simpson outlined three tasks for the "seeker after Righteousness": (1) read the Bible, (2) pray to God for a true interpretation of the biblical texts, and (3) reflect upon life, death, and eternity and our relation to things past, present, and to come.

This seemed to me reasonable. I wished to go—I was very much agitated—I could see my heart beating—and yet I stood there apparently calm and careless & *resisted*. No, I did not go, I did not try for forgiveness as I have often thought I would. I stood in my place very quietly. Fool! Fool! I shall never again think it idle to openly declare oneself on the Lord's side. I think I will go tonight. And yet I may not. I cannot tell. Alas the day has come when I cannot rely on myself—cannot master myself![32]

Willard, frustrated with her inability to make a public declaration of faith, and still attempting to reconcile her intellectual process with her spiritual beliefs having not yet received assurance of her salvation, concluded this journal entry with the words, "Sighing, cursing this undying Human Pride."

The mood of the next journal entry shifted dramatically. "I have commenced! O Lord!" On December 16, 1859, Willard recorded, "I have publicly declared my determination to forsake my sins—to seek forgiveness for the past and help for the future; to endeavor with Christ's help,—always with Christ's help,—to live a good, true, valuable life—a life that shall glorify God and be a blessing to my fellow toilers and sufferers on the earth." But Willard quickly qualified her experience: "I have not yet the change of heart that Christ has promised to those who ask Him rightly, but I expect it."[33] She clarified further: "I feel inclined to do right more than I ever did before;—it is *easy* for me to be obliging and patient today, and it was never easy before. This is not of myself. I know that the *third person of the Trinity* is helping me, even as Christ has said."[34] Despite Willard's qualification taken together, the descriptions of her experience closely resemble what John

---

[32] Gifford, *Writing Out My Heart*, 54.

[33] Gifford, *Writing Out My Heart*, 54. This episode of Willard's conversion is recollected by Professor W. P. Jones and included in Willard's autobiography, *Glimpses of Fifty Years*, 123. Willard noted that Jones incorrectly dated the event a year prior to its occurrence. "It was Sunday evening. A large congregation in the Methodist church had listened to an ordinary sermon and seemed somewhat impatient for dismissal, when the pastor, to the surprise of every one, extended an invitation to those who wished to unite with the church on probation to meet him at the altar. The revival wave of the last winter had rolled by; there had been no special meetings; not a ripple of religious excitement was discoverable on the smooth current of the church. Under the circumstances, no one was expected to respond to the pastor's invitation. A moment's pause, and a single young woman moved out into the main aisle and with a firm step approached the altar. Instantly, all eyes converged on her. There was no mistaking that form and face; it was Miss Willard."

[34] Gifford, *Writing Out My Heart*, 54. Perhaps a reference to John 14:26.

Wesley called "justification": Willard offered a public confession of faith in Jesus Christ and repentance of her sins; and acknowledging God's forgiveness in Christ, she requested Christ's subsequent "help" through the Holy Spirit to live a holy and faithful life. She professed the major components of justification, including the commencement of "sanctification," or the work of the Holy Spirit within her.

However, one component of justification remained absent in Willard's testimony, an experience of "assurance": "Though I have yet no evidence of that change of purpose—that reconciliation to God— that active Peace—which I believe accompanies conversion, I am not discouraged. I see many reasons to hope that gradually I shall come to be 'in the light as He is in the light.' "[35] Willard expressed some confidence in the gradual nature of her continued process of faith, namely sanctification, later adding the following commentary to this series of events, "For fourteen nights in succession I thus knelt at the altar, expecting some utter transformation—some portion of heaven to be placed in my inmost heart, as I have seen the box of valuables placed in the corner-stone of a building firmly set, plastered over and fixed in its place for ever. This is what I had determined must be done, and was loath to give it up. I prayed and agonized, but what I sought did not occur."[36] In the midst of this frustration and disappointment, she withdrew to her room wearily after an evening's service and knelt beside her bed in prayer. "It came to me quietly that this was not the way; that my 'conversion,' my 'turning about,' my religious experience (*re-ligare*, to bind again), had reached its crisis on that summer night when I said 'yes,' to God. A quiet certitude of this pervaded my consciousness, and the next night I told the public congregation so, gave my name to the church as a probationer."[37]

[35] Gifford, *Writing Out My Heart*, 55.

[36] Willard, *Glimpses of Fifty Years*, 623. Incidentally, although John Wesley's teaching on justification included assurance along with the components mentioned in the chapter, Wesley struggled persistently throughout his spiritual journey with the dynamics of doubt and assurance, though he remained a confirmed member and ordained clergy in the Church of England for the entirety of his life. See R. P. Heitzenrater, *Wesley and the People Called Methodists* (Nashville: Abingdon, 1976), 77, 80–82, 85, 87, 89, 90, 103, 153, 201, 224, and a collection of essays on the topic edited by R. Maddox, *Aldersgate Reconsidered* (Nashville: Abingdon, 1990).

[37] Willard, *Glimpses of Fifty Years*, 623. R. S. Keller describes Willard's conversion as a "willful act," rather than a "warmed heart," a phrase used by John Wesley to describe his assurance of faith. See R. S. Keller, "Conversions and Their Consequences: Women's Ministry and Leadership in the United Methodist Tradition," in *Religious Institutions and Women's Leadership: New Roles Inside the*

She held this relationship for one year while waiting for her sister Mary, who later commenced the required six-month probation. "I was baptized and joined the church, May 5, 1861, 'in full connection.'" Through weekly class meetings Willard interacted with others seeking to deepen their faith and cultivate Christian character. "Prayer-meeting, class-meeting (in which Rev. Dr. Hemenway was my beloved leader), and church services were most pleasant to me, and I became an active worker, seeking to lead others to Christ."[38] Willard, despite substantial struggle, received assurance and began her faith journey in earnest. Having proclaimed faith in Jesus Christ, Willard recognized the evangelistic purpose of that Christian faith for others, integrating the intellectual and the useful in her emerging vocation of doing good.

Theological and Other Influences

Phoebe Palmer, during a visit to Evanston in 1866, facilitated Willard's receiving a "second blessing" of entire sanctification.[39] Willard later claimed to lose this because she did not testify to the experience as Palmer had admonished. Although Willard struggled with religious experience and its loss, her faith framed her later interests in and practices of reform that would create a space for a profound evangelistic ministry. Within this frame, Willard's European travels encouraged a growing gender ideology that alongside a frustrated vocation to ordained ministry informed the development of her multifaceted evangelistic ministry. Over the next almost ten years Willard filled a series of teaching positions in the Chicago area, Pittsburgh, and Lima, New York, among others.[40] Willard continued to nurture her Christian faith with more or less effectiveness depending upon the context and its resources.

By 1866 Willard was actively seeking information and guidance on the doctrine of holiness. She confessed, "I began to desire and pray for holiness of heart." She reported reading books often mentioned by

---

Mainstream, ed. C. Wessinger (Columbia: University of South Carolina Press, 1996), 113.

[38] Willard, *Glimpses of Fifty Years*, 624.

[39] Hardesty, *Women Called to Witness*, 4. See also Gifford, *Writing Out My Heart*, 200.

[40] From the 1830s and 1840s, teaching began to open alongside nursing as a possible vocation for educated women. H. Sigerman, "An Unfinished Battle: 1848–1865," in *No Small Courage: A History of Women in the United States*, ed. N. Cott (Oxford: Oxford University Press, 2000), 264–65.

women of the period as resources on the doctrine and experience of holiness and engaging in conversation and prayers with Melinda Hamline.[41] "My earnest prayer is that we may all be more & more like Christ—our Divine *Exemplar*—That is what life is for—To *be* & to *do* good. Whatever I forget, may I remember this."[42]

But Willard's quest for holiness was beset by questions: "I wish I understood not what anybody in particular thinks, but what is the truth about 'the full assurance of faith.' Is it instantaneous or progressive? Can one be free from inward temptation? This is 'a deep' to me. Surely if I pray & am teachable, & bring forth in my daily living 'fruits meet for repentance' I shall not be left unenlightened?"[43] Her prayers were seemingly answered early in the year, when Hamline assumed an influential role in organizing religious meetings in Evanston. According to her journal, Willard encountered Phoebe Palmer at a Ladies' Prayer Meeting conducted by Palmer and Hamline.

Although Willard's journal leaves the date and description of her receipt of entire sanctification unclear, her autobiography provides the following account recollected years later.

> Soon after [I began to desire and pray for holiness of heart], Dr. and Mrs. Phebe [*sic*] Palmer came to Evanston as guests of Mrs. Hamline, and for weeks they held meetings in our church. This was in the winter of 1866; the precise date I can not give. One evening, early in their meetings, when Mrs. Palmer had spoken with marvelous clearness and power, and at the close, those desirous of entering into the higher Christian life had been asked to kneel at the altar, another crisis came to me. It was not so tremendous as the first, but it was one that solemnly impressed my spirit. . . . At last I turned to my mother (who was converted and joined the church when she was only twelve years old) and whispered, "Will you go with me to the altar?" She did not hesitate a moment. . . . Kneeling in utter self-abandonment, I consecrated myself anew to God.[44]

Willard described a "deep welling up of joy that gradually possessed" her. She claimed to be "utterly free from care" and "blithe as a bird that is good for nothing except to sing." Willard explained that she no

---

[41] Willard, *Glimpses of Fifty Years*, 625. Melinda (Johnson) Hamline (1801–1881) was the recent widow of Methodist Episcopal bishop Leonidas L. Hamline (1797–1865). Mrs. Hamline moved to Evanston shortly after her husband's death and held holiness meetings in her home. See Gifford, *Writing Out My Heart*, 202 n 3.

[42] Willard, *Glimpses of Fifty Years*, 222; journal entry January 12, 1866.

[43] Willard, *Glimpses of Fifty Years*, 223; journal entry January 15, 1866.

[44] Willard, *Glimpses of Fifty Years*, 625.

longer asked herself, "Is this my duty?" since she "intuitively knew" what she was called upon to do. Willard's description echoed components of the holiness doctrine of entire sanctification, namely the presence and work of Christ in people through the Holy Spirit that destroys the root of sin so that love is one's defining attribute. "The conscious, emotional presence of Christ through the Holy Spirit held me. I ran about upon His errands 'just for love.' "[45]

Although Willard claimed in her autobiography written and published decades later that she experienced a second blessing of holiness or entire sanctification during the meeting conducted by Phoebe Palmer in the winter of 1866, her journals provide a slightly different chronology. On April 17, 1866, she wrote:

> I shall never, never forget how, yesterday, the clouds dispersed from my mind—the light that never was on sea or shore shown in to my dark heart, & Jesus, man's Saviour, was revealed to me as I had not before seen Him *for myself*. So now, to use dear Mother's favorite illustration, "I am like air to sunshine";—that is, I am continually helped to yield my being as the medium through which Christ's strength & righteousness may shine. This is all that I do, or can do, thanks be to God!—am *wished* to do. The hand of *faith* grasps the spotless robe of my Redeemer—the eye of faith rests on His matchless face—the heart of faith murmurs "Not as I will, but as *thou wilt* O, Saviour!"[46]

With her faith propelled by Christian holiness, Willard began to develop and reveal her complex evangelistic ministry. Whatever the actual date of her sanctification, in "this holy, happy state," Willard departed Evanston for Lima, New York, an area torn by deep theological divisions, serving as preceptress of Genesee Wesleyan Seminary.[47]

As a result of heated polemics largely over doctrinal issues, friends advised Willard to be discreet about her understanding and experience of holiness, since the Palmers' ministry and writings were a source of antagonism. In her autobiography, Willard described a

---

[45] Willard, *Glimpses of Fifty Years*, 626.

[46] Willard, *Glimpses of Fifty Years*, 227–28. ??Italics?? See also S. O. Garrison, ed., *Forty Witnesses* (New York: Hunt & Eaton, 1888), 69–77.

[47] Hardesty, *Women Called to Witness*, 4. The Genesee Conference of the Methodist Episcopal Church suffered from volatile polemics. According to Hardesty, there was "first the controversy over abolition in 1844 that resulted in Orange Scott's formation of the Free Methodist Church and then the holiness controversy of 1860 that spawned B. T. Roberts's and Luther Lee's Wesleyan Methodist Connection."

scene at Lima in which she witnessed a professor and good friend "whose subsequent experience has been such a blessed heritage to Christians, [reply] to a student who rose to inquire about holiness: 'It is a subject we do not mention here.'"[48] However, such discretion ran contrary to the Palmers' teachings that suggested testimony to one's experience was required for its retention.[49] "Young and docile-minded as I was . . . I 'kept still' until I soon found I had nothing in particular to keep still about. The experience left me." Willard quickly added that in spite of her "stillness," she thought her students would bear witness because "for their conversion and spiritual up building I was constantly at work."[50]

In her autobiography, Willard further qualified this "stillness": "Since then I have sat at the feet of every teacher of holiness whom I could reach; have read their books and compared their views. I love and reverence and am greatly drawn toward all, and never feel out of harmony with their spirit." Willard's Christian faith and practices remained consistent with her understanding and experience of holiness, despite the loss of feeling. "But that sweet pervasiveness, that heaven in the soul, of which I came to know in Mrs. Palmer's meeting, I do not feel." Despite her bereavement at the loss of a distinctive experience of holiness, Willard connected her Christian faith and study with her thoughts and practices related to doing good, particularly social reform, which would contribute substantially to her evangelistic ministry. "In the temperance, labor and woman questions I see the stirring of Christ's heart."[51]

By 1867 Willard began to focus on issues related to women's opportunities within the frame of her Christian faith and quietly

---

[48] Willard, *Glimpses of Fifty Years*, 626.

[49] Hardesty, *Women Called to Witness*, 4. Palmer's advice seems to resonate with Kallenberg's emphasis upon narrative and language: "divine revelation comes to us in the form of a story because God's dealings with us are narratively shaped rather than theoretically driven" (Kallenberg, *Live to Tell*, 37).

[50] Willard, *Glimpses of Fifty Years*, 626–27. In one sense, Willard had not acquired proficiency in the conceptual language of "holiness" as prescribed by Palmer. "If Lindbeck is correct about the significant role language plays in enabling religious experience, then it follows that religious conversion necessarily includes the acquisition of the appropriate conceptual language" (Kallenberg, *Live to Tell*, 41).

[51] Willard, *Glimpses of Fifty Years*, 626–27. Interestingly, later in life Willard became an "interested investigator" of Spiritualism, a movement that contributed, if as merely one small factor, to the suffrage movement. See A. Braude, *Radical Spirits: Spiritualism and Women's Rights in Nineteenth-Century America*, 2d ed. (Bloomington: Indiana University Press, 2001), 196.

emerging vocation. In preparation for a lengthy tour of Europe and the Middle East with friend and colleague Kate Jackson, Willard attended a speech advocating women's suffrage entitled, "The American Woman," by Theodore Tilton, a well-known women's rights speaker.[52] "I never heard anything better—or that so much inspired me." Willard included other suffrage-related conversations and vignettes in her journal entries: for example, a letter from Charles Fowler inquiring, "Have you not some brave possibility of work for women's suffrage, with your pen? It is to be *the question* of your prime & mine." Willard described her traveling companion's strong and at times even amusing favor for the woman question, as Kate "lies on the lounge now, reading John Stuart Mill's speech in Parliament on the subject & 'interlarding' with original observations." Willard included a statement of some levity from her brother Oliver: "I'm sure I've no objection to women's voting only so it don't interfere with the *insurance business!*"[53] Tilton's speech seemed to affirm Willard's emerging ideas and further focus the interests she pursued in her international travels, during which she carefully examined the status and roles of women.[54] "Some how since I heard Tilton lecture, my purpose is confirmed—my object in life clearer than ever before. What I can do in large & little ways, by influence, by pen, by observation, for *woman*, in all Christian ways, that I will do. And may God help me!"[55]

[52] Gifford, *Writing Out My Heart*, 202. Theodore Tilton (1835–1907), an abolitionist prior to the Civil War, later turned his attention to other issues including woman's suffrage, even joining the Equal Rights Association. The first Woman's Rights Convention was held in Seneca Falls, the Wesleyan Chapel, beginning July 19, 1848. For a comprehensive historical analysis of the dynamics leading to and including the convention, see J. Wellman, *The Road to Seneca Falls: Elizabeth Cady Stanton and the First Woman's Rights Convention* (Urbana: University of Illinois Press, 2004).

[53] Gifford, *Writing Out My Heart*, journal entry, March 9, 1868, pp. 265–66. Oliver Willard worked for a New York-based insurance company in Wisconsin during the late 1860s.

[54] Gifford, *Writing Out My Heart*, 202. Gifford notes that in a journal entry dated February 21, 1860, Willard, age twenty, mentioned "her agreement with the popular liberal minister Henry Ward Beecher that women should have the right to vote." "'The Woman's Cause Is Man's'?" 23.

[55] Gifford, *Writing Out My Heart*, journal entry March 20, 1868, p. 266. See Gifford, "'The Woman's Cause Is Man's'?" 23. Willard's commitment to women's issues resonates with the integration of evangelism and social service addressed in the scholarly conversation in the area of evangelism. See Abraham, *The Logic of Evangelism*, 45; Jones, *The Evangelistic Love*, 16, 45–64. According to Lesslie Newbigin, "There is no knowledge of God apart from the love of God, and there is no love of God apart from the love of the neighbor" (*The Open Secret: An Introduction to the Theology of Mission*, rev. ed. [Grand Rapids: Eerdmans, 1995], 97).

Willard's international travels informed her desire to do good. During her travels she learned to identify the connection of educational opportunities and economic resources (or the lack thereof) to women's opportunities (or oppression). After a year's delay, occasioned by the illness and death of Willard's father, Willard and Kate Jackson departed in May 1868 for nearly two and one-half years of travel abroad, staying for months at a time in Rome, Berlin, and Paris. In addition to extensive sightseeing, Willard enrolled in language and introduction classes in these locations, studying history and culture, most often focusing on women's issues.[56] Her journals record conversations about women's situations in France, England, and Italy, including meetings in Paris with women's rights advocates from France and the United States.[57] She described her purpose:

> To study as far as possible by reading, learning of languages and personal observation, the aspects of the "Woman Question" in France—Germany & England, & when I return to America after two or three years absence, studying the same subject carefully in relation to my own land, to *talk in public* of the matter, and cast myself with what weight or weakness I possess against the only foe of what I conceive to be the justice of the subject—unenlightened public opinion.[58]

Committed to this purpose during and after her travels, Willard recorded a vast number of observations, compiling substantial material for future reference as well as for articles she sent home for publication. Despite her relatively sheltered background as a middle-class American Protestant, Willard began to make astute connections. For example, she seemed to have first analyzed the situation of women from an economic perspective while in Paris.[59] "If all ladies would be as kind to one another as [Mlle. Daubie, author of "La Pauvre Femme de Dix-Neuviem Siecle"] to us what strength they would find in union! She said the greatest evil here was the seduction of young girls—who worked for their living—by rich men. Wages were so low that the poor things often sold their honor to eke out the pittance they could *honorably* earn. . . ."[60] Through her travels Willard honed

---

[56] Gifford, *Writing Out My Heart*, 272.
[57] Gifford, "'My Own Methodist Hive,'" 88.
[58] Gifford, *Writing Out My Heart*, journal entry February 6, 1869, Paris, p. 292.
[59] Gifford, *Writing Out My Heart*, 273–74.
[60] Gifford, *Writing Out My Heart*, 305.

her ideas and focused her direction, having discerned for herself the significance of women's issues.

Upon returning to the United States in 1870, Willard composed a speech on the plight of women, "The New Chivalry." Based on her journal notes, her observations, and reflections during her travels,[61] the speech opened with an endearing description of Willard's own work in the education of young women.[62] She then moved to vivid descriptions of women's oppression in the "old world," discussing the lack of economic, social, and educational opportunity for women in Egypt, Italy, France, Germany, and England. In this way Willard composed an argument advocating women's education in light of the better opportunities for women in the United States, but acknowledging the room for further work, and strategically encouraging men of the "new chivalry" to join her.[63]

In the following years, Willard explored various vocational opportunities within education, reform, and Christian ministry. Each experience subsequently contributed to her provocative vision for evangelistic ministry. The next year Willard accepted the presidency of the newly established Evanston College for Ladies.[64] Her role as college president devolved into the office of dean of the Women's College at Northwestern University where she also had teaching responsibilities. In light of such opposition to a future in academic

[61] Gifford, "'The Woman's Cause Is Man's'?" 24. Willard first delivered this speech in March 1871. The text is also reprinted in Willard's autobiography, *Glimpses of Fifty Years*, 576–89; see also Hardesty, *Women Called to Witness*, 6–7.

[62] Willard, "The New Chivalry," in *Glimpses of Fifty Years*, 576–77.

[63] Gifford, "'The Woman's Cause Is Man's'?" 24–25.

[64] The Evanston College for Ladies was founded with the initial meeting of its board late in 1868, followed by the acquisition of a state charter in March 1869. Interestingly, the trustees of Northwestern University voted in June 1869 (1) to elect to the presidency Erastus O. Haven, known for his progressive advocacy of coeducation, and (2) to admit women as students. In June 1870, the board of Evanston College for Ladies proposed a merger with Northwestern. This was agreed upon the condition that the Ladies' College provide a dormitory for its students; the trustees of Northwestern responded with a promise to raise fifty thousand dollars toward the cause. Willard excelled in her leadership role and worked well with Haven. The Ladies' College faced severe difficulties as a result of the Chicago Fire of 1871 that consumed the once-generous pledges. Northwestern's subsequent president (and Willard's former fiancé) Charles Fowler facilitated a merger with the Ladies' College, the university assuming financial responsibilities and shifting Willard's role to dean of the Women's College with a professorship in the university. See H. Williamson and P. Wild, *Northwestern University: A History 1850–1975* (Evanston, Ill.: Northwestern University Press, 1976), 24–25, 28–29.

leadership[65] or ordained ministry, Willard turned her attention to doing good through the NWCTU.[66]

Elected president of the Chicago chapter of the Woman's Christian Temperance Union (WCTU), Willard also served as a delegate to the first national convention in 1874, where she was elected corresponding secretary for the NWCTU.[67] Willard recollected the first national gathering in her autobiography.

> Very few could make a speech at that early period—we gave speechlets instead, off-hand talks of from five to fifteen minutes. The daily prayer-meetings were times of refreshing from the presence of the Lord. There was no waiting, everything was fresh, tender and spontaneous. Such singing I never heard; the Bible exposition was bread to the soul. Everybody said it "wasn't a bit like men's conventions." "And it's all the better for that," was the universal verdict.[68]

The Christian ethos of the organization is apparent from Willard's remarks, and the only resolution Willard recalled writing illustrates the Christian foundation of the organization's agenda: "*Resolved*, That, recognizing that our cause is, and will be, combated by mighty, determined and relentless forces, we will, trusting in Him who is the Prince of Peace, meet argument with argument, misjudgment with patience, denunciation with kindness, and all our difficulties and dangers with prayer." Willard added in her autobiographical account, "There was some debate about inserting the word 'Christian' in the name of our society." She explained that to leave out "Christian" would "broaden and thus benefit the platform," yet, then "as always since, the Convention said by its deeds, 'We are not here to seek a large following, but to do what we think is right.'"[69]

As Willard's leadership began to expand within the local, but more importantly the national, WCTU, the issue of women's suffrage would become paramount to her platform and agenda.[70] The follow-

[65] Most likely as a result of conflicting personalities between Fowler and Willard, several disagreements over issues of administration emerged, eventually resulting in Willard's resignation in June 1874 (Williamson and Wild, *Northwestern University*, 29).

[66] Willard's mother participated in the founding of the Evanston Temperance Society. Hardesty, *Women Called to Witness*, 5.

[67] Willard, *Glimpses of Fifty Years*, 348–50.

[68] Willard, *Glimpses of Fifty Years*, 349.

[69] Willard, *Glimpses of Fifty Years*, 350.

[70] Although several scholars such as Epstein, *The Politics of Domesticity*, and R. Bordin, *Frances Willard: A Biography* (Chapel Hill: University of North Carolina Press, 1986) describe the early Woman's Crusade of 1873–1874 and the subsequent

ing autobiographical account explicitly used the language of faith, again linking her personal vocation with the developing temperance movement manifest in the NWCTU.

> Upon my knees alone, in the room of my hostess, who was a veteran Crusader, there was borne in upon my mind, as I believe, from loftier regions, the declaration, "You are to speak for woman's ballot as a weapon of protection to her home and tempted loved ones from the tyranny of drink," and then for the first and only time in my life, there flashed through my brain a complete line of argument and illustration—the same that I used a few months later before the Woman's Congress, in St. George's Hall, Philadelphia, when I first publicly avowed my faith in the enfranchisement of women.[71]

Willard promptly sent correspondence to Annie Wittenmeyer, president of the NWCTU, outlining her desire to speak on "The Home Protection Ballot" at the upcoming International Temperance Convention. Wittenmeyer "mildly, but firmly" declined. But later that year, at the third national convention in Newark, October 1876, Willard "disregard[ed] the earnest, almost tearful pleading" of her friends and delivered her "suffrage speech."[72] Willard claimed that upon arrival she deeply felt, "Woe is me if I declare not this gospel."[73] Though she could feel the "strong conservatism of an audience of Christian women," she felt "more strongly the undergirdings of the Spirit."[74] Willard recalled, "At the close I was applauded beyond my

---

WCTU as protofeminist in ideology, Blocker argues for a further facet in light of the relations between women participating in late-nineteenth-century temperance and suffrage movements. At this time the majority of "Crusaders" avoided the topic of women's suffrage, though the crusade was largely considered a women's rights movement. For further discussion, see J. Blocker Jr., *"Give to the Winds Thy Fears": The Women's Temperance Crusade, 1873–1874* (Westport, Conn.: Greenwood Press, 1985).

[71] Willard, *Glimpses of Fifty Years*, 351.

[72] Willard, *Glimpses of Fifty Years*, 351. Interestingly, in 1882 Willard proposed a partial suffrage for women that would exclude "illiterate women, women who drank, and prostitutes" (Ginzberg, *Women and the Work of Benevolence*, 187).

[73] Frances Willard, quoted in Hardesty, *Women Called to Witness*, 7.

[74] Willard, *Glimpses of Fifty Years*, 352. See also Hardesty, *Women Called to Witness*, 7. Willard's platform for women's suffrage, though political in focus, was theological in purpose, and guided by the Spirit. The women in this study demonstrate robust pneumatologies. The role of the Spirit and its implications bring complexity to understandings and practices of evangelism. For example, according to Newbigin, "Mission is not just church extension. It is something more costly and more revolutionary. It is the action of the Holy Spirit, who in his sovereign freedom both convicts the world (John 16.18-11) and leads the church toward the fullness of

hopes." In the midst of this affirmation, the chairwoman, Mrs. Allen Butler, swiftly offered the qualification, "I wish it clearly understood that the speaker represents herself and not the Woman's Christian Temperance Union, for we do not propose to trail our skirts through the mire of politics." Willard claimed that these words were received in silence by those gathered, and she "knew then that the hearts of the women were with the forward movement,"[75] even if the leadership was not.

Willard's growing commitment to women's rights, particularly suffrage, was grounded in her Christian faith and informed by her international travels. Both in Willard's ministry practices and in the NWCTU's agenda and work, an evangelistic program, initially centered on the declaration of the gospel message, reached far beyond verbal proclamation.

Evangelistic Practices

Willard has been described as an "evangelist"[76] in a traditional sense, meaning that she regularly spoke in public, and at times preached, even itinerantly. Although she and other women "evangelists" in the NWCTU spoke publicly in favor of temperance and other social issues, preaching the Christian gospel as a component of their task, Willard's work and the developing agenda of the NWCTU were not limited to verbal proclamation. This section, first, describes Willard's training in ministry practices, including evangelistic public speaking and preaching encouraged by famed evangelist Dwight L. Moody (1837–1899).[77] While Willard's advocacy for women focused initially

---

the truth that it has not yet grasped (John 16.12-15)" (*The Open Secret*, 59). See also I. Dietterich, "Missional Community: Cultivating Communities of the Holy Spirit," in Guder and Barret, *Missional Church*, 142–82.

[75] Willard, *Glimpses of Fifty Years*, 352. See also Hardesty, *Women Called to Witness*, 7. Butler, a Presbyterian from Syracuse, was at that time president of the New York WCTU.

[76] Hardesty, *Women Called to Witness*, 7–9.

[77] Dwight Lyman Moody was one of the most influential evangelicals of his generation, though with no formal theological training. Initially a shoe clerk and salesman, Moody became an incredibly well-known itinerant preacher. Recognized early in his career, initially in Great Britain, for his simple message without denominational affiliation that stressed Christian virtues and personal salvation, his influence spread throughout the United States. See M. E. Lender, *Dictionary of American Temperance Biography: From Temperance Reform to Alcohol Research, the 1600s to the 1980s* (Westport, Conn.: Greenwood Press, 1984), 343–45.

on accessibility to education and suffrage, she later admitted in
Woman in the Pulpit (1889) a frustrated call to the ordained ministry
and proposed a case for women's ecclesiastic rights. Second, this section describes the evangelistic purpose for Willard's advocacy of
ecclesiastic rights for women. For church structures to constrain
women from assuming leadership roles was, for Willard, to constrain
the church from fulfilling its evangelistic purpose to share the gospel
of Jesus Christ and participate in realizing the reign of God on earth.
Third, this section briefly explores the evangelistic themes behind the
NWCTU's ethos and agenda and the influence of Willard's leadership. The NWCTU initially advocated methods of verbal proclamation that had revivalist echoes. As the Christian identity and witness
of the organization strengthened, its evangelistic purpose became
more pronounced, allowing for the cultivation of a wide range of
evangelistic ministry opportunities. With the help of a comprehensive
training program, NWCTU speakers pursued deep theological
reflection alongside pragmatic ministry practices to support the
marginalized, practices that addressed the sinful systems of poverty.
As a result of these emphases, solidified and expanded during
Willard's presidency, the NWCTU instituted ecclesiological elements (aspects of a woman's church) to reclaim the church's mission
for the world following the example of Jesus Christ.[78] In this way,
Willard facilitated not only the evangelistic ministry of individuals,
but also the evangelistic witness of communities of faith.

Moody's Meetings

In January 1877, after returning from his preaching tour in Great
Britain (1873–1875), the internationally renowned revivalist Dwight
L. Moody invited Willard to join his work. Willard resigned as president of the Chicago WCTU and departed for Boston, commencing
her work with Moody in February. In her autobiography, Willard
wrote, "I find this entry, my only record of that fruitful three months
of work and study."

> My first *whole day* of real, spiritual, joyful, loving study of the ker-
> nel of God's word, simply desirous to learn my Father's will, is this
> 17th of February, 1877, with the Boston work just begun. And on

[78] Willard, one of the most radical leaders of the WCTU, also supported an
institutionalization of religious belief. See Ginzberg, *Women and the Work of
Benevolence*, 206.

this sweet, eventful day, in which, with every hour of study, the
Bible has grown dearer, I take as my life-motto henceforth, humbly
asking God's grace that I may measure up to it, this wonderful passage from Paul: *"And whatsoever ye do, in word or deed, do all in the
name of the Lord Jesus, giving thanks to God and the Father by him."*—
Col. 3:17.[79]

Every day Willard studied the Scriptures from eight until noon,
then spoke without manuscript to an audience, and conducted an
inquiry meeting afterward. It is likely that Willard's role in these
meetings was parallel to that of Moody and other male revivalists:
preaching or exhorting biblical texts, leading to an invitation to personally declare faith in Jesus Christ, followed by further conversation
with inquirers. In the afternoons Willard attended to correspondence
for the NWCTU, "save when I had an extra meeting, which was not
infrequently, and made a temperance address, usually in the suburbs,
at night." According to Willard, there were "four or six hundred,
often a thousand, and occasionally twelve or fourteen hundred women
in my meetings at Berkeley Street and Park Street Congregational
Churches." Willard usually spoke on Sunday evenings at Clarendon
Street Baptist Church, and occasionally participated in "Temperance
Conferences" planned by Moody, in which her name was placed on
the program. During one of these meetings Moody, "had me literally
preach—though I did not call it that."[80]

Despite Willard's apparent delight in both the study and practice
of evangelism, she left Moody's team later that summer, returning to
Evanston. Moody had disapproved Willard's sharing the platform
with Mary Livermore (1820–1905), a Universalist minister, committed suffragist, and temperance leader.[81] "He held with earnestness that
I ought not to appear on the same platform with one who denied the
divinity of Christ." Initially, Willard "deferred to [Moody's] judgment, partly from conviction and partly from a desire to keep the
peace." But the deference didn't last. After her departure, Willard
expressed gratitude for her short time in ministry with Moody: "I
deem[ed] it one of the choicest seals of my calling that Dwight L.

---

[79] Willard, *Glimpses of Fifty Years*, 356. Willard confessed, "I had lacked specific
Bible teaching, having almost never attended Sunday-school, because of being
brought up in the country." See also Hardesty, *Women Called to Witness*, 7–8, and D.
Martin, *Moody Bible Institute: God's Power in Action* (Chicago: Moody Press, 1977), 18.

[80] Willard, *Glimpses of Fifty Years*, 357.

[81] Willard, *Glimpses of Fifty Years*, 359. Livermore was then president of the
Massachusetts WCTU.

Moody should have invited me to cast in my little lot with his great one as an evangelist."[82]

After reflecting on the issue of her departure for some time, Willard wrote a letter of explanation to Moody's wife, Emma. In this letter dated September 5, 1877, Willard outlined her thinking regarding opportunities for women, particularly opportunities for ministry in the church, introducing the evangelistic impetus of the argument that she later elaborated in *Woman in the Pulpit*.

> All my life I have been devoted to the advancement of women in education and opportunity. I firmly believe God has a work for them to do as evangelists, as bearers of Christ's message to the ungospeled, to the prayer meeting, to the church generally and the world at large, such as most people have not dreamed. It is therefore my dearest wish to help break down the barriers of prejudice that keep them silent.[83]

Willard explained that Moody approached the temperance movement as a revivalist, focusing upon the regeneration of souls. Willard argued that although this was the most important component of the work, other ministry practices also contributed significantly.

> Mr. Moody views the temperance work from the standpoint of a revivalist, and so emphasizes the regeneration of men. But to me as a woman, there are other phases of it almost equally important to its success, viz., saving the *children*, teaching them never to drink; showing to their mothers the duty of total abstinence; rousing a dead church and a torpid Sunday-school to its duty; spreading the facts concerning the iniquitous traffic far and wide; influencing legislation so that what is physically wrong and morally wrong shall not, on the statute books of a Christian land, be set down as legally right;—and to this end putting the ballot in woman's hand for the protection of her little ones and of her home.[84]

---

[82] Willard, *Glimpses of Fifty Years*, 359. Willard concluded that had she stayed with Moody, her work for the NWCTU and the world's WCTU "would have been immeasurably greater than it is now," since (1) he did not seem to object to her work there, and (2) it would therefore have allowed for international exposure. Friends claimed her decision was a mistake, but "[f]or myself I only knew that, liberal as he was toward me in all other things, tolerant of my ways and manners, generous in his views upon the woman question, devotedly conscientious and true, Brother Moody's Scripture interpretations concerning religious toleration were too literal for me; the jacket was too straight—I could not wear it" (361).

[83] Willard, *Glimpses of Fifty Years*, 360.

[84] Willard, *Glimpses of Fifty Years*, 360. Abraham argues for a shift in emphasis

Implying a feminist critique of Moody's approach, Willard sought to form practices of Christian temperance among individuals and the nation alongside the vital task of "regeneration" of souls. In expressing her loss at leaving this ministry work, Willard explicitly named the evangelistic purpose of her own ministry: "[B]est of all I love to declare the blessed tidings of salvation, and would gladly do so still, if I might act in my own character."[85] Thus, perhaps influenced by biblical study, but certainly by the experience of sharing in Moody's evangelistic ministry, Willard began to construct her own evangelistic theology and practice that appreciated and included, but differentiated from, Moody's revivalist themes. For that purpose she returned to Evanston to lay the foundation of the work that would occupy her until her death.

In her autobiography, Willard noted that she resigned her position as corresponding secretary of the NWCTU at the convention in 1877 and declined to have her name submitted as a candidate for president.[86] In 1878 she accepted the presidency of the Illinois WCTU, from which she campaigned for "home protection" and for women's right to vote on temperance issues in local elections.[87] Under Willard's rallying cry, "For God and Home and Native Land" (composed for the Chicago chapter of the WCTU), the women of Illinois collected 180,000 signatures in three months to support state legislation on these issues. Though their efforts failed, since that session denied the bill, the message was delivered and legislation eventually passed.[88]

---

from theology to practice among nineteenth-century evangelists. "The most striking feature of the landscape is the steady decline in the theological abilities of the better-known evangelists over the generations" (*The Logic of Evangelism*, 8–9). Abraham identifies the beginnings of this shift with Charles Finney. "By the time we come to his successors, D. L. Moody and Billy Sunday, there is no serious theological substance at all. Moody is a fascinating figure who did gather around him at times scholars of considerable distinction, but his theological interests were limited in the extreme" (9). While Willard's reasons did not explicitly identify theological differences, or the lack of theological reflection on Moody's part, Abraham's observation clarifies the possibility of additional facets to Willard's decision.

[85] Willard, *Glimpses of Fifty Years*, 360.

[86] Willard, *Glimpses of Fifty Years*, 361. During 1878 Willard enlisted with the Lyceum Lecture Bureau, speaking prolifically nationwide.

[87] Hardesty, *Women Called to Witness*, 9.

[88] It was endorsed by the national convention in 1876; Hardesty, *Women Called to Witness*, 9.

Willard's evangelistic understanding and practice, moving beyond Moody's, consisted of an embodiment of the Christian faith in individual as well as corporate practices.

Woman in the Pulpit

In her text *Woman in the Pulpit*, Willard presented a comprehensive argument for women's ecclesiastic rights, particularly the right to preach and receive ordination. Willard published the text for at least two reasons: the MEC's refusal to recognize her as an elected lay delegate to the 1888 General Conference,[89] and her unanswerable call to ordained ministry.

> But even my dear old mother-church (the Methodist) did not call women to her altars. I was too timid to go without a call; and so it came about that while my unconstrained preference would long ago have led me to the pastorate, I have failed of it, and am perhaps writing out all the more earnestly for this reason thoughts long familiar to my mind. Let me, as a loyal daughter of the church, urge upon younger women who feel a call, as I once did, to preach the unsearchable riches of Christ.[90]

The book outlines the contemporary arguments for and against women's ordination, supported by testimony from male and female voices of expertise and authority. In the midst of this structure, Willard built her argument upon biblical foundations, exegetically and hermeneutically, demonstrating the necessity of women's participation in both ministry practices as well as biblical interpretation. For Willard, the underlying impetus for women's contributions in all areas of church life was evangelistic—not merely the verbal proclamation of

---

[89] In 1888 the ME General Conference ruled that women holding local church offices could be members of quarterly conferences and therefore would eventually allow for women to be elected as lay delegates to General Conference, which occurred in 1888—Frances Willard was one of five women elected as lay delegates from annual conferences. Though Willard could not be present for the tumultuous proceedings due to her mother's illness, the female delegates were not permitted to take their seats. James Buckley, a leading opponent on the question of women's ecclesiastic rights published numerous editorials in part responding to Willard's published advocacy of women's ecclesiastic rights, in *Woman in the Pulpit*. In 1900 the General Conference voted to allow women lay delegates, and in 1904 twenty-four women were elected. See J. M. Schmidt, *Grace Sufficient: A History of Women in American Methodism 1760–1939* (Nashville: Abingdon, 1999), 217–24.

[90] Willard, *Woman in the Pulpit*, 62.

the gospel, but its embodiment in individual and communal practices.[91] By excluding women from ministry roles, the church limited its ability to evangelize.

In the initial chapter, Willard critiqued the "two conflicting methods of exegesis, one of which strenuously insisted on a literal view, while the other played fast and loose with God's word according to personal predilection." Using numerous Scripture examples interpreted with one or the other of these methods, Willard demonstrated that a more nuanced and sensible method was needed. "We need women commentators to bring out the women's side of the book; we need the stereoscopic view of truth in general, which can only be had when woman's eye and man's together shall discern the perspective of the Bible's full-orbed revelation."[92] Though Willard acknowledged that women are not innately better than men in faithfulness or biblical exegesis, she highlighted the limitations of exegetical practice by men alone. "It [exegesis by men] has broken Christendom into sects that confuse and astound the heathen world, and to-day imposes the heaviest yoke now worn by woman upon that most faithful follower of Him who is her emancipator no less than humanity's Saviour." Willard continued, "But as the world becomes more deeply permeated by the principles of Christ's Gospel, methods of exegesis are

[91] Many writing in the area of evangelism acknowledge the essential role of the congregation in faithful and effective evangelistic practices. For Abraham, there are four agents involved in the process of evangelism: the triune God, the church, the evangelist, and the person or persons evangelized (see Abraham, *The Logic of Evangelism*, 103–4). Generally, the evangelistic ministry of the women in this study includes at least three of the four agents, since many find themselves marginalized from Christian congregations. However, Willard demonstrates the strongest ecclesiastical commitments.

[92] Willard, *Woman in the Pulpit*, 21. Elizabeth Cady Stanton built her "sustained ideological assault on religious orthodoxy" in part on the publication of *The Woman's Bible* (1895–1898). E. C. Stanton, *The Woman's Bible*, foreword by M. Fitzgerald (Boston: Northeastern University Press, 1993), viii. While providing a comprehensive commentary on the entire canon, Old and New Testaments, Stanton reminded her readers of women's presence and participation in Jesus' life and ministry; see B. B. Zikmund, "Biblical Arguments and Women's Place in the Church," in *The Bible and Social Reform*, ed. E. Sandeen (Philadelphia: Fortress, 1982), 94–95. Zikmund identifies at least five typologies of biblical arguments for change, referring to Willard's argument in *Woman and the Pulpit* as an example of the first: an appeal to and experience of the Holy Spirit. However, Willard seems to touch upon additional typologies identified by Zikmund, including a pragmatic argument claiming that women were already participating in such ministries, and another that reinterpreted biblical texts (88–93).

revised. The old texts stand there, just as before, but we interpret them less narrowly. Universal liberty of person and of opinion is now conceded to be Bible-precept principles."[93]

From this critical position of contemporary exegesis, specifically one that subordinated or excluded women from ministry practices, Willard reminded her readers:

> Now, let any reasonable human being read this exegesis, and remember that two-thirds of the graduates from our great system of public education are women; that two-thirds of the teachers in these schools are women; that nearly three-fourths of our church members are women; that through the modern Sunday-school women have already become the theological teachers of the future church.[94]

Willard responded to the constraining interpretation that limited women's roles by noting examples of women's contributions in the biblical texts. Willard argued, "The whole subjection theory grows out of the one-sided interpretation of the Bible by men." Willard conceded that in humanity's lapsed state man "will rule over woman." However, "God does not speak with approbation of this act, and the whole tenor of the Scriptures is to show that in Christ the world is to be restored to the original intent of its creation."[95]

From the biblical texts she also drew her own exegetical conclusions to support women's ministries. "There are thirty or forty passages in favor of woman's public work for Christ, and only two against it, and these not really so when rightly understood." Willard boldly asserted, "Christ, not Paul, is the source of all churchly authority and power." Referring to Christ's multiple interactions and commissions to women, Willard responded to the opposition: "It is objected that he called no woman to be an apostle. Granted, but he himself said that he chose one man who had a devil; is this a precedent?" Willard reminded her reader of Martha, the woman at the well in Samaria,

---

[93] Willard, *Woman in the Pulpit*, 23.

[94] Willard, *Woman in the Pulpit*, 25. Willard continues with a somewhat presumptuous argument: "[A]nd that, *per contra*, out of about sixty thousand persons in our penitentiaries fifty-five thousand are men; that whisky, beer, and tobacco to the value of fifteen hundred million dollars per year are consumed almost wholly by men; and then see if the said reasonable human being will find much mental or spiritual pabulum in the said learned exegesis" (25–26). Perhaps more significantly, Willard's argument and the WCTU benefited from the remarkable ability of women to organize, creating an accessibility to influence church and society not otherwise afforded to women individually; see Scott, *Natural Allies*, 2–3.

[95] Willard, *Woman in the Pulpit*, 37.

and Mary, among others, to whom Jesus Christ gave "the first commission to declare his resurrection." Willard pointed out that Jesus
Christ "did not designate women as his followers; they came without
a call."[96]

Willard then shifted from biblical interpretation to reflections
upon the social constructions of gender, both critiquing and embracing the expectations of femininity of her period. "The position, in fact
(never formulated, of course, by any ministerial association, and probably not realized by our honored brethren), is just this: Christian
women are at liberty to work in any way that does not interfere with
ecclesiastical prerogative, and does help to build up the interests of
the church, financially or spiritually."[97] Willard incisively critiqued
the less-ideal tendencies of human nature:

> It is a whimsical fact that men seem comparatively willing that
> women should enter any profession except their own. The lawyer is
> willing that they should be doctors, and the doctor thinks they may
> plead at the bar if they desire to do so, but each prefers to keep them
> out of his own professional garden-plot. This is true of ministers
> with added emphasis, for here we have the pride of sex plus the
> pride of sacerdotalism. "Does a woman think to rank with *me*?"
> That is the first question, and the second is like unto it as to its ani-
> mus: "Does a woman think she has a right to stand with *me* in the
> most sacred of all callings?"[98]

In a characteristically skillful turn, she embraced what might
appear to be confining gender expectations, turning them into
enabling possibilities: "But if the purest should be called to purest
ministries, then women, by men's own showing, outrank them in
actual fitness for the pulpit, and the fact is that woman's holiness and
wholesomeness of life, her clean hands and pure heart, specially
authorize her to be a minister of God." In a sweeping generalization,
Willard proposed that men "have taken the simple, loving, tender
Gospel of the New Testament . . . and given us the dead letter rather
than the living Gospel." Alternatively for Willard, "The mother-heart
of God will never be known to the world until translated into terms
of speech by mother-hearted women." Willard further argued that
religion is an affair of the heart. "Men have always tithed mint and rue
and cumin in their exegesis and their ecclesiasticism, while the world's

[96] Willard, *Woman in the Pulpit*, 34, 40–41.
[97] Willard, *Woman in the Pulpit*, 38–39.
[98] Willard, *Woman in the Pulpit*, 39.

heart has cried out for compassion, forgiveness, and sympathy." In a skillful feint, Willard seemed to capitulate to the reigning gender expectations for women of the time, but she used this rationale instead to support the inclusion of women in ministry. "The world is hungry for the comfort of Christ's Gospel, and thirsty for its every-day beatitudes of that holiness which alone constitutes happiness."[99]

Focusing her argument upon the needs of the world and the ills of society, Willard expounded upon greed, impurity, and intemperance. She wrote, "The masses of the people have forsaken God's house, and solace themselves in the saloons or with the Sunday newspaper." In light of this unfaithfulness, her argument, woven throughout with feminine and maternal threads, introduced the pervasive evangelistic purpose of her proposal for women's ministry roles. "But the masses will go to hear women when they speak, and every woman who leads a life of weekday holiness, and has the Gospel in her looks, however plain her face and dress may be, has round her head the sweet Madonna's halo, in the eyes of every man who sees her, and she speaks to him with the sacred cadence of his own mother's voice." Willard observed, "Men have been preaching well-nigh two thousand years, and the large majority of the converts have been women. Suppose now that women should share the preaching power, might it not be reasonably expected that a majority of the converts under their administration would be men?" Unlike many other proponents of woman's rights, even ecclesiastic rights, Willard embraced a biblical and evangelistic argument for women's ministry that did not ignore the natural philosophy of individual rights, without allowing this latter ideology to take precedence. "Indeed, how else are the latter [men] to have a fair chance at the Gospel? The question is asked in all seriousness, and if its practical answer shall be the equipping of women for the pulpit, it may be reasonably claimed that men's hopes of heaven will be immeasurably increased."[100]

Willard argued for the inclusion of women in ministry roles, highlighting verbal proclamation but joining it with compassionate practices. Willard argued that the church sustains "immeasurable

[99] Willard, *Woman in the Pulpit*, 46–47. In her presidential address to the 1891 NWCTU gathering Willard stated, "How home-like the good news becomes when brought by the motherly voices of women! From our own ranks we now send out bearers of the grand evangel to soldiers and sailors, miners and lumbermen, cow-boys and paupers and prisoners. The question of Christian unity would be settled in a single year if white-ribboners had the handling of it" (*NWCTU Minutes*, 1890, 121).

[100] Willard, *Woman in the Pulpit*, 48–49.

losses . . . by not claiming for her altars these loyal, earnest-hearted daughters, who, rather than stand in an equivocal relation to her polity, are going into other lines of work." And a series of rhetorical questions crystallized the underlying dynamics of women's ministry: "Are they willing that woman should go to the lowly and forgotten, but not to the affluent and powerful? Are they willing that women should baptize and administer the sacrament in the zenanas of India, but not at the elegant altars of Christendom?" The implicit answer is, yes—the church of Willard's time was willing for women to minister, but only along the margins. Despite the church's disenfranchisement of women, Willard revealed that numerous women had already answered their vocational call to pastoral ministry. "Are they aware that thousands of services are held each Sabbath by white-ribbon women, to whom reformed men and their wives have said: 'We will come if you will speak. We don't go to church, because they have rented pews, and because we cannot dress well enough; but we'll come to hear you'?"[101]

Quick to mention that these women often took "their commission from the evangelistic department of the Woman's Christian Temperance Union," Willard began to lay the groundwork not merely for women's inclusion in the ministry of established churches, but for the possibility of a woman's church. "Have they observed that W.C.T.U. halls, reading-rooms, and tabernacles for the people are being daily multiplied, in which the poor have the Gospel preached to them?"[102] She argued that women were already practicing fruitful ministry in the WCTU among other contexts.

> The National Woman's Christian Temperance Union has a depart-
> ment of evangelistic work, of Bible Readings, of Gospel Work for
> railroad employees, for soldiers, sailors, and lumbermen; of prison,
> jail, and police-station work; each of these departments being in
> charge of a woman called a national Superintendent, who has an

[101] Willard, *Woman in the Pulpit*, 55.

[102] Willard, *Woman in the Pulpit*, 55–56. Willard's question proceeds from her at times implicit critique of the church's ineffectiveness at fulfilling its purpose. This resonates with a similar argument proposed by Abraham regarding the failure of the church. "The solution is to recognize that the problem is ecclesiological: failure to focus on the kingdom is precisely a failure in ecclesiology. It is to ignore the fact that the church exists in and for service to the kingdom out of which it originated" (W. Abraham, "On Making Disciples of the Lord Jesus Christ," in *Marks of the Body of Christ*, ed. C. Braaten and R. Jenson [Grand Rapids: Eerdmans, 1999], 160–61, quoted in Jones, *The Evangelistic Love*, 71).

assistant in nearly every State and Territory, and she, in turn, in every local union. These make an aggregate of several thousands of women who are regularly studying and expounding God's word to the multitude, to say nothing of the army in home and foreign missionary work, and who are engaged in church evangelism.[103]

Willard also astutely noted that John Wesley, the founder of Methodism, defied the ecclesiastic hierarchy, though reluctantly as a last resort, for an evangelistic purpose. According to Willard, Wesley's decision to ordain and consecrate leadership for the United States "cost the Episcopal Church its future in the New World, as time has proved." Willard boldly compared Wesley's dilemma with that of her contemporary church on the issue of woman's ordination and took the argument one provocative step further: "To ministerial leaders who have been profoundly impressed by the difficulties of the question, 'Shall women be ordained to preach?' another question is hereby propounded: 'Shall women ordain themselves?'"[104]

Willard's advocacy for women's ecclesiastic rights was not without its edge. She suggested the possibility that these several thousand women, two-thirds of the church's membership, "who 'now publish the glad tidings' are quite beyond the watch-care of the church, not because they wish to be so."[105] And she seemed to hold out the possibility that these women, so vital to the effectiveness of the church, could leave the church to fulfill their vocations to Christian ministry.

A Woman's Church

Willard's administration of the NWCTU demonstrated both in the United States and internationally a clear evangelistic purpose based on a concept of evangelism that reached beyond verbal proclamation.[106] Under her leadership as corresponding secretary (1874–1877), and later as president (1879–1898), Willard strongly supported the evangelistic work of the movement through the Committee on Gospel Temperance, which later expanded into the Evangelistic Department. Willard claimed and would often repeat, "The Evangelistic

[103] Willard, *Woman in the Pulpit*, 57.
[104] Willard, *Woman in the Pulpit*, 57.
[105] Willard, *Woman in the Pulpit*, 57.
[106] See Garner, "The Woman's Christian Temperance Union," 278. According to Garner, "The women did not confine their 'evangelistic work' to the walls of the church. WCTU members expanded this category of work to include prison reform,

Department is the basis of all our varied lines of work."[107] The 1879 *NWCTU Minutes* track the work of the Evangelistic Department. Although there was some initial concern over this department's scope,[108] the appended reports feature consistent references to the salvation of souls,[109] which was echoed in subsequent reports.[110] Through the Christian ethos and evangelistic purpose of the NWCTU, Willard and others created a space within which women could respond to their vocations to pastoral and evangelistic ministry, contributing to the possibility of a woman's church.[111] Despite Willard's provocative proposal in *Woman in the Pulpit*, the participants in the NWCTU's work were careful not to compete with established denominations. Their aim instead was to complement the established church's ministry, particularly of evangelism, while critiquing its shortcomings from within.[112]

The first national convention of the WCTU (Cleveland, 1874) proposed methods similar to those of Charles Finney's revivals from earlier in the century. These methods located the ministry of the NWCTU within local churches with some success: "Endeavoring to secure from pastors everywhere frequent temperance sermons, and special services in connection with the weekly church prayer-meeting and the Sabbath-school."[113] However, the scope of the work would soon reach beyond the church walls. In addition to "Home Missionary Work" (consisting of "private visitation of those who drink and those who sell, we contemplate still further, our aim being to go in spirit of prayerful and helpful kindness"), the NWCTU's plan of work included "Gospel Temperance Meetings." Also reminiscent of Finney's revivals,

---

ensuring the observance of the sabbath, lobbying to include Bible study in public schools, and cooperation with women's missionary societies, among other concerns. This is specifically where they translated their religious ideas into a political agenda that amounted to their uniquely feminine version of the Social Gospel."

[107] F. Willard, "Do Everything: A Handbook for the World's White Ribboners," in *Women in American Protestant Religion 1800–1930*, ed. C. D. Gifford (New York: Garland, 1987), 92.

[108] *NWCTU Minutes*, 1879, 16.

[109] *NWCTU Minutes*, 1879, 121–24.

[110] See, for example, *NWCTU Minutes*, 1880–1900, Evangelistic Department Report Summary, and subsequent elaboration in the appendix of each volume.

[111] See T. Larsen, "'How Many Sisters Make a Brotherhood?' A Case Study in Gender and Ecclesiology in Early Nineteenth-Century English Dissent," *Journal of Ecclesiastical History* 49 (1998): 282–92, for an interesting and provocative study of similar themes in a Baptist context with the specific question of whether only female membership may constitute a congregation.

[112] Garner, "The Woman's Christian Temperance Union," 274.

[113] *NWCTU Minutes*, 1874 Convention, 25.

these meetings held "in the streets, billiard halls, and churches" could be "protracted if the interest warranted it." The purpose of these meetings was to offer "the Gospel cure for intemperance" and, through the integration of compassionate ministries, to address the brokenness of bodies and souls.[114] During the meetings, the leader would often go "through the audience to get persons to come forward and sign the pledge, to the tune of 'Jesus, Lover of my soul,' investing the act with all the solemnity and enthusiasm of a religious service."[115] Although the account in the *NWCTU Minutes*, 1874, seems reluctant to claim the religious and therefore evangelistic potential of the gathering, later descriptions would boldly claim these themes.

In 1877 the first indications of a woman's church emerged.[116] The *NWCTU Minutes* not only reported upon "a woman's church" in Ohio, but also included this paradigm among the "Suggestions for 1878." The report described evangelistic services connected to "Friendly Inns" in Cleveland, at which it was estimated that fifty thousand had attended and two hundred professed conversion. "Out of these services has grown a woman's church—with articles so Scriptural, so simple, so undenominational that all can subscribe to them—with but an informal government, and no pastor save the shepherdess, who may be delegated by the Union." The description also included the "spiritual and temporal interests" cared for by the women, who could be called "deaconesses."[117] Gospel Temperance Meetings proved a valuable evangelistic method, expanding the notion of evangelism beyond verbal proclamation. "Tens of thousands have been saved, and redeemed from the appetite of rum . . . multitudes who came only for the bread and meat stayed to pray and were saved." The account further claimed that believers were baptized, the

---

[114] *NWCTU Minutes*, 1874 Convention, 27. This is a consistent theme throughout the *NWCTU Minutes*, for example: "Let our WCTU women systematically and repeatedly visit these homes, studying spiritual and temporal needs, and carrying an atmosphere of health and hope, for spirit, mind and body" (*NWCTU Minutes*, 1894, 357).

[115] *NWCTU Minutes*, 1874, 27. Then President Annie Wittenmyer echoed this reluctance in her somewhat qualifying statement, "By a wonderful dispensation of the Divine Ruler, attended by unmistakable signs of power and approval, the women of this nation have been set apart as the apostles of the temperance gospel" (24).

[116] First NWCTU President Annie Wittenmyer's address is seasoned with the language of commission and salvation. For example, see *NWCTU Minutes*, 1877, 142–43.

[117] *NWCTU Minutes*, 1877, 190. See also Garner, "The Woman's Christian Temperance Union," 272–74.

Lord's Supper administered, and the dead were buried. While the "Suggestions for 1878" encouraged the model of the Cleveland work, it was tempered by a recommendation: "Let us especially insist on Sunday meetings held at such an hour as will not interfere with regular church services." The women were attempting to reclaim the basic identity and mission of the church without going head-to-head with the established churches. As the work expanded into a complicated infrastructure of departments and committees, the evangelistic purpose of the organization became more prominent. "This temperance movement means soul-saving."[118]

Finally convinced that both she and the organization were ready for the work she had in mind, Willard answered the NWCTU's call and was elected president. Her first presidential address delivered at the sixth national convention (Indianapolis, 1879) and inspired by Matthew 25 explicitly built upon the evangelistic purpose: "In as much as ye have done it unto one of the least of these, ye have done it unto Me."[119]

> Thousands lost in the mazes of drunkenness, guided by their beacon fires, have found their way to the cross of Christ, and to a new and redeemed life; other thousands beaten, and robbed, and cast out, and ready to perish, have been found and ministered to and saved. In no work has God's power been more clearly seen in these last few years than in the work of this Society. The rude halls and mission-chapels where the workers have held their meetings for the salvation of souls have seemed favored places of heaven, where God has let down His ladder for the swift feet of the angels of forgiveness and mercy.[120]

Willard passionately communicated the gravity of the task ahead. "There is no system of iniquity that so successfully antagonizes the Christian church as the drink traffic." And she skillfully built her argument on equally dramatic statistics: "For every church there are twenty-five saloons, for every Sabbath-school teacher a bartender. The church, open two or three times each week, sends out a dim,

---

[118] *NWCTU Minutes*, 1877, 143, 190–91, 197, 211. "It is one of the methods God is using to usher in His later day glory. Let us praise Him that He has permitted us to be co-workers with Him in this great work of saving human souls."

[119] *NWCTU Minutes*, 1879, 12. Willard introduced her maternal appeal, "What America wants more than silver or gold is good mothers." She also named the previous focus upon men's intemperance to the exclusion of women's reformation.

[120] *NWCTU Minutes*, 1879, 15.

uncertain light through its stained glass memorial windows—the saloons, open night and day, Sunday and week day, throw their glare of false light across the pathway of the innocent and unwary."[121]

In response to these tragic circumstances and guided by Willard's bold leadership, the NWCTU organized its efforts under three divisions, "Evangelistic, Moral Suasion, and Legal Suasion," with a recommendation in 1879 for the appointment of standing committees "that may be duplicated in the States," significantly expanding the national infrastructure.[122] In her 1880 presidential address, Willard described the "Evangelistic Work" as "faith and works [going] hand in hand" after the example of Jesus Christ.[123] For Willard the "Evangelistic Department" pursued the following aims: (1) "to keep brightly burning upon our altars the sacred fire which was kindled in the Crusade," (2) "to train spiritually the individual worker," (3) "to permeate, by its devotional services, Bible readings and consecration, all other departments with the evangelistic spirit," (4) "to secure the establishment of the 11 a.m. devotional hour in all conventions," (5) "to emphasize the importance of the Noontide Prayer," (6) "to arouse the Church," (7) "to reach the masses by visitation, Gospel missions and conferences, crusade bands, wayside services, services in jails, halls, cottages, railway stations, etc.," and (8) "to enlist more women who shall preach the Gospel, and to train the workers."[124] The 1883 *NWCTU Minutes* reported, "This [the Evangelistic] Department out of which have grown all the others, is still the foundation of all our efforts."[125] The superintendent of the Evangelistic Department, Hannah Whitall Smith, echoed this sentiment:

> The evangelistic work of the W.C.T.U. lies at the foundation of all the other departments, and it is difficult, therefore, to make a separate report. *All* our work is evangelistic, whether it be legal,

---

[121] *NWCTU Minutes*, 1879, 15.

[122] *NWCTU Minutes*, 1879, 160.

[123] *NWCTU Minutes*, 1880, 14. In 1880 the organization acknowledged the need of trained evangelistic workers for conducting evangelistic meetings (146–47). In 1881 the "Report of the Superintendent of the Department of Friendly Inns, Restaurants, Etc." revealed that "this branch of temperance work in our country is not, as yet, an assured success," while similar ventures in England proved very effective (*NWCTU Minutes*, 1881, 59). The *NWCTU Minutes*, 1881, also mention the preparation of a "Manual of Evangelistic Temperance Work" for use in institutes and local W.C.T.U., xx (Appendix).

[124] Willard, "Do Everything," 92.

[125] *NWCTU Minutes*, 1883, 101.

educational, hygienic, or on any other of our many valuable lines, or whether it has reference to politics, to the home, to the prayer meeting, to the children, the drunkard, or to our workers themselves. If our religion is really our life, and not merely something extraneous tacked on to our life, it must necessarily go into everything in which we live.[126]

Willard predicted in her presidential address, "By Christmas, we shall have the outline of a WCTU in every State and Territory of the Republic."[127]

The next year the NWCTU provided a certificate to those with appropriate training and credentials who were sent into the field for evangelistic work. "This [certificate] elicited many grateful responses from women whose hearts have heard the Divine call, and who have been praying and waiting for some such open door into the world's great harvest field."[128] The evangelistic work of the NWCTU created both structure and space for women to respond to their vocations to evangelistic Christian ministry, the effects spreading nationwide.

A "Brief History of the Past Ten Years," included in the appendix of the *NWCTU Minutes*, 1884, outlined an evolution of the work: "At the outset we knew little of what had been accomplished in the past and were alike ignorant of methods. In our ignorance and wrought upon by the knowledge of personal suffering rather, perhaps, than by the broader feeling of philanthropy, we made the saloon our objective point and out of this grew our *Evangelistic Work*, which has formed the basis of all our operations."[129] Despite the women's unfamiliarity with "methods," their experience and knowledge of the personal suffering of those most captive to the ills of intemperance, coupled with their Christian faith and works, shaped their response, resulting in a multifaceted evangelism. The report of one woman's work in Pennsylvania demonstrated this multifaceted concept of evangelism: "Visits paid since last report 48; Services held 96; literature distributed, 19,000

---

[126] *NWCTU Minutes*, 1883, i (Appendix). Smith goes on to make an allusion to sanctification: "[I]f it is to be Christ working in the Christian who is to make the sermon effectual, or the prayer-meeting a success, it must also be Christ working in the Christian who is to make any other work valuable or effective."

[127] *NWCTU Minutes, 1883*, 54. Willard described in her presidential address that the work of the Evangelistic Department continued to increase in every branch. "If the statistics could be ascertained it would amaze us. But as yet our women are far better at doing than at recording, we can only approximate" (*NWCTU Minutes*, 1884, li [Appendix]).

[128] *NWCTU Minutes*, 1884, liii (Appendix).

[129] *NWCTU Minutes*, 1884, cxxxv (Appendix).

pages; bibles given 6; other books added to the library 100; pledges taken 80; families of prisoners helped 34; letters written for prisoners 86; number of interviews with prisoners in cells 400; number at cell doors 960; helped to their homes 38; situations found for 23; spent of my personal funds $130.00."[130]

Mindful of the importance of her training at Moody's institute and ever the educator, Willard noted the importance of biblical training for white ribboners. According to Willard, "the more we know about the Bible the better we can teach."[131] At the NWCTU gathering in 1887, a resolution entitled "Assistance in Evangelistic Work" expressed gratitude to Dean A. A. Wright of Cambridge, Massachusetts, "for the generous interest in our evangelistic work which led him to give his presence and work in teaching Greek to members of the Convention, and that we believe there will be fruits seen in the increased efficiency of this earliest and most fundamental of our departments."[132] Wright tutored nearly one thousand students, and those from the NWCTU at no cost. The resolution represents an astounding connection between serious biblical study and the formation of evangelistic practices. Perhaps this biblical study informed the understanding of salvation expressed in one state's report: "The burden coming from our workers is for more consecration and better fitness for the work, realizing salvation of both body and souls to be the desired end of the great WCTU work."[133] Willard's presidential address that year resonated with these themes, "The building up of Christ's kingdom, in the solid, practical, every-day fashion of which His words and life give us the working plans."[134] In 1888 the theological instruction expanded from New Testament Greek studies to a comprehensive "Evangelistic Institute."[135]

---

[130] *NWCTU Minutes*, 1885, ii (Appendix). The Pennsylvania report also stated that "grand work is being done by our Committee in the jails and alms-houses . . . the Bible lies on the shelf of every cell."

[131] *NWCTU Minutes*, 1884, 86.

[132] *NWCTU Minutes*, *1887*, 47. The Rev. Dr. A. A. Wright was dean of the Chautauqua School of Theology.

[133] *NWCTU Minutes*, 1884, clxxxiv (Appendix).

[134] *NWCTU Minutes*, 1884, 72. Willard also stated, "The Bible is the most political of books" (73).

[135] *NWCTU Minutes*, 1888, 51, 94–95. "Our evangelists must aid in bringing about that order of things in the church . . . when Christianity shall mean everywhere the protection of the helpless and the prohibition of crime. It must be the work of our evangelism to exalt Christ in all the law of every land, and so crown him Lord of all."

A four years' course should be arranged, during which the student may spend a good share of time in actual service—being employed where she will be best able to apply the gifts and knowledge. . . . A system of Bible study and a course in New Testament Greek under the leadership of Dean Wright, is in preparation which shall be brought within reach of our women, both as regards methods and expense.[136]

By 1889, eighty-three women had enrolled in the course of study led by Wright, with the anticipation that the training would be set on a permanent basis.[137] The four-year curriculum covered the whole Bible, and emerged as a significant component of the evangelistic work.

Willard's provocative proposal for a woman's church did not result in a fracturing of mainline Protestantism along gender lines, but it, along with the organizational and evangelistic program emphases of the NWCTU, provided theological training to women seeking to answer their vocations to Christian ministry. In this space, women were empowered to develop evangelistic practices to care for the souls and bodies of perhaps millions of individuals.[138] In her 1894 presiden-

[136] *NWCTU Minutes*, 1884, 95. The following plan of work was proposed for the Evangelistic Board, "(1) An evangelistic institute course of reading in every local union, conducted by correspondence with the National Board, including a systematic course in the Bible, temperance and history, and studies in W.C.T.U. history and all lines of Department Service; (2) That some definite plan for Evangelistic Institutes shall be devised, in which a thorough training in the application of gospel truth to W.C.T.U. work can be given to those who would be recognized as W.C.T.U. evangelists; (3) That the plan of the establishment of an order of W.C.T.U. deaconesses be made a subject of special study and discussion by State and local unions during the coming year. These deaconesses to be commissioned such, upon passing examination in all required intellectual and spiritual gifts, and for whom recognition shall be asked from all ecclesiastical bodies, and who shall be subject to call and appointment for pastoral service whenever needed" (51).

[137] *NWCTU Minutes*, 1889, 142. Greenwood, the Superintendent of the Evangelistic Department, also included the following information in her report: "Miss Greenwood reports about 600 women preachers and evangelists, some of them ordained pastors, and will print the list next year. . . . Hartford Theological Seminary (Congregational) has opened its doors to women this year. Those of Boston and Evanston, Ill., have been open always. The Free Baptist church has admitted women to its General Conference this year for the first time. The office of Deaconess has been officially restored by the Episcopal Church, and several homes for Deaconesses established by the Methodists this year. It seems as if more women have been ordained than in any previous year, and Mr. Moody has established a Bible Institute in Chicago, to which men and women are admitted on equal terms" (142–43).

[138] *NWCTU Minutes*, 1894, 145. The Evangelistic Department reported: "The Need: Never has the need been greater for such ministry to the poor, the sorrowing,

tial address, Willard expressed the integrated character of the Evangelistic Department as well as her own work: "To enlist more women who shall preach the Gospel to the drinking-classes and to help in the great movement that shall some day obliterate the sex line in the realm of ecclesiastical office and power, is the practical purpose of this department."[139]

A prominent international leader in the temperance reform movement, Willard's Christian faith, including her own precarious early spiritual journey, framed her advocacy for women that focused upon education, suffrage, and ecclesiastic rights. Under Willard's leadership, Christian practices and ministry emerged among the priorities of the NWCTU's Evangelistic Department. Through the auspices of this massive organization Willard encouraged the implementation of ecclesiological elements to reclaim the church's mission, particularly among the poor and marginalized through aspects of a woman's church.

> *I firmly believe God has a work for [women] to do as evangelists, as bearers of Christ's message to the ungospeled, to the prayer-meeting, to the church generally and the world at large, such as most people have not dreamed.*[140]

---

the sinning. Think of the ninety-five thousand families in one city with only one room to a family; of two hundred and ten thousand human beings in New York City last winter on the verge of starvation; of little children in factories when they should be in school; of women with children to support, making shirts at ten cents a piece, finding their own rent, fuel, light, clothing, everything out of this wage, and remember that this wretchedness can be duplicated all over our land. Think of the corruption in high places . . . think of the sorrowing, hard-worked, ignorant, sick and weary, of those who cheer the name of Jesus but hiss the mention of the church. Of whole wards in our cities, and whole sections in our states where no ray of hope falls, and you have a picture of the need for our ministry" (355).

[139] *NWCTU Minutes*, 1894, 146.

[140] Willard, *Glimpses of Fifty Years*, 360.

Helen Barrett Montgomery, Rochester Regional Library Council,
Rochester Public Library Local History Division

5

᷍HELEN BARRETT MONTGOMERY᷍

The clear teaching in regard to the holiness of God has made impossible the divorce between religion and ethics wherever the Bible is adequately taught or obeyed.[1]

Helen Barrett Montgomery's (1861–1934) vocational pilgrimage enabled her to craft a Trinitarian biblical theology of evangelism. An influential leader in the women's ecumenical missionary movement, Montgomery traveled widely and wrote copiously, including one of the earliest New Testament translations by a female scholar, the *Centenary Translation of the New Testament* (1924).[2] Montgomery

---

[1] H. B. Montgomery, *The Bible and Missions* (West Medford, Mass.: The Central Committee on the United Study of Foreign Missions, 1920), 13.

[2] H. B. Montgomery, trans. *Centenary Translation of the New Testament* (Philadelphia: The American Baptist Publication Society, 1924). This publication commemorated the first hundred years of the American Baptist Publication Society. According to Dana Robert, Montgomery's *Centenary Translation* is "the first translation of the Bible into English that translated Pheobe's role as 'minister' rather than 'deaconess'" (*American Women in Mission: A Social History of Their Thought and Practice* [Macon, Ga.: Mercer University Press], 281 n 60). Robert mentions Katherine Bushnell and her biblical study text, *God's Word to Women: One Hundred Stories on Woman's Place in the Divine Economy*, 2d ed. (Mooseville, Ill.: God's Word to Women Publishers, 1923), calling it "the most noteworthy attempt by a missionary woman to comment on the Bible from a cross-culturally aware, proto-feminist perspective." Dowd points out that Montgomery's purpose in translating the New Testament was evangelistic. She goes on to trace Montgomery's dependence upon Bushnell in her New Testament translation. Bushnell's biblical commentary is strikingly similar to Montgomery's translation in the case of 1 Corinthians 14:34-36. Montgomery

seems to break new theological ground for evangelism studies in her biblical theology, *The Bible and Missions* (1920), which predates similar themes echoed by Karl Barth (1886–1968) almost a decade later. Montgomery's biblical theology is also notable for its attention to the Old Testament, which continues to lack sufficient consideration in the current study of evangelism.

Montgomery is often recognized as the first woman elected to serve as president of the Northern Baptist Convention (1921–1922)—the first woman to hold such a leadership position in a major Christian denomination.[3] Very active in the women's ecumenical missionary movement, Montgomery's writing figured prominently in a book series published annually from 1900 to 1938 by the Central Committee on the United Study of Foreign Missions. Montgomery's election to the presidency occurred in the midst of a difficult time for women's missions as a result at least in part of tensions provoked by controversies between competing fundamentalist and liberal agendas.[4]

According to Montgomery, a significant aspect of her formation in faith was the influence of her family, particularly her father. In her

---

reviewed Bushnell's *God's Word to Women* for *The Baptist* in July 1924—Montgomery's translation was published in December 1924. In her review article, Montgomery refers to Bushnell's treatment of Romans 16:1 and Phoebe's role. Though Montgomery does not cite Bushnell, Montgomery's notes also demonstrate a strong resemblance to Bushnell's. S. Dowd, "Helen Barrett Montgomery's *Centenary Translation* of the New Testament: Characteristics and Influences," *Perspectives in Religious Studies* 19 (1992): 135, 143–48. For further discussion of women's roles and ministry in Montgomery's New Testament translation, see Dowd's subsequent article, "The Ministry of Women in Montgomery's *Centenary New Testament*: The Evidence of the Autograph," *American Baptist Quarterly* 20 (2001): 320–28.

[3] R. Omanson, "Bible Translation: Baptist Contributions to Understanding God's Word," *Baptist History and Heritage* 31 (1996): 14. The NBC formed in 1908, but the constituencies had already affiliated as a result of schism in 1845 that also produced the Southern Baptist Convention. According to McBeth, the divisions between the Northern and Southern bodies were less pronounced in 1845 than in 1900 when many major denominations experienced healing of mid-century divisive wounds. The schism of 1845, according to some, seemed to facilitate greater missional possibilities. Subsequently the NBC would adopt a new name, American Baptist Convention, implemented in 1950 (H. L. McBeth, *The Baptist Heritage: Four Centuries of Baptist Witness* [Nashville: Broadman, 1987], 392, 463, 564, 578–79). Interestingly, *The New York Times* honored Montgomery with an announcement from the American Baptist Publication Society. However, the announcement did not mention her presidency of the NBC or her translation of the New Testament (*The New York Times*, February 10, 1924, sec. 1, part 2, p. 6; quoted in Roger Bullard, "Feminine and Feminist Touches in the Centenary New Testament," *The Bible Translator* 38 [1987]: 119).

[4] Robert, *American Women in Mission*, 307–9.

autobiography, Montgomery highlighted the value her family placed on education. Following many years as a teacher, her father completed seminary and answered a call to serve as pastor of Lake Avenue Baptist Church in Rochester, New York. At age fifteen, Montgomery, with her two siblings, made professions of faith, were baptized, and received into church membership. In recounting the pivotal experience of her profession of faith, Montgomery expressed her hope and anticipation for a joyful memory. Instead, the memory was a severely painful one. Montgomery's narrative of this event, specifically her exchange with the presiding deacon, provides a hermeneutical key for understanding Montgomery's later ministry vocation within the women's missionary movement. The experience contributed to her interest in reading and interpreting biblical texts, and enabling others to do the same for the purpose of cultivating Christian faith, providing the foundation for her biblical theology of evangelism. In addition to her vocation as a leader and scholar within the women's missionary movement, Montgomery received a license to preach in 1892 from Lake Avenue Baptist Church. While Montgomery occasionally preached "as pulpit supply" following her father's death,[5] she is best remembered for her role as teacher, faithfully leading a weekly Sunday school class for over four decades.

Further informing the hermeneutical key of Montgomery's painful memory of her baptism and profession of faith, her interest in biblical texts intertwined with formative life experiences. During Montgomery's undergraduate studies at Wellesley (1880–1884), she learned both (1) the significance and complexity of living within a community of Christians, as well as (2) the importance of engaging those on the margins. The Wellesley student body included a variety of Protestant constituencies, the distinctions of which often surfaced around questions of Christian practices such as the sacraments. In this context, punctuated by biblical study and prayer, Montgomery began to acquire skills not only for debate, but careful and attentive dialogue related to controversial issues.

Growing up in Rochester, Montgomery lived and served in the midst of the emerging social gospel movement. She crossed paths with early social gospel leaders such as Walter Rauschenbusch and

---

[5] H. B. Montgomery [with tributes by her friends], *From Campus to World Citizenship* (New York: Fleming H. Revell, 1940), 93. About half of this work is Montgomery's story told in her own words, and the remaining half consists of tributes from her friends. This particular remark was recorded by Rev. Albert W. Beaven, D.D. Rev. Beaven served as Montgomery's pastor from 1909 to 1929.

Susan B. Anthony. After marrying and returning to Rochester, Montgomery participated in numerous local reform efforts, from educational policy to women's suffrage. The first woman elected to the Rochester City School Board in 1899, Montgomery served for ten years, implementing numerous innovations. As a friend of Anthony, Montgomery supported a variety of programs and policies to increase opportunities for women, including education and suffrage.

After graduating from Wellesley, Montgomery received opportunities to assume administrative posts in women's education. Instead, her interest in reading and interpreting biblical texts and her vocational desire to work among the margins led her to employ her leadership skills within the women's ecumenical missionary movement. Montgomery led a transnational tour in 1910–1911 celebrating the Jubilee of women's missions. During the tour she delivered an estimated two hundred speeches, her book *Western Women in Eastern Lands* (1910) sold one hundred thousand copies within the year, and the campaign raised over one million dollars.[6]

The foundation of Montgomery's remarkable leadership and vocation within the women's ecumenical missionary movement remained her reading and interpreting of biblical texts. Upon this foundation Montgomery crafted her biblical theology of evangelism, outlined in *The Bible and Missions*, a contribution to the Central Committee's book series. In this text, Montgomery broke new theological ground by reclaiming the Trinity's missional character as a paradigm for evangelistic ministry. Taking seriously the Old Testament alongside the New as biblical Scripture, Montgomery offered a canonical perspective, providing a faithful reorientation of the Church as sent by God in mission to the world, rather than the Church sending missions, for the ministry of evangelism as a holistic and transformative witness to the reign of God.

Formation and Vocation

Helen "Nellie" Barrett was born 1861, in Kingsville, Ohio, the eldest of three children, two daughters and a son.[7] She was raised for much

---

[6] N. Hardesty, "The Scientific Study of Missions: Textbooks of the Central Committee on the United Study of Foreign Missions," in *The Foreign Missionary Enterprise at Home: Explorations in North American Cultural History*, ed. D. Bays and G. Wacker (Tuscaloosa: University of Alabama Press, 2003), 109.

[7] Montgomery, *From Campus to World Citizenship*, 19, 21. According to Montgomery, "I was named Nellie" (19). Barrett's brother, Storrs Barrett, later served on the faculty at University of Chicago (18, 21, 140).

of her childhood in Lowville, New York.[8] In her autobiographical remarks published with commentary from peers as *Helen Barrett Montgomery: From Campus to World Citizenship*,[9] Barrett claimed to enjoy a close Christian family that provided a strong formation focused largely upon education. This focus guided Barrett's life work in Christian service. Barrett's father, Adoniram Judson Barrett (1832–1889),[10] provided a particularly strong influence and example.[11] The significance of his influence and the unfolding of what Barrett would recount as a painful memory regarding her baptism and profession of faith provide a hermeneutical key to understanding her ministry vocation and subsequent evangelistic theology and practice.

A schoolteacher with a keen interest in the classics, Barrett's father later entered the Christian ministry after graduating from Rochester Theological Seminary in 1876.[12] From his graduation until his sudden death in 1889 he served Lake Avenue Baptist Church in Rochester. Demonstrating a strong fondness for her father, Barrett remarked in her autobiography:

> I loved both my parents with all the affection within me. But I am not quite sure that my mother's authority was completely successful. She was obeyed because she belonged. My father, on the other hand, was adored. To this child God always looked like her father, and obedience to her father became the basis of submission to the

[8] Montgomery, *From Campus to World Citizenship*, 23.

[9] Prior to the text's first chapter the following comment is printed, "From notes that Mrs. Montgomery dictated and family letters that were edited by her brother, Professor Storrs Barrett, it has been possible to gather in her own words, adjusted only to continuity, an account of her childhood, college days, and marriage" (Montgomery, *From Campus to World Citizenship*, 18).

[10] Brackney points out that Barrett's father came from a long ancestry of Baptists and was named after the early and much-admired Baptist missionary to Burma, Adoniram Judson (1788–1850). W. Brackney, "The Legacy of Helen B. Montgomery and Lucy W. Peabody," *International Bulletin of Missionary Research* 15 (1991): 174.

[11] Barrett made at least one somewhat veiled reference to her mother's role in Christian formation: "Like Ruskin, she [Barrett] valued the education that comes when a mother reads the Bible to her children" (Montgomery, *From Campus to World Citizenship*, 23).

[12] Montgomery, *From Campus to World Citizenship*, 28. The University of Rochester and Rochester Theological Seminary developed at the same time. In May 1850 a New York Baptist Union for Ministerial Education Society formed with the intention of establishing an institution to train pastors (A. May, *A History of the University of Rochester 1850–1962* [Rochester, University of Rochester Press, 1977], 21).

will of God. There was reverence, there was fear, the right kind of fear, a dread of doing what was wrong in my father's sight.[13]

Barrett's desire to excel in her father's eyes informed her emerging ministry vocation reflecting his love of education and reading biblical and classical texts.

This emphasis on education woven together with Christian formation shared by father and daughter was demonstrated in previous generations. Two of Judson Barrett's five brothers, in addition to himself, attended college, a fourth went to medical school, and the remaining two went into business.[14] According to Barrett in her autobiography, "Grandfather Barrett did his part in the work of education. Every night the children were lined up along a crack and made to spell, there was instruction in the Bible, there were family prayers." Memories of her Grandmother Barrett retreating "to a small outhouse for her daily season of prayer,"[15] taught Barrett how to pray. "I used to steal after her and stand outside the closed door where I could listen to her dear voice as she prayed for each of her family in turn." Visits with her maternal grandparents were also formative. "Grandfather Barrows was a handsome old man, with intellectual interests."[16] She recounted time spent immersed in reading texts from the Christian tradition.

> At Grandfather Barrow's, I was not much interested in the Reports of the Smithsonian Institute, nor in Young's *Night Thoughts*, nor in Butler's *Analogy* and the *Call to the Unconverted*. But Foxe's *Book of Martyrs* was by no means to be sniffed at, and there was *Pilgrim's Progress*. We skipped the piety and dramatized the narrative, playing it day after day throughout the house. The City of Destruction was in the cellar, the Celestial Regions on the third floor. A pillow-case provided the burden of sin that rolled away on the first turn of the second-floor stairs, and Appolyon lurked in the clothes closet near

---

[13] Montgomery, *From Campus to World Citizenship*, 22. Similar to Ripley in chapter 1, Barrett is strongly influenced by her father's example, echoing to a lesser extent Wilken's observations regarding Christian hagiography (R. L. Wilken, *Remembering the Christian Past* [Grand Rapids, Eerdmans, 1995], 121–44). According to Wilken, "Of the several paths that lead to virtue, the broadest and the most obliging is the way of imitation. By observing the lives of holy men and women and imitating their deeds, we become virtuous" (121).

[14] Montgomery, *From Campus to World Citizenship*, 19.

[15] Montgomery, *From Campus to World Citizenship*, 20.

[16] Montgomery, *From Campus to World Citizenship*, 25.

by. The Delectable Mountains were viewed after crawling through
a trap door onto the parapet below the roof.[17]

Barrett seemed to argue that her formation also benefited from her
maternal grandmother's organizational skills and diligence. "If one of
my grandmothers taught me to pray, the other taught me to work.
. . . I used to spend months at a time with her, helping her to knit and
sew, bake bread and cake, make soup and sausages, feed the hens and
the pigs, dig the potatoes, shell the peas, hunt for eggs, collect the cows,
and harness old Doll." However, revealing a glimpse of a sense of
humor, Barrett admitted, "I was fonder of reading than housework."[18]
The frame of Barrett's formation in faith, namely an emphasis upon
education, was highlighted by threads of personal piety and diligence.

Her father's graduation from Rochester Theological Seminary and
subsequent role as pastor at Lake Avenue Baptist Church represented
a climactic point within Barrett's formation in faith. "At the age of fifteen I was thus the eldest daughter of a pastor, and from that day
onwards this church became one of my reasons for existence. During
my father's first winter, about one hundred and fifty new members
were added to the church, including the pastor's three children. We
were baptised [*sic*] by my father."[19] The following demonstrates a significant contrast in Barrett's experience related to her baptism and profession of faith from other spiritual autobiographical discourses.[20]

---

[17] Montgomery, *From Campus to World Citizenship*, 26. Montgomery referred to
John Bunyan (1628–1688), *Pilgrim's Progress* (London: 1678); Joseph Butler
(1692–1752), *The Analogy of Religion to the Constitution and Course of Nature*
(Philadelphia: 1867); and Richard Baxter (1615–1691) *Call to the Unconverted* (1658);
John Foxe (1516–1587), *Book of Martyrs* (1684); and Edward Young (1683–1765),
Night Thoughts (1741). These resonate with Barrett's Puritan ancestry, the predeces-
sors of both parents arriving in New England in the early seventeenth century
(Montgomery, *From Campus to World Citizenship*, 19). Barrett goes on to reference "a
worn little volume called Letty's Gold Locket." The story tells of a thoughtful young
girl who wore a locket. Letty performed a variety of good deeds narrated throughout.
The story concludes with the locket open, containing the words, "he pleased not himself." Recounting the memory from a later vantage point, Barrett explained, "It [the
volume] was doubtless one of those despised books that were written for the Sunday
school but it fascinated me. It made more of an impression on me than many another
volume of greater literary merit. A thorn-bush may be, I suppose, a cathedral to a
sparrow" (*From Campus to World Citizenship*, 26–27).

[18] Montgomery, *From Campus to World Citizenship*, 25, 26.

[19] Montgomery, *From Campus to World Citizenship*, 28.

[20] For further discussion on evangelical autobiography, see Susie Stanley, *Holy
Boldness* (Knoxville: University of Tennessee Press, 2002). Most often spiritual autobiographies, such as those of women in the Wesleyan/Holiness traditions studied by

One cloud darkens the remembrance of that moving experience. Candidates came before the deacons to be questioned as to their Christian experience. One old deacon put to me his unfailing enquiry, "My young sister, did you feel the burden of sin roll away?" Those were his exact words to me, a child of fifteen growing up in a Christian home! Trembling, I answered, "Yes, sir," and realized at once that I had told a lie in order to get into the church. It filled me with bitterness at the very moment when a gracious father was welcoming me into the household of faith.[21]

Barrett's narration of the event expressed substantial ambivalence in response to her exchange with the deacon. She struggled with the local church's expectation represented by the deacon's inquiry and subsequently with the meaning of the event. For Barrett, the women's missionary organization in large part became the community within which she was able to reinterpret this past event to make sense of her later ministry vocation.[22]

Barrett's narration of this experience serves as a hermeneutical key for understanding her ministry vocation and evangelistic theology and practices. A memory prior to her baptism and profession of faith recalled by Barrett demonstrates her early devotion to biblical texts: "This child noted a difference between what the minister read out of the big red Bible and what he read from his sermon paper laid across the volume. She thought the Bible much superior."[23] Much if not all of Barrett's life's work reflected upon theological questions related to God's invitation to enjoy a reconciled relationship and humanity's response. For Barrett, the primary means of addressing these questions was through reading and interpreting biblical texts, the primary context was among women in foreign mission fields as well as the women supporting those missions.

Stanley, depict a conviction of sin, but subsequent joy at receiving justification and professing Christian faith.

[21] Montgomery, *From Campus to World Citizenship*, 28. Barrett continued her recollections of that year. "At the age of fifteen I recovered from pneumonia and had to get my strength back on a farm. I went through a serious mood. . . . " (29).

[22] See A. F. Segal, *Paul the Convert: The Apostolate and Apostasy of Saul the Pharisee* (New Haven: Yale University Press, 1990), 294, 296.

[23] Montgomery, *From Campus to World Citizenship*, 23.

Wellesley

After attending Livingston Park Seminary[24] Barrett received tutoring from her father to prepare her for studies in classical literature at Wellesley College (1880–1884).[25] She had read the required Latin before the age of fifteen. Soon after arriving at Wellesley, in correspondence with her parents, Barrett initially resisted the president's strong recommendation to enroll in Greek, since her father seemed unsupportive of such a decision.[26] Barrett apparently transferred into a Greek class soon after the exchange and excelled in its study, going on to publish the first known translation of the New Testament by a woman.[27] Barrett's time at Wellesley informed her emerging vocation and interest in biblical studies beyond scholarly subjects in at least two ways. First, Barrett was impressed by the complexities of living in a relatively diverse community of Christians. She encountered theological

[24] Livingston Park Seminary was opened in Rochester, New York from 1861 to 1930.

[25] W. Hudson, "Helen Barrett Montgomery," in *Notable American Women 1607–1950* (Cambridge, Mass.: Belknap Press of Harvard University Press, 1971), 2:566. According to Brackney, she entered an M.A. degree program at Brown University after completing her studies at Wellesley (Brackney, "The Legacy of Helen B. Montgomery and Lucy W. Peabody," 174). However, Hudson does not make mention of the M.A., although he does name Brown among the institutions from which Montgomery received honorary degrees—namely Brown University, Franklin College, Denison University, and Wellesley (567). Montgomery's autobiography with tributes includes the following on the frontispiece, "Helen Barrett Montgomery graduated as Bachelor of Arts with the Class of 1884 at Wellesley College. She took her Master's degree at Brown University. She was granted, honoris causa, the degrees of Doctor of Laws by Denison University, Doctor of Humane Letters by Franklin College, and Doctor of Laws by Wellesley, her Alma Mater. Five times only had this degree been conferred by Wellesley on a woman, and one of the five women thus honored was Madame Curie" (Montgomery, *From Campus to World Citizenship*, frontispiece). See also C. D. H. Abbott, *Envoy of Grace: The Life of Helen Barrett Montgomery* (Valley Forge, Pa.: American Baptist Historical Society, 1997), 15. Henry Fowle Durant, a lawyer elected as a trustee to Mt. Holyoke, founded Wellesley Female Seminary in 1870. Wellesley's Board of Trustees included both men and women and opened its doors September 8, 1875, to 314 female students. See F. Converse, *Wellesley College: A Chronicle of the Years 1875–1938* (Wellesley, Mass.: Hathaway House Bookshop, 1939), 12, 16–17, 19.

[26] Montgomery, *From Campus to World Citizenship*, 31, 36–37. "I left the Livingston Park Seminary where I had been a student, and was put through a course of mathematics" (31).

[27] Montgomery, *From Campus to World Citizenship*, 44. In this letter, Montgomery acknowledges that she is in a Greek class (*Centenary Translation of the New Testament*; see n 2, this chapter).

questions and issues not merely in the abstract, but within relationships with friends and teachers. Second, through the guidance of an
instructor, Barrett engaged in ministry on the margins, awakening in
her a desire to pursue such ministry in her future vocation.

At Wellesley, students practiced a silent time of twenty minutes
before breakfast, reserved for Bible reading and prayer. According to
Barrett, "I cannot remember that any of us felt that this was an imposition. Some may have spent the time on lessons, but the girls I knew
best garnered a rich harvest of acquaintance with the Bible."[28]
Although for the most part Barrett's time at Wellesley seemed to edify
her Christian faith, it was not without complexity. In a letter written
to her family shortly after arriving (September 1881), Barrett depicted
tensions related to doctrinal differences:

> Oh, you don't know how it seems to *feel* that you are an *out* set, that
> you are regarded as narrow, bigoted, etc. . . . I had felt so lonesome
> and homesick in the morning. A peculiar feeling of being left out,
> being different and a little despised, but when I found others of this
> sect 'that is everywhere spoken against' my heart warmed and filled
> with the happiness of human companionship. . . . Before service
> Birdie and I had a long talk and a very earnest one, though both of
> us kept perfectly cool. Finally she agreed to read *Grace Truman* if I
> would read *Theodore*, and that she would send for the Westminster
> Confession of Faith, and I for our Covenant and Articles of Faith.[29]

Perhaps the challenge of navigating the treacherous waters of theological issues from early in her time at Wellesley helped to cultivate
her sensitivity to difference as well as skills for building community.
Barrett added in January 1881, "It's good discipline for me to get used
to letting people be just as positive in their beliefs as I am in mine."[30]
Barrett built upon her reflections:

> It may be wrong but I do love argument. I feel just in my element.
> I sniff the battle from afar. But I have come round to Papa's view
> that argument simply as argument very seldom does any good.
> Unless both parties are anxious to learn something and are in a
> mood to accept truth wherever they find it, argument only
> strengthens the prejudices of both sides.[31]

---

[28] Montgomery, *From Campus to World Citizenship*, 33. "In chapel we heard many
splendid sermons." Among the preachers were Lyman Abbott and Bishop Brooks.

[29] Montgomery, *From Campus to World Citizenship*, 38.

[30] Montgomery, *From Campus to World Citizenship*, 48.

[31] Montgomery, *From Campus to World Citizenship*, 55.

During the same month, Barrett recorded that she was invited to lead the evening prayer meeting before dinner and took for her subject, "We are workers together for God."[32] In September 1882, Barrett seemed unusually distressed on the matter of Holy Communion in a letter to her father.

> It has been a most trying day for us. There is malignant diphtheria at Natick so we could not go there for communion. After Dr. [Lyman] Abbott's sermon he said that the sacrament here was less a church than a family ordinance—in fact, as Christ gave it. He invited to the table all who loved the name of Christ—whether having openly professed it or not. Then he invited all who did not care to partake to remain, and I wanted to, but all the Baptist girls went out—so did we. I could never go through the like again. Ought we to have communed? Is it not carrying the point too far when we see we can't go elsewhere, to refrain from communing outwardly as well as in heart?
>
> I am sadly shaken and confused, I fear. Generally outside, in the world, I can hold firmly to the principle. But here all seems changed—for four years we all work together, with no thought of sect except at the communion table, when I am shut out from all other Christians. You cannot understand how it seems. I never should have unless I had been here.[33]

Barrett's excerpt reveals the power of the community to shape theology through its pursuit of faithful practices, which would continue to inform Barrett's evangelistic ministry, including her scholarship, and particularly her biblical theology.

In addition to cultivating her sensibilities and skills, Wellesley nurtured Barrett's emerging vocation with those on the margins. On a Sunday in November 1880, she wrote of spending time with three students and Professor Whiting, an astronomy instructor:

> Miss Whiting read to us a little story from the *Christian Union* called *Summers in Huckleberry Cut* by Jane Grey. It was a brief forceful account of the experience of two women in temperance work among the lowly. At times moving to laughter, again to tears, it told how two ladies, neither "strong-minded" nor "reformers" labored among

---

[32] Montgomery, *From Campus to World Citizenship*, 56.

[33] Montgomery, *From Campus to World Citizenship*, 61–62. Among Baptist traditions the Northern Baptists were the most deeply involved in the ecumenical movement; see W. Brackney, ed., *Baptist Life and Thought: 1600–1980, A Source Book*, rev. ed. (Valley Forge, Pa.: Judson Press, 1998), 355, 365.

men who were drunkards. . . . Deep down in my heart there was born a purpose that said, "Yes, Lord, when Thou dost call me."[34]

This episode underlined Barrett's earlier experience teaching a Sunday school class of "underprivileged boys" at the Lyell Avenue Mission two miles from her father's church in Rochester. "I told of my little trial in working for my neighbor, how I had found that the power of much love for a few rough street boys helped them to know of the love which enfolds all loves in its bosom."[35] Thus, Barrett's ministry of compassion informed her experience of God's love and Christian faith, motivating her evangelistic ministries. In September 1881, Barrett expressed her vocational interests.

> There are so many ways of doing good in the world and so much need in every direction that I feel bewildered in trying to decide in which way to turn my attention. When I hear about the South, it seems to me I must go there; when of the Indians, I don't see how I can stay away from them. And now the Mormons, they need teachers so much. I wish I could divide myself up and do work in every direction at once.[36]

In February 1884, Barrett went with a friend "to the Saturday Night Club for the working girls of South Natick," where Barrett gave a temperance talk that was well received. In that same month Barrett recorded, "ten of us went over to the prison to give an entertainment for the women."[37] Thus, as a young woman Barrett not only began to discern her Christian vocation for an evangelistic ministry, but had already embarked upon the journey working to weave together her gifts for teaching and heart for compassionate ministries. Claiming the authority of God's call upon her life, the confluence of Barrett's honest biblical exegesis and compassion for the disenfranchised both locally and globally would merge into a powerful ministry with profound implications for the discourses of evangelism.

After graduation, Barrett spent a year teaching in the high school in Rochester and another two years serving as coprincipal of the Wellesley Preparatory School in Philadelphia.[38] Although presented

---

[34] Montgomery, *From Campus to World Citizenship*, 42–44.

[35] Montgomery, *From Campus to World Citizenship*, 29, 43, 55.

[36] Montgomery, *From Campus to World Citizenship*, 55

[37] Montgomery, *From Campus to World Citizenship*, 68.

[38] Montgomery, *From Campus to World Citizenship*, 70. According to Brackney, Barrett began as principal of Wellesley Preparatory School in Philadelphia in 1887 ("The Legacy of Helen B. Montgomery and Lucy W. Peabody," 174).

with numerous possibilities—including returning to Wellesley as a member of the faculty, and two presidencies at women's colleges—Helen Barrett chose to marry William Montgomery (1854–1930), a businessman and widower seven years her senior, on September 6, 1887.[39] William was exceptionally supportive of his spouse's gifts and opportunities. In offering a tribute to Barrett, their pastor described William's relationship to her. "She was able to do what she did only because he was one hundred percent a partner with her in the enterprises to which she gave her brilliant mind. He rejoiced in her ability, gloried in the opportunities which came to her, happily supported her in every possible way, and cheered her on in every struggle."[40] Together, each with their particular gifts, the Montgomerys worked for the realization of God's reign in their local community of Rochester and around the world.

Rochester

Growing up and living most of her life in Rochester, Montgomery was surrounded by the emerging social gospel movement. Montgomery's leadership ability was recognized as she participated in numerous reform efforts, from educational policy to women's suffrage. While Montgomery remained committed to local efforts, these experiences gave focus to her biblical scholarship and leadership in the women's missionary movement, which received international recognition.

Montgomery's vocation, including her interest in biblical texts, remained grounded in her active church membership. A popular Bible teacher, Montgomery received a license to preach from her local congregation, Lake Avenue Baptist Church in 1892.[41] An extremely rare

[39] Barrett's parents doubted the success of the contemplated marriage, in her words "anxious" that she should pursue the teaching opportunities (Montgomery, *From Campus to World Citizenship*, 72).

[40] Montgomery, *From Campus to World Citizenship*, 94. The tribute included in the appendix to Montgomery's autobiography is written by Rev. Albert W. Beaven, DD., president of the Colgate Rochester Divinity School, of which William Montgomery was chairman of the Board of Trustees, and pastor of the Lake Avenue Baptist Church from 1909 to 1929. The Montgomerys contributed funds to build a new president's home, later named Montgomery House, following the merger resulting in Colgate Rochester Theological Seminary (Brackney, "The Legacy of Helen B. Montgomery and Lucy W. Peabody," 174).

[41] W. Hudson, "Helen Barrett Montgomery," in *Notable American Women 1607–1950*, vol. 2 (Cambridge, Mass.: Belknap Press of Harvard University Press, 1971), 567. See also Abbott, *Envoy of Grace*, 4. According to Lynch, there are approximately fifty-eight women's ordinations in Baptist traditions for which the year is

occurrence among Southern Baptists even today, women occasionally received preaching licenses and ordination from local congregations and associations in the North during the middle to late nineteenth century.[42] Miss Alice Chester, church historian of the Lake Avenue Baptist Church, described Montgomery's preaching ministry.

> She was licensed to preach; and it was not at all an unusual thing for her, from the period following her father's death and throughout the next pastorate, to serve as pulpit supply—preaching the sermon and conducting the service—in the absence of the pastor, either in his vacation or for any other Sunday in the year. And it is safe to say that in the first decade of the twentieth century it was still an unusual thing to find a woman fitted and called upon to render that sort of service.[43]

The church historian also described Montgomery's Sunday school class, the Barrett Bible Class, which Montgomery taught for forty-four years, numbering at one time 250 members, with usual attendance of at least 150. Not only did Montgomery give the members of her class and the larger church an idea of the possibilities for Christian womanhood, but "she loved her Bible, inspired her hearers with a love for it, and trained them to use it intelligently."[44]

Although women's contributions to the social gospel are only beginning to be recognized in contemporary scholarship, Montgomery's formation in faith provided a significant framework for her participation in the social gospel movement's objectives. Montgomery's vocation unfolded into a ministry that took seriously both personal and systemic social sins locally and globally. An influential leader in the women's ecumenical missionary movement, Montgomery's contributions to the social gospel expand previously truncated notions while at the same time indicating future trajectories in the study of evangelism.

known; the earliest in the Northern Baptist tradition was Mary C. Jones on July 9, 1882, at a meeting of the Baptist Association of Puget Sound. The earliest known recorded formal licensed woman is Mrs. Ruby Bixby around 1846. Penfield provides helpful and organized data on specific categories of women's ministry roles. See J. Lynch, "Baptist Women in Ministry through 1920," *American Baptist Quarterly* 13 (1994): 308–11. This particular edition of the journal is devoted to Baptist women in ministry.

[42] Lynch, "Baptist Women in Ministry through 1920," 304–9.

[43] Rev. Albert W. Beaven in Montgomery, *From Campus to World Citizenship*, 93.

[44] Rev. Albert W. Beaven in Montgomery, *From Campus to World Citizenship*, 92–93.

Arguably the most influential figure of the American social gospel, Walter Rauschenbusch's (1861–1918) leadership emerged with his publication *Christianity and the Social Crisis* in 1907.[45] The primary goal of the social gospel, typically dated as emerging after the Civil War and developing over the next fifty years,[46] is often described as effecting "widespread Christian salvation aimed at transforming both personal lives and the social order."[47] This emphasis upon a societal eschatology or fulfillment of God's will that involved the creation of a just social order, namely the reign of God on earth, was a significant theological component of the movement.[48] Montgomery was a contemporary of Walter Rauschenbusch and Susan B. Anthony (1820–1906), with whom she participated in social activism and religious life in Rochester.[49] Some scholars give the impression that

[45] W. Rauschenbusch, *Christianity and the Social Crisis* (New York: Macmillan, 1907). According to Marsden, Rauschenbusch's "optimistic social theology" opposed an individualistic and otherworldly emphasis often associated with evangelical revivalism (G. Marsden, *Fundamentalism and American Culture: The Shaping of Twentieth-Century Evangelicalism 1870–1925* [Oxford: Oxford University Press, 1980], 105). Rauschenbusch's text, with another published by George Foster (1858–1918) of the University of Chicago in 1906, agitated conservatives among Northern Baptists. Rauschenbush's indictment of the church's focus upon a message about Jesus, rather than the message of Jesus, was not warmly received by all (McBeth, *The Baptist Heritage*, 569). In 1913 moderate conservatives founded Northern Baptist Seminary as an alternative to the modernist agenda of University of Chicago Divinity School (Marsden, *Fundamentalism and American Culture*, 108). These developments contributed to early tensions that preceded later fundamentalist and modernist controversies among Northern Baptists in the 1920s, which included the investigation of Baptist educational institutions for suspected doctrinal infidelity, the charges of which were largely false, based on the subsequent 1921 report (McBeth, *The Baptist Heritage*, 571–72). For attention to the fundamentalist attacks against social Christianity and Rauschenbusch in particular, see G. Dorrien, *The Making of American Liberal Theology: Idealism, Realism, and Modernity 1900–1950* (Louisville, Ky.: Westminster/John Knox, 2003), 124–28.

[46] W. D. Edwards and C. D. Gifford, introduction to *Gender and the Social Gospel* (Urbana: University of Illinois Press, 2003), 3.

[47] Edwards and Gifford, introduction to *Gender and the Social Gospel*, 3. See C. H. Hopkins, *The Rise of the Social Gospel in American Protestantism, 1865–1915* (New Haven: Yale University Press, 1940), and R. White and C. H. Hopkins, *The Social Gospel: Religion and Reform in a Changing America* (Philadelphia: Temple University Press, 1976).

[48] Edwards and Gifford, introduction to *Gender and the Social Gospel*, 3. White and Hopkins summarize, "Always more than a traditional religious movement, the Social Gospel stepped outside the churches to intersect the political, social, and economic forces of changing America" (*The Social Gospel*, xi).

[49] Bullard, "Feminine and Feminist Touches," 119. See also Hudson, "Helen Barrett Montgomery," in *Notable American Women*, 567. According to Hudson,

Montgomery became involved in the social gospel as a result of Rauschenbusch's influence. Rauschenbusch taught seminary in Rochester from 1897 to 1918.[50] However, Montgomery was already working in Rochester for religious and social reform when Rauschenbusch was only beginning to address the systemic social oppression of Hell's Kitchen.[51] Living and ministering within this harsh context, Rauschenbusch began to formulate programs for social action and later a theological rationale for such work.[52]

Incredibly productive, Montgomery gave her attention to faith and social concerns both locally in Rochester as well as on the international landscape of the women's missionary movement.[53] A friend of Susan B. Anthony, Montgomery supported women's suffrage. Anthony urged her to help found the Women's Educational and Industrial Union of Rochester in 1893. Montgomery chaired the committee that raised the funds, approximately one hundred thousand dollars, to make possible open admission of the University of Rochester to women.[54] Montgomery, an admired local lecturer and

---

Montgomery founded the Women's Educational and Industrial Union of Rochester in 1893 and joined the Woman's Political Equality League of Rochester.

[50] Robert, *American Women in Mission*, 268–69 n. 33.

[51] Dowd, "Helen Barrett Montgomery's Centenary Translation of the New Testament," 133–34 n. 3. Dowd claims: "The best critical treatment of Montgomery that I have seen is an unpublished paper by Julie Fewster, 'Helen Barrett Montgomery: A Disciple of Jesus Christ, 1861–1934,' written at Colgate Rochester Divinity School as a class assignment in 1981 and available only from the author. Fewster corrects the impression given by Hudson that Montgomery became involved in the 'social gospel' movement under the influence of Rauschenbusch. In fact, Montgomery and her cohorts were already changing the shape of religion and politics in Rochester while Rauschenbusch was cutting his teeth on the problems of Hell's Kitchen." According to White and Hopkins, *The Social Gospel*, xv, Rauschenbusch commenced his pastoral duties at the Second German Baptist Church on June 1, 1886.

[52] White and Hopkins, *The Social Gospel*, xv, xvi. According to White and Hopkins, "Did not Walter Rauschenbusch, certainly the foremost theologian of the Social Gospel—so the argument runs—admit in the opening sentences of his A Theology for the Gospel: 'We have a Social Gospel. We need a systematic theology large enough to match it and vital enough to back it'? But this was in 1917, Rauschenbusch was dead within a year, and no serious theological formulation was then forthcoming."

[53] F. Hewitt, "Mining the Baptist Tradition for Christian Ethics: Some Gems," *Perspectives in Religious Studies* 25 (1998): 76–77. Hewitt briefly highlights Montgomery's sometimes forgotten social activism. However, in highlighting Montgomery's social reform efforts, Hewitt claims these were limited to Rochester and the state of New York.

[54] Brackney, "The Legacy of Helen B. Montgomery and Lucy W. Peabody," 174.

frequent figure in local newspapers, in 1899 became the first woman elected to the Rochester City School Board.[55]

Montgomery's theology seems to resonate with the connection Rauschenbusch made between the reign of God and social issues.[56] For Rauschenbusch, the reign of God included both the spiritual life of the individual and the social life of the community, which embraced the political, social, and economic aspects of the larger social system. According to Rauschenbusch, the starting point of the reign of God is in the soul of the individual, which then expands into the world.[57] As demonstrated in her writings, particularly *The Bible and Missions*, Montgomery's theology as well as her ministry practices coincided with many of the major components of the social gospel.[58]

As some social gospel historians recognize, the most prominent definitions of the movement have not explicitly excluded women or gender issues. Rather, given the time and context, including the dominant male characters and focus, the definitions are notably "non-gender specific." Although such definitions could indicate gender inclusivity, in the historiography of the social gospel movement the absence of identifying the presence of women in pertinent definitions can actually reinforce the practice of overlooking women's contributions that characterize the movement's main themes. Like Frances

[55] K. Mobley, "The Ecumenical Women's Missionary Movement: Helen Barrett Montgomery and *The Baptist*, 1920–30," in Edwards and Gifford, *Gender and the Social Gospel*, 167. See also Hudson, "Helen Barrett Montgomery," 567. According to Abbott, "Her ten years of service on the board brought many innovations to the schools: kindergartens, vacation schools, manual and domestic training, school lunches, night schools, and mother's clubs. The schools became neighborhood social centers used by the growing immigrant populations. She helped establish school clinics, the first factory school in America, and playground plans" (*Envoy of Grace*, 5).

[56] Robert names the reflection of social gospel themes, particularly related to the kingdom of God, in Montgomery's writings (*American Women in Mission*, 268–69 n. 33).

[57] Hewitt, "Mining the Baptist Tradition for Christian Ethics," 73–74. See also Rauschenbusch, *Christianity and the Social Crisis*, particularly chaps. 2–3, and 7.

[58] According to Mobley, though, Montgomery was not technically included in the social gospel movement by definition, due to its exclusion of women's missions. See Mobley, "The Ecumenical Women's Missionary Movement," for a detailed comparison of Montgomery's position articulated in the ecumenical women's missionary movement in the pages of *The Baptist* and the key elements of social gospel theology. According to Mobley, "These three dimensions of Montgomery's life—personal involvement in social reform, advocacy for world mission on the ecumenical level, and lifelong leadership and service among Baptists—shared a single, overarching purpose in Montgomery's mind: the emancipation of women through the power of the gospel of Jesus Christ" (168).

Willard and numerous others, Montgomery resonated with and even contributed to the social gospel, proclaiming a Christ-centered gospel that was both personally and socially transforming. Consistent with the historical trends of the time, Montgomery was concerned for social purity and other issues pertaining directly to the well-being of women and children at home and abroad.[59] However, less characteristic of women of the time, Montgomery, with Willard, published theological treatises, encouraged women to participate in ministry, and subtly challenged the middle-class Victorian ideals of gender.[60]

A colleague in the Baptist denomination and women's missionary movement recounted Montgomery's prayer for men, women, and children to build up "the Kingdom of God throughout the world—a kingdom of freedom, health, enlightenment, industry, reverence, happiness, service, mutual consideration."[61] Lucy Waterbury Peabody (1861–1949), once a missionary, worked closely with Montgomery, and relayed Montgomery's words, "missions were shown to be 'great social settlements suffused with the religious motive.'"[62] Peabody and

[59] Edwards and Gifford, introduction to *Gender and the Social Gospel*, 3–4, 5. According to Edwards and Gifford, "Women rarely ventured to tamper with these male prerogatives [oversight of industrial, political, and theological concerns], except when they perceived and could demonstrate that the well-being of women, children, or the family was at stake. Women were more likely than men to address social purity issues, including promotion of sex education, opposition to the double sexual standard for men and women, raising of the age of consent, and prevention of prostitution."

[60] Edwards and Gifford, introduction to *Gender and the Social Gospel*, 5. According to Edwards and Gifford, "Women were less likely, with some notable exceptions, to publish theological treatises and philosophical books than men, who were] trained and validated in these areas. Men were less disposed than women, again with some exceptions, to use social gospel principles to argue for woman suffrage or for women's ordination or right to preach. Nor would they easily challenge the middle-class Victorian ideals of manhood and womanhood that shaped the popular understanding of the family and its role in society."

[61] Montgomery, *From Campus to World Citizenship*, 106. Mrs. Curtis Lee Laws was Montgomery's colleague. Mr. Curtis Lee Laws, editor of the popular independent conservative paper *The Watchman Examiner*, coined the term *Fundamentalist*, in an editorial he authored following the 1920 NBC in Buffalo. He expanded upon the meaning of the term "fundamental" previously in use, which referred to doctrines, to refer to individuals with the new term "fundamentalist." Laws with 154 other signatories called for a General Committee on Fundamentals to precede the NBC. See "Convention Side Lights," *Watchman-Examiner*, July 1, 1920, 834; quoted in and discussed by Marsden, *Fundamentalism and American Culture*, 159–60.

[62] Mrs. Henry W. Peabody, in Montgomery, *From Campus to World Citizenship*, 121. At least one scholar notes affinities with the fundamentalist agenda on the part of Peabody. However, her main concern was maintaining women's role in evangelism,

Montgomery met as early as 1887, in Penfield, New York, at a county gathering of Baptists to support outreach ministries. Peabody later wrote of the occasion, "What the audience felt we never knew. We were conscious only of terrible stage fright and a mutual sympathy and love."[63] Peabody and Montgomery would go on to assume significant leadership roles and work together within their Baptist denomination and the ecumenical women's missionary movement.

Women's Missions

The international missionary gathering at Edinburgh in 1910 is considered by most mission histories the starting point for the twentieth-century ecumenical movement from which the World Council of Churches emerged in 1948. However, the largely forgotten Women's missionary Jubilee of 1910–1911, led by Montgomery, among others, marked fifty years, a longer sustained period of ecumenical cooperation up to that time.[64] The women's missionary societies numbered approximately forty, with active membership in the millions, in addition to fifty-five women sent as missionaries in 1910, among a typical total of one hundred denominational missionaries.[65] Within the women's ecumenical missionary movement, Montgomery lived into her vocation, which was grounded in reading and interpreting biblical texts for the purpose of addressing questions of faith that included ministry with those on the margins.

The Central Committee on the United Study of Foreign Missions was formed in 1900, including representatives from Congregationalist,

---

specifically on the mission field. See M. L. Bendroth, *Fundamentalism and Gender: 1875–Present* (New Haven: Yale University Press, 1993), 62.

[63] L. Peabody, "Helen Barrett Montgomery," *The Watchman Examiner*, November 1, 1934, 1158, quoted in L. Cattan, *Lamps are for Lighting: The Story of Helen Barrett Montgomery and Lucy Waterbury Peabody* (Grand Rapids: Eerdmans, 1972), 22.

[64] Robert, *American Women in Mission*, 256. For a helpful introduction and essays examining missionary women from 1920, see D. L. Robert, *Gospel Bearers, Gender Barriers: Missionary Women in the Twentieth Century* (Maryknoll, N.Y.: Orbis Books, 2002).

[65] Robert, *American Women in Mission*, 256. "Its grassroots unity from the bottom up had an immediate effect on far more Americans than Edinburgh's ecumenics from the top down. Yet the Jubilee of 1910, and the movement it symbolized, was forgotten precisely because it represented a popular groundswell rather than an elitist intellectualism, because it involved women rather than men, and because while the issues with which it was concerned have endured, its organizational base eroded over time" (256–57).

Methodist, Presbyterian, Baptist, and Episcopalian churches for the purpose of compiling "reliable material about missions."[66] With the leadership of Peabody, the Central Committee initiated a series, annually publishing textbooks to be used by local women's missionary groups.[67] Elected in 1914 as the first president of the newly formed Woman's American Foreign Mission Society, Montgomery served as the uncontested presidential choice for ten years (with the exception of the year she served as president of the NBC).[68] Her writing figured prominently in the Central Committee's series, including her biblical theology of evangelism, *The Bible and Missions* (1920). These books each sold tens of thousands of copies to local church women eager not only to learn about foreign missions, but also how to support such efforts with and for women as they explored and lived into their own faiths.[69]

The ecumenical study movement was probably the most effective grassroots ecumenism of the time. For example, in 1917, alongside millions of active members, nearly twelve thousand women and girls attended twenty-five summer schools around the country that included mission study, Bible study, pageants, and fellowship. Although the Central Committee originally planned on publishing seven books, the success of these resulted in the continuation of the series. Beginning with historical background, the first text, *Via Christi* by Louise Manning Hodgkins, sold fifty thousand copies. By 1921, twenty-one texts were published, the total sales reaching approxi-

---

[66] Cattan, *Lamps Are for Lighting*, 38. The original name was Central Committee on the United Study of Missions, which according to Hardesty became the Central Committee on the United Study of Foreign Missions sometime between 1912 and 1915 ("The Scientific Study of Missions," 106). According to Brackney, the Central Committee began in 1900 as a committee of the New York Ecumenical Missionary Conference and was sponsored by the Woman's Union Missionary Society ("The Legacy of Helen B. Montgomery and Lucy W. Peabody," 175).

[67] For instructive appendices regarding the series, see Hardesty, "The Scientific Study of Missions," 119–22. Hardesty also provides a brief but informative description of additional emphases of the Central Committee, such as preparation of teachers for service within the educational program of the missionary movement at home, initiating the still-celebrated Women's World Day of Prayer in 1919, local publications for women and children around the world, and periodical series. The largest women's movement in America, over three million women from forty denominations were involved by 1915 (109–11).

[68] Brackney, "The Legacy of Helen B. Montgomery and Lucy W. Peabody," 175. According to Brackney, "She wrote countless editorials, filled pulpits, and presided over meetings that sought to organize women's work in local church circles, associational bands, and in a national network."

[69] Robert, *American Women in Mission*, 261.

mately two million dollars.[70] The entire series from 1901 to 1938 published a total of four million volumes.[71]

During the jubilee celebration, Montgomery featured prominently among the speakers, delivering approximately two hundred speeches.[72] Beginning October 12, 1910, in Oakland, California, the jubilee culminated in New York in April 1911, with Montgomery delivering the closing address of the celebration at Carnegie Hall.[73] The traveling celebration, featuring Montgomery and Peabody, as well as active women missionaries, facilitated forty-eight two-day "great Jubilees" in major cities and numerous one-day events in less populated locales.[74] The sale of her book written for the series and the occasion, *Western Women in Eastern Lands*, sold fifty thousand copies

[70] Robert, *American Women in Mission*, 261–62 n. 14. The texts in chronological order as listed by Robert (1901–1921): L. M. Hodgkins, *Via Christi*; C. A. Mason, *Lux Christi*; A. Smith, *Rex Christus*; W. Griffis, *Dux Christus*; E. Parsons, *Christus Liberator*; H. B. Montgomery, *Christus Redemptor*; A. R. B. Lindsay, *Gloria Christi*; A. J. Brown and Samuel Zwemer, *The Nearer and Farther East*; Dr. and Mrs. F. Clark, *The Gospel in Latin Lands*; H. B. Montgomery, *Western Women in Eastern Lands*; R. Speer, *The Light of the World*; I. Headland, *China's New Day*; Mrs. P. Raymond, *The King's Business*; M. S. Platt, *The Child in the Midst*; H. B. Montgomery, *The King's Highway*; C. A. Mason, *World Missions and World Peace*; J. K. Mackenzie, *An African Trail*; M. Burton, *Women Workers of the Orient*; Dr. B. Allen, *A Crusade of Compassion*; H. B. Montgomery, *The Bible and Missions*; and E. North, *The Kingdom and the Nations*. Hardesty's appendix A lists titles and authors for 1901–1938 ("The Scientific Study of Missions," 119–20). The following are texts from 1922 to 1938: A. B. Van Doren, *Lighted to Lighten the Hope of India*, and D. J. Fleming, *Building with India*; C. De Forest, *The Woman and the Leaven in Japan*, and G. Fisher, *Creative Forces in Japan*; M. N. Gamewell, *Ming-Kwong: City of the Morning Light*; H. B. Montgomery, *Prayer and Missions*; A. E. and S. Zwemer, *Moslem Women*; M. S. Platt, *A Straight Way toward Tomorrow*; J. K. Mackenzie, *Friends of Africa*; H. B. Montgomery, *From Jerusalem to Jerusalem*; E. Singmaster, *A Cloud of Witnesses*; M. Schauffler, ed., *Christ Comes to the Village: A Study of Rural Life in Non-Christian Lands*; M. B. Hollister, *Lady Fourth Daughter of China: Sharer of Life*; R. F. Woodsmall, *Eastern Women Today and Tomorrow*; Michi Kawai and Ochimi Kubushira, *Japanese Women Speak: A Message from the Christian Women of Japan to the Christian Women of America*; M. R. Miller, *Women under the Southern Cross*; J. L. Kellersberger, *Congo Crosses: A Study of Congo Womanhood*; [1937 no title]; Madame Chiang Kai-shek et al., *Women and the Way: Christ and the World's Womanhood*.

[71] Brackney, "The Legacy of Helen B. Montgomery and Lucy W. Peabody," 175.

[72] According to Lucy Peabody, she delivered 197 speeches in two months, while Abbott claims Montgomery delivered 209 speeches during the jubilee celebration. Cf. Montgomery, *From Campus to World Citizenship*, 124, and Abbott, *Envoy of Grace*, 8.

[73] Brackney, "The Legacy of Helen B. Montgomery and Lucy W. Peabody," 175.

[74] Hardesty, "The Scientific Study of Missions," 109. According to Hardesty, local missionary committees with as many as four hundred members participated.

in the first six weeks of publication, one hundred thousand copies during the first year, and continued to sell.[75] The jubilee national campaign raised over one million dollars, most of which supported women's education internationally, specifically in Asia.[76]

While Montgomery's role in the jubilee celebration did not directly engage those on the margins, her efforts not only generated awareness and enthusiasm for women's missionary efforts around the world, it also provided the financial means to implement those ministry programs with women and children internationally.[77] In this way, Montgomery continued to demonstrate her commitment to ministry on the margins resonating with social gospel themes. While Montgomery and other contributors to the Central Committee's book series critiqued consequences of Western imperialism, this is not to say that Montgomery with her missionary colleagues did not perpetuate some aspects of cultural imperialism. Within the limitations of the time and context, Montgomery and the ecumenical women's missionary movement advocated for social reform through evangelistic educational ministries in foreign mission contexts while holding middle-class Euro-American women accountable to their complicity in sinful social systems.[78]

[75] Montgomery, *From Campus to World Citizenship*, 120, 124. A challenge grant from Abbie Rockefeller enabled the Jubilee celebration to raise $1.03 million ("The Scientific Study of Missions," 109).

[76] According to Lucy Peabody, $871,000 was raised by the national campaign (Mrs. Henry W. Peabody in Montgomery, *From Campus to World Citizenship*, 124). However, Cattan claims, "The women had raised $1,030,000 for missions, most of which would go to Christian colleges for women in Asia. More important than the money, however, were the increase in membership in the local societies, the national awareness of the women's missionary movement, and for each woman involved, a new sense of power in unity" (*Lamps Are For Lighting*, 60).

[77] Though Montgomery figures prominently among the recognized leaders, this dynamic of women not merely raising funds, but sending female missionaries to minister to and with women in foreign contexts, was not uncommon. See S. Garrett, "Sisters All: Feminism and the American Women's Missionary Movement," in *Missionary Ideologies in the Imperialist Era: 1880–1920*, ed. T. Christensen and W. Hutchinson (Århus, Denmark: Aros, 1982), 223. Garrett goes on to argue for the place of feminism in the women's missionary movement, which Jane Hunter would later refute in her careful and groundbreaking study, *The Gospel of Gentility: American Women Missionaries in Turn-of-the-Century China* (New Haven: Yale University Press, 1984).

[78] Robert, *American Women in Mission*, 267–68. Robert refers to Montgomery's *Western Women in Eastern Lands* to demonstrate the mission strategy of education. Robert summarizes the many balanced facets within the movement, "spiritual and physical, evangelism and education, personal work and social work" (272). As Tucker notes, Montgomery's first text published by the Central Committee, *Christus*

While Montgomery's leadership within the women's missionary movement and later biblical theology resonated with social gospel themes, it also included components of personal evangelism. She maintained that one's personal faith in Jesus Christ could not rightfully be separated from a personal commitment to social activism.[79] Montgomery's writings were punctuated with this balanced theme. For example, Montgomery prefaced her *Centenary Translation of the New Testament* published in 1924 with the following:

MY DECLARATION OF DISCIPLESHIP

I desire to enroll myself as a disciple of Jesus Christ. I trust in His promise that He will reject none who come to Him. I confess my sins, and rely on His promise of forgiveness to all who repent and confess. I renounce self and will seek to follow Jesus. I claim the promised guidance of the Holy Spirit into all truth. I promise to make love the law of my life, and to accept my Master's oft-reiterated invitation to prayer and communion.

Name, ...

Date, ..."[80]

Despite the effectiveness of the jubilee and the widespread women's ecumenical missionary movement, the movement's momentum was eroded at least in part by the fundamentalist-modernist controversy. Until the jubilee celebration the women's missionary movement was characterized by holism, which included holding together the women's leadership with the authority of Scripture. However, the fundamentalist-modernist controversy seriously wounded the women's missionary movement by cutting off the Bible as a foundation for women's ministry roles.[81] In general, the fundamentalists strongly affirmed the literal

---

Redemptor, gives an account of the problems created by Western imperialism (R. Tucker, "Female Mission Strategists: A Historical and Contemporary Perspective," *Missiology: An International Review* 15 [1987]: 78). Mobley summarizes Montgomery's ministry purpose: "the emancipation of women through the power of the gospel of Jesus Christ" ("The Ecumenical Women's Missionary Movement," 168).

[79] Mobley, "The Ecumenical Women's Missionary Movement," 176.

[80] Montgomery, *Centenary Translation of the New Testament*, n.p.

[81] Robert, *American Women in Mission*, 307–8. Robert argues that the decline of the women's missionary movement was largely a result of male opposition rooted in fundamentalism. Hardesty adds to the possibilities outlined by Robert including the

character of Scripture and an understanding of evangelism as solely verbal proclamation.[82] Although some fundamentalist Baptist leaders assumed Montgomery naïve, generally they did not associate her with the liberal and modernist agenda.[83] However, another component of the fundamentalist agenda was damaging to the women's missionary movement: its perceived need to regain the church for men. This would be accomplished by (1) diminishing the influence of women by limiting the roles accessible to them, and (2) replacing what some perceived as a feminized Christianity with masculine language of virility and strength.[84] The modernists focused on the social implications of the reign of God, questioning the need for evangelizing individuals.[85] Therefore, both platforms left little room for the holism of women's missionary work. The dual emphasis upon evangelism and social issues demonstrated by Montgomery, and key to the success of the women's missionary movement, ultimately became estranged.[86]

While earlier tremors of the fundamentalist-modernist controversies can be traced back into the nineteenth century, tensions within the NBC surfaced profoundly in the 1920s. The fundamentalists chal-

---

following: explaining the influence of historical events such as World War I, shifting roles and opportunities for women in missions, controversies related to fundamentalism, and the changing mediums from periodicals to texts and beyond print materials to radio, films, and television. Perhaps her most insightful explanation for the demise of the women's foreign missionary enterprise was that it had run its course; the movement had served its purpose. See Hardesty, "The Scientific Study of Missions," 115–19. Robert and Hardesty note the following texts for further discussion of fundamentalism and gender: B. DeBerg, *Ungodly Women: Gender and the First Wave of American Fundamentalism* (Minneapolis: Fortress, 1990), and Bendroth, *Fundamentalism and Gender*.

[82] See Brackney, ed., *Baptist Life and Thought*, 356. Brackney's volume includes brief but illustrative primary sources with insightful introductions and contextual commentary.

[83] Bendroth, *Fundamentalism and Gender*, 59–60.

[84] DeBerg, *Ungodly Women*, 76. DeBerg bases her argument for this additional component to the fundamentalists' agenda on close reading of the fundamentalist press. The Men and Religion Forward Movement, consisting largely of evangelicals, shared this purpose (96). Over one million people attended events in 76 major cities and 1,083 small towns related to this interdenominational religious revival that occurred in 1911–1912. According to *Collier's*, "The women have had charge of the church work long enough" (A. Gleason, "Going After Souls on a Business Basis," *Collier's*, December 23, 1911, 14; quoted in G. Bederman, "'The Women Have Had Charge of the Church Work Long Enough': The Men and Religion Forward Movement of 1911–1912 and the Masculinization of Middle-Class Protestantism," *American Quarterly* 41 [1989]: 432–65. Rauschenbusch numbered among its participants (434).

[85] See Brackney, *Baptist Life and Thought*, 356.

[86] Robert, *American Women in Mission*, 307.

lenged the NBC by raising charges of heresy in three areas: (1) in educational institutions, specifically seminaries, (2) among foreign missionaries, and (3) in literature produced by the Board of Publication.[87] While the charges against Baptist educational institutions by fundamentalists were largely false, as reported by the investigating committee to the NBC in 1921, an antiintellectual attitude toward biblical scholarship and academic theology underlined the tensions.[88] As one Baptist scholar notes, foreign missionaries seldom suffered from such suspicions, unlike their educator counterparts for whom it was not unusual to be called upon in this way. The Foreign Mission Board attempted to allay suspicions raised previously by fundamentalists in debates over mission policy in a report to the 1922 NBC, but fundamentalists wanted access to correspondence from missionaries to the board. Despite restrictions of confidentiality, damaging quotes were subsequently obtained. The quotes demonstrated the assumed doctrinal infidelity, which included denial of (1) biblical inspiration, (2) the virgin birth, (3) the deity of Christ, and (4) the resurrection—similar to the accusations articulated in the pamphlet series of the prior decade. Following an investigation, only a small number of missionaries were found to demonstrate the suspected doctrinal inconsistencies, while the large majority, and the movement generally, was exonerated at the 1924 NBC in Milwaukee.[89]

In the meantime, fundamentalists continued to raise concerns while they also worked to organize a coherent strategy. The Fundamentalist Fellowship, as they came to be called, began meeting prior to the NBC in 1920, during which significant support emerged for proposing the adoption of a creed to the NBC. Fundamentalist leadership delayed the proposal for one year, in further efforts to

[87] McBeth, *The Baptist Heritage*, 571. See Brackney, *Baptist Life and Thought*, 356–59, for the text of the resolutions identifying these three areas. See also Marsden, *Fundamentalism and American Culture*, 159–61, 165–68, 171–72, 180–83.

[88] Bendroth, *Fundamentalism and Gender*, 4. Bendroth goes on to observe that this antiintellectualism persisted even though fundamentalists were not the rural or backward constituency described by its opponents. Marsden and DeBerg concur that fundamentalist-modernist debates occurred among scholars and ecclesiastic leaders, not among those in the pews (Marsden, *Fundamentalism and American Culture*, 106; DeBerg, *Ungodly Women*, 4).

[89] McBeth, *The Baptist Heritage*, 572, 573. Terms related to (1)–(4) came into more regular use with the publication of a widely circulated set of pamphlets entitled *The Fundamentals: A Testimony to Truth* published between 1910 and 1915. See M. A. Noll, *A History of Christianity in the United States and Canada* (Grand Rapids: Eerdmans, 1992), 381–86.

organize.[90] W. B. Riley then proposed the adoption of a creed to the NBC in 1922. When Cornelius Woelfkin, a pastor from New York, offered a substitute motion, indecision among the fundamentalists essentially split the movement.[91] Woelfkin proposed "The Northern Baptist Convention affirms that the New Testament is the all-sufficient ground of our faith and practise [*sic*], and we need no other statement." The substitute motion was adopted by a margin of 2-1 after heated debate.[92] Many fundamentalists, though eager for a creed, found it difficult to improve upon the New Testament.

During this tumultuous period, in 1921 Montgomery was elected president of the NBC, the first woman to lead a major American denomination.[93] With an invitation in 1923 to address the Baptist World Alliance, together these roles signified high regard for the women's missionary movement by a substantial number in the midst of heresy allegations relating to foreign missions.[94] During

---

[90] Marsden, *Fundamentalism and American Culture*, 166–67. The creed adopted for proposal incorporated elements from the Philadelphia and New Hampshire Confessions with other broad Baptist themes. In the midst of postponing the creed's proposal, a donor offered two million dollars to Baptist missions on the condition that it only be distributed to those subscribing to "orthodox beliefs."

[91] Marsden, *Fundamentalism and American Culture*, 172.

[92] Cornelius Woelfkin, "Resolution," *Annual of the Northern Baptist Convention 1922 Containing the Proceedings of the Fifteenth Meeting Held at Indianapolis, Indiana, June 14 to 20, 1922* (American Baptist Publication Society, 1922), 133. The vote result was 1,264-637. For further discussion of the two proposals, see 129–34.

[93] By the middle to late 1980s, American Baptists (the successor of the NBC following the changed name in 1950) had elected five women to serve as president. The Southern Baptist Convention, although it had nominated a woman (Marie Mathis in 1972), has not elected a woman to serve as its president. See C. D. Blevins, "Women in Baptist History," *RevExp* 83, no. 1 (1986): 59. Blevins's study is an interesting survey, but it seems to lack historical clarity by not providing consistent information, such as first roles for women (as missionaries, preachers, ordained ministers, etc.) across the Baptist bodies. Major Baptist historical surveys from southern presses and/or authors do not mention Montgomery's election and presidency; see McBeth, *The Baptist Heritage*; and W. J. Leonard, *Baptist Ways: A History* (Valley Forge, Pa.: Judson Press, 2003). While McBeth does not mention Montgomery, Leonard makes only brief mention of her in a paragraph highlighting her accomplishments (with the exception of her election as president to the NBC) and as secretary to a woman's meeting related to the Baptist World Alliance at its Third World Congress in 1923 (*Baptist Ways*, 222, 382). However, William Brackney, an American Baptist, mentions Montgomery's role as president in his source book (*Baptist Life and Thought*, 368).

[94] Robert, *American Women in Mission*, 307. In "A Postconvention Message to the Women of the Churches," as president of the NBC, Montgomery wrote, "First let me thank you all for the wonderful support that you have given me. I know that I was

Montgomery's presidency the NBC adopted an "inclusive policy," rather than a creed as proposed by fundamentalists. In her presidential address, Montgomery, surprising to some more conservative Baptists, denounced the fundamentalists' proposal.[95] In reference to the great opportunity of Europe's liberation for religious freedom following World War I, Montgomery asked, "Have we, ourselves, a firm hold of the principle of toleration and religious freedom so that we can help them to establish it? Are we free from religious intolerance and bigotry? Pray God that we may purge ourselves of any root of bitterness and rise to the fulness [*sic*] of this great opportunity."[96] In "A Postconvention Message to the Women of the Churches," Montgomery recounted, "There was earnest conviction on both sides, but there was also courtesy and fairness and a spirit of mutual forbearance and helpfulness. God has been speaking through this Convention. He has preserved us from schism. He has enabled us to emphasize the things on which we do not differ."[97] Having navigated the complex terrain of such opposing fundamentalist and liberal agendas, Montgomery worked diligently to clear a middle ground not compromising on either of the above biblically grounded positions to advocate a third option,[98] demonstrated in her text *The Bible and Missions*.

---

your representative; that my selection was a recognition on the part of the denomination of the effective work done by the women's organization at home and abroad" ("A Postconvention Message to the Women of the Churches" [1922] in *Women and Religion in America 1900–1968*, ed. R. R. Ruether and R. S. Keller, vol. 3 [San Francisco: Harper & Row, 1986], 285–86).

[95] Bendroth, *Fundamentalism and Gender*, 60. This inclusive policy allowed for the acceptance of members from other Christian bodies without requiring them to be baptized again by immersion. See Brackney, *Baptist Life and Thought*, 355, 359–60.

[96] H. B. Montgomery, "President's Address," in *Annual of the Northern Baptist Convention 1922 Containing the Proceedings of the Fifteenth Meeting Held at Indianapolis, Indiana, June 14 to 20, 1922* (American Baptist Publication Society, 1922), 39.

[97] Montgomery, "A Postconvention Message," 286.

[98] Robert, *American Women in Mission*, 309. Montgomery's holism sought to maintain a space for women's participation in foreign missions. Montgomery warned the church in 1923 that it would bear the loss of power resulting from not matching the world's acceptance of women in leadership roles. H. B. Montgomery, "The New Opportunity for Baptist Women," *Watchman-Examiner*, July 26, 1923, 950, quoted in Bendroth, *Fundamentalism and Gender*, 55. In spite of Fundamentalism's seeming claims to the contrary, Riley would admit later in an editorial that women were sometimes called by God to become evangelists (W. B. Riley, "Women in the Ministry," *Christian Fundamentalist* [1928]: 21, quoted in DeBerg, *Ungodly Women*, 79).

A Biblical Theology of Evangelism

Montgomery's attention to biblical texts, exposures at Wellesley and in Rochester related to the social gospel movement, as well as her leadership within the women's ecumenical missionary movement shaped a Trinitarian biblical theology of evangelism, the themes of which seem to predate similar themes later echoed by Karl Barth in 1928. In the midst of the international missionary movement strongly influenced by images of colonization that perceived the church as the sending agent and steward of the gospel, Montgomery composed a biblical theology of evangelism that challenged such a perspective reclaiming the Trinity's missional character.

Her biblical theology, particularly contained in *The Bible and Missions*, gives not only a female voice, but also a nuanced contribution to the contemporary discourse on evangelism. Emerging from a careful canonical reading of Scripture, her biblical theology did not overlook Old Testament texts in its construction of a nuanced theology of witness to the reign of God. Beginning with God's initiation of relationship with humankind, Montgomery faithfully oriented the Church as sent by God in mission to the world. Her theological reflection upon the nature of God as both immanent and transcendent provided a frame within which to critique the fundamentalist-modernist polemic of her time. From Jesus' revelation of the Father's holiness, Montgomery's theological reflection shaped implications for humanity's redemption and relationships with God and neighbor in the context of the reign established by Jesus Christ.[99] Leaving appropriate space for proclamation, the culmination of Montgomery's biblical theology is a holistic and transformative witness to the reign of God that is not without practical strategies such as giving money as an aspect of preaching the gospel and the prevalence of lay ministers, specifically women—both missional practices of the early Church.[100]

---

[99] Montgomery does not seem to discuss distinctions between the church and the reign of God.

[100] H. B. Montgomery, *The Bible and Missions* (West Medford, Mass.: The Central Committee on the United Study of Foreign Missions, 1920), 85–86. Montgomery published an article entitled "Civic Opportunities for Christian Women," *The Baptist* 1 (1920): 1073. It encouraged women to include legislative committees in their organizations to shape public policy. See Brackney, *Baptist Life and Thought*, 368–70.

Mission and Evangelism?

The use of the term *evangelism* and its relation to *mission* often lacks consistency.[101] Evangelism and mission are at times used synonymously, and at other times a distinction is made between them. In the latter case, evangelism may be understood as an activity in a domestic context—for example, one's country, to those already baptized, but estranged from the Church. Mission is then, at times, understood as preaching usually accompanied by outreach activities such as educational and medical assistance in urban or more often foreign contexts. Mission has its root in the Latin phrase *missio dei* (the mission of God). According to the commission text in the gospel of John, the mission of God is to send Jesus Christ to the world, and with the Holy Spirit to send the Church to the world. As Montgomery demonstrates, a relatively recent but important shift has occurred within the Church's self-understanding from the Church sending missions to the world, to God sending the Church in mission to the world.[102]

While mission includes evangelism, evangelism is an essential dimension of the total activity of the Church that does not allow the compartmentalization of evangelism separate from social action.[103] Separating the language of evangelism from social action is not consistent with biblical foundations. Instead, evangelism must remain at the heart of the Church's mission, sent by God in service to the world to proclaim repentance and forgiveness, inviting individuals to live changed lives by the power of the Holy Spirit within Christ's Church initiated into the reign of God.[104]

---

[101] This essay's use of the terms *mission* and *evangelism* is consistent with David Bosch's explanation, which is definitive for the academic study of mission and evangelism. According to Bosch, "Mission means being involved in the redemption of the universe and the glorification of God. . . . Evangelism is the *core*, *heart*, or *center* of mission; it consists in the proclamation of salvation in Christ to nonbelievers, in announcing forgiveness of sins, in calling people to repentance and faith in Christ, in inviting them to become living members of Christ's earthly community and to begin a life in the power of the Holy Spirit" ("Evangelism: Theological Currents and Cross-currents Today," *International Bulletin of Missionary Research* [1987]: 100).

[102] D. J. Bosch, *Transforming Mission: Paradigm Shifts in Theology of Mission* (Maryknoll, N.Y.: Orbis Books, 1991), 377–78.

[103] Bosch, *Transforming Mission*, 412. This understanding of evangelism is opposed to John Stott's position articulated in the Lausanne Covenant. Stott claims that evangelism is one of two components of mission, with social action as the other component. Bosch refers to the World Council of Churches' statement on evangelism made at the 1954 gathering in Evanston, Ill.

[104] Bosch, *Transforming Mission*, 10. This conception of evangelism combines those of Bosch, William Abraham, and Scott Jones.

A Trinitarian Canonical Reading

One of Montgomery's most significant contributions to evangelistic theology and practice is her early use of the language of missionary to describe the nature of the Bible, as well as the Church, with God as the origin of mission. This insightful nuance grew from her canonical and theological reading of the biblical texts, especially attention to its narrative quality, including the Old Testament.[105] Most studies in Christian evangelistic theology and practice do not sufficiently take into account the Old Testament. [106] Even the most helpful theological projects in the study of evangelism are informed by biblical foundations that seldom reach beyond the New Testament.[107] In contrast,

---

[105] While Montgomery's use of footnotes does not directly reveal her sources, her inclusion of the following in the reading list at the close of the volume seem to indicate her dependence upon these texts in constructing her biblical theology: Horton, *The Bible a Missionary Book* (Pilgrim Press, 1908), and Beach, *New Testament Studies in Missions* (Student Volunteer Movement, 1900). For mission history she referred to Mason, *Outlines of Missionary History* (Doran, 1912), and Barnes, *Two Thousand Years of Missions before Carey* (Chicago: Christian Culture Press, 1900).

[106] David Barrett devotes only a few paragraphs, the majority of one page, to "usages before Christ," with a survey of occurrences in 2 Samuel, Psalms, Writings, and Prophets; see D. B. Barrett, *Evangelize!: An Historical Survey of the Concept* (Birmingham, U.K.: New Hope, 1987), 10. David Bohr begins chap. 1 with an etymology of the language of evangelism with a few paragraphs on Old Testament foundations. The language can mean any good news (Nahum 1:15), but it develops into good news of the reign of God (Isa 40:9-10, 52:7-8). See also D. Bohr, *Evangelization in America: Proclamation, Way of Life and the Catholic Church in the United States* (New York: Paulist, 1977), 11–12. Bohr also mentions the universal/particular elements of the Old Testament, specifically Abraham as a blessing to all the nations (13). In Walter Klaiber, (*Call and Response: Biblical Foundations of a Theology of Evangelism* [Nashville: Abingdon, 1997]), the author's etymology begins with evangelism's root in the Old Testament followed by discussion of Isaiah's implications for the practice (21–22). Although described as biblical foundations for a theology of evangelism, Klaiber's text does not engage the Old Testament in any depth until pages 102–7, which is a discussion of judgment and the preaching of the prophets. Klaiber tends to alternate chapters/sections between biblical exegesis and theological reflection. However, the theological reflection focuses primarily on the New Testament with little if any mention of the Old Testament. See also Bosch, *Transforming Mission*, 15–31. While Bosch acknowledges that for the Christian church there is no New Testament divorced from the Old, "on the issue of mission we run into difficulties here, particularly if we adhere to the traditional understanding of mission as the sending of preachers to distant places (a definition which, in the course of this study, will be challenged in several ways)" (16–17). The argument of this essay, with Bosch, is critical of such a traditional understanding, but at the same time moves beyond his comparatively brief treatment of the Old Testament to a canonical and theological approach.

[107] Abraham, Arias, and Jones, for example, while acknowledging the Old

Montgomery begins her project with a constructive theological reading of the Old Testament to illumine theology and practice. In her text both the Old Testament and the New Testament are given approximately the same space.[108]

Montgomery made the following observation in *The Bible and Missions* on the opening page of chapter 1: "Reading the Bible meticulously for proof texts and argument, it is possible to escape its unmistakable drift; reading it in the large and simply as it was written, its missionary message is inescapable."[109] Beginning with the Old Testament (chap. 1)—including the Law, History, Prophets, and Writings—and culminating in the New Testament (chap. 2), Montgomery surveyed the whole of the biblical text to construct her biblical theology.

Montgomery used the term *missions* to denote activities of North American and Western European churches in foreign (or international) contexts. Therefore, her language of "missionary" included this aspect of late nineteenth- and early twentieth-century missions. However, it also emphasized God's action of sending, not only Jesus Christ and the Holy Spirit to the church, but the sending of the

---

Testament frame as a reference for comprehending the reign of God, concentrate their biblical exegesis and theological reflection in the New Testament. For references to the Old Testament in their studies, see W. J. Abraham, *The Logic of Evangelism* (Grand Rapids: Eerdmans, 1989); for understanding the reign of God, 23–25, 31; for etymological study of evangelism related to proclamation in fulfillment of Old Testament prophecy, 40–43; in reference to the Shema in Mark 12:29-31 to demonstrate the implications for love of God and neighbor in Christian conversion and initiation, 134–35; with regard to a theology of world religions, 219–20, 222. See also S. J. Jones, *The Evangelistic Love of God and Neighbor: A Theology Witness and Discipleship* (Nashville: Abingdon, 2003). For the starting point of evangelism in God's love (which leads to God's reign) in brief surveys of the Old and New Testament, see 33–38; like Abraham, referring to Jesus' quotation of Deuteronomy 6:5 (Shema) in Mark and Matthew and his inclusion of Leviticus 19, making note of Jesus' explanation in Matthew that on these "hang all the law and the prophets" and reminding the reader that these were the entirety of the Jewish Scriptures at the time, 50–51; beginning his discussion of "God's Mission and the Mission of the Church" with reference to God's election of Israel "as a key turning point in the history of salvation" and the blessing of the nations through Abraham's faithfulness, 53; describing the NT as a missionary document, 55. Mortimer Arias likewise refers to a relatively small number of Old Testament references, particularly in initial chapters, to establish the nature of God's reign. See M. Arias, *Announcing the Reign of God: Evangelization and the Subversive Memory of Jesus* (Philadelphia: Fortress, 1984; repr., Eugene, Ore.: Sipf & Stock, 1999), 4, 14–15, 19–24, 28–29, 52, 85, 89–90.

[108] Forty-seven and forty-two pages respectively.

[109] Montgomery, *The Bible and Missions*, 7.

church in ministry to the world. For Montgomery, God is the origin
of mission, "The Pentateuch plants itself squarely on Theism, and
that in itself is a fundamental missionary message."[110] Montgomery
recognized God as the origin of mission rather than the church. This
is an important distinction, which allows for an internal theological
critique of the church's now much-contested role in nineteenth- and
early-twentieth-century international missions. By naming God as the
origin of mission, the Trinity becomes the paradigm for human relationships both with God and with one another. Thus, the church is
held accountable to God's mission rather than the inevitable temptation to pursue a mission distinct from God's mission and defined by
human sin. Montgomery's use of mission seems to predate the larger
trend that scholars have dated to the missiologist Hartenstein, who
developed the term to describe Barth's teaching on the topic.[111]

Expanding this point with New Testament texts related to the
nature of God, she claimed, "the Bible records God's search for
[humanity] for the purpose of redemption and fellowship. . . . Other
sacred books record the story of [humanity's] search for God. The
Bible reverses the process."[112] This prioritizing of God's action reach-

---

[110] Montgomery, *The Bible and Missions*, 17. This shift is later demonstrated
among World Council of Churches' documents in the second half of the twentieth
century (Bosch, *Transforming Mission*, 377–78).

[111] According to Chris Wright, "The phrase *Missio Dei*, 'the mission of God', has
a long history. It seems to go back to a German missiologist, Karl Hartenstein. He
coined it as a way of summarizing the teaching of Karl Barth 'who in a lecture on mission in 1928 had connected mission with the doctrine of the trinity. . . . The phrase
became popular in ecumenical circles after the Willingen world mission conference
in 1952, through the work of Georg Vicedom" ("Mission as a Matrix for
Hermeneutics and Biblical Theology" [unpublished paper presented at the
University of St. Andrews: Scripture and Hermeneutics Seminar, August 2003], 72).
Wright looks to L. A. Hoedemaker's survey of the historical use of the phrase *missio
dei*, which according to Hoedemaker is not necessarily the key theological concept,
but points to the essential starting point of mission and evangelistic ministry—God;
God sends the church in mission to the world. Hoedemaker argues that to speak of
mission the ecumenical movement must be taken into account ("The People of God
and the Ends of the Earth," in A. Camps et al., eds., *Missiology, an Ecumenical
Introduction: Texts and Contexts of Global Christianity* [Grand Rapids: Eerdmans, 1995],
161–65, 171). For further discussion, see W. Scott, "Karl Barth's Theology of
Mission," *Missiology: An International Review* 3, no. 2 (1975): 209–24; G. Schwarz,
"The Legacy of Karl Hartenstein," *International Bulletin of Missionary Research* 8
(1984): 125–31; and C. Braaten, "The Triune God: The Source and Model of
Christian Unity and Mission," *Missiology: An International Review* 18 (1990): 415–27.

[112] Montgomery, *The Bible and Missions*, 16. Montgomery also claimed, "From
first to last [the Bible] is Christocentric." Although such a general statement leaves

ing out to humanity continues to provide significant theological resources for understanding evangelistic theology and practice as a faithful response to God. Humanity's beginning experience of faith is to receive God's unconditional love, rather than to pursue any particular task of obedience. Therefore, humanity's relationship with God begins with the kenotic (self-emptying) love of God, made manifest in the creation of the world ex nihilo (out of nothing), which then culminates in Jesus Christ's inauguration of the reign of God in his earthly ministry. Christian faith cannot begin with self-sufficiency demonstrated in a human's search for God, it must begin with God.

Returning to the Old Testament, Montgomery acknowledged the greater difficulty in tracing the missionary character of the historical books. Montgomery persevered in drawing attention to 1 Kings 8:41-43, in which Solomon's prayer of dedication illuminated Israel's vocation to provide the nations with a witness to God, "that all the peoples of the earth may know thy name, to fear thee, as doth thy people Israel and that they may know that this house which I have built is called by thy name." Although each genre of literature within the Old Testament includes a missionary component according to Montgomery, she acknowledged the particular clarity of the missionary message in the Psalms and the Prophets.[113] In these texts the missionary teachings include the following seven lessons:

1. A statement of the blessing for all the race held in trust by the chosen people.
2. A growing belief in the coming of a universal Kingdom of God under the sway of a Messianic ruler.
3. The universality of the Providential Government of God among the nations.
4. The emergence of a message for the individual believer as well as for the nation.
5. The distinct teaching that heathen nations are instruments of God.
6. The preaching of God's purposes of mercy to those outside the law.
7. The sudden coming of the Messenger, and the setting up of the Kingdom of God.[114]

---

room for critique, Montgomery's biblical theology seems to read the canonical (Old and New Testaments) texts theologically and narratively as Christian Scripture, while keeping in view the role of Torah as Jewish Scripture (16–17).

[113] Montgomery, *The Bible and Missions*, 24, 25, 27–51.

[114] Montgomery, *The Bible and Missions*, 51.

Despite the occasional limitations of her period, namely language and scholarship, by claiming the Old Testament as a resource for biblical theology, Montgomery's position adds substantially to the contemporary discourse. The use of the Old Testament as a basis for evangelism is rare even within current conversations.[115]

Turning her attention to the New Testament, she described her aim: "To show that the missionary principles laid down in the Old Testament are fully revealed in the New in the fundamental teachings of Jesus; in his life; and in his commands to his disciples; and that these principles are exemplified in the life of the Apostolic Church." The Church's missionary identity finds its foundation in the ministry and person of Jesus Christ. Montgomery outlined two foci for Jesus' thought: "(1) The Father God, whom he has come to reveal, and (2) The Kingdom of God, which he has come to establish."[116] Montgomery held in creative dialectic tension God's immanence and transcendence.[117]

> Only in the teachings of Jesus does [human]kind find a revelation of God infinite in holiness and absolute in power, who is also the Father, more eager than are earthly fathers to give good gifts to their little children, whose love runs out to the prodigal while still in the far country, and whose Holy Spirit makes his dwelling place in the hearts of his humble worshippers.[118]

Montgomery constructed a foundation for ministry, based on the holiness of God the Father, extended to humankind through Jesus Christ, and available through the Holy Spirit, thus reiterating the missionary character not only of the Bible, but of the triune God.

---

[115] Few scholars in the academic study of evangelism refer to Old Testament texts—creating a potentially Marcionite ethos. Walter Brueggemann's text, *Biblical Perspectives on Evangelism* (Nashville: Abingdon, 1993), is a notable exception. Bosch includes one of the few and more substantial references. He initially claims that "in the normal sense of the word" the Old Testament has nothing to do with mission, although he comments parenthetically that such a "normal" or "traditional" definition of mission "will be challenged in several ways" by his study. Bosch does concede, "Even so, the Old Testament is fundamental to the understanding of mission in the New" (*Transforming Mission*, 17).

[116] Montgomery, *The Bible and Missions*, 52, 56.

[117] Montgomery, *The Bible and Missions*, 57. For example, according to Montgomery, "In the religions that emphasize God's immanence, as does Hinduism, [they] tend constantly to drift into pantheism, and to lose any clear conception of the . . . power of sin, or the necessity of personal righteousness. In a religion that emphasizes God's transcendence, as does Islam, [they] tend to drift into formalism and fatalism."

[118] Montgomery, *The Bible and Missions*, 57.

God's grace has found a way so to express itself through the person and words of Christ that the resources of Divinity are placed at the disposal of [all]. It is in Christ we have our access, in Christ we realize our [role as children], in Christ we put off the old [self] and put on that new life born from above; in Christ we who were dead in trespasses and sins are made alive by the power of God; in Christ the love of God is shed abroad in our hearts. This is what the New Testament calls The Good News. This it is that we are commissioned to tell to the whole, wide world, that God was in Christ reconciling the world to himself.[119]

According to Montgomery, in Christ individuals receive new life through the love of God, which then leads to the sharing of this good news with the world. So, in Jesus' revelation of the Father and establishment of the reign, which grows forth from the revelation of the Father, individuals are invited into a new relationship both with God and humanity. Montgomery observed, "Throughout the Gospel narrative Jesus is engaged in teaching his disciples the true meaning of this Kingdom of God which he has already set up among them. His teachings form the very heart of our Christian message."[120]

In briefly describing Jesus' teachings on the reign of God, Montgomery begins by highlighting the theme of peace, responding specifically to her post-World War I context. "Jesus refused to bring in the reign of God by a revolution. . . . The Kingdom of God is, indeed, a revolutionary force in the world, but it is not to be set up by revolution."[121] She added, "The follower of Jesus can never expect to advance his Kingdom by a resort to violence; [one] must always believe in the might of meekness, and seek to transform life from the centre outward." Montgomery continued her characterization of the reign of God established by Jesus Christ citing Jesus' words from Luke 7:22-23. "Go and report to John what you have seen and heard; that the blind see, the lame walk, lepers are cleansed, the deaf hear, the dead are raised, and the poor have the Good News proclaimed to them. And blessed is every one who does not stumble because of my claims."[122]

---

[119] Montgomery, *The Bible and Missions*, 60.

[120] Montgomery, *The Bible and Missions*, 63.

[121] Montgomery, *The Bible and Missions*, 63–64. She continued, "There is a constant temptation to forget this and to seek to win the world to Christ by the very methods he pushed one side; to trust to political reform, to social amelioration, to better environment (things all good in themselves, and to be desired), to bring the Kingdom, and to despise or to overlook the very simple measures on which Jesus relied" (64).

[122] Montgomery, *The Bible and Missions*, 64, 66.

Montgomery read her context and responded to the fundamentalist-modernist controversy with her discussion of the missionary
character of the reign of God. "The clear teaching in regard to the
holiness of God has made impossible the divorce between religion
and ethics wherever the Bible is adequately taught or obeyed."[123]
Seemingly without taking sides in the polemic, she focused upon
aspects of each platform. To those focused upon narrow truths lacking in compassion she argued: "The Son of Man still goes about our
streets, still rebukes our narrow ideas of his heavenly Kingdom, still
calls us to look up from our preoccupation with secondary truths, and
look through his eyes of love at [human]kind. We are trustees of the
gospel, not its owners." And, to those focused upon the sufficiency of
a simple code of ethics, she argued: "In our Christian faith we have no
simple system of ethics, no noble ritual of religious faith. We have a
great overturning, transforming, revolutionary power to be released
throughout the world."[124] Montgomery then integrated her position
highlighting the role of the Holy Spirit:

> The Kingdom now is. Its King is present, working by the Spirit of
> the Living God on the hidden foundations of the unseen Empire of
> Jesus Christ. With no littleness, no sectarian bitterness, no nation-
> alistic limitations, all Christians everywhere are summoned to share
> in the works which our Lord taught us are the marks of his present
> Kingdom.[125]

Montgomery claimed, "[T]he Church has failed, up to the present
moment, to interpret her own worldwide mission. She has spent her
strength on definitions while the world lay in agony."[126] She presented
this dramatic exchange:

> I am asked, "Do you believe in foreign missions?" I answer, "Do you
> believe in the gospel of Christ?" For be assured of this, if foreign
> missions, when considered in the large, are a failure, the gospel is a
> failure. If Jesus Christ has no message for the [person] in Shanghai

---

[123] Montgomery, *The Bible and Missions*, 13. She added, "For there is a Plan,
although the phrase 'plan of salvation,' so popular in times past, is now seldom heard.
The trouble is not with the phrase or the idea behind it, but with its misapplication
and misuse. We do not send out missionaries to proclaim a 'plan of salvation,' but
Christ and the power of his resurrection. We are not saved by a 'plan,' but by a
Person" (14–15).

[124] Montgomery, *The Bible and Missions*, 65, 66, 66–67.

[125] Montgomery, *The Bible and Missions*, 66–67.

[126] Montgomery, *The Bible and Missions*, 22–23, 37–38.

that is worth giving my life, if need be, to get it to [him or her], he has no message for the [person] in London that I need bother about. He is either the Saviour of the whole world or he is no one's Saviour.[127]

In Montgomery's assessment, although the Church has failed thus far, "The gospel will not fail."[128] For Montgomery, the inescapable missionary character of the Bible included the missionary message that penetrates the book's entire structure,[129] Jesus' and the disciples' roles as missionaries,[130] the missionary role of the reign of God and of the early Church enabled by the Holy Spirit.[131]

> The Early Church did not alone support missionaries; it was missionary. It did not take pride in the heroic faith of the missionaries but feel that its own part was fulfilled if it paid the bills and listened with languid interest to the stories the missionaries told of their successes. These little churches were themselves missionary beehives. Everybody felt called to tell the Good News.[132]

Montgomery boldly claimed that when proclaiming the gospel as witness to the reign of God, only a compromising Church would find no opposition. "A compromising church finds smooth sailing. A missionary church can always count on her full share of head winds and tempests." She expanded this claim:

> The gospel is seen as no beautiful, ethical statement to be admired and written about. It is a desperate cause to be fought for and died for. Christ's message is presented not as something which wins easy acceptance, but as a challenge standing squarely athwart human selfishness and greed and sin, and so meeting deep hostility and opposition. The instinctive recognition, on the part of evil forces, of the gospel as a deadly foe is disclosed again and again in this mission text-book.[133]

Through this multifaceted missionary work, the early Church persisted in proclaiming a holistic witness to the reign of God.

---

[127] Montgomery, *The Bible and Missions*, 37–38.

[128] Montgomery, *The Bible and Missions*, 23.

[129] Montgomery, *The Bible and Missions*, 82.

[130] Montgomery, *The Bible and Missions*, 71, 73.

[131] Montgomery, *The Bible and Missions*, 66–70.

[132] Montgomery, *The Bible and Missions*, 88–89.

[133] Montgomery, *The Bible and Missions*, 84–85. This is admittedly a change in tone from the previous theme of the reign of God as a peaceful embodiment.

Montgomery, looking through the lens of Revelation, recited these words to the Church of her time: "In spite of enthroned evil, in spite of apparent failure and defection, the Kingdom of Christ will triumph. It is a universal Kingdom. [Persons] come into it out of every kingdom and tribe and tongue and nation."[134]

Evangelistic Practice

Montgomery allowed this theological framework of her scholarship to directly form strategies for evangelistic practice. At times in the current discourse, the theological and the strategic practices remain distinct and even estranged. Rather than succumbing to ideological presuppositions or trendy techniques, Montgomery maintained a rigorous theological reflection that directly informed active and effective ministry in a creative dialectic relationship.

For example, she lifted up fund-raising and lay leadership, including women, not as a result of rational problem-solving or a capitalist/market-driven ideology valuing assets and extensive work forces. These strategies emerged from her exegesis of the biblical texts. Montgomery reminded the reader that immediately following his proclamation of the gospel in Romans 10:11-13, Paul adds a practical note regarding fund-raising in Romans 10:14-15.

> These words and those others of Paul in regard to the missionary contributions which he was gathering among his Gentile converts to take to the poor saints in Jerusalem have been read in innumerable missionary meetings, and have stirred many sluggish consciences in our days to realize that giving money is a part of preaching the gospel.[135]

Likewise, Montgomery recognized the broad-based responsibility of Christians to nurture others in the faith, rather than focusing this substantial task solely among the clergy.

> A beautiful sidelight on the fellowship of ministry which prevailed in the Early Church is found in the personal greetings with which Paul closes his letters. Here is reflected no hierarchy propagating

---

[134] Montgomery, *The Bible and Missions*, 91.

[135] Montgomery, *The Bible and Missions*, 85. Montgomery adds the following texts related to giving money: Romans 15:26; 1 Corinthians 16:1-21; 2 Corinthians 8:1-15; Acts 11:29.

the faith through solemnly official channels, but groups of men and women bound by one fraternal purpose.[136]

Montgomery elaborated her argument referring to numerous lay-women such as Phoebe, Priscilla, Mary, Junia, Tryphaena, Tryphosa, Rufus's mother, and Lydia. "In fact, the prominence of women workers in these early lists is little less than amazing, when the social customs of the times are considered."[137] Montgomery then continued the comprehensive list, adding many male counterparts and concluding with the following.

> The study of this Missionary Church of the Apostolic Age is sorely needed in the present age. The greatest danger of the missionary enterprise is that it may be officialized, externalized, becoming the cult of a group rather than the expression of the church's life. No missionary study can so powerfully counteract this danger as the study of New Testament Christianity both as interpreted by Christ himself, and in the life of the Apostolic Church.[138]

Montgomery offered a carefully crafted biblically grounded theology and practice that contributed to the woman's international ecumenical missionary movement before navigating the difficult landscape of the fundamentalist-modernist polemic. This exquisite combination of theologically astute scholarship and savvy practical strategies could make rich offerings to the contemporary discussion on evangelistic theology and practice.

> *A compromising church finds smooth sailing. A missionary church can always count on her full share of head winds and tempests.*[139]

---

[136] Montgomery, *The Bible and Missions*, 85–86.
[137] Montgomery, *The Bible and Missions*, 86.
[138] Montgomery, *The Bible and Missions*, 88.
[139] Montgomery, *The Bible and Missions*, 85.

Mary McLeod Bethune, Library of Congress

6

⤙Mary McLeod Bethune⤚

The church is beginning to acquire new courage in the application to life of the great moral truths. . . . But too often these principles are merely preached in beautiful language when there is the pressing need to set them forth in the specific language of deed.[1]

Mary McLeod Bethune (1875–1955) achieved an astonishing amount in her lifetime. She was the first African-American woman to establish a four-year institution of higher learning,[2] to found a national organization to lobby the federal government,[3] and the first African American to hold such a high-level government appointment as director of the Negro Division of the National Youth Administration.[4] She

---

[1] M. M. Bethune, "Girding for Peace," Mary McLeod Bethune Foundation Papers, Daytona Beach, Florida, n.d., 6, quoted in C. Newsome, "Mary McLeod Bethune and the Methodist Episcopal Church North: In but Out," in *This Far by Faith: Readings in African-American Women's Religious Biography*, ed. J. Weisenfeld and R. Newman (New York: Routledge, 1996), 137.

[2] Bethune-Cookman College located in Daytona Beach, Florida.

[3] The National Council of Negro Women lobbied primarily on behalf of African-American women and children.

[4] This post was held during the presidency of Franklin Delano Roosevelt. "As the highest ranking black in the New Deal, Bethune met with President Roosevelt six or seven times a year and pushed privately and publicly to make the New Deal more sensitive to the issue of race. Bethune commanded considerable attention in the black community as leader of a group of black federal officials known as the Black Cabinet and as a champion for a variety of civil rights causes, including antilynching activities, the Scottsboro boys, and rights for black sharecroppers. She ended her work in Washington in 1944 and returned to Florida where she lived until her death in 1955"

advised three presidents and received numerous awards.[5] Between 1933 and 1945, Bethune was arguably the most powerful African-American person in the United States, and according to Bethune, this was largely due to the exercise of her Christian faith.[6] Bethune's Christian faith and the evangelistic ministry it inspired are most clearly demonstrated in her educational contributions, which are intimately related to her commitment to political action, specifically civil rights and racial justice.

While scholars acknowledge Bethune's open religiosity, a lifelong church member often publicly professing her Christian faith, much of the historiography related to Bethune emphasizes her efforts for social and economic justice related to racial reconciliation, which were staggering.[7] However, when viewed through Bethune's accounts these efforts grew from her Christian faith and included an evangelistic impetus. For example, Bethune clearly articulated her faith in Jesus Christ in her "Spiritual Autobiography," written at the age of seventy-one, in which she acknowledged her experience of faith and described her vocation.[8] In this piece, with complementary remarks from other materials written throughout her life, she revealed aspects of a simple con-

---

(O. Graham and M. R. Wander, eds., *Franklin D. Roosevelt: His Life and Times: An Encyclopedic View* [Boston: G. K. Hall, 1985], 26; see also 38–39, 278–80).

[5] Herbert Hoover, Franklin Delano Roosevelt, and Harry S. Truman. See Newsome, "Mary McLeod Bethune and the Methodist Episcopal Church North," 125.

[6] Newsome, "Mary McLeod Bethune and the Methodist Episcopal Church North," 125.

[7] For example, see A. T. McCluskey and E. Smith, eds., *Mary McLeod Bethune Building a Better World: Essays and Selected Documents* (Bloomington: Indiana University Press, 2001); R. Holt, *Mary McLeod Bethune: A Biography* (Garden City, N.Y.: Doubleday, 1964); G. Lerner, ed., *Black Women in White America: A Documentary History* (New York: Vintage Books, 1992); A. Broadwater, *Mary McLeod Bethune: Educator and Activist* (Berkeley Heights, N.J.: Enslow Publishers, 2003), Graham and Wander, *Franklin D. Roosevelt*. An exception is Newsome's essays "Mary McLeod Bethune and the Methodist Episcopal Church North" and "Mary McLeod Bethune as Religionist," in *Women in New Worlds: Historical Perspectives on the Wesleyan Tradition*, ed. Hilah F. Thomas and Rosemary Skinner Keller, vol. 1 (Nashville: Abingdon, 1981).

[8] M. M. Bethune, "Spiritual Autobiography," in *American Spiritual Autobiographies: Fifteen Self-Portaits*, ed. L. Finkelstein (New York: Harper & Row, 1948), 182–90. In reflecting upon Bethune's spiritual autobiography, it is important to acknowledge the opportunities and limitations of the material. As has been previously noted, according to Paula Fredriksen, "The historian works with the available evidence, the conversion narrative; and that narrative can reveal to him only the retrospective moment, and the retrospective self" ("Paul and Augustine: Conversion Narratives, Orthodox Traditions, and the Retrospective Self," *Journal of Theological Studies* 37 [1986]: 34).

structive ecclesiology that took seriously eschatology as the theological framework for her evangelistic ministry, focusing upon education.

Bethune committed her life to education after struggling with its inaccessibility as a result of race and class discrimination. Raised in a loving Christian family, Bethune gladly accepted educational opportunities in Christian mission contexts, initially through a small local school staffed by a Presbyterian missionary. Bethune later attended Scotia Female Seminary and eventually received admission to what would become Moody Bible Institute. She interpreted such opportunities as a setting apart. Although she felt a call to missionary work in Africa, the Presbyterian Foreign Mission Board denied her participation. As a result, she redirected her vocational trajectory to serve among African Americans in the South.

Her early vision identified the need among African-American girls for evangelistic education. This vision expanded into a denominationally sponsored institution for higher education. Throughout her decades-long leadership of the educational institution she founded, Bethune engaged in evangelistic education through the school's curriculum, equipping African-American youth for service in families, churches, and the world.

Formation in Faith

Mary Jane McLeod was born near Maysville, South Carolina, on July 10, 1875, to Patsy and Samuel McLeod, the fifteenth of seventeen children, following the Civil War in the waning years of Reconstruction, in the midst of the racial discrimination that touched every part of life.[9] When freed from slavery, her parents were active participants and leaders in an African-American Methodist congregation, which they may have also helped to organize.[10] According to her "Spiritual Autobiography," McLeod claimed that before birth she was

[9] Newsome, "Mary McLeod Bethune and the Methodist Episcopal Church North," 124. Her parents were most likely formed by the Christian ethos of the men to whom they belonged until the abolition of slavery. See also Bethune in "Charles S. Johnson, Interview with Bethune [abridged]" (1940), in McCluskey and Smith, "My mother kept in rather close contact with the people she served as a slave. She continued to cook for her master until she [saved enough to purchase] five acres of land. [Her former master] deeded her five acres. . . . She kept up these relations" (*Mary McLeod Bethune Building a Better World*, 36).

[10] Newsome, "Mary McLeod Bethune and the Methodist Episcopal Church North," 126.

given an unusual advantage. Her mother was "a consecrated, clear-thinking, careful woman," and her father "a principled man with more than average devotion to his family."[11] McLeod cherished her parents' loving examples that provided the foundation for her evangelistic vocation in which she claimed to emulate them. "I was loved before I came into being, and I have treasured this heritage of love and have made it the foundation of my life."[12] McLeod described her formation raised in a loving Christian home and in local church communities in which she learned disciplined Christian practices that provided the foundation for her evangelistic ministry vocation.

From her parents' loving example, McLeod explained that her "spiritual vigor" was "quickened and energized" through the discipline she received in her formation, particularly from her mother.[13] "Before I fully knew myself, my mother disciplined my life in order that I might know humility, stamina, faith, and goodness. I was shown goodness by precept and example."[14] McLeod was profoundly influenced by the depth and strength of her mother's Christian faith. "My mother had a great philosophy of life. She came down from one of the great royalties of Africa. She could not be discouraged. No matter what kind of plight we found ourselves in, she always believed there was, through prayer and work, a way out."[15] McLeod's formation in faith was characterized by her mother's cultivation of disciplined practices.

> Early in my childhood, my mother taught me to hold the little New Testament, which the minister brought around, and to sit quietly in

[11] Bethune, "Spiritual Autobiography," 182.

[12] Bethune, "Spiritual Autobiography," 182.

[13] Bethune, "Spiritual Autobiography," 183. Similar to Dorothy Ripley's relationship with her father, McLeod claimed to look to her parents, particularly her mother, for role models in the Christian faith; see R. L. Wilken, *Remembering the Christian Past* (Grand Rapids: Eerdmans, 1995), 122, 127, 131–32. According to Wilken, "Of the several paths that lead to virtue, the broadest and the most obliging is the way of imitation. By observing the lives of holy men and women and imitating their deeds, we become virtuous" (121). Like Ripley, McLeod's description of her mother's ministry and her influence upon her commission and evangelistic ministry exemplifies Wilken's description of the rise of Christian hagiography by the early fourth century and its two characteristic features: (1) imitation as the path to virtue, and (2) subjects with whom the author was acquainted (127, 131–32). John Westerhoff also names "Role Models" as an important component, among many, for catechesis, which for him follows evangelism and evangelization ("Evangelism, Evangelization, and Catechesis," *Interpretation* 48 [1994]: 164).

[14] Bethune, "Spiritual Autobiography," 183.

[15] Bethune in "Charles S. Johnson, Interview with Bethune [abridged]," 36–37.

communion with it and God, even before I could read. My tongue was ready to recite the 23rd Psalm and other precious passages from the written page, when once my intellect was prepared to meet the yearnings of my heart—to read the Scriptures.[16]

McLeod expounded the point of her formation in the Christian practices of her parents and community, "The *word* had been hidden in my heart by that knowing which is not literacy, but which is so basic to literacy." She invoked the example of spirituals to demonstrate such early and deep formation in faith. "As we sing the beautiful spirituals and remember that they flowed from unlearned hearts, we can appreciate more deeply how their social significance is interwoven with their spiritual understandings."[17]

Among the significant Christian practices that grew out of a life shaped by the Bible and modeled by her mother was daily prayer. For example, when her mother thought all in the house were asleep, she would hold vigil in prayer to God. McLeod's recollection echoes themes that appear in her constructive ecclesiology, which is discussed in a subsequent section.

There she was in the dark, on her knees. I knew the form, sometimes silhouetted by the moonlight which poured in upon her kneeling there—sometimes beside her bed, sometimes beside a chair. She would ask God for faith, for strength, for love, for forgiveness, for knowledge, for food and clothing—not for herself but for her children, and for all the poor people.[18]

McLeod, in reflecting upon her life in "Spiritual Autobiography," explained the significance of "meditation and communion" alone with God for her continued spiritual growth after the example of her mother. "I feel Him working in and through me, and I have learned to give myself—freely—unreservedly to the guidance of the inner

[16] Bethune, "Spiritual Autobiography," 183. McLeod's recollections seem to resonate with Brad Kallenberg's claim: "fluency is gained by participation in the linguistic community's form of life—that weave of activity, relationships, and speech that gives the community its unique personality." Kallenberg makes a related point, "The characteristic pattern of life of the entire believing community is to its speech what style is to a message" (*Live to Tell: Evangelism for a Postmodern Age* [Grand Rapids: Brazos, 2002], 41, 49).

[17] Bethune, "Spiritual Autobiography," 183. All italics in quotations are original unless otherwise noted. For further discussion on the role of spirituals in African-American Christian tradition, see J. Cone, *The Spirituals and the Blues: An Interpretation*, rev. ed. (Maryknoll, N.Y.: Orbis Books, 1991).

[18] Bethune, "Spiritual Autobiography," 185.

voice in me."[19] McLeod acknowledged that she gained faith from
watching her mother pursue Christian practices, such as reading the
Bible and prayer, and in witnessing those prayers answered.

> Many a poor man left our home happy because Mother and Father
> had given some simple thing that met his need. Many were the
> times that our little family was happy when a gift of something we
> needed came almost miraculously. And my mother's "Thank you,
> Father," made me realize—early in my life—that all things must
> come from God.[20]

These practices shaped by regular reading of the biblical texts and
prayer were not isolated from material needs, but rather demonstrated the necessary connection between practices of love of God and
neighbor within a specific context.

Although McLeod does not name a precise conversion experience
in her "Spiritual Autobiography," her description from late in life of
coming to faith in her youth alluded to theological themes of justification and sanctification. "My birth into wisdom and spiritual acceptance is a very real fact to me. Out of the womb of salvation and truth
my new life was born, and it is in that life that I live and move and
have my being."[21] Her "birth into spiritual acceptance" and its being
"a very real fact to me" seem to resemble a receiving of assurance, an
aspect of justification. McLeod remembered a longing "to know the
inner voice" and searching for the meaning of faith. The answer
"came about in the late hours of those nights when I listened to my
mother."[22] While watching her mother's example of Christian practices of biblical reading, prayer, and mutuality, McLeod searched for
faith and found it.

> As I grew I knew what it meant to absorb my will into the will of
> God, Whom I claimed as my Father. Where He reigned at first, I

---

[19] Bethune, "Spiritual Autobiography," 185

[20] Bethune, "Spiritual Autobiography," 185–86. Scott Jones offers further theological reflection on the multidimensional character of evangelism: "Evangelism must
be seen as both a divine activity and a human activity. . . . A holistic understanding of
evangelism is best understood as an interrelated set of practices in a congregational
context." Jones concludes that to evangelize is to love well (*The Evangelistic Love of
God and Neighbor: A Thology of Witness and Discipleship* [Nashville: Abingdon, 2003],
16–17, 21).

[21] Bethune, "Spiritual Autobiography," 182. Jones argues that "evangelism is best
understood as an aspect of the church's mission that seeks to help persons enter into
Christian discipleship" (*Evangelistic Love of God and Neighbor*, 65).

[22] Bethune, "Spiritual Autobiography," 185.

do not know; I am sure my child mind personalized Him, but when I knew Him to be a great Spirit, His fatherhood increased because His spirit could dwell in me and go with me and never leave me to my own devices.[23]

Educated in primarily Reform theological contexts, in both the mission school and female seminary, McLeod's later narration acknowledged aspects of justification, namely assurance and sanctification, namely the imparting of the Holy Spirit in her, which echo Wesleyan themes. Additionally, while a student in her early twenties she experienced a subsequent work of the Holy Spirit in a dramatic event, possibly indicating a receipt of entire sanctification.[24] Interestingly, McLeod's religious experiences reflect the expectations of the communities with which she affiliated either at the time, or as she narrated these in retrospect (e.g., her inclusion of Wesleyan doctrinal perspectives in her spiritual autobiography and her receiving a second distinct work of the Holy Spirit while studying at what would become Moody Bible Institute).

From childhood McLeod, formed in Christian practices, knew both what it was to seek God in the silence of solitude, as well as in communal relationships of mutuality after the example of her mother. She proclaimed a personal relationship with God, strongly influenced by the faith of her family and rural Christian community.[25] According to McLeod, "because my parents believed so implicitly in me and my understanding, I learned to believe in other people."[26] Through her formation in faith encouraged by her parents' example, a foundation was laid for her later vocation and evangelistic ministry.

Education

McLeod struggled with the inaccessibility of education largely as a result of racism. Around her eighth or ninth birthday she became self-aware of this lack of opportunity.[27]

---

[23] Bethune, "Spiritual Autobiography," 186.

[24] See A. F. Segal, *Paul the Convert: The Apostolate and Apostasy of Saul the Pharisee* (New Haven: Yale University Press, 1990), particularly 294 for further discussion of the community's effect upon the meaning of conversion.

[25] McCluskey, "Introduction," in McCluskey and Smith, *Mary McLeod Bethune Building a Better World*, 13.

[26] Bethune, "Spiritual Autobiography," 183.

[27] Newsome, "Mary McLeod Bethune as Religionist," 104–5.

I think that possibly the first and real wound that I could feel in my soul and mind was the realization of the dense darkness and ignorance that I found myself—when I did find myself—with the seeming absence of a remedy. What I mean by that was the recognition of the lack of opportunity. I could see little white boys and girls going to school every day, learning to read and write; living in comfortable homes with all types of opportunities for growth and service and to be surrounded as I was with no opportunity for school life, no chance to grow—I found myself very often yearning all along for the things that were being provided for the white children with whom I had to chop cotton every day, or pick corn, or whatever my task happened to be.[28]

On occasion, McLeod's mother returned to her former master's residence for work, and McLeod accompanied her.

I went out into what they called their play house in the yard where they did their studying. They had pencils, slates, magazines and books. I picked up one of the books and one of the girls said to me—"You can't read that—put that down. I will show you some pictures over here," and when she said to me, "You can't read that—put that down," it just did something to my pride and to my heart that made me feel that some day I would read just as she was reading.[29]

Such experiences deeply wounded McLeod, leaving her with vivid memories of the sharp pain of disenfranchisement as a result of racism. At the same time, those vivid images grew into passionate energy, motivating her later evangelistic vocation. "When I had my first experiences with people who could read, when I could not, and with seeing fine churches when my people worshipped in shacks, I asked God to open to me the opportunity to do something about that."[30] An interesting point of connection for the women in this study

[28] Bethune in "Charles S. Johnson, Interview with Bethune [abridged]," 35.

[29] Bethune in "Charles S. Johnson, Interview with Bethune [abridged]," 36.

[30] Bethune, "Spiritual Autobiography," 186. While the situation of education for African Americans at the turn of the twentieth century was not void of bright spots, it was extremely difficult. Church-related educational programs led early efforts that attempted to bring education among African Americans alongside efforts among all disenfranchised. However, African-American education seemed to remain "on the heels" of mainstream educational programs that continued to harbor white racism. Even when attention shifted away from Christian affiliations or focus, Christian leaders and themes continued to provide momentum and structure—for example, the Capon Springs Conferences initiated by Edward Abbott, brother of Lyman Abbott. See R. White Jr., *Liberty and Justice for All: Racial Reform and the Social Gospel (1877–1925)*, rev. ed. (Louisville, Ky.: Westminster/John Knox, 2002), 78, 77–90.

is the significance of education to their formations in faith and subsequent vocations, many of which like McLeod integrated education into their evangelistic ministries.

An answer to McLeod's persistent childhood prayers, the Presbyterian Board for Freedmen opened a school in October 1884 in Maysville's Trinity Presbyterian Church, an African-American congregation affiliated with the Presbyterian Church, USA.[31]

> One day we were out in the field picking cotton and the mission teacher came from Maysville, five miles away, and told mother and father that the Presbyterian church had established a mission where the Negro children could go and that the children would be allowed to go. I was among the first of the young ones to enroll.[32]

McLeod, though one of the youngest in her family, was chosen by her parents to enroll in school, the first in her family to receive any formal education. Therefore, McLeod perceived that God had set her aside for a special purpose.[33] McLeod first glimpsed what that purpose might be in the role model of Miss Emma Wilson, the African-American and Presbyterian missionary sent to conduct the school. In McLeod's words, "The Presbyterian church sent a woman, Miss Emma Wilson, a very fa[i]r Negro—couldn't tell her from white. [S]he was the first [black] person we knew to call 'Miss.' "[34] Wilson provided guidance for both McLeod's intellectual and spiritual growth grounded in the Golden Rule, an important biblical and theological framework within which her vocation and evangelistic ministry would emerge.[35]

Although the initial setting was modest, the mission school provided the context in which McLeod began her early education.

---

[31] Newsome, "Mary McLeod Bethune and the Methodist Episcopal Church North," 126. Within ten years of the Civil War's end, northern missionaries had established more than one thousand schools in the South for emancipated African Americans. However, momentum was quickly lost, and major organizations dissolved by 1870, leaving denominational efforts the strongest among Methodists, Baptists, and Presbyterians. These educational missions led to the establishment of local churches. While Methodists were very effective in recruiting southern African-American membership, African-American Presbyterians never accounted for more than 1 percent of total denominational membership (White, *Liberty and Justice for All*, 62, 63, 64; see also 61–74).

[32] Bethune in "Charles S. Johnson, Interview with Bethune [abridged]," 36.

[33] Newsome, "Mary McLeod Bethune as Religionist," 105.

[34] Bethune in "Charles S. Johnson, Interview with Bethune [abridged]," 40.

[35] Newsome, "Mary McLeod Bethune as Religionist," 105.

It was a small church. There were some home-made benches, a little table, and desks, a little pulpit, a little wood stove in the corner
. . . had a blackboard on the wall. . . . The first morning I went in,
Miss Wilson was standing at the door and received me. There was
a crowd of boys and girls. [M]ost of them [were] very crudely
dressed, just as you find in any rural school today. We had our little
singing that morning, prayer, Bible lesson. We were started on our
way to learning![36]

In the school's second year of operation, Maysville Institute occupied
its own two-room yellow-brick facility adjacent to the church.
Through her enrollment at the school, McLeod became involved
with the congregation of Trinity Presbyterian Church, attending
Sunday worship and participating in Sunday school and numerous
other programs.[37] Upon graduating from Maysville Institute, McLeod
and her classmates professed their faith before the elders of the congregation. Each student was questioned regarding their belief in God
and assurance of eternal salvation. The students were examined
according to a catechism, and each publicly professed a confession of
faith, upon which at age twelve McLeod was received as a member of
Trinity Presbyterian Church.[38]

    After completing her education at the mission school, which
equated to approximately the sixth or seventh grade, McLeod
returned to work in the cotton fields. In later remarks she claimed to
continue to encourage "the community to keep alive the interest in
education." McLeod explained that her experience of education at the
mission school did not ostracize her from her family and community,
but rather endeared her. "I became a very definite favorite in the family—my mother, father, sisters and brothers, people in the community
all loved me."[39] She described her motives as serious and unselfish in
wanting to contribute to the life and work of the community.

When I got so I could do the counting, all the papers—of both the
whites and colored people—were put into my lap—the papers
showing the weights of the cotton. . . . When we went to pick cotton for white people they said, 'Let Mary Jane put down the number of pounds.' I became useful. . . . I won the[ir] respect and

[36] Bethune in "Charles S. Johnson, Interview with Bethune [abridged]," 40.
[37] Newsome, "Mary McLeod Bethune and the Methodist Episcopal Church
North," 126–27.
[38] Holt, *Mary McLeod Bethune*, 29.
[39] Bethune in "Charles S. Johnson, Interview with Bethune [abridged]," 42, 39.

admiration. I made my learning, what little it was, [help others. I did nothing] that would put me above the people about me.[40]

Although pleased that her community appreciated her education and respected her contributions, McLeod continued her intercessions for further educational opportunities, adding for the purpose "that I might be of service to others." Thus, by her recollection McLeod seemed to wish to communicate that her pursuit of further education was not a selfish endeavor but rather a means of equipping her for ministry. Her prayers were again answered on an October day when Miss Wilson came to speak with McLeod's parents in the field where McLeod and her family were working.

> They had been sending out literature about the work done at Maysville mission and a piece of the literature had gotten into the hands of a white woman in Denver, Colorado, Miss Mary Chrisman—a rural school teacher who would often do dress-making after school hours—who became interested in what had been done for the Negro children in South Carolina and wrote to the teachers asking if they could find a little girl who would make good if given a chance, and that out of the money she was earning, she would give for the little girl's education.[41]

Miss Wilson had come to give McLeod's parents the news—their daughter had been selected to attend Scotia Seminary for Negro Girls in Concord, North Carolina. Like Maysville Institute, Scotia Seminary was also supported by the Presbyterian Church, USA.[42]

> It was a thrilling day for me, when I was called from the field by my father and teacher said, "Mary Jane, would you like to go to Scotia?" I asked, "What is Scotia?" and they told me it was a school in Concord, North Carolina, and that a good woman was going to send me. I pulled my cotton sack off, got down on my knees,

[40] Bethune in "Charles S. Johnson, Interview with Bethune [abridged]," 39.

[41] Bethune in "Charles S. Johnson, Interview with Bethune [abridged]," 42.

[42] Bethune in "Charles S. Johnson, Interview with Bethune [abridged]," 42, 44. Scotia Seminary was renamed Barber-Scotia College in 1932; it became coeducational in 1955. The school was chartered by the state of North Carolina in 1870 and founded in 1867 by Luke Dorland, an European American leader in the Presbyterian Church. During McLeod's enrollment the school was governed by Dr. David Satterfield. See also Newsome, "Mary McLeod Bethune and the Methodist Episcopal Church North," 127.

clasped my hands, and turned my eyes upward and thanked God for the chance that had come.[43]

McLeod prepared to begin Scotia Seminary in the early autumn of 1888. Not only her parents but also friends and neighbors helped with the preparations, contributing clothes and other supplies for her new endeavor.

> So mother and father started getting me ready to go. I did not have a trunk. We used to have cracker boxes. We kept our clothing in them, so my father went down and got me a little trunk. Some neighbors knitted a pair of stockings, some gave me a little linsey dress, little aprons, this that and the other, and when that October day came I can see myself now, going down to Maysville to take the train for the first time in my life.[44]

A moving memory for McLeod, numerous neighbors stopped their work on the afternoon of her departure, some rode in wagons and ox-carts, others on mules and horses, while still others walked. "They were going to Maysville to put me on the train to go to school." McLeod experienced a strange feeling as she wondered what it was all about. "My little heart was going pit-a-pat. I can see my mother as she clasped me in her arms and she said, 'God bless my child.' Tears and hand-shakes; all bidding little Mary good-bye."[45] Even as a young adolescent, McLeod sensed the enormity of her opportunity and the

---

[43] Bethune in "Charles S. Johnson, Interview with Bethune [abridged]," 42.

[44] Bethune in "Charles S. Johnson, Interview with Bethune [abridged]," 42–43.

[45] Bethune in "Charles S. Johnson, Interview with Bethune [abridged]," 43. In an interesting study of the Presbyterian periodical, *The Church at Home and Abroad* (1890–1898), Anne Blue Wills reveals the difficulty of mapping missionary identity in Presbyterian missions to freedpeople. Her reflection analyzes the complexity of an incarnational Christian evangelistic ministry with an acknowledged integration of American citizenship (A. B. Wills, "Mapping Presbyterian Missionary Identity in *The Church at Home and Abroad*, 1890–1898," in *The Foreign Missionary Enterprise at Home: Explorations in North American Cultural History*, ed. D. H. Bays and G. Wacker [Tuscaloosa: University of Alabama, 2003], 95–105). While education among African Americans at the turn of the century seemed to advocate the industrial model after the example of Tuskegee, for McLeod and others, education represented opportunity for a holistic transformation inclusive of spiritual and economic implications; see White, *Liberty and Justice for All*, 89. According to Ernest Thompson's study, education and evangelism among African Americans in Presbyterian traditions was closely intertwined, particularly in the south after the Civil War; see E. T. Thompson, "Black Presbyterians, Education and Evangelism after the Civil War," *Journal of Presbyterian History* 51 (1973): 174–98.

implications not only for her future but also what her opportunity represented for her community.

Upon arriving at Scotia Seminary, McLeod encountered numerous new experiences and unfamiliar surroundings, but a sense of excitement pervaded all.

> I got to Concord, was met at the station [and] taken to this beautiful brick building. I had never been in a brick building before. I was taken upstairs. I had never been upstairs before. I was taken into a beautiful little room, with two beds; [there was a] pretty spread on my bed. Oh, it was different, so different. I was received by the matron, and my roommate who was named Janie Shankle. Oh, she was so patient and kind to me. I got down on my little knees and thanked God.[46]

McLeod remembered her first morning at the school and her eagerness to engage in the community's life. She described the beautiful dining room, with white tablecloths, knives, and forks. "I made so many blunders not knowing whether to use my knife or fork." McLeod seized every activity and task no matter how menial as an opportunity to learn, whether in the chorus or on the debate team, doing laundry, baking, or scrubbing. McLeod perceived her time at Scotia Seminary, as she perceived all her education, as a preparation for the tasks awaiting her. McLeod made note that her time at Scotia Seminary "was the first time I had had a chance to study and know white people. They had a mixed faculty at Scotia. I can never doubt the sincerity and interest of some white people when I think of my experience with my beloved, consecrated teachers who took so much time and patience with me at a time when patience and tolerance were needed." For McLeod, the highlight of her six years at Scotia Seminary was her contact with the teaching faculty. These women gave her vision, ability, incentive, and empowerment.[47] McLeod's relationships and rapport with the relatively diverse faculty may have contributed some precedent for her efforts toward racial cooperation.

Her time at Scotia Seminary further shaped her emerging Christian vocation to an evangelistic educational ministry. Miss Wilson and more specifically the Scotia Seminary curriculum's dual

---

[46] Bethune in "Charles S. Johnson, Interview with Bethune [abridged]," 43. Admittedly, Newsome claims the Maysville Institute moved into a yellow-brick building in its second year of operation ("Mary McLeod Bethune and the Methodist Episcopal Church North," 126–27).

[47] Bethune in "Charles S. Johnson, Interview with Bethune [abridged]," 43–44.

focus upon academic and vocational training of "head, heart, and hand" contributed to her later educational leadership. In addition to this dual focus, Scotia Seminary, and later Lucy Laney, for whom McLeod later apprenticed at Haines Institute, encouraged a philosophy of "female uplift," which trained girls and young women for civic leadership.[48]

Following her graduation from Scotia Seminary in 1894, McLeod attended the training school founded by Dwight L. Moody, which would become Moody Bible Institute.[49] She was the first African American to enroll there.[50] While pursuing her training, McLeod received a "mighty baptism of the Holy Spirit,"[51] resembling an experience of entire sanctification. Years later she confessed that this pivotal spiritual experience, mediated by Dwight Moody's intercessions, made all her thoughts, words, and actions effective.[52]

Vocation

McLeod's interest in mission and eventual training in that area was awakened at the age of twelve when she heard an address on Africa's "need of missionaries to carry them the light":

> It was a rainy, cold night, we had driven from Maysville, ten miles, with father, who was going to sell cotton the next day. We found

[48] McCluskey, "Introduction," in McCluskey and Smith, *Mary McLeod Bethune Building a Better World*, 4–5.

[49] In addition to his fame as an itinerant preacher, Moody also established schools for young people in Northfield, Illinois, his hometown, and a bible training school in Chicago that targeted students without the financial means to attend college. The latter institution was renamed by the trustees in honor of Moody after his death. According to Grant Wacker, in the twentieth century, Moody Bible Institute would thrive as one of the "wealthiest, strongest, most prestigious of the conservative Protestant colleges" (*Religion in Nineteenth-Century America* [New York: Oxford University Press, 2000], 143).

[50] McCluskey, "Introduction," in McCluskey and Smith, *Mary McLeod Bethune Building a Better World*, 4–5; Newsome, "Mary McLeod Bethune and the Methodist Episcopal Church North," 127. Interestingly, Moody Bible Institute graduated its last woman from the Pastor's Class in 1929, according to Betty DeBerg (*Ungodly Women: Gender and the First Wave of American Fundamentalism* [Minneapolis: Fortress, 1990], 84).

[51] M. M. Bethune, untitled autobiographical statement, Mary McLeod Bethune Foundation papers, Daytona Beach, Florida, n.d., 4–5; quoted in Newsome, "Mary McLeod Bethune and the Methodist Episcopal Church North," 127.

[52] Newsome, "Mary McLeod Bethune and the Methodist Episcopal Church North," 127.

that Dr. Bowen was to speak at the Methodist church. I got with Sister and went over to hear him. As I heard him tell about African people and the need of missionaries, there grew in my soul the determination to go some day and it has never ceased, and I sent up a prayer to God to give me the light, to show me the way that I, in turn, might show others.[53]

As a result of this presentation, McLeod felt a strong vocation to foreign mission work in Africa. However, upon completion of her evangelistic training at Moody in 1895 the Presbyterian Board of Mission refused her application. "They informed me that no openings were available where they could place Negro missionaries."[54] Although disappointed she would not have the opportunity to introduce Africans to Christianity, she returned south to assume a teaching position, eventually realizing a clarification of her missional call to serve among persons of African descent in the American South.[55] "And for years I just had a yearning to go to Africa and thought that when I was through with my education I could be sent, but instead, I found my way into the deep South."[56] She apprenticed in several Christian educational missions in the Southeast before establishing her own in Daytona, Florida, in 1904.

McLeod described early evidences of her vocation in childhood. "I had more of a missionary spirit—the spirit of doing things for others. Any one sick in the community, I would tantalize my mother to make them some soup. If any child had no shoes, I always wanted to share my shoes. She had to watch me to keep me from giving away things that were mine."[57] In her early twenties and having completed substantial education, including theological, McLeod's vocation turned definitively toward Christian service. Although not fully clarified, her vocation included a component of evangelistic ministry despite her thwarted expectation of pursuing this ministry primarily in the African mission field. McLeod's vocation would not be fully clarified until early in the twentieth century. However, after the denial of the Presbyterian Board of Foreign Missions to appoint her to mission work in Africa, McLeod accepted an appointment in 1895, by the

[53] Bethune in "Charles S. Johnson, Interview with Bethune [abridged]," 42.
[54] Bethune in "Charles S. Johnson, Interview with Bethune [abridged]," 42.
[55] Newsome, "Mary McLeod Bethune as Religionist," 107.
[56] Bethune in "Charles S. Johnson, Interview with Bethune [abridged]," 42.
[57] Bethune in "Charles S. Johnson, Interview with Bethune [abridged]," 38.

Presbyterian Board of Education to a teaching position at Haines Institute in Augusta, Georgia.[58]

Haines Institute was founded and led by Lucy Croft Laney, a former slave. As Laney's apprentice, McLeod was further directed toward serving among African Americans in the South. Laney's mentoring built upon the previous foundation of Miss Wilson and Scotia Seminary, reiterating the notion that through education African-American women should assume the "burden" of uplift for their families. Such women would then provide Christian and moral leadership both at home and in their communities. Laney added to this familiar foundation a nuance of political activism by women for the purpose of alleviating social and economic oppression.[59]

Laney was a significant influence upon McLeod's vision for the Christian formation of African-American youth, especially girls. Laney started Haines Institute in the basement of her church. McLeod recalled Laney, with other strong women of faith she encountered—"All were a great inspiration to me":

> I was so happy for the chance to blend my life with the lives of those women—Lucy Laney with her spirit of service, quick steps, determination, will, alert mind, again demonstrated to me that it could be done. I studied her, watched her every move and gave myself full to the cause she represented.[60]

While working alongside Laney, McLeod put into practice some of her training from what would become Moody Bible Institute. Haines Institute was located in a densely settled African-American community with numerous children who played in the streets on Sunday afternoons. Feeling there was a chance to help these children, McLeod requested permission of Laney to start a mission Sunday school. "I took the girls of . . . my own class and went out and combed

---

[58] Newsome, "Mary McLeod Bethune and the Methodist Episcopal Church North," 128.

[59] McCluskey, "Introduction" in McCluskey and Smith, *Mary McLeod Bethune Building a Better World*, 5. See also Bethune, "A Philosophy of Education for Negro Girls" (1926) in McCluskey and Smith, *Mary McLeod Bethune Building a Better World*, 84–86.

[60] Bethune in "Charles S. Johnson, Interview with Bethune [abridged]," 50. McLeod also named Mamie McCrory Jackson and Irene Smallwood Bowen. "How Mrs. Jackson stood side-by-side with Lucy Laney, gave twenty-five years of her life helping build Haines Institute, and Irene Smallwood who gave years and years."

the alleys and streets and brought in hundreds of children until we had a Sunday School of almost a thousand young people."[61]

McLeod continued during the next several years mostly in similar missional and Christian educational roles living in Georgia, South Carolina, and Florida while caring for her aging parents, meeting and marrying Albertus Bethune in 1898, and giving birth to her only son, Albert, in 1899.[62] After working with a Presbyterian minister in Palatka, Florida, who invited her to organize a school in connection with his local church, she moved to Daytona Beach late in the summer of 1904.[63] In October of that same year she opened Daytona Educational and Industrial School for Negro Girls.[64]

Claiming a missionary spirit from childhood, Bethune integrated this inclination with her desire to seek and provide education, as well as to work against the racial oppression and disenfranchisement of African Americans.

> When I look back 79 years ago, I see myself coming from the home life of slaves. My mother and father were slaves in America. We were hungry and thirsting for help, for light, for that thing that would help us to grow and become what we believed our God and your God wanted us to be. We wanted light, intelligence; we

[61] Bethune in "Charles S. Johnson, Interview with Bethune [abridged]," 50.

[62] McCluskey, "Introduction" in McCluskey and Smith, *Mary McLeod Bethune Building a Better World*, 5; see also Newsome, "Mary McLeod Bethune and the Methodist Episcopal Church North," 127–29.

[63] Newsome, "Mary McLeod Bethune and the Methodist Episcopal Church North," 127–29. See also McCluskey, "Introduction" in McCluskey and Smith, *Mary McLeod Bethune Building a Better World*, 5; and Bethune: "I got to Palatka and started . . . this community school and worked in the jails two and three times a week. [I went] out to the sawmills there and, in general, among the young people in clubs there, and built up a very interesting setting. I stayed there for five years. Then I made up my mind to go down on the East coast and study the situation there and see what was being done, and found very little being done" (in "Charles S. Johnson, Interview with Bethune [abridged]," 47).

[64] McCluskey, "Introduction" in McCluskey and Smith, *Mary McLeod Bethune Building a Better World*, 5. The school's establishment is discussed in more detail in the final section: "Albertus helped with the school initially and was listed as a member of the board of trustees in 1906, but he clearly played a minor role in his wife's expanding orbit. Albertus Bethune left the family in 1907 and returned to South Carolina. Although they never divorced, Mary Bethune's apparent uneasiness about how the social ramifications of marital failure reflected upon her image led to her being listed in the 1910 U.S. census as a widow even before Albertus died in 1918."

wanted that spiritual guidance that would guide us into that full manhood and womanhood that could help bless the world.[65]

In these remarks she intentionally connected the material and pragmatic needs of her community, represented by the language of "light," which in this context she seemed to equate with intelligence and spiritual guidance. In her ministry, an intentional though at times more implicit evangelistic component emerged in this integral connection of spiritual and material needs of individuals and communities. "Because of what God has done for me, because of the spiritual guidance I sought to the extent of my ability, I felt called of Him . . . to go out and open a way, make a path, that they could follow."[66] Bethune characterized her life's work of establishing and leading an educational institution for African Americans, in addition to her political advocacy for racial justice and reconciliation, as the fulfillment of her Christian calling. In one of her last speeches, Bethune again recounted her life of service, expressing her humble gratitude to God. "Be quiet, let the tears of gratitude flow because you have been humble enough to permit a great God to take a life, reshape it and mold it and send it out to give off sunshine and love, peace, [and] brotherhood among all men regardless of their creed, their caste, their color."[67]

Theological Emphases: An Eschatological Ecclesiology

Bethune's unfolding evangelistic theology informed by the biblical foundation of the "Golden Rule" addressed the often debilitating systemic sins of racism with a simple constructive ecclesiology that took seriously a robust eschatology in its dual emphasis upon present Christian discipleship and the fulfillment of God's reign yet to come. Bethune did not offer substantial detail regarding theological influences to confidently locate her spiritual formation in a particular doctrinal tradition. By piecing together various themes of a more general theological tenor—for example, the framework for her life's work: love and the Golden Rule—with aspects of the socioeconomic land-

---

[65] Bethune, "Address to a World Assembly for Moral Re-Armament" (Caux, Switzerland, July 27, 1954), in McCluskey and Smith, *Mary McLeod Bethune Building a Better World*, 56.

[66] Bethune, "Address to a World Assembly for Moral Re-Armament," 56–57.

[67] Bethune, "Address to the National Council of Negro Women Brotherhood Luncheon" (1955), in McCluskey and Smith, *Mary McLeod Bethune Building a Better World*, 281.

scape of her life and time, elements of a simple ecclesiology emerges. Bethune's constructive ecclesiology offers a critique of those within contemporary American Protestantism that emphasize an eschatology of the world to come, overlooking the present implications for Christian discipleship in communities of faith.

Biblical Foundations

Bethune's evangelistic vocation that witnessed to a multidimensional gospel of Jesus Christ functioned within a simple, but significant, understanding of the church.[68] Although Bethune's materials offer substance for theological reflection, these are not systematic, nor sophisticated in argument. However, with some attention to similar themes in light of the social and political context of the church in the late nineteenth and first half of the twentieth centuries, some significant contributions can be distilled for contemporary evangelistic theology and practices. Bethune's contributions, which emerge from her emphasis upon Christian practices for faith formation, focus upon the implications of these practices in response to one's salvation for justice and reconciliation within Christian communities and beyond.

According to Bethune, "Love is a universal factor." She claimed love transcends "pettiness, discrimination, segregation, narrowness, and unfair dealings" with regard to one's opportunities to grow and serve. Indeed, she identified love as the basis of her faith formation as mentioned earlier: "I was loved before I came into being, and I have treasured this heritage of love and have made it the foundation of my life."[69] From this formation in faith her vocation then grew in love to humankind. "It seems to me that from the very beginning I have practiced the affirmation of my devotion to love of humanity, and I have precious contentment in my realization of God as my spiritual Father." Bethune's profound impact on the social, political, and economic lives

---

[68] Bethune's constructive response resonates with Abraham's analysis, "The solution is to recognize that the problem is ecclesiological: failure to focus on the kingdom is precisely a failure in ecclesiology. It is to ignore the fact that the church exists in and for service to the kingdom out of which it originated" (W. Abraham, "On Making Disciples of the Lord Jesus Christ," in *Marks of the Body of Christ*, ed. C. E. Braaten and R. W. Jenson [Grand Rapids: Eerdmans, 1999], 160–61; quoted in Jones, *Evangelistic Love of God and Neighbor*, 71).

[69] Bethune, "Spiritual Autobiography," 188, 182.

of African Americans in the first half of the twentieth century grew
from her Christian faith, receiving and expressing such love.[70]

Guided by "the principle of the Golden Rule," Bethune cemented
the connection between her personal faith and ministry with others.

> In my spiritual life, the ideal of the Golden Rule charges me to con-
> tend for the products of whatsoever things are fair and whatsoever
> things are just, and for the quality of opportunities to become my
> best self—not Peter, not John, not Ruth, not Esther, but Mary
> McLeod Bethune. [. . .] As I received those things that are true, hon-
> est, lovely, and beautiful, I pray that others shall have them, too. Oh,
> how I love to open the doors to let people in to a fuller experience.[71]

As evidenced in the above, Bethune demonstrated a healthy sense of
self, which in a context of racial and gender discrimination provided an
important resource for her ministry. She supposedly often said, "I have
faith in God, and in Mary Bethune."[72] Bethune understood the
tremendous toll racial oppression excised from African Americans, not
only in social disenfranchisement from ordinary privileges of citizenship, but the constant weight that pressed upon individuals. "Faith in
God is the greatest power, but great, too, is faith in oneself."[73]

---

[70] For further discussion of the comprehensive witness (addressing spiritual and
material aspects of the gospel) in women's ministries in the midst of the divisiveness
of the period, see J. M. Schmidt, "Reexamining the Public/Private Split: Reforming
the Continent and Spreading Scriptural Holiness," in *Perspectives on American
Methodism: Interpretive Essays*, ed. Russell Richey et. al. (Nashville: Abingdon, 1993),
228–47; D. Dayton, *Discovering an Evangelical Heritage* (New York: Harper & Row,
1976), chaps. 8–10; and Douglas Strong's nuanced argument building on Dayton and
others in "The Crusade for Women's Rights and the Formative Antecedents of the
Holiness Movement," *Wesleyan Theological Journal* 27 (1992): 132–60.

[71] Bethune, "Spiritual Autobiography," 189. McLeod in referring to the "Golden
Rule" did not seem to include its text in her written materials or transcribed interviews implying an assumed formation in the biblical texts by writer and reader. The
"Golden Rule" according to Matthew 7:12 (NRSV) is "In everything do to others as
you would have them do to you."

[72] McCluskey, "Introduction," in McCluskey and Smith, *Mary McLeod Bethune
Building a Better World*, 8.

[73] Bethune, "My Last Will and Testament" (1955), in McCluskey and Smith,
Mary McLeod Bethune Building a Better World, 60. Her statement is not dissimilar to
the Grimkés' plea to "use the talents committed to thy charge" and Luce Irigaray's
lack of skin to envelope. See chap. 2 of this study and Serene Jones, *Feminist Theory
and Christian Theology: Catographies of Grace*, Guides to Theological Inquiry Series
(Minneapolis: Fortress, 2000), 42–43, 48, 49, 62, 67, 69. An even more pertinent
interpretation of Bethune's statement is D. Williams's groundbreaking work of womanist theology, *Sisters in the Wilderness: The Challenge of Womanist God-Talk*

"Boundless love ripens the ordinary life into one that is fuller and sweeter." This emphasis upon love can seem to have a pious façade, creating a seeming distance from the certain pain and suffering experienced in her struggles for justice. "Love, not hate has been the fountain of my fullness. In the streams of love that spring up within me, I have built my relationships with all [hu]mankind." Bethune's role model of such love is the person and ministry of Jesus Christ. "When hate has been projected toward me, I have known that the person who extended it lacked spiritual understanding. I have had great pity and compassion for them. Our Heavenly Father pitieth each one of us when we fail to understand. Jesus said of those who crucified Him, *Father, forgive them, For they know not what they do.*" Bethune called others to imitate the example of Jesus Christ in fashioning "spiritual tools" and cultivating "leadership" and "courage":[74]

> I think our Master, Jesus Christ, showed how the use of [spiritual tools] in His life brought courage and determination and even the quality of righteous indignation, when it was necessary to call people to a sense of their duty. I have not cringed; I have been a fighter for the things that are just and fair for myself and for my people—yes for *all* [hu]mankind.[75]

Bethune invoked the example of Jesus Christ, not only for courage and practices of righteous indignation for herself, the African-American community, and all humankind, but also for her understanding of Christian discipleship.[76] Bethune understood the

---

(Maryknoll, N.Y.: Orbis, 1993). For example, in her chapter "Color Struck: A State of Mind" (84–107), Williams demonstrates the impact of race and gender upon racial oppression in America; see also p. 9.

[74] Bethune, "Spiritual Autobiography," 187–88.

[75] Bethune, "Spiritual Autobiography," 188

[76] Similar emphases to Bethune's later echo in black liberation and womanist theologies. For example, James Cone also emphasizes the ministry and example of Jesus Christ. For Cone, "The grounding of liberation in God's act in Jesus Christ is the logical consequence of any Christian theology that takes Scripture seriously as an important source for the doing of theology" (*God of the Oppressed*, rev. ed. [Maryknoll, N.Y.: Orbis Books, 1997], 128). Interestingly, Albert Cleage expands upon the positions of many of the women in this study (some explicit and others implicit) related to the apostle Paul. "On the other hand, there is the spiritualized Jesus, reconstructed many years later by the Apostle Paul who never knew Jesus and who modified his teachings to conform to the pagan philosophies of the white gentiles. Considering himself an apostle to the gentiles, Paul preached individual salvation and life after death. We, as black Christians suffering oppression in a white man's land, do not need the individualistic and otherworldly doctrines of Paul and the white man" ("The

gospel of Jesus Christ as multidimensional, feeding both the spirit and the body with life-giving sustenance. "But the hungry cannot listen well to any teaching but that which relieves their hunger. Jesus knew this when he fed the multitude."[77] Her vocation to care for whole persons in the midst of social and economic oppression pervaded her life work and consciously offered an evangelistic witness. She included the following verses from a hymn she learned to sing "during the formative years of [her] life":

> Take time to be holy
> Speak oft with Thy Lord.
> Spend much time in secret
> With Jesus alone.
> By looking to Jesus
> Like Him thou shalt be.
> Thy friends in thy conduct
> His likeness shall see.[78]

Bethune's Christian discipleship, which sought to imitate Jesus Christ's life and ministry in love to humankind, formed not only her own relationship with God in Jesus Christ, but within a framework of love and the Golden Rule led her to pray and act evangelistically for others to receive that redemption. Bethune often expressed her gratitude for the opportunities and education that allowed her to open opportunities for others. Bethune perceived such preparation—for example, "in head, in hand and in heart"—to be for the purpose of leading humankind "from darkness and sin and point [them] to the light."[79] This quiet evangelistic component in Bethune's life work informed her remarkable public leadership efforts, specifically her efforts in educating young African Americans.

In order to make such a difference, Bethune advocated for the cultivation of Christian virtue in response to one's salvation as an aspect of sanctification, specifically among African-American youth. For

---

Black Messiah," in *Black Theology: A Documentary History*, ed. J. Cone and G. Wilmore, 2nd ed., vol. 1 [Maryknoll, N.Y.: Orbis Books, 1993], 101–2).

[77] Bethune, "Yes, I Went to Liberia" (1952), in McCluskey and Smith, *Mary McLeod Bethune Building a Better World*, 276.

[78] Bethune, "Spiritual Autobiography," 185. The words to the hymn based on Leviticus 19:2 were written by William D. Longstaff in 1882 to the tune "Holiness," composed by George C. Stebins in 1890.

[79] Bethune, "Address to a World Assembly for Moral Re-Armament," 56.

example, Bethune unpacked her notion of training in a speech entitled "The Lesson of Tolerance," delivered in 1952.

> Training ourselves and our children to have both tolerance and respect for opinions diverging from our own, is one of the best possible ways to promote brotherhood—among the peoples of the world, and among our neighbors in our block! They who admit righteousness, sincerity, good intentions, understanding—*and loyalty*—in no one but themselves . . . are unprepared for Democratic living.[80]

Bethune's emphasis upon democracy seemed to grow from her Christian formation and its implications for justice and reconciliation during a particular time in American history and identity. At times, democracy seemed a subset of Christianity for Bethune.

> Tyranny of opinion must never be our goal, for it is not the goal of Democracy or of Christianity. We must learn to *differ without denouncing; to listen without distrust; to reserve judgment.* "Judge not that ye be not judged. For with what judgment ye judge ye shall be judged. And with what measure ye mete, it shall be measured unto you again." You know the words, my friends.[81]

Though her political and ideological affirmations, and perhaps religious assumptions, may seem contradictory or confusing to some contemporary readers, Bethune's witness against tyranny of opinion was a profound one. Through Christian practices that responded to one's experience of salvation, which was not limited to an individual's spirituality, for the purpose of cultivating Christian virtues of tolerance, righteousness, attentiveness, patience, and forgiveness, Bethune labored to change the world for the better.

Bethune consistently integrated biblical allusions to Christian faith and discipleship in her writing and remarks, even in the midst of substantial openness—"I am strongly *inter*-denominational, *inter*-racial, and *inter*-national"[82]—in a larger Christian context of inclusivity. Bethune's openness and inclusivity must be located within her time and place, which was characterized by suspicion, fear, and oppression, particularly related to race and class, but also with regard to religious and political ideologies. Although her remarks at times

---

[80] Bethune, "The Lesson of Tolerance" (1952), in McCluskey and Smith, *Mary McLeod Bethune Building a Better World*, 267.

[81] Bethune, "The Lesson of Tolerance," 267.

[82] Bethune, "Spiritual Autobiography," 189.

expressed such broad religious and ideological openness that contemporary readers may conclude that an evangelistic component to her Christian faith was dubious, as an African-American woman, Bethune was writing and speaking in perilous times. Bethune left evidence of a powerful Christian witness to which she gave audible voice and substantial status as a national political and ecclesiastical leader. In her "Address to the National Council of Negro Women Brotherhood Luncheon" in 1955, Bethune expressed gratitude for the women's support of the effort to bring humankind closer together, "to rid them of hate and to fill them with love, to take away the spirit of segregation [and] discrimination and bind us together as one in a great democracy made by a great God."[83] For Bethune, democracy and openness in the context of faithful Christian practices were not merely a capitulation to social or political trends, but perhaps a prophetic witness against nominal Christian practices, most notably of racial segregation and discrimination.

An Eschatological Ecclesiology

Bethune left important pieces of a provocative ecclesiology for her time and context.[84] The early twentieth century witnessed some of the most atrocious violence against African Americans in widespread lynching, the most prevalent of any period; oppressive social restraints of segregation; and continued economic disenfranchisement for most.[85] "Our forefathers had been freed from the yoke of bondage

[83] Bethune, "Address to the National Council of Negro Women Brotherhood Luncheon," 281.

[84] Bethune's ecclesiological themes seem consistent with Kallenberg's later remarks, "In other words, the church is the foundation of the truth rather than the other way around. . . . [T]he world will not be able to evaluate the claims of the gospel unless they understand clearly what is the nature of the community that speaks these claims" (*Live to Tell*, 50).

[85] From 1891 to 1901, over 100 individuals were lynched each year. The numbers reached their reported high in 1892, when 226 were lynched—with 155 of these African Americans. While the number of reported lynchings declined, the number of African-American deaths rose with the total number of lynchings between 1889 and 1918 at 3,224, 78.2 percent African-American (see White, *Liberty and Justice for All*, 11–12). For an excellent historical study of women's efforts against lynching, see J. D. Hall, *Revolt Against Chivalry: Jessie Daniel Ames and the Women's Campaign Against Lynching*, rev. ed. (New York: Columbia University Press, 1993). See also D. Mathews, "Lynching Is Part of the Religion of Our People: Faith in the Christian South," in *Religion in the American South: Protestants and Others in History and Culture*, ed. B. B. Schweiger and D. Mathews (Chapel Hill: University of North Carolina

about twelve years when I was born. My early heritage was the spirit of fight and determination which had helped my parents and others to fight for freedom, and which was during my childhood helping them to build security for their children." Thus, when Bethune offered an interpretation of the "Church militant wherein we have membership until we are called to the Church triumphant which is without spot or wrinkle,"[86] there were clear implications for faithful Christian practices among African and specifically European Americans in the United States. These practices should be shaped, according to Bethune, "through love and faith and determination," which empowered her persistently to face obstacles both large and small. For Bethune, therefore, the church is called to presently struggle against such obstacles as an aspect of its faithful Christian discipleship and evangelistic witness.[87]

According to Bethune the mission of the church and its gospel mandate is the welfare and total well-being of each individual. Throughout her career she claimed that the church fell short of its calling because it tended not to proclaim "a religion that had meaning for this world and the present age."[88] For Bethune, "The truth is the

---

Press, 2004), 153–94. Mathews argues that American religion must take into account the experiences of the disenfranchised. He focuses on lynching as key.

[86] Bethune, "Spiritual Autobiography," 183, 189.

[87] Bethune's constructive eschatological ecclesiology emphasized both the future hope of the reign of God and the present missional role of the Church in the world, resonating with contemporary theological reflection upon salvation and its implications. For example, David Bosch argues that salvation, specifically in the gospel of Luke, has at least six dimensions: "economic, social, political, physical, psychological, and spiritual," and seems to pay special attention to the initial three. Bosch claims in relation to Luke that personal conversion is not a goal in itself. Rather, receiving Christian faith moves the individual believer into the community of faith and includes a real change of heart and life that brings moral responsibilities that distinguish Christians from "outsiders," while not abandoning those "outsiders." In this vein, Bethune seemed to expect more from the Christian community, and at times even her Christian nation, beyond testimonies of spiritual awakening and conversion into the frontier of Christian discipleship practices that make a difference. See D. J. Bosch, *Transforming Mission: Paradigm Shifts in Theology of Mission* (Maryknoll, N.Y.: Orbis Books, 1991), 117.

[88] Newsome, "Mary McLeod Bethune and the Methodist Episcopal Church North," 136. According to James Cone, "While white preachers and theologians often defined Jesus Christ as a spiritual Savior, the deliverer of people from sin and guilt, black preachers were unquestionably historical. . . . That was why the black Church was involved in the abolitionist movement in the nineteenth century and the civil rights movement in the twentieth" (*God of the Oppressed*, 51). William Abraham expresses the significance of eschatology to understanding evangelism by reflecting

Negro long lived a revivalistic emotion and was taught to think of heaven as a land of luxury to which he would pass after a life of burden in this world. The Negro needs an equality of religion. He needs a religion in which his religious feeling has matured into social passion." Bethune argued that the church should participate in the "full teaching of Jesus concerning the abundant life."[89] In a speech entitled "Girding for Peace" she asserted, "the church is beginning to acquire new courage in the application to life of the great moral truths. . . . But too often these principles are merely preached in beautiful language when there is the pressing need to set them forth in the specific language of deed."[90] Thus, Bethune called the Christian community to a present accountability.

---

upon the evangelistic ministry of early Christians. "[Eschatology] was not just a matter of some future hope that lay out there on the horizon of history and from which they then made certain inferences about a change in life-style. Eschatology was something that had already dawned and had brought a whole new direction and power into their lives. God had moved decisively to establish his reign; the events of the new age were already under way; the kingdom had come already in Jesus Christ; they now experienced the fullness of the Holy Spirit in their personal lives, in their corporate worship, and in their service to the world; and they eagerly looked forward to the full dawning of the consummation of God's final act when at long last his purposes for the cosmos would be realized" (*The Logic of Evangelism* [Grand Rapids: Eerdmans, 1999], 19).

[89] E. Martin, "Mary McLeod Bethune: A Prototype of the Rising Social Consciousness of the American Negro" (master's thesis, Northwestern University, 1958), 73, quoted in Newsome, "Mary McLeod Bethune and the Methodist Episcopal Church North," 136. For William Abraham, "Evangelism should be housed very firmly within the dynamic rule of God on earth" (*The Logic of Evangelism*, 18). Gayraud Wilmore offers the following commentary that seems to explain Bethune's earlier point: "Blacks in the United States and the Caribbean are, for the most part, Christians. But they are Christians in a way different from what we usually understand by the term. The nonsystematic, ambivalent Christianity of blacks has been understood in terms of evangelicalism or otherworldliness, but it has produced one of the most this-worldly, empirical religious traditions in the New World" (*Black Religion and Black Radicalism: An Interpretation of the Religious History of Afro-American People*, rev. ed. [Maryknoll, N.Y.: Orbis Books, 1993], 227).

[90] Martin, "Mary McLeod Bethune," 73, quoted in Newsome, "Mary McLeod Bethune and the Methodist Episcopal Church North," 137. Abraham reminds, "It is surely clear to the observant student that much of the evangelistic preaching of the last two hundred years in the West has failed to deal seriously with the eschatological content and reality of the gospel." Abraham continues making reference to a shift demonstrated by Finney and Moody to a focus upon "techniques that will bring about conversion and personal renewal, even though Finney has a fine record in his fight for the transformation of society. Once the latter element drops out, as it does toward the end of the last century, there is little left but a message of sin and salvation that has relegated eschatology to the last days of history, as we can see happening in the fragile theology of D. L. Moody" (*The Logic of Evangelism*, 58–59).

Bethune characterized this dynamic in her personal faith. "I am not waiting for peace and happiness to come to me in another world. I am enjoying it here day by day." This comment does not indicate an omission of the full realization of the reign of God to come. Rather, Bethune's understandings of personal Christian faith and discipleship, as well as the mission of the church, provide a needed corrective to the inattention given by the church in Bethune's experience to the faithful embodiment of the gospel, which includes practices of justice and reconciliation. "I am ready to act with faith and love and wisdom for justice and progress and peace." Bethune likened the educational concept of readiness to her spiritual readiness. "We hear much about 'readiness' today in the field of education; readiness to read, readiness to act; readiness to learn. I am in a state of spiritual readiness at all times. I am ready to read the signs of the times and interpret them for my people, for the world."[91] Bethune concluded "Spiritual Autobiography" with these words: "I am ready to keep an open mind—to follow the guides toward upward trends and forward progress which will make our world the ONE GREAT WORLD—a world where all men are brothers."[92] Invoking hope for the ultimate realization of God's reign on earth, Bethune offered a nuanced Christian perspective that sought racial justice and reconciliation.

In 1936, after arriving in Washington, D.C., Bethune gave a speech entitled "Closed Doors," in which she outlined the strict restraints imposed upon African Americans in the United States. Her opening statements were striking:

> Frequently from some fair minded speaker who wishes his platform utterances to fall on pleased ears, comes this expression—"Do not continually emphasize the fact that you are a Negro, forget that," and quite as frequently there is always the desire to hurl back this challenge, "You be a Negro for just one short twenty-four hours and see what your reaction will be." A thousand times during that

[91] Bethune, "Spiritual Autobiography," 190. For Abraham, evangelism "is not just a matter of getting the word out to all who will listen, using any means of communication that comes to hand. It is a matter of the power of the living God, unveiling himself to the minds and hearts of the listeners as the gospel is taught and made known" (*The Logic of Evangelism*, 60).

[92] Bethune, "Spiritual Autobiography," 190. According to Jones, "whatever privileged position we understand the church to hold in God's mission, it is highly presumptuous to suppose that God is not at work outside the church. That view unacceptably limits God's saving activity to the church's ministry" (*Evangelistic Love of God and Neighbor*, 73).

twenty-four hours, without a single word being said he would be reminded and would realize unmistakably that he is a Negro.[93]

Bethune made the obvious observation to her nation and church that to possess American citizenship was theoretically to have life, liberty, and the pursuit of happiness "without anyone else's let or hindrance," yet she astutely and boldly claimed that this rule did "not apply equally to the Negro as it does to the white man." Bethune testified: "Whether it be my religion, my aesthetic taste, my economic opportunity, my educational desire, whatever the craving is, I find a limitation because I suffer the greatest known handicap, a Negro—a Negro woman."[94] For Bethune the inconsistencies not only of race but also of gender and their implications for citizenship and residency in the United States were unacceptable, especially in light of her understanding of the church's mission to pursue the gospel mandate for the total well-being of every individual.

Despite intolerably deficient medical care and living conditions resulting in poor health, depleted quality of life, and premature death in the midst of a self-proclaimed Christian nation of considerable resources, many African Americans maintained their Christian faith in God. In the midst of this tenacity of faith African Americans lived in forced segregation that perpetuated these inequities even in the supposed sacred confines of the church.

> The Negro must go to a separate church even though he claims to be of the same denomination [as some whites]. He is not allowed to sing, in unison with the white man, the grand old hymns of Calvin, the Wesleys—the triumphant songs of Christ and eternal glory. When at last he is called to his final resting place on earth even his ashes are not allowed to mingle with those of his white brother, but are borne away to some remote place where the white man is not even reminded that this Negro ever lived. Judging from all that has preceded the Negro in death, it looks as if he has been prepared for

[93] Bethune, "Closed Doors" (1936), in McCluskey and Smith, *Mary McLeod Bethune Building a Better World*, 207.

[94] Bethune, "Closed Doors," 208–9. Delores Williams corroborates, "It is no wonder that a theology of liberation has been birthed by Black American theologians and that a theology with emphasis upon survival and quality of life has been spawned by some Black Christian women naming their theological movement, 'womanist'" ("Straight Talk, Plain Talk: Womanist Words about Salvation in a Social Context," in *Embracing the Spirit: Womanist Perspectives on Hope, Salvation, and Transformation*, ed. E. Townes [Maryknoll, N.Y.: Orbis, 1997], 118).

a heaven, separate from the one to which the white man feels he alone is fit to inhabit.[95]

Bethune's life work struggled against these inconsistencies fueled by racism in the United States and its churches.[96] "This is a high challenge to America—to the church—and to the State."[97]

Following the Methodist Episcopal Church's sponsorship of Bethune-Cookman College, Bethune became very involved in the denomination, participating at all levels of church life. Within five years of her joining the Methodist Episcopal Church she was elected as a delegate to General Conference, the denomination's national policy-making body. Between 1928 and 1952, she served as a delegate to each General Conference and as a delegate to each Annual and Jurisdictional Conference from 1924 until her death in 1955.[98]

In 1938 preparations were in process for the reunification of the Methodist Episcopal Church, the Methodist Episcopal Church, South, and the Methodist Protestant Church. Although the divisions were caused largely as a result of polity issues, these issues were not void of theological and ethical implications. While the Methodist Protestant Church divided from the Methodist Episcopal Church in 1820 as a result of stronger democratic tendencies, the role of race in the separation of the Methodist Episcopal Church and Methodist

[95] Bethune, "Closed Doors," 211.

[96] James Cone's provocative early work articulates the underlying issue, "The white church has not merely failed to render services to the poor, but has failed miserably in being a visible manifestation to the world of God's intention for humanity and in proclaiming the gospel to the world. It seems that the white church is not God's redemptive agent but, rather, an agent of the old society. It fails to create an atmosphere of radical obedience to Christ. Most church fellowships are more concerned about drinking or new buildings or Sunday closing than about children who die of rat bites or men who are killed because they want to be treated like men" (*Black Theology and Black Power* [New York: Seabury, 1969], 71); similar themes are echoed in Cone's more recent publication: "There is a credibility gap between what we say and what we do as the church" (*Risks of Faith: The Emergence of a Black Theology of Liberation, 1968–1998* [Boston: Beacon, 1999], 111).

[97] Bethune, "Closed Doors," 212. According to Lesslie Newbigin, "The reign of God that the church proclaims is indeed present in the life of the church, but it is not the church's possession. It goes before us, summoning us to follow" (*The Open Secret: An Introduction to the Theology of Mission*, rev. ed. [Grand Rapids: Eerdmans, 1995], 64).

[98] Newsome, "Mary McLeod Bethune and the Methodist Episcopal Church North," 130. According to Newsome, "During this time she also served on a number of important committees that addressed such issues as education, federation, books, episcopacy, foreign missions, hospitals and homes, itinerancy, pensions and relief, state of the Church, temperance, prohibition, public morals, and temporal economy."

Episcopal Church, South from each other in 1844 was more apparent.[99] At the 1938 Methodist Episcopal General Conference, 250 African-American leaders, including Bethune, met to protest the provisions for segregation and creation of a Central Jurisdiction based solely on race, one of six jurisdictions, the remaining five determined by geography.[100] Bishop Robert E. Jones, Bishop Matthew W. Clair, and Mary McLeod Bethune voiced opposition to this plan to institutionalize segregation within the Methodist Episcopal Church.[101] In 1939, the merger occurred and the Central Jurisdiction was established, institutionalizing segregation. While many rejoiced at this ecumenical accomplishment, standing and singing "We Are Marching to Zion," others, mainly African Americans and their friends, grieved in their seats; some wept.[102]

Although Bethune was an incredibly influential public figure, especially considering her race, gender, and context, it was her Christian faith and vocation that focused and gave momentum to the trajectory of her life's work. Strong in her faith, Bethune was also wise and prophetic in seeing the greater implications of that faith for an evangelistic education for the Christian formation of African-American youth. Her simple but constructive ecclesiology, which understood the church as a triumphant future hope, as well as a present reality struggling for justice and reconciliation in its faithful practices, contributes significantly to a rich understanding of eschatology and salvation in the effort to retrieve theology and practices of evangelism.

[99] See F. A. Norwood, *The Story of American Methodism: A History of the United Methodists and Their Relations* (Nashville: Abingdon, 1974), 164–209; for primary source material see R. E. Richey, K. E. Rowe, and J. M. Schmidt, eds., *The Methodist Experience in America: A Sourcebook*, vol. 2 (Nashville: Abingdon, 2000).

[100] African Americans had applied and received autonomy in separate annual conferences in the Methodist Episcopal Church from 1864 and in the (currently named) Christian Methodist Episcopal Church from 1870. However, despite the application of these African Americans, their creation along with the creation of the Central Jurisdiction imposed by the white majority all evidence the systemic sin of racism. For further explanation, see J. Thomas, *Methodism's Racial Dilemma: The Story of the Central Jurisdiction* (Nashville: Abingdon, 1992), 9–47.

[101] A. Knotts, *Fellowship of Love: Methodist Women Changing American Racial Attitudes, 1920–1968* (Nashville: Kingswood Books, 1996), 135.

[102] Thomas, *Methodism's Racial Dilemma*, 43. *The Journal of the First General Conference of the Methodist Church*, 1940, ed. L. Estes, E. Heckman, and H. Upperman, included the following, "That the Secretary of the General Conference be requested to send the greetings of the body to Mrs. Mary McLeod Bethune, lay delegate from the South Florida Conference, detained at home by illness" (Nashville: Methodist Publishing House, 1940), 290.

Evangelistic Education

Throughout her decades-long leadership, Bethune engaged in Christian formation equipping African-American youth for service in families, churches, and the world. Bethune's formation in faith, education, and vocational trajectory wove together biblical themes with a constructive ecclesiology that insisted on faithful Christian practices that took seriously the eschatological implications of one's salvation for the present life and discipleship of the church in the world. In later remarks from June 22, 1947, Bethune's more complex vision is apparent:

> The world needs audacity. . . . We must be audacious in fighting for Christian principles and dominating moral and spiritual enemies. The instrument used in the fight is faith. This will lift us to the far goal and carry us to goals that seem in[ac]cessible. We call upon the people of the nation to assist in bringing leadership and strong public sentiment to lead us on the high road where peace, security and justice will be found for all minority groups here in America.[103]

Bethune saw far-reaching implications of not only Christian formation, but education, and democracy specifically for the African-American community, which would then influence the nation and the world. "Today we will not only help a race to secure the fruits of full Democracy, but we will be cleansing the soul of a nation that would lead the world to peace." Seeing this as no small task, Bethune boldly named those, in her opinion, upon whom the responsibility could be trusted, echoing earlier themes of her own Christian education.

> And, again, as we have always done, it must be the women of our race and our nation that must supply the driving force and the inspiration needed as we take the up-hill road to peace. The united effort of women is paramount. For women have always been concerned with putting a floor on the necessities of life—namely, food, clothing, shelter. We can help provide the spiritual strength that buoyed up our fathers and grandfathers before us. We must help our boys and our men to know the way and find the light.[104]

---

[103] Bethune, "Americans All: Which Way, America???" (1947), in McCluskey and Smith, *Mary McLeod Bethune Building a Better World*, 188.

[104] Bethune, "Americans All: Which Way, America???" (1947), in McCluskey and Smith, *Mary McLeod Bethune Building a Better World*, 188.

Although written more than forty years after the opening of her school, these remarks help to focus Bethune's vocational trajectory and its implications not merely for the evangelistic education of African-American youth, specifically female, but for the realization of the broadest implications of that Christian formation for the church, the nation, and the world.

Bethune's vocational direction took definitive shape with the establishment of a school for African-American girls, which she brought to fruition in Daytona Beach, Florida, on October 3, 1904.[105] "As I studied the situation I saw the importance of someone going down there doing something. So I selected Daytona Beach."[106] She envisioned the Daytona Normal and Industrial Institute for Negro Girls as a response to the spiritual, intellectual, and cultural barrenness that had not improved substantially since the days of slavery. In the context of this school Bethune created an evangelistic education that took seriously the social and economic circumstances of racial oppression in the southeastern United States at the beginning of the twentieth century. In the school's curriculum, the familiar themes of Bethune's Christian formation and vocation to ministry integrate with her passionate and prophetic constructive ecclesiology, which understood the church's gospel mandate to pursue the well-being of every individual through faithful practices.

Bethune often narrated the events that led up to and immediately followed the opening of the school, reminding the hearer that the school was opened very much on faith. "When I got to Daytona I had only one dollar and a half left in cash." Unable to pay the rent of a small house that belonged to John Williams, an African American, he told Bethune he trusted her. "I had no furniture. I begged dry good boxes and made benches and stools; begged a basin and other things

---

[105] Newsome, "Mary McLeod Bethune and the Methodist Episcopal Church North," 128.

[106] Bethune, "Charles S. Johnson, Interview with Bethune [abridged]," 47. Bethune chose Daytona as the location for her school based on better donor prospects because of the affluence of the area as compared with her previous settings. "So I selected Daytona Beach, a town where very conservative people lived and where James M. Gamble (of the Procter and Gamble Company of Cincinnati); Thomas White (of the White Sewing Machine Company of Cleveland) and other fine people [owned homes]. A fine club of white women in that section formed a philanthropic group, [the] Palmetto Club, through whom I thought approaches could be made." See also McCluskey, "Introduction" in McCluskey and Smith, *Mary McLeod Bethune Building a Better World*, 5.

I needed and in 1904, five little girls there started school."[107] Bethune recounted numerous episodes of exhausted resources, including lack of food for the children and the desperate need of roof repairs, approaching the brink of closure on more than one occasion. However, in each case Bethune benefited from gifts of mutuality that provided for every need. "That is the kind of faith that has built Bethune-Cookman."[108]

The earliest complete available catalogue for Bethune's school, for 1910–1911, demonstrates the swift growth of the faculty and student body. The faculty consisted of six female teachers. In the school's initial six years, the enrollment increased 500 percent.[109] The aim of the school prioritized the spiritual uplift of its students and significantly placed the development of their Christian character.

> The aim of the institution is to uplift Negro girls spiritually, morally, intellectually and industrially. The school stands for a broad, thorough practical training. To develop Christian character, to send forth women who will be rounded home-makers and Christian leaders is the aim of its founder and supporters, a trained mind, heart and hand being their idea of a complete education.[110]

The curriculum of the school seemed somewhat confined to race and gender constructs with roots mainly in the nineteenth century.[111]

[107] Bethune, "Charles S. Johnson, Interview with Bethune [abridged]," 48.

[108] Bethune, "Charles S. Johnson, Interview with Bethune [abridged]," 50.

[109] McCluskey, "Introduction" in McCluskey and Smith, *Mary McLeod Bethune Building a Better World*, 70.

[110] Bethune, "Sixth Annual Catalogue of the Daytona Educational and Industrial Training School for Negro Girls" (1910–11), in McCluskey and Smith, *Mary McLeod Bethune Building a Better World*, 77–78. In the first part of the twentieth century African Americans in the South migrated north, women in greater number than men. While African-American men found a broader range of job opportunities, "the restriction of white immigrant women during World War One relegated Black women to the domestic jobs which northern white women scorned or considered demeaning." Sexist and racist attitudes created complicated gender constraints for African-American women. See K. Cannon, *Black Womanist Ethics*, American Academy of Religion Academic Series 60 (Atlanta: Scholars Press, 1988), 60.

[111] As Gerda Lerner notes, "Black women have had an ambiguous role in relation to white society. Because they were women, white society has considered them more docile, less of a threat than black men. It has 'rewarded' them by allowing—or forcing—black women into service in the white family. . . . At the same time, they have struggled in partnership with their men to keep the black family together and to allow the black community to survive. This dual and often conflicting role has imposed great tensions on black women and has given them unusual strength" (preface to *Black Women in White America*, xxiii).

However, Bethune, with other women in this study, gently yet firmly pushed previously conceived expectations.[112] "They [female students] are needed as home makers, wives, teachers and missionaries in destitute places."[113] Although the Christian formation of the students echoed such gendered limitations, resembling Bethune's own Christian educational formation, the curriculum also grew from Bethune's prophetic vision for cultivating Christian women leaders for the African-American community.

The catalogue clearly acknowledged Christian formation as the most important aspect of the school's work. "It is our object to give a thorough religious training." This statement opened a section dedicated to describing the prominent theme "Our Religious Work":

> The supreme need of our people beyond doubt is Christian leadership. There is a crying need among us for women qualified as moral and Christian leaders. We are endeavoring to teach an every-day practical religion. The Bible is prominent in every department of our work. It is the guide of our lives. We feel more keenly than we can express the necessity of preparing the girls entrusted to our care for the great religious duties of life.[114]

Cultivation of leaders formed in the Christian faith is the priority of the curriculum. Neither Bethune nor the catalogue boldly articulated the evangelistic purpose of the school, and its curriculum in language understood as such in the current context. However, there is a strong evangelistic component throughout, demonstrated in the objective of forming the students in the Christian faith and equipping them for Christian leadership in their families and communities. "The very

---

[112] Bethune opened her address before the Chicago Women's Federation, June 30, 1933, with a plea attributed to Frederick Douglass, that "the Negro be not judged by the heights to which he is risen, but by the depths from which he has climbed." According to Bethune, "Judged on that basis, the Negro woman embodies one of the modern miracles of the New World" (M. M. Bethune, "A Century of Progress of Negro Women," in Lerner, *Black Women in White America*, 579–80).

[113] Bethune, "Sixth Annual Catalogue of the Daytona Educational and Industrial Training School for Negro Girls," 79.

[114] Bethune, "Sixth Annual Catalogue of the Daytona Educational and Industrial Training School for Negro Girls," 79. Bethune employed the terms *religious, spiritual,* and *Christian* throughout her writings. In describing the curriculum she seemed to interchange the language of *religious* and *Christian*, only specifying the particularity of nonsectarian, implying a possible synonymous use of the terms.

atmosphere of our school has a tendency to draw them [students] nearer the path of right."[115]

The school's course of study included three areas: English, Industrial, and Biblical. The English and Industrial departments provided intellectual and practical formation, respectively. The Biblical Department intentionally formed the students in Christian practices.

Biblical Department

> This work is strictly non-sectarian. We seek guidance rather than creed. Daily instruction is given in the study of the Bible. Two quiet periods are observed each day for quiet Bible reading. Regular attendance at church and Sunday school is required. Sunday afternoon practical mission work for street children is conducted by advanced pupils and teachers.[116]

The Biblical Department, while self-consciously "non-sectarian" at this early date, formed the students in the Christian faith through daily instruction on the Bible and reading, weekly worship, and Sunday school, as well as modeling practical mission work each Sunday afternoon. Bethune prominently incorporated Christian practices into the daily life of the school for the evangelistic purpose of initiating and forming students in the Christian faith. In addition to Bible reading, time was also set aside for daily prayer. "Two periods a day, morning and evening, are given to each student to tarry alone in the great school of prayer." Not only were the students expected to take individual time for prayer, they were also expected to "give some public thought each day as a result of private study,"[117] sharing with the community reflections from their times of personal prayer. These individual and communal Christian practices seemed to grow from Bethune's own formation in faith through Christian practices modeled after the examples of her mother and family.

As a part of her Christian formation, Bethune learned traditional spirituals that wove together the spiritual and social significance of an embodied Christian faith and discipleship for African Americans. "My

[115] Bethune, "Sixth Annual Catalogue of the Daytona Educational and Industrial Training School for Negro Girls," 79.
[116] Bethune, "Sixth Annual Catalogue of the Daytona Educational and Industrial Training School for Negro Girls," 77.
[117] Bethune, "Sixth Annual Catalogue of the Daytona Educational and Industrial Training School for Negro Girls," 79.

dear old grandmother told me the stories because she thought I would understand, and hold the idea until I was mature enough to do something about it." Similarly, Bethune taught spirituals to her students. Remembering a traditional spiritual sung by her ancestors and continued by her community, "*Nobody knows the trouble I see*," she explained. "they did not stop on a note of complaint." This line was immediately followed with "*Glory Hallelujah.*" Bethune claimed this as a definite part of her spirit. "To be sure I have seen trouble, I have had difficulty, the way has not been easy . . . but I have thanked God and said, 'Glory Hallelujah!' "[118] Thus, she incorporated "the spirit of the spiritual" in the Alma Mater Hymn. "There may be sacrifices and tears, there may be disappointments and difficulties, but let us give praise for these, for in them is enrichment and power."[119]

In the "Twenty-fifth Annual Report of the President" submitted in 1929, the growth of the school and the development of its curriculum are apparent. "From the status of one teacher and an enrollment of five, it has grown to a place where twenty-five well-trained, consecrated men and women are employed on the teaching staff, and two hundred thirty-five boys and girls are enrolled in the departments ranging from the eighth grade through the Junior College."[120] Although opened with no sponsorship (religious or otherwise), Bethune nurtured the school into a junior college by 1924. At this

---

[118] Bethune, "Spiritual Autobiography," 183. Williams discusses the role of wilderness in the religious character of spirituals, thereby claiming wilderness as space in the presence of God, even indicating an element of freedom. Although Williams identifies the mystery of many spirituals that remains uninterpreted, the spiritual seems generally to demonstrate a recognition of God's presence and possibility of redemption; see *Sisters in the Wilderness*, 110–12, 189–90. For Wilmore, spirituals pointed to the complexity of African-American religious experience. Spirituals, not merely songs, included "singing feet" and moved from "melancholy" and "unrelieved gloom and grief" to "affirmation and joy" (*Black Religion and Black Radicalism*, 12).

[119] Bethune, "Spiritual Autobiography," 184. "At the College, my students sing in their Alma Mater Hymn: *Thou art results of toil and pain, And tears came in a stream.* . . . But they end that stanza by saying: *Thou are the answered prayer of a dream!* The affirmative realization is that though I dreamed and prayed, my prayers were answered, my dreams became realities, and the sons and daughters who sing to their Alma Mater are enjoying the fruits of those dreams. In the second stanza of that Hymn which I love to hear my children sing, the first verses are made into a prayer: *O God protect dear B.C.C., Crown her with love and cheer.* But at the end of that stanza, which they sing in a quiet, prayerful tone, they burst forth into: *All Hail to thee, dear B.C.C.*"

[120] Bethune, "Twenty-fifth Annual Report of the President [abridged]" (1929), in McCluskey and Smith, *Mary McLeod Bethune Building a Better World*, 96.

point she decided to seek denominational support, inquiring into sponsorship from Presbyterian, Episcopal, and Methodist churches. The ME Church responded first to Bethune's request. With sponsorship, the MEC proposed a merger with Cookman Institute, a Methodist coeducational school. Although initially reluctant to consider such a merger, Bethune accepted the proposal and the invitation to serve as president of the new institution.[121]

In 1928–1929, according to the president's report, Bethune-Cookman College consisted of two departments, academic and industrial. Although not featured as prominently in the reported material, the religious life of the school still provided the foundation for the school's overall purpose of evangelistic education of leaders for the church and community. "Bethune-Cookman, founded on faith and prayer, has always been permeated with the spirit of religious fervor." The report described the school's Christian character carried on through the years by faculty and students through daily communal worship, weekly Sunday morning church services, and mid-week prayer and singing, in addition to the presence of Young Men's and Young Women's Christian Associations. The report stated that the Christian work of the school was also pursued in the curriculum. Courses in religious education and Bible history were described as taught "on the par" with academic and industrial courses. "Development of the 'heart' for Christian service and moral uplift, is one of Bethune-Cookman's three main factors [with academic and industrial]."[122]

Bethune continued to emphasize Christian formation in her educational work. In remarks entitled "The Educational Values of the College-Bred" offered in 1934, Bethune listed three factors "that have contributed to make Education the great enterprise it is today." According to Bethune, the three factors were (1) Science, "with its powers of production, distribution, transportation and communication," (2) Democracy, "In former years education was a luxury to be enjoyed by the members of higher castes; now it is within the reach of the masses," and (3) Religion, "All science points toward God—God the Maker, the Preserver, the Director of all of our lives. As you grow in the knowledge of Science, young people, strive to grow more like God. Amid the collapse and crumbling of economic and social structures, religion is the vitalizing element in all education."[123] Bethune

---

[121] Newsome, "Mary McLeod Bethune and the Methodist Episcopal Church North," 133.

[122] Bethune, "Twenty-fifth Annual Report of the President [abridged]," 99.

[123] M. M. Bethune, "The Educational Values of the College-Bred" (1934), in

then asked her audience to take on specific qualities to better the performance of the task of evangelistic education. First, through preparation and spiritual determination, hearts may be consecrated to make difficult but necessary sacrifices. Other qualities included a sympathetic attitude, industry, idealism, courage, and finally faith. Bethune defined faith in general terms but relied on an allusion to the New Testament epistle to the Hebrews providing a Christian context. "Has it ever occurred to you that Faith—simple Faith—so often made complex by our own clumsy efforts to force it into our consciousness—is merely the serene confidence, the inward smiling assurance of rightness begetting rightness? Faith is the substance of things hoped for, the evidence of things not seen."[124]

In conclusion, Bethune continued on this theme of faith. "May I earnestly exhort YOU to have Faith—in God, in yourselves, your possibilities—faith in [Hu]Mankind."[125] Another address also resonated with these themes and made explicit the evangelistic component that remained a thread throughout her life and work. "God bless you. God inspire you. God dedicate every single one of you [to] a new today, to go out and shine! shine! so that your light may be seen in distant places and men and women everywhere will know the spirit of brotherhood, the spirit of the great Christ who gave Himself that we might have life and have it more abundantly."[126]

Mary McLeod Bethune's Christian witness included both a strong faith and substantial openness in the public and political arena. Bethune took seriously evangelistic education and its relationship to practices of justice and reconciliation. With the other women in this study, Bethune contributes to an understanding of evangelism that requires a multifaceted set of practices. For Bethune and her educational endeavor, African-American youth were initiated and formed in the Christian faith over time through practices of daily Bible reading, prayer, and singing alongside weekly worship and service opportunities. Bethune provides a role model for the Christian community to take its complex eschatological role in the world more seriously as an

---

McCluskey and Smith, *Mary McLeod Bethune Building a Better World*, 109; also published in *The Southern Workman* 63 (1934): 200–204.

[124] Bethune, "The Educational Values of the College-Bred," 111.

[125] Bethune, "The Educational Values of the College-Bred," 111.

[126] Bethune, "Address to the National Council of Negro Women Brotherhood Luncheon," 282.

evangelistic witness not only to what God has done and will do, but is doing in Jesus Christ through the Holy Spirit.

> *Personally and racially, our enemies must be forgiven. Our aim must be to create a world of fellowship and justice where no man's skin color or religion, is held against him. 'Love thy neighbor' is a precept which could transform the world if it were universally practiced.*[127]

---

[127] Bethune, "My Last Will and Testament," 59.

CONCLUSION

The church is mighty orthodox in notions, but very heretical in practice, but the time must come when the church will be just as vigilant in guarding orthodoxy in practice as orthodoxy in doctrine, and just as prompt to turn out heretics in practice as heretics that corrupt the doctrines of the gospel. In fact, it is vastly more important.[1]

Evangelism, largely construed as preaching throughout Christian tradition, has generally excluded women from its study and practice. The evangelistic ministries of these women contribute important insights to contemporary understandings and practices of evangelism, expanding traditional notions often still captive to connotations of merely verbal proclamation.[2] Although the evangelistic ministries of the women in this study included public speaking—and often preaching—their practices moved beyond merely verbal proclamation to a rich synthesis. As mentioned in the introduction, William Abraham clarifies the problem: "at issue is the appropriation of what evangelism has actually meant in the early church and in history, not judged by

---

[1] C. G. Finney, *Lectures on Revivals of Religion*, ed. William G. McLoughlin (Cambridge, Mass.: Belknap Press, 1960), 401. As mentioned in the introduction, William Abraham argues that Finney marks a shift away from serious theological reflection among practitioners of evangelism. He summarizes, "In other words, we not only need to attend to the experiential, communal, and moral dimensions of initiation; we also need to deal with its intellectual, operational, and disciplinary aspects" (*The Logic of Evangelism* [Grand Rapids: Eerdmans, 1989], 9, 142).

[2] See Abraham for a discussion of evangelism as proclamation and the limitations of such a connotation; *The Logic of Evangelism*, 40–69, particularly 44, 47, 50–59.

the etymology of the word *evangelism* and its rather occasional use in Scripture, but by what evangelists have actually done in both proclaiming the gospel and establishing new converts in the kingdom of God."[3]

The women in this study provide examples of "what evangelists have actually done. . . ." The women preached and published, advocated and served, proclaiming the gospel of Jesus Christ in their words and lives to a variety of constituencies in numerous contexts: from Ripley's evangelistic political action among enslaved Africans, Native Americans, and those sentenced to death; to Bethune's evangelistic education, which, while offering African American youth Christian formation and leadership skills, called the church to take seriously a comprehensive eschatological witness. As Abraham argues, these women seem to embody an evangelism that "is not just simply a matter of getting the word out. . . . It is a matter of the power of the living God, unveiling himself to the minds and hearts of the listener as the gospel is taught and made known."[4] For these women, evangelism consisted of sharing the gospel message and participating in God's transformation of individuals and communities as well as themselves.

The women in this study faced two main obstacles challenging faithful and effective evangelism in their times and contexts that persist today: (1) antiintellectualism, including a lack of theological reflection,[5] and (2) an objectification of the "other" related to class, race, and/or gender discrimination.[6] Not only was elementary and higher education generally less accessible to persons outside the more affluent classes, it was significantly less accessible to women.[7] This

---

[3] Abraham, *The Logic of Evangelism*, 69; italics in the original.

[4] Abraham, *The Logic of Evangelism*, 60.

[5] As mentioned in the introduction, Abraham argues that John Wesley (1703–1791) and Jonathan Edwards (1703–1758) are among the last serious theologians associated with the practice of evangelism. With Finney's influence, a pragmatic and even antiintellectual shift followed. Abraham, *The Logic of Evangelism*, 9.

[6] While Abraham is not opposed to social action and argues that evangelism does not preclude such "laudable and urgent tasks" as medical, educational or social, there remains room to build upon Abraham and others for further theological and critical reflection of evangelistic practices beyond proclamation that overcome such an objectification of the "other": related to class, race, and gender discrimination (*The Logic of Evangelism*, 45). A central reason for this remaining room for study was the prevalence of the church growth movement and need for critical responses. Although remnants of church growth methodologies linger, momentum related to its study has largely passed and/or shifted into new directions opening possibilities for other conversation partners and trajectories.

[7] According to Nancy Cott, "The improvement of women's higher education in the half-century after the Revolution was an uphill battle. The best-educated women

lack of education magnified an increasing weakness of theological foundations related to evangelistic theology and practices. Additionally, the discrimination faced by the women in this study and those to and with whom they ministered reflected that of their time and contexts. Despite a seeming esteem for the female gender,[8] women, particularly African American women,[9] faced considerable disenfranchisement from social and ecclesiastic structures.[10] As previously noted, for example, while women within the Society of Friends regularly preached, unlike most other Christian traditions of the early nineteenth century, for Ripley and the Grimkés this did not necessarily presume support for such vocations.[11] Although the holiness movement of the mid- and late nineteenth century carved a qualified space for women's preaching, ordination remained a complex enterprise, only received by Julia Foote among the women in this study, though ecclesiastic rights of various forms were sought by each.[12]

---

in those years were self-taught, or tutored at home by teachers or relatives, although institutions offering secondary education for girls began to be founded" (*The Bonds of Womanhood: Women's Sphere in New England, 1780–1835*, 2nd ed. [New Haven: Yale University Press, 1977], 112). See also Charles R. Foster, and Fred Smith with Grant S. Shockley, *Black Religious Experience: Conversations on Double Consciousness and the Work of Grant Shockley* (Nashville: Abingdon, 2003), 35.

[8] According to Catherine Brekus, the shift in gender expectations from the eighteenth to the nineteenth century is "one of the most important ideological transformations in American history" (*Strangers and Pilgrims: Female Preaching in America 1740-1845* [Chapel Hill: University of North Carolina, 1998], 146). "Unlike the Puritan clergymen of New England, or the Separates of the first Great Awakening, or the Founding Fathers of the American Revolution, nineteenth century ministers believed that women were as virtuous, if not more virtuous, than men."

[9] Delores S. Williams, *Sisters in the Wilderness: The Challenge of Womanist God-Talk* (Maryknoll, N.Y.: Orbis Books, 1993), 84–107.

[10] For example, see S. H. Lindley, *"You Have Stept Out of Your Place": A History of Women and Religion in America* (Louisville: Westminster/John Knox, 1996); B. Collier-Thomas, *Daughters of Thunder: Black Women Preachers and Their Sermons, 1850-1979* (San Francisco: Jossey-Bass, 1998); W. L. Andrews, ed., *Sisters of the Spirit: Three Black Women's Autobiographies of the Nineteenth Century* (Bloomington: University of Indiana Press, 1986).

[11] As mentioned in chap. 1, women, in particular, who experienced such discernment individually, confronted the precarious situation of losing or not attaining the support of their meeting. See S. M. Stuard, "Women's Witnessing: A New Departure," in *Witnesses for Change: Quaker Women over Three Centuries*, ed. E. P. Brown and S. M. Stuard (New Brunswick: Rutgers University Press, 1989), 12.

[12] While Dorothy Ripley did not specifically mention a desire for ordination, she sought endorsement from the Quaker meeting in Whitby. Sarah Grimké and Frances Willard acknowledged a call to a formal ministry role including ordination. Helen

In professional and practical texts on evangelistic methods, substantial responses to these obstacles generally seem to remain absent. This highly subscribed genre of resources often perpetuates these and other enduring obstacles that can result in problematic and truncated understandings of evangelism. To envision evangelism beyond such confines opens possibilities for more faithful practices shaped by biblical and theological foundations and the transforming power of God in Jesus Christ through the Holy Spirit.

Saving Women

In spite of such obstacles, the women in this study came to embrace their evangelistic vocations through a dialectic of biblical and theological reflection that informed and was informed by related practices. With little if any encouragement for or cultivation of their vocations to ministry, the women relied heavily upon simple personal practices of devotion such as prayer and Bible study. These practices informed significant and often powerful conversion experiences. Largely as a result of the lack of community support and encouragement for vocational discernment, many of the women confronted menacing doubts related to their faiths. Challenging prescribed roles held by church and society based on gender, class, and racial constructs led to tremendous anxiety and fear for their own salvations.[13] This anxiety

---

Barrett Montgomery received a licensed to preach. Although Mary McLeod Bethune seemed least interested in ordination, she served as a lay delegate to General Conference, the major policymaking body of the Methodist Church.

[13] One contemporary study concludes that adolescents exhibiting "mild" doubts, expressed religious doubt related to "religion's failure to make people 'better,'" the claimed infallibility of scriptures, and pressures to accept religious teachings." Doubt consistently corresponded to decreased personal religiosity and with greater doubt in problematic family environments echoing themes observed in many of the women's formations in faith (B. Hunsberger, M. Pratt, and S. M. Pancer, "A Longitudinal Study of Religious Doubts in High School and Beyond: Relationships, Stability, and Searching for Answers," *Journal for the Scientific Study of Religion* 41:2 [2002]: 255–66). Another study explores the connection between religious doubt and health, specifically symptoms of depression (N. Krause and K. M. Wulff, "Religious Doubt and Health: Exploring the Potential Dark Side of Religion," *Sociology of Religion* 65:1 [2004]: 35–56). Interestingly, an earlier though tangential study identifies the inconclusive nature of studies investigating the relationship of socioeconomic status and belief-orthodoxy to religious participation demonstrating the possibility of educational rather than economic factors. S. Gaede, "Religious Participation, Socioeconomic Status, and Belief-Orthodoxy," *Journal for the Scientific Study of Religion* 16:3 (1977): 245–53.

for their eternal well-beings pushed them further into personal practices of prayer and Bible study, resulting in a dialectic not only of theology and practice—but of *evangelistic* theology and practice. With little if any encouragement, much less guidance from communities of faith, *the women's doubts and anxieties for their salvations resulted in their facilitating God's salvation for others.*

Armed with biblical texts, the women rethought Christian salvation for themselves without the mediation of preachers or scholars, and in the process discovered their vocations. For example, Foote's evangelistic ministry began in her youth with practices of prayer and visitation. Complemented by biblical study and impacted by life events such as an eye injury resulting in partial blindness, Foote's faith grew deeper and her evangelistic ministry added facets related to her experience of entire sanctification. Encountering the divine in religious experiences, not through or with those entrusted with her pastoral care, led her to move beyond an opposition to female preaching as well as informing ministries of racial reconciliation. This dynamic of reflection and practices was at times fostered by women's greater marginalization and therefore distance from the monopoly of verbal proclamation related to understandings of evangelism. *The women's evangelistic ministries demonstrate an inability to separate Christian conversion from condition, their own and others.* While influenced by theological themes and biblical interpretation generally characteristic of their times and contexts, each woman realized the centrality of evangelistic ministry to her vocational trajectory in spite of the imposition of ecclesiastic and societal limitations.

Retrieving Evangelistic Theology for Faithful Practices

Each woman's vocation to evangelistic ministry was framed by at least one area of Christian doctrine (e.g., universal atonement, sin, eschatology) with implications for contemporary evangelistic theology and practices. These theological components respond to the obstacles faced by the women in their times and contexts as well as those persistent in the contemporary discussion related to the study of evangelism. The following, first, offers constructive possibilities for understandings, theology, and practices of evangelism drawn from each woman's writings and ministry, noting points of resonance among select scholarship in the study of evangelism. Then, four contributions of the women's examples to the contemporary discussion follow, which resonate with helpful themes and push the conversation further.

Offering the Gospel to All

Dorothy Ripley traveled tirelessly throughout the United States at the turn of the nineteenth century responding to a divine commission to preach the gospel among slaves and slave owners—including President Jefferson. While seemingly bound to traditional notions of evangelism as verbal proclamation through preaching and publication, Ripley embodied the Christian gospel in ministries of compassionate presence and evangelistically motivated political action. *Ripley's example legitimates an evangelistic theology that subverts the tradition of limited atonement by offering the gospel to all.*

Though ultimately concerned for the conversion of numerous individuals, Ripley did not succumb to a truncated understanding of Christian faith or evangelism simply for the purpose of achieving selective or quantitative results. Instead, she faithfully responded to her evangelistic vocation, inviting persons from a range of constituencies regardless of social or political status—ideally all God's children—into reconciled relationships with Jesus Christ through the Holy Spirit. Ripley's invitation included an expectation of participation in a new life, very similar to that described by Julia Foote.

Neither the gospels nor Pauline epistles require the increase of membership at the expense of participation in and acknowledgment of the reign of God in lives of Christian faithfulness. Ripley's concerns resonate with those of Lesslie Newbigin echoed in the contemporary study of evangelism. According to Newbigin, although the earliest accounts of the Christian church in Acts highlight numerical growth, "the rest of the New Testament furnishes little evidence of interest in numerical growth." Newbigin argues, "The emphasis falls upon the faithfulness of the disciples rather than upon their numbers." Because of Ripley's possible post-millennialism, it is unclear whether Ripley's perspective is largely consistent with Newbigin's additional argument, "In no sense does the triumph of God's reign seem to depend upon the growth of the church." In spite of this latter claim, with Newbigin, for Ripley evangelistic theology and practice did not prioritize numerical growth to the exclusion of faithfulness.[14]

---

[14] Lesslie Newbigin, *The Open Secret: An Introduction to the Theology of Mission*, rev. ed. (Grand Rapids: Eerdmans, 1978, 1995), 125. Newbigin offers these remarks in a constructive response to Donald McGavran and The Institute of Church Growth of the School of World Missions at Fuller Theological Seminary, particularly content of a presentation by McGavran made to the International Congress on World Evangelization (Lausanne, 1974).

Sadly, many local churches in their desire to add members look only to similar demographics and/or similar or higher social status, neglecting Jesus' ministry with the marginalized.[15] Often such strategies resemble lingering remnants of church growth methodologies, the rationales of which neglect comprehensive biblical and theological foundations. As Ripley demonstrates, a theological frame—specifically universal atonement—cannot ignore the significance of sharing the gospel message with marginalized constituencies. Ripley models a comprehensive awareness of biblical texts and theological themes that directly impact her vocation and provocative evangelistic practices. The biblical emphasis upon such an orientation arguably focuses as much if not more upon the changed lives and existing need of those sharing the gospel, than those receiving. Ripley's offering the gospel to all contributes to this helpful reorientation, shifting attention from the evangelized to both the evangelized and evangelizer in God's work of salvation.

Selfless Sinning

Sarah and Angelina Grimké are well known for their contributions to antislavery and women's rights causes in the nineteenth century. The Grimkés were particularly concerned for women's adherence to biblical texts, particularly the parable of the talents, urging the use of gifts including one's intellect in faithful responses. A radical proposal for Christian communities well before the gathering in Seneca Falls, the Grimkés encouraged disenfranchised white women to read and study biblical texts, cultivating their faith and identity in the image of God and empowering them for faithful and compassionate witness. *Within their evangelistic theology the Grimkés defined sin in its many dimensions—personal, social, institutional.*

The Grimkés outlined an evangelistic theology and practices for women, but with relevance to other constituencies, which included the redemption of those not only captive to pride, but to lack of self. Serene Jones has composed a careful harmony of feminist theory and Christian theology that addresses women's experience of justification and sanctification, among other theological issues, illuminating the Grimkés' early reflections.[16] The Grimkés' evangelistic theology

---

[15] Scott L. Jones, *The Evangelistic Love of God and Neighbor: A Theology of Witness and Discipleship* (Nashville: Abingdon, 1990), 41–42.

[16] See Serene Jones, *Feminist Theory and Christian Theology: Cartographies of Grace* (Minneapolis: Fortress, 2000), 55–68, 110–11.

resonates with Serene Jones's remarks, "Although Luther no doubt meant to include woman in his account of 'the sinner,' his conceptual focus on man suggests that she is only guilty and saved by association. Luther's story leaves no place for her specificity as 'woman.'" Jones nuances the traditional understanding of conversion imaged by Luther in conversation with feminist theory, shedding light on the implications of the Grimkés' contribution. When "woman" inhabits this story of conversion, "she finds herself judged by a God who is imaged in distinctly male terms: he (God) is the mighty tribunal patriarch of Roman law. She will fit the role of the defendant insofar as she identifies herself as part of Luther's masculine subject."[17]

In select writings the Grimkés offer a complex and textured understanding of sin beyond flat images of pride and excess self. The dominant metaphor for conversion in contemporary circles seems still to rely upon Luther's image of the courtroom. The defendant standing before God, the judge, found guilty of arrogant self-sufficiency having turned away from God, awaits the proclamation of punishment.[18] As scholars have acknowledged, the proliferation of this metaphor often excludes those who suffer not from the sin of excess self, but lack of self—selfless sinning. As mentioned in chapter 2, Sarah, building on Angelina's previous arguments for the empowerment of women, offers glimpses of insights later expanded by Valerie Saving's groundbreaking thesis regarding women's particular experience in theology, specifically sin.

The Grimkés' understanding of sin contributes important texture to a constructive evangelistic theology. While some scholars in the study of evangelism acknowledge the increased difficulties related to understandings of original sin and guilt, there is room for further consideration.[19] For evangelistic ministries to remain faithful and effective, alternative and even contrary perspectives to that of a European American affluent masculinity must be engaged. This is not to argue

---

[17] S. Jones, *Feminist Theory and Christian Theology*, 61. See also R. R. Ruether, *Women and Redemption: A Thological History* (Minneapolis: Fortress, 1998), 127–35.

[18] S. Jones, *Feminist Theory and Christian Theology*, 55–57.

[19] For example, Abraham, *The Logic of Evangelism*, 123. Abraham not only acknowledges the difficulties in his text, cited above, but also assisted me in identifying the implications of women's distinctive experience of sin for evangelism. For other examples of diverse readings and perspectives related to concepts of sin and salvation for evangelism, see O. E. Costas, "Evangelism and the Gospel of Salvation," *International Review of Mission* 63 (1974): 24–37; and idem., *Liberating News: A Theology of Contextual Evangelization* (Grand Rapids: Eerdmans, 1989).

for a dilution or undermining of substantial biblical theological reflection but rather for a robust critical engagement of particularities that benefit from serious exegetical and theological work. Such reflection and engagement are not only optimal but essential for faithful and effective evangelism in the contemporary context. For the Grimkés, the conversion of individuals—whether men or women, free or enslaved—directly affected and challenged the material and physical conditions of Christians as well as their organizations and institutions.

Living Transformation

For Julia Foote, breaking the power of sin was realized most fully through the doctrine of entire sanctification that resulted in transformation—*real change*—in and between persons. Foote's evangelistic ministry expected this real change to include transformed relationships within church and society, with implications for how Christians live in the world. *A careful evangelistic theology avoids both extremes of works righteousness and antinominianism allowing persons and communities to experience a living transformation.*

Conversion is a complex and mysterious event and/or process that is often misunderstood and even trivialized.[20] A significant resource in approaching this important concept and its implications for lives of Christian faithfulness are basic theological teachings related to the Trinity through prayerful formation of biblical texts.[21] The truth that God in Jesus Christ, fully human and fully divine, is present and active in the world through the Holy Spirit has tremendous implications for ministry and specifically evangelism.

While Christians facilitate ministries of evangelism, inviting others into relationship with Jesus Christ in God's reign, God, not human beings, offers salvation.[22] However, on occasion Christians and communities of faith continue to live into truncated theological

[20] According to Abraham, "attempts to articulate the morphology of conversion have turned much of the theology of evangelism, which this language fosters, into an introspective anthropocentrism that neglects the richer tapestry of Christian theology and encourages the development of a narrow and inadequate piety" (*The Logic of Evangelism*, 122).

[21] B. J. Kallenberg, "The first lesson for evangelism to be gleaned from postcritical philosophy, then, is the importance of embodying the story of Jesus in our communal life" (*Live to Tell: Evangelism for a Postmodern Age* [Grand Rapids: Brazos Books, 2002], 54).

[22] Abraham, *The Logic of Evangelism*, 92, 64–65.

understandings often resembling one of two extremes: (1) works righteousness: attempting to earn relationship with and salvation from God, or (2) antinomianism: ignoring the baptismal commission to practices of love of God and neighbor.

Foote's conversion and vocation to evangelistic ministry, informed by Wesleyan themes of holiness, embodied a careful balance, avoiding either extreme. Although questions of faithful discipleship are complex, accepting God's unconditional love in Jesus Christ through the Holy Spirit and living into one's baptism invites the proclamation of the gospel in words and lives.[23] This complex witness reveals a living transformation of God's sanctification in persons and communities, demonstrated in changed lives and relationships. Despite the complexities of Christian witness in the contemporary context, understandings and practices of evangelism shaped by forces other than the Holy Spirit, emerging from identities other than persons and communities made holy through experiencing a real change, will yield other than faithful Christian disciples. After Foote's example, Christians are invited to receive and enjoy a living transformation.

A Serving Church

Frances Willard's leadership of the National Woman's Christian Temperance Union cultivated the organization's Christian identity and facilitated a broad evangelistic ministry. As a result numerous women were trained, encouraged, and enabled to participate in a variety of ministry roles, enhancing the evangelistic witness of American Protestantism in the concluding years of the nineteenth century. Best known as an educator and reformer, Willard's provocative agenda for women's suffrage at the close of the nineteenth century emerged from her Christian faith, frustrated vocation to ordained ministry, and understanding of the church's purpose in the world. *Such a comprehensive evangelistic theology refuses to separate social responsibility from evangelism.*

Willard's critique of the church of her time led her to cultivate ecclesiological components within the NWCTU mobilizing an effort to fulfill the church's purpose by essentially creating space for women in ministry—components of a woman's serving church. Dating from Willard's lifetime, many Protestant denominations in America con-

---

[23] For Abraham, "evangelism is a polymorphous activity," and it is "impossible to claim that one act alone is enough to constitute evangelism" (*The Logic of Evangelism*, 104–5).

tinue to suffer from the estrangement of evangelism (as merely personal salvation) and social responsibility. However, such a compartmentalization, which is often antagonistic is neither biblically nor theologically consistent.[24] Willard's contribution resonates with George Hunsberger's admonition that focuses upon the faithful responses and practices of local congregations which constitute an embodied witness. According to Hunsberger:

> We also catch the pulse of the work of the four "evangelists" in the written gospels they have given us. . . . Yet, our perspectives will be skewed if we do not take note of the evangelists that did not write letter [e.g., Paul] or gospels. It is to the specific congregations that I refer. Clues about them may be more faint, but the substructure of living congregations bearing faith, love, and hope provides the foundational witness of the first-century church. . . . Whatever else may be said about modes of articulation appropriate to the gospel's announcement, embodiment is the essential feature of them all.[25]

Willard enlisted women within the WCTU in evangelistic ministry that did not succumb to the emerging and eventually reigning dichotomy of proclamation and social action. She implemented such opportunities for women's ministry while seeking to embody the gospel message in communities of faith, despite the institutional church's basic reluctance to encourage such leadership by women.

Although scholarship in the study of evangelism for the most part acknowledges the inadequacy of truncated understandings of evangelism as verbal proclamation alone that stand in opposition to social action, institutional structures and conversations generally maintain this estrangement. The restoration of this divide inspired by biblical and theological reflection is imperative for the integrity of the church's embodiment of the gospel and evangelistic witness. With Willard and Hunsberger, the church's identity and purpose, namely evangelism, must emerge from such careful reflection in conversation with diverse constituencies. This reflection informed by a variety of voices will substantially strengthen the integrity of a more complex

---

[24] Abraham, *The Logic of Evangelism*, 40–61; D. J. Bosch, *Transforming Mission: Paradigm Shifts in Theology of Mission* (Maryknoll, N.Y.: Orbis Books, 1991), 377–78, 412; See also R. J. Sider, P. N. Olson, and H. B. Unbuh, *Churches That Make a Difference: Reaching Your Community with Good News with Good Works* (Grand Rapids: Baker Books, 2002).

[25] George Hunsberger, "Is there Biblical Warrant for Evangelism?" *Interpretation* 48 (1994): 141.

witness of the gospel in words and lives beyond simplistic categories that continue to pervade.

Narrating Salvation

Helen Barrett Montgomery provided a theological and narrative reading of the biblical text, giving similar consideration to both Old and New Testaments in her biblical theology of evangelism. While there is substantial controversy related to biblical interpretation and theological commitments, the increasing estrangement between Christian theology and church practices particularly related to evangelism is alarming. *An authentic evangelistic theology relies upon the whole salvation narrative, rather than a myopic Marcionism.*

The biblical text is an essential resource for discerning Christian faith and practices, particularly evangelism. Despite canonical assumptions, the Bible, namely Old and New Testaments, provides vital, inspired, and authoritative texts for understanding the triune God as well as God's relationship to the chosen people of Israel and the early Christian church. Surprisingly nearly all critical and theological studies related to evangelism overlook large sections of the biblical canon. The majority of studies related to evangelism focus predominantly upon the New Testament to the exclusion of the Old, thereby neglecting much of God's salvation narrative and the rich possibilities for evangelistic ministries.[26]

To overcome obstacles related to faithful and effective practices of evangelism, Christian communities must take seriously thoughtful and comprehensive biblical theological reflection for the purpose of receiving formation from and living into that narrative.[27] So much of contemporary preaching, and even pastoral training, focuses upon alternative disciplines that begin with perceived needs of individuals.

---

[26] As mentioned in chapter 5, few scholars in the academic study of evangelism refer to Old Testament texts—creating a potentially Marcionite ethos. Walter Brueggemann's text, *Biblical Perspectives on Evangelism: Living in Three-Storied Universe* (Nashville: Abingdon, 1993) is a notable exception. Bosch includes one of the few and more substantial references. He initially claims that "in the normal sense of the word" the Old Testament has nothing to do with mission, although he comments parenthetically that such a "normal" or "traditional" definition of mission "will be challenged in several ways" by his study. Bosch does concede, "Even so, the Old Testament is fundamental to the understanding of mission in the New" (*Transforming Mission*, 17).

[27] See G. Lindbeck, "Scripture, Consensus, and Community," in *Biblical Interpretation in Crisis*, ed. R. J. Neuhaus (Grand Rapids: Eerdmans, 1989), 74–101.

Anthropological and experiential starting points prioritize disciplines tangential and sometimes contrary to Christian theology and the biblical texts. Instead, Christian leaders need to begin *theologically* with God and the salvation narrative from biblical texts. This is not to argue that the Bible is the sole source for Christian identity, as the fundamentalism Montgomery encountered claimed, or that Christian communities need not listen with attentive openness to other communities of faith narrate God's salvation in Jesus Christ through the Holy Spirit. Rather, alternative disciplines, whether marketing and finance or psychology and self-help, must be read through a theological lens crafted by the salvation narrative that unfolds in the biblical texts.

Such a paradigm shift then informs not only our understanding and practices of evangelism and its relationship to Christian discipleship but the church's identity and purpose. Understanding the church as sent by God in service to the world, not as the sender and/or keeper of a parochial gospel, carries tremendous implications for evangelistic practice.[28] Faithful and effective evangelistic practices are unlikely if not impossible without an understanding of the church's identity in relation to God in Jesus Christ through the Holy Spirit. The church is sent to share the gospel of God's reign with the world after the example of Christ, in humble and sacrificial service. And, through the mysterious presence of the Holy Spirit before and behind, the reign of God is revealed not only to the receivers and hearers but to the sharers and bearers as well.

Salvation Now

Mary McLeod Bethune, perhaps the most influential African American person of her generation, pursued a ministry of evangelistic education, establishing a school for girls that later emerged as Bethune-Cookman College in Daytona, Florida. This evangelistic education embodied Bethune's simple yet profound theological observation that the church must understand itself eschatologically in ministry to the present world alongside preparation for the next. For Bethune, the church must not only proclaim a gospel of distant reward and paradise but must proclaim and live a gospel that points to the unfolding reign of God—salvation now. *A faithful evangelistic the-*

---

[28] See D. L. Guder, ed., *Missional Church: A Vision for the Sending of the Church in North America* (Grand Rapids: Eerdmans, 1998).

ology does not ignore the present implications of salvation for an eschatology that merely looks to a future reward.

Bethune's clarity on the implications of losing such a perspective continues to resonate among mainline denominations still suffering from the remnants of institutionalized racism within complex socio-economic realities.[29] It is difficult and sometimes presumptuous to dictate content and methods that represent a faithful eschatological reflection of the gospel for today. Yet such a delicate but theologically astute orientation by Christians within communities of faith carves an essential space for evangelistic ministry.[30] Eschatological evangelism, after the example of the early church, does not merely correspond to a future hope but also a changed present reality.[31]

Within American Protestantism, this changed present reality must include racial justice and reconciliation. The study and practice of evangelism generally overlooks issues of race specifically black and womanist liberation theologies, creating a chasm in its scholarship and ministries.[32] The evangelistic ministries of Bethune, and Foote, resonate with fundamental assertions in these fields. For example, according to James Cone, "While white preachers and theologians often defined Jesus Christ as a spiritual Savior, the deliverer of people from sin and guilt, black preachers were unquestionably historical. . . . That was why the black Church was involved in the abolitionist movement in the nineteenth century and the civil rights movement in the twentieth."[33] For the church to faithfully embody the gospel message—presently—Christians in America must confront and respond to this omission in scholarship, as well as the persistence of segregation whether voluntary or economic. As Christians commissioned to evangelistic ministry by our baptisms, we are called to live—

[29] J. N. K. Mugambi, "A Fresh Look at Evangelism in Africa," *International Review of Mission* 87 (1998): 353–54.

[30] Abraham, *The Logic of Evangelism*, 17. For Abraham, eschatology "cannot be the last word but rather must be the first word on evangelism," which must be understood in the context of the dynamic reign of God on earth.

[31] Abraham, *The Logic of Evangelism*, 19, 17–39.

[32] L. Warner, "Reconsidering Evangelism: Lessons from Black Liberation and Womanist Theologies," in *Living Stones in the Household of God: The Legacy and Future of Black Theology*, ed. L. E. Thomas (Minneapolis: Fortress, 2003), 71–82.

[33] J. H. Cone, *God of the Oppressed* (New York: Seabury, 1975; rev. ed, Maryknoll, N.Y.: Orbis Books, 1997), 51. Foote and Bethune seem to resonate with Jacquelyn Grant's critique of attempt for racial reconciliation without liberation. See J. Grant, *White Women's Christ and Black Women's Jesus: Feminist Christology and Womanist Responses* (Atlanta: Scholars Press, 1989), 146.

presently—in the midst of the unfolding reign of God reflecting the resurrected Christ guided by the witness of the Holy Spirit.[34]

Contributions

The women's evangelistic ministries both resonate with recent helpful themes and make contributions to the contemporary study of evangelism. The four contributions address the obstacles faced by those committed to embodying faithful and effective evangelistic practices, namely lack of theological reflection and objectification of the other.

(1) Their synthesis of practices, most often with proclamation at the heart, necessarily blurs the boundaries between evangelism and discipleship. Many studies on evangelism labor to keep evangelism and discipleship discreet despite more complex biblical foundations and precedents within the life of the church.[35] The women in this study give comprehensive, nuanced, and contextualized examples that demonstrate the inadequacy of such simplistic compartmentalization.[36]

The marginalization of the study of evangelism within practical theology at times results in a possessiveness or even antagonism between subareas. This animosity can hinder the fruitful interface of these areas of study and the recognition of interdependence in the lived practices of communities of faith. To reduce evangelistic practices to a discreet set (for example, verbal proclamation, apologetics, and invitation to decision) further perpetuates the marginalization of the study of evangelism and its truncated practice.

---

[34] For a thoughtful and moving discussion of the reign of God and its implications for evangelism see M. Arias, *Announcing the Reign of God: Evangelism and the Subversive Memory of Jesus* (Philadelphia: Fortress , 1984; repr., Eugene, Ore.: Wipf & Stock, 1999).

[35] For example, Jones's work ably builds upon Abraham's foundation, broadening Abraham's concept of evangelism which is limited to "initiating people into the kingdom of God for the first time," but continues to work towards the clarification of evangelism as distinct from though in relation to discipleship. Abraham, *The Logic of Evangelism*, 95; and S. J. Jones, *Evangelistic Love of God and Neighbor*, 99–118.

[36] B. J. Kallenberg, *Live to Tell: Evangelism for a Postmodern Age* (Grand Rapids: Brazos Press, 2002), 54. Kallenberg admits the inevitable blurring of boundaries between evangelism and discipleship. While Abraham (and Jones cited above) argues for a set of intentional practices for initiating individuals into the reign of God, he seems more concerned with distinguishing evangelism as initiation from discipleship and nurturing of individuals in the faith. Abraham, *The Logic of Evangelism*, 95, 108. The women in this study, with Kallenberg, demonstrate a more complex position.

As discussed in chapter 5, evangelism must remain at the heart of the church's mission, sent by God in service to the world to proclaim repentance and forgiveness inviting individuals to live changed lives by the power of the Holy Spirit within Christ's church initiated into the reign of God.[37] Just as evangelism is the heart of the church's mission or purpose, so evangelism is the core of ecclesial practices. If practices of worship, discipleship, and outreach are pursued without an evangelistic component, namely an intentional proclamation and/or embodiment of the gospel of Jesus Christ, then such practices not only lose their motivation and power but arguably cease to function as Christian practices.

Each of the women looked to the ministry of Jesus Christ described in the gospels as the ultimate example of such a synthesis of evangelistic ministry practices for their vocations. Interestingly, most of the women also made a distinction between the method and content of Jesus' ministry from that of Paul's when defending their vocations—since the Pauline epistles, though a popular inspiration for contemporary evangelistic practices, were and continue to be used by critics of women's ministry vocations.[38]

Most of the women articulated a desire for educational opportunities, and most often focused such energies on literacy, particularly biblical study. Montgomery provided the most substantial argument for the significance of biblical study for evangelistic theology and practices. (2) Beyond the simple, but profound, importance of biblical foundations for evangelism, the study of evangelism must acknowledge the significance of the Old Testament alongside the New. A canonical and narrative reading of the Bible provides a narrative perspective for our shared Christian identity as well as theological resources for shaping faithful and effective practices of evangelism in a diverse and changing world.

---

[37] Bosch, *Transforming Mission*, 10. This conception of evangelism combines those of Bosch, William Abraham and Scott Jones.

[38] As mentioned in chap. 6, Albert Cleage expands upon the positions of many of the women in this study (some explicit and others implicit) related to the apostle Paul. "On the other hand, there is the spiritualized Jesus, reconstructed many years later by the Apostle Paul who never knew Jesus and who modified his teachings to conform to the pagan philosophies of the white gentiles. Considering himself an apostle to the gentiles, Paul preached individual salvation and life after death. We, as black Christians suffering oppression in a white man's land, do not need the individualistic and otherworldly doctrines of Paul and the white man" ("The Black Messiah," in *Black Theology: A Documentary History*, ed. J. Cone and G. Wilmore, 2d ed., vol. 1 (Maryknoll, N.Y.: Orbis Books, 1993) 101–2.

Each woman advocated aspects of various social agendas related to race (such as antislavery and civil rights) or gender (such as women's ecclesiastic rights and suffrage). (3) Yet, while advocating for social agendas, the women's ministries remained grounded in theological frames with evangelism as the primary purpose. Many of the women alluded to or echoed natural rights arguments grounded in Enlightenment themes. However, each woman's primary purpose remained evangelistically focused upon God's salvation for her and the salvation of others.[39]

A consistent theme throughout the selected women's evangelistic ministries is an inability to separate Christian conversion from condition, their own and others. This theme echoes feminist, black liberation, and womanist theologies in particular. Respectful consideration of these and other disciplines can offer important perspectives and contributions to evangelistic theology and practice.[40] Admittedly, distinctions of methodologies and implications exist, some of which may not allow for extensive collaboration. Awareness, if not respectful conversation, can also sharpen and deepen reflection and embodiment of

[39] Letty M. Russell, "Liberation and Evangelization—A Feminist Perspective," *Occasional Bulletin of Missionary Research* (October 1974): 129. According to Russell, "Liberation theologies can be helpful in maintaining the full dimensions of evangelization. They begin from a theocentric basis as reflection on the liberating action of God, and seek by means of praxis to focus on social as well as individual needs of persons and groups." Such a "theocentric" basis of reflection upon practices relating to social and individual needs are very important. However, Russell's argument seems flat. Based on the women in this study, a more nuanced perspective emerging from the Trinity, including particularly christological and pneumatological themes, provides rich theological resources to address not only individual and social needs emerging from human experience but a more complex dynamic of accountability of humans to God and one another within which to frame that experience.

[40] For example, Russell, "Liberation and Evangelization—A Feminist Perspective," 128. Russell argues for "the unity of and interrelationship of liberation and evangelization," including the significance of "our own context, our own life story, and the ways in which we struggle together with others to live out the gospel message." She then asserts, "The ultimate meaning of liberation or evangelization is not determined, however, by one's perspective, be it feminist, black, Third World, or whatever. The meaning comes from the biblical story of what God is doing in bringing about the New Creation of Jesus Christ. Yet that meaning must be interpreted in relation to our various 'worldviews' and 'church views.'" According to Rosemary Ruether, a key paradigm shift related to women and redemption occurred with seventeenth-century Quakers that acknowledged the created equality of men and women and a second key shift in the seventeenth to the nineteenth centuries with a turn "from an otherworldly to a this-worldly view of redemption" (*Women and Redemption*, 273). See also Grant, *White Women's Christ and Black Women's Jesus*.

evangelistic theology and practice. Ignoring insights and arguments of other disciplines no longer seems an option in light of our complex global context.

(4) The women's evangelistic ministries responded to a comprehensive concept of sin beyond individual pride. While the Grimké sisters most directly addressed the experience of sin among disenfranchised constituencies and its implications for evangelistic theology and practice, many of the women reflect similar themes. Additional reflection upon such themes related to a multidimensional understanding of sin—which takes seriously not only sinful systems but also the impact of lack of self upon individuals and communities—provides important insights for the study and practice of evangelism. While some scholars resonate with such themes, reflecting theologically upon evangelistic ministries that cross boundaries and engage "the other," a particular focus upon the theological implications of a more comprehensive understanding of sin is essential.

In light of the persistent obstacles to faithful and effective evangelistic understandings and practices, an eschatological evangelism informed by these women (1) offers the gospel of Jesus Christ to all, (2) in the midst of sins both of pride and lack of self, (3) facilitates a real change in and among persons, (4) enables churches and the multiplicity of its members to understand and fulfill their evangelistic purpose to love and serve the world, and (5) while receiving formation from and living into the salvation narrative of the biblical text.

As concepts and practices of evangelism move beyond verbal proclamation to embrace a more complex theological future, I hope that additional attention will be given to the contributions of disenfranchised or not yet engaged constituencies in these efforts. While the gospel message is intended to meet individuals and communities in their present contexts, serious biblical and theological reflection that begins with God's creation out of nothing and subsequent invitation into reconciled relationship provide an essential foundation to faithful and effective evangelism. Therefore, I also hope that evangelism among the ecclesial practices will benefit from faithful stewardship in maintaining strong biblical and theological foundations within and among communities of faith. Ideally, after the example of these "Saving Women," the contemporary church might embrace a dynamic process in which theology and practices shape and inform each other, leading to an evangelism embodied in vital communities of faith.

BIBLIOGRAPHY

Primary Sources

Asbury, Francis. *The Journal and Letters of Francis Asbury*, vol. 1. Edited by Elmer T. Clark. London: Epworth, 1958.

Bethune, Mary McLeod. "A Century of Progress of Negro Women." In *Black Women in White America*, edited by Gerda Lerner. New York: Vintage Books, 1992.

———. *Mary McLeod Bethune Building a Better World: Essays and Selected Documents*. Edited by Audrey Thomas McCluskey and Elaine M. Smith. Bloomington: Indiana University Press, 1999.

———. "Spiritual Autobiography." In *American Spiritual Autobiographies: Fifteen Self-Portraits*, edited by Louis Finkelstein. New York: Harper & Row, 1948.

Clowes, William. *The Journals of William Clowes*. London: Hallam & Holliday, 1844.

Edmonds, John N. *Statutes at Large of the State of New York*. Albany, N.Y.: Weave C. Little, Law Bodeseller, 1863.

Finney, Charles Grandison. *Lectures on Revivals of Religion*. Edited by William G. McLoughlin. Cambridge: Belknap Press, 1960.

Foote, Julia. "A Brand Plucked from the Fire: An Autobiographical Sketch by Mrs. Julia A. J. Foote." In *Sisters of the Spirit: Three Black Women's Autobiographies of the Nineteenth Century*, edited by William L. Andrews. Bloomington: University of Indiana Press, 1986.

Garrettson, Freeborn. *A Dialogue Between Do-Justice and Professing Christian*. Wilmington, Del.: Peter Brynberg, 1805.

———. *The Experience and Travels of Mr. Freeborn Garrettson, Minister of the Methodist Episcopal Church in North America*. Philadelphia: Parry Hall, 1791.

Grimké, Angelina E. "Appeal to Christian Women of the South." *The Anti-Slavery Examiner* 1 (September 1836).

Grimké, Sarah. Diary, 1827. Theodore Dwight Weld Collection, William L. Clements Library, The University of Michigan, Ann Arbor, Mich.

———. *Letters on the Equality of the Sexes and Other Essays*. Edited by Elizabeth Ann Bartlett. New Haven: Yale University Press, 1988.

Laws of the State of New York. Albany, N.Y.: Websters & Skinners, 1815.

Montgomery, Helen Barrett. *The Bible and Missions*. West Medford, Mass.: The Central Committee on the United Study of Foreign Missions, 1920.

———. "Civic Opportunities for Christian Women." *The Baptist* 1 (28 August 1920).

——— [with tributes by her friends]. *From Campus to World Citizenship*. New York: Fleming H. Revell, 1940.

———. "A Postconvention Message to the Women of the Churches" (1922). In *Women and Religion in America, 1900–1968*, vol. 3, edited by Rosemary Radford Ruether and Rosemary Skinner Keller. San Francisco: Harper & Row, 1986.

———. "President's Address." In *Annual of the Northern Baptist Convention 1922 Containing the Proceedings of the Fifteenth Meeting Held at Indianapolis, Indiana, June 14 to 20, 1922*. American Baptist Publication Society, 1922.

———, trans. *Centenary Translation of the New Testament*. Philadelphia: The American Baptist Publication Society, 1924.

National Woman's Christian Temperance Union. Annual Convention's Minutes and Addresses. Chicago, 1874–1910.

Palmer, Phoebe. *The Way of Holiness, with Notes by the Way; Being a Narrative of Experience Resulting from A Determination to Be a Bible Christian*. New York: Piercy & Reed, 1843.

Payne, Daniel A. *History of the African Methodist Episcopal Church*. Nashville: Publishing House of the AME. Sunday-school Union, 1891.

Ripley, Dorothy. *An Account of Rose Butler, Aged Nineteen Years, Whose Execution I Attended in the Potter's Field*. New York: John C. Totten, 1819.

———. *The Bank of Faith and Works United*. Philadelphia: J. H. Cunningham, 1819.

———. *The Extraordinary Conversion, and Religious Experience of Dorothy Ripley, with Her First Voyage and Travels in America*. New York: G&R Waite, 1810.

———, ed. *Letters, Addressed to Dorothy Ripley from Several Africans and Indians on Subjects of Christian Experience &C*. Chester, U.K.: J. Hemingway, 1807.

Smith, Charles Spencer. *A History of the African Methodist Episcopal Church: Supplemental Volumes*. Philadelphia: Book Concern of the AME Church, 1922.

Stanton, Elizabeth Cady. *The Woman's Bible*. Foreword by Maureen Fitzgerald. Boston: Northeastern University Press, 1993.

Taft, Zachariah. *Biographical Sketches of the Lives and Public Ministry of Various Holy Women*. Vols. 1 and 2. London: Kershaw, Baynes & Sons, 1826.

Weld, Theodore Dwight. *The Bible Against Slavery: An Inquiry into the Patriarchal and Mosaic Systems on the Subject of Human Rights*, 3rd ed. New York: American Anti-Slavery Society, 1838.

———, ed. *American Slavery As It Is: Testimony of a Thousand Witnesses*. 1839. Reprint, Salem, N.H.: Ayer, 1991.

Wesley, John. *The Journal of the Rev. John Wesley, A.M.* Edited by Nehemiah Curnock. 1916. Reprint, London: Epworth, 1938.

———. *The Letters of the Rev. John Wesley, A.M.* Edited by John Telford. London: Epworth, 1931.

———. "A Plain Account of Christian Perfection." In *The Works of John Wesley, 1872*. Reprint, Grand Rapids: Zondervan, 1958–1959.

———. Sermon 43, "The Scripture Way of Salvation." In *Sermons II*, vol. 2 of *The Bicentennial Edition of the Works of John Wesley*, edited by Albert C. Outler. Nashville: Abingdon, 1976.

———. *Thoughts upon Slavery*. London: R. Hawes, 1774.

Willard, Frances E. "Do Everything: A Handbook for the World's White Ribboners." In *Women in American Protestant Religion 1800–1930*, edited by Carolyn DeSwarte Gifford, N.Y.: Garland, 1987.

———. *Glimpses of Fifty Years: The Autobiography of an American Woman*. Chicago: Woman's Temperance Publication Association, 1889.

———. *Woman in the Pulpit*. 1889. Reprint, Washington, D.C.: Zenger, 1978.

Woolman, John. *The Works of John Woolman*. Edited by William A. Beardslee. 1774. Reprint, New York: Garrett Press, 1970.

Secondary Sources

Abbott, Conda Delite Hitch. *Envoy of Grace: The Life of Helen Barrett Montgomery*. Valley Forge, Pa.: American Baptist Historical Society, 1997.

Abraham, William J. *The Logic of Evangelism*. Grand Rapids: Eerdmans, 1989.

———. "On Making Disciples of the Lord Jesus Christ." In *Marks of the Body of Christ*, edited by Carl E. Braaten and Robert W. Jenson. Grand Rapids: Eerdmans, 1999.

Andrews, William L., ed. *Sisters of the Spirit: Three Black Women's Autobiographies of the Nineteenth Century*. Bloomington: Indiana University Press, 1986.

Arias, Mortimer. *Announcing the Reign of God: Evangelism and the Subversive Memory of Jesus*. Philadelphia: Fortress. Reprint, Eugene, Ore.: Wipf & Stock, 1999.

Arias, Mortimer, and Alan Johnson. *The Great Commission: Biblical Models for Evangelism*. Nashville: Abingdon, 1992.

Bacon, Margaret Hope. *Mothers of Feminism: The Story of Quaker Women in America*. San Francisco: Harper, 1986.

Barbour, Hugh, et al., eds. *Quaker Crosscurrents: Three Hundred Years of Friends in the New York Yearly Meetings*. Syracuse, N.Y.: Syracuse University Press, 1995.

Barnes, Gilbert H. *The Anti-Slavery Impulse, 1830–44*. New York: D. Appleton-Century, 1933. Reprint, New York: Harcourt, Brace, 1964.

Barnes, Gilbert H., and Dwight L. Dumond, eds. *Letters of Theodore Dwight Weld, Angelina Grimké Weld, and Sarah Grimké 1822–1844*. New York: D. Appleton-Century, 1934.

Barrett, David B. *Evangelize! A Historical Survey of the Concept*. Birmingham, U.K.: New Hope, 1987.

Bassard, Katherine Clay. *Spiritual Interrogations: Culture, Gender, and Community in Early African American Women's Writing*. Princeton: Princeton University Press, 1999.

Bebbington, D. W. *Evangelicalism in Modern Britain: A History from the 1730s to the 1980s*. London: Unwin Hyman, 1989.

———. "Holiness in the Evangelical Tradition." In *Holiness Past and Present*, edited by Stephen C. Barton. London: T&T Clark, 2003.

Bederman, Gail. " 'The Women Have Had Charge of the Church Work Long Enough': The Men and Religion Forward Movement of 1911–1912 and the Masculinization of Middle-Class Protestantism." *American Quarterly* 41 (1989): 432–65.

Bendroth, Margaret Lamberts. *Fundamentalism and Gender: 1875–Present*. New Haven: Yale University Press, 1993.

Bevans, Stephen B., and Roger P. Schroeder. *Constants in Context: A Theology of Mission for Today*. Maryknoll, N.Y.: Orbis Books, 2004.

Birney, Catherine H. *The Grimké Sisters: Sarah and Angelina Grimké, The First Women Advocates of Abolition and Woman's Rights*. Boston: Lee & Sheppard, 1885.

Bjorklund, Diane. *Interpreting the Self: Two Hundred Years of American Autobiography*. Chicago: University of Chicago Press, 1998.

Blevins, Carolyn DeArmond. "Women in Baptist History." *Review and Expositor* 83 (1986): 51–61.

Blocker, Jack S., Jr. *"Give to the Winds Thy Fears": The Women's Temperance Crusade, 1873–1874*. Westport, Conn.: Greenwood Press, 1985.

Bohr, David. *Evangelization in America: Proclamation, Way of Life and the Catholic Church in the United States*. New York: Paulist, 1977.

Bondi, Roberta C. *To Pray and to Love: Conversations on Prayer with the Early Church*. Minneapolis: Fortress, 1991.

Bordin, Ruth. *Frances Willard: A Biography*. Chapel Hill: University of North Carolina Press, 1986.

Bosch, David Jacobus. "Evangelism: Theological Currents and Cross-currents Today." *International Bulletin of Missionary Research* (1987): 98–103.

———. "The Structure of Mission: An Exposition of Matt. 28: 16-21." In *Exploring Church Growth*, edited by Wilbert R. Shenk. Grand Rapids: Eerdmans, 1983.

———. *Transforming Mission: Paradigm Shifts in Theology of Mission.* Maryknoll, N.Y.: Orbis Books, 1991.

Braaten, Carl E. "The Triune God: The Source and Model of Christian Unity and Mission." *Missiology: An International Review* 18 (1990): 415–27.

Braaten, Carl E., and Robert W. Jenson, eds. *The Strange New Word of the Gospel: Re-Evangelizing in the Postmodern World.* Grand Rapids: Eerdmans, 2002.

Brackney, William H. "The Legacy of Helen B. Montgomery and Lucy W. Peabody." *International Bulletin of Missionary Research* 15 (1991): 174–78.

———, ed. *Baptist Life and Thought: 1600–1980, A Source Book*, rev. ed. Valley Forge, Pa.: Judson, 1998.

Braude, Ann. *Radical Spirits: Spiritualism and Women's Rights in Nineteenth-Century America*, 2d ed. Bloomington: Indiana University Press, 2001.

———. "Women's History Is American Religious History." In *Retelling U.S. Religious History*, edited by Thomas A. Tweed. Berkeley: University of California Press, 1997.

Brekus, Catherine. "Female Evangelism in the Early Methodist Movement, 1784–1845." In *Methodism and the Shaping of American Culture*, edited by Nathan O. Hatch and John H. Wigger. Nashville: Kingswood Books, 2001.

———. A. *Strangers and Pilgrims: Female Preaching in America 1740–1845.* Chapel Hill: University of North Carolina Press, 1998.

Broadwater, Andrew. *Mary McLeod Bethune: Educator and Activist.* Berkeley Heights, N.J.: Enslow Publishers., 2003.

Brown, Ira V. "'Am I not a Woman and a Sister?' The Anti-Slavery Convention of American Women, 1837–1839." In *Abolitionism and Issues of Race and Gender*, edited by John R. McKivigan. New York: Garland, 1999.

Brueggemann, Walter. *Biblical Perspectives on Evangelism: Living in Three-Storied Universe.* Nashville: Abingdon, 1993.

Bullard, Roger. "Feminine and Feminist Touches in the *Centenary New Testament*." *The Bible Translator* 38 (1987): 118–22.

Bushnell, Katherine. *God's Word to Women: One Hundred Stories on Woman's Place in the Divine Economy*, 2d ed. Mooseville, Ill.: God's Word to Women Publishers, 1923.

Cannon, Katie G. *Black Womanist Ethics.* American Academy of Religion Academic Series 60. Atlanta: Scholars Press, 1988.

Cattan, Louise A. *Lamps Are for Lighting: The Story of Helen Barrett Montgomery and Lucy Waterbury Peabody.* Grand Rapids: Eerdmans, 1972.

Ceplair, Larry, ed. *The Public Years of Sarah and Angelina Grimké: Selected Writings 1835–1839.* New York: Columbia University Press, 1989.

Chilcote, Paul Wesley. *Her Own Story: Autobiographical Portraits of Early Methodist Women.* Nashville: Kingswood Books, 2001.

———. *John Wesley and the Women Preachers of Early Methodism.* Metuchen, N.J.: Scarecrow, 1991.

———. *She Offered Them Christ: The Legacy of Women Preachers in Early Methodism.* Nashville: Abingdon, 1993.

Child, Alfred Thurston, Jr. "Prudence Crandall and the Canterbury Experiment." *Bulletin of the Friends Historical Association* 22 (1933): 35–55.

Cleage, Albert. "The Black Messiah." In *Black Theology: A Documentary History,* 2d ed., vol. 1, edited by James Cones and Gayraud Wilmore. Maryknoll, N.Y.: Orbis Books, 1993.

Collier-Thomas, Bettye. *Daughters of Thunder: Black Women Preachers and Their Sermons, 1850–1979.* San Francisco: Jossey Bass, 1998.

Cone, James H. *Black Theology and Black Power.* New York: Seabury Press, 1969.

———. *God of the Oppressed,* rev. ed. Maryknoll, N.Y.: Orbis Books, 1997.

———. *Risks of Faith: The Emergence of a Black Theology of Liberation, 1968–1998.* Boston: Beacon Press, 1999.

———. *The Spirituals and the Blues: An Interpretation,* rev. ed. Maryknoll, NY: Orbis Books, 1991.

Connor, Kimberly Rae. *Conversions and Visions in the Writings of African-American Women.* Knoxville: University of Tennessee Press, 1994.

Converse, Florence. *Wellesley College: A Chronicle of the Years 1875–1938.* Wellesley, Mass.: Hathaway House, 1939.

Costas, Orlando E. "Evangelism and the Gospel of Salvation." *International Review of Mission* 63 (1974): 24–37.

———. *Liberating News: A Theology of Contextual Evangelization.* Grand Rapids: Eerdmans, 1989.

Cott, Nancy F. *The Bonds of Womanhood: "Woman's Sphere" in New England, 1780–1835,* 2d ed. New Haven: Yale University Press, 1997.

Cullmann, Oscar. *Peter, Apostle, Disciple, Martyr: A Historical and Theological Study.* Philadelphia: Westminster, 1953.

Davidoff, Leonore, and Catherine Hall. *Family Fortunes: Men and Women of the Middle Class 1780–1850.* London: Hutchinson Education, 1987. Reprint, London: Routledge, 2002.

Dayton, Donald W. *Discovering an Evangelical Heritage.* New York: Harper & Row, 1976.

———, ed. *"The Higher Christian Life"; Sources for the Study of Holiness, Pentecostal and Keswick Movements. Holiness Tracts Defending the Ministry of Women.* New York: Garland, 1985.

DeBerg, Betty. *Ungodly Women: Gender and the First Wave of American Fundamentalism.* Minneapolis: Fortress, 1990.

Dieter, Melvin, ed. *The 19th-Century Holiness Movement.* Great Holiness Classics, vol. 4. Kansas City: Beach Hill Press, 1998.

Dietterich, Inagrace T. "Missional Community: Cultivating Communities of the Holy Spirit." In *Missional Church: A Vision for the Sending of the Church in North America,* edited by Darrell L. Guder and Lois Barret. Grand Rapids: Eerdmans, 1988.

Dodson, Jualynne. "Nineteenth-Century A.M.E. Preaching Women." In *Women in New Worlds. Historical Perspectives on the Wesleyan Tradition,* vol. 1, edited by Hilah F. Thomas and Rosemary Skinner Keller. Nashville: Abingdon, 1981.

Dorrien, Gary. *The Making of American Liberal Theology: Idealism, Realism, and Modernity 1900–1950.* Louisville, Ky.: Westminster John Knox, 2003.

Dowd, Sharyn. "Helen Barrett Montgomery's Centenary Translation of the New Testament: Characteristics and Influences." *Perspectives in Religious Studies* 19 (1992): 133–50.

———. "The Ministry of Women in Montgomery's Centenary New Testament: The Evidence of the Autograph." *American Baptist Quarterly* 20 (2001): 320–28.

Edwards, Wendy Deichmann, and Carolyn De Swarte Gifford. *Gender and the Social Gospel.* Urbana: University of Illinois Press, 2003.

Epstein, Barbara Leslie. *The Politics of Domesticity: Women, Evangelism, and Temperance in Nineteenth-Century America.* Middletown, Conn.: Wesleyan University, 1981.

Fede, Andrew. *People without Rights: An Interpretation of the Fundamentals of the Law of Slavery in the U.S. South.* New York: Garland, 1992.

Finney, Charles Grandison. *Lectures on Revivals of Religion.* Edited by William G. McLoughlin. Cambridge: Belknap, 1960.

Fiorenza, Elisabeth Schussler. *In Memory of Her: A Feminist Theological Reconstruction of Christian Origins.* New York: Crossroad, 1983.

Foster, Charles R., and Fred Smith, with Grant S. Shockley. *Black Religious Experience: Conversations on Double Consciousness and the Work of Grant Shockley.* Nashville: Abingdon, 2003.

Fox-Genovese, Elizabeth. *Within the Plantation Household: Black and White Women of the Old South.* Chapel Hill: University of North Carolina Press, 1988.

Fredriksen, Paula. "Paul and Augustine: Conversion Narratives, Orthodox Traditions, and the Retrospective Self." *Journal of Theological Studies* 37 (1986): 3–34.

Frost, J. William, ed. *The Quaker Origins of Antislavery.* Norwood, Pa.: Norwood, 1980.

Gaede, Stan. "Religious Participation, Socioeconomic Status, and Belief-Orthodoxy." *Journal for the Scientific Study of Religion* 16, no. 3 (1977): 245–53.

Garner, Nancy G. "The Woman's Christian Temperance Union: A Woman's Branch of American Protestantism." In *Re-forming the Center: American Protestantism, 1900 to the Present*, edited by Douglas Jacobsen and William Trollinger. Grand Rapids: Eerdmans, 1998.

Garrett, Shirley S. "Sisters All: Feminism and the American Woman's Missionary Movement." In *Missionary Ideologies in the Imperialist Era: 1880–1920*, edited by Torben Christensen and William R. Hutchison. Århus, Denmark: Aros, 1982.

Garrison, Stephen Olin, ed. *Forty Witnesses.* New York: Hunt & Eaton, 1888.

Gaventa, Beverly Roberts. *From Darkness to Light: Aspects of Conversion in the New Testament.* Philadelphia: Fortress, 1986.

Gifford, Carolyn. "'My Own Methodist Hive': Frances Willard's Faith as Disclosed in Her Journal, 1855–1870." In *Spirituality and Social Responsibility: Vocational Vision of Women in The United Methodist Tradition*, edited by Rosemary Skinner Keller. Nashville: Abingdon, 1993.

———. "'The Woman's Cause Is Man's'? Frances Willard and the Social Gospel." In *Gender and the Social Gospel*, edited by Wendy J. Deichmann Edwards and Carolyn DeSwarte Gifford. Urbana: University of Illinois Press, 2003.

———, ed. *Writing Out My Heart: Selections from the Journal of Frances E. Willard, 1855–96.* Urbana: University of Illinois Press, 1995.

Gill, Sean. *Women and the Church of England: From the Eighteenth Century to the Present.* London: SPCK, 1994.

Ginzberg, Lori D. *Women and the Work of Benevolence: Morality, Politics, and Class in the 19th-Century U.S.* New Haven: Yale University Press, 1990.

Graham, E. Dorothy. "Chosen by God: The Female Itinerants of Early Primitive Methodism." Ph.D. diss., University of Birmingham, 1987.

———. "Chosen by God: A List of the Female Travelling [*sic*] Preachers of Early Primitive Methodism." Wesley Historical Society. North Lodge, U.K.: Bankhead, 1989.

———. "Methodist Women Local Preachers." *Wesley Historical Society Proceedings* (New Zealand) 68 (July 1999): 35pp.

———. "Women Local Preachers." In *Workaday Preachers: The Story of Methodist Local Preaching*, edited by Geoffrey Milburn and Margaret Batty. Petersborough, U.K.: Methodist Publishing House, 1995.

Graham, Otis L., and Meghan Robinson Wander, eds. *Franklin D. Roosevelt: His Life and Times: An Encyclopedic View.* Boston: G. K. Hall, 1985.

Grant, Jacquelyn. *White Women's Christ and Black Women's Jesus: Feminist Christology and Womanist Response.* Atlanta: Scholars Press, 1989.

Guder, Darrell L., and Lois Barret, eds. *Missional Church: A Vision for the Sending of the Church in North America.* Grand Rapids: Eerdmans, 1988.

Hall, Jacquelyn Dowd. *Revolt Against Chivalry: Jessie Daniel Ames and the Women's Campaign Against Lynching*, rev. ed. New York: Columbia University Press, 1993.

Hardesty, Nancy. "The Scientific Study of Missions: Textbooks of the Central Committee on the United Study of Foreign Missions." In *The Foreign Missionary Enterprise at Home: Explorations in North American Cultural History*, edited by Daniel H. Bays and Grant Wacker. Tuscaloosa: The University of Alabama Press, 2003.

———. Hardesty, Nancy. *Women Called to Witness: Evangelical Feminism in the Nineteenth Century*. 2d ed. Knoxville: University of Tennessee Press, 1999.

Hardesty, Nancy, Lucille Sider Dayton, and Donald W. Dayton. "Women in the Holiness Movement: Feminism in the Evangelical Tradition." In *Women of Spirit*, edited by Rosemary Ruether and Eleanor McLaughlin. New York: Simon & Schuster, 1979.

Harvey, Paul. "The Christian Doctrine of Slavery." In *Religions of the U.S. in Practice, Princeton Readings in Religions*, edited by Collen McDannell, vol. 1. Princeton: Princeton University Press, 2001.

Haywood, Chanta M. "Prophesying Daughters: Nineteenth-Century Black Religious Women, the Bible, and Black Literary History." In *African Americans and the Bible: Sacred Texts and Social Textures*, edited by Vincent L. Wimbush. New York: Continuum, 2000.

Heasman, Kathleen J. *Evangelicals in Action: An Appraisal of Their Social Work in the Victorian Era*. London: Geoffrey Bles, 1962.

Heitzenrater, Richard P. *Wesley and the People Called Methodists*. Nashville: Abingdon, 1976.

———, ed. *The Poor and the People Called Methodists*. Nashville: Kingswood Books, 2002.

Hersh, Blanche Glassman. *The Slavery of Sex: Feminist Abolitionists in America*. Urbana: University of Illinois Press, 1978.

Hewitt, Furman. "Mining the Baptist Tradition for Christian Ethics: Some Gems." *Perspectives in Religious Studies* 25 (1998): 63–80.

Heyrman, Christine Leigh. *Southern Cross: The Beginnings of the Bible Belt*. New York: Alfred A. Knopf, 1997.

Hill, Anthony. "After Baptizatus: or, The Negro turn'd Christian" (London, 1702). In *American Religion: Literary Sources & Documents*, vol. 1, edited by David Turley. Mountfield, U.K.: Helm Information, 1998.

Hoedemaker, L. A. "The People of God and the Ends of the Earth." In *Missiology, an Ecumenical Introduction: Texts and Contexts of Global Christianity*, edited by A. Camps et al. Grand Rapids: Eerdmans, 1995.

Holifield, E. Brooks. *Theology in America: Christian Thought from the Age of the Puritans to the Civil War*. New Haven: Yale University Press, 2003.

Holt, Rackman. *Mary McLeod Bethune: A Biography*. Garden City, N.Y.: Doubleday, 1964.

Hopkins, C. Howard. *The Rise of the Social Gospel in American Protestantism, 1865–1915*. New Haven: Yale University Press, 1940.

Hudson, Winthrop. "Helen Barrett Montgomery." In *Notable American Women 1607–1950*, vol. 2. Cambridge, Mass.: Belknap Press of Harvard University Press, 1971.

Humez, Jean M. "'My Spirit Eye': Some Functions of Spiritual and Visionary Experience in the Lives of Five Black Women Preachers, 1810–1880." In *Women and the Structure of Society: Selected Research from the Fifth Berkshire Conference on the History of Women*, edited by Barbara J. Harris and JoAnn K. McNamara. Durham, N.C.: Duke University Press, 1984.

Hunsberger, Bruce, Michael Pratt, and S. Mark Pancer. "A Longitudinal Study of Religious Doubts in High School and Beyond: Relationships, Stability, and Searching for Answers." *Journal for the Scientific Study of Religion* 41, no. 2 (2002): 255–66.

Hunsberger, George. "Is There Biblical Warrant for Evangelism?" *Interpretation* 48 (1994): 131–44.

Hunter, Jane. *The Gospel of Gentility: American Women Missionaries in Turn-of-the-Century China*. New Haven: Yale University Press, 1984.

Jacobs, Janet. "The Economy of Love in Religious Commitment: The Deconversion of Women from Nontraditional Religious Movements." *Journal for the Scientific Study of Religion* 23 (1984): 155–71.

Japp, Phyllis M. "Esther or Isaiah?: The Abolitionist-Feminist Rhetoric of Angelina Grimké." *Quarterly Journal of Speech* 71 (1985): 335–48.

Jennings, Theodore. *Good News to the Poor: John Wesley's Evangelical Economics*. Nashville: Abingdon, 1990.

Jones, Scott J. *The Evangelistic Love of God and Neighbor: A Theology of Witness and Discipleship*. Nashville: Abingdon, 2003.

Jones, Serene. *Feminist Theory and Christian Theology: Cartographies of Grace*. Guides to Theological Inquiry Series. Minneapolis: Fortress, 2000.

Juster, Susan. "'In a Different Voice': Male and Female Narratives of Religious Conversion in Post-Revolutionary America." *American Quarterly* 41 (1989): 34–62.

Kallenberg, Brad J. *Live to Tell: Evangelism for a Postmodern Age*. Grand Rapids: Brazos Press, 2002.

Keller, Rosemary Skinner. "Conversions and Their Consequences: Women's Ministry and Leadership in the United Methodist Tradition." In *Religious Institutions and Women's Leadership: New Roles Inside the Mainstream*, edited by Catherine Wessinger. Columbia: University of South Carolina Press, 1996.

Keller, Rosemary Skinner, and Rosemary Radford Ruether, eds. *In Our Own Voices: Four Centuries of American Women's Religious Writing*. San Francisco: HarperSanFrancisco, 1995. Reprint, Louisville, Ky.: Westminster John Knox, 2000.

Klaiber, Walter. *Call and Response: Biblical Foundations of a Theology of Evangelism*. Nashville: Abingdon, 1997.

Knotts, Alice. *Fellowship of Love: Methodist Women Changing American Racial Attitudes, 1920–1968*. Nashville: Kingswood Books, 1996.

Krause, Neal, and Keith M. Wulff. "Religious Doubt and Health: Exploring the Potential Dark Side of Religion." *Sociology of Religion* 65, no. 1 (2004): 35–56.

Larson, Rebecca. *Daughters of Light: Quaker Women Preaching and Prophesying in the Colonies and Abroad, 1700–1755*. New York: Alfred A. Knopf, 1999.

Larson, Timothy. "'How Many Sisters Make a Brotherhood?' A Case Study in Gender and Ecclesiology in Early Nineteenth-Century English Dissent." *Journal of Ecclesiastical History* 49 (1998): 282–92.

Leclerc, Diane. "The Spirit's Cry in the Soul." In *"Heart Religion" in the Methodist Tradition and Related Movements*. Pietist and Wesleyan Studies 12, edited by Richard B. Steele. Lanham, Md.: Scarecrow Press, 2001.

Lender, Mark Edward. *Dictionary of American Temperance Biography: From Temperance Reform to Alcohol Research, the 1600s to the 1980s*. Westport, Conn.: Greenwood Press, 1984.

Leonard, William J. *Baptist Ways: A History*. Valley Forge, Pa.: Judson Press, 2003.

———. "Evangelism and Contemporary Life." *Review and Expositor* 77 (1980): 493–506.

Lerner, Gerda. *The Feminist Thought of Sarah Grimké*. New York: Oxford University Press, 1998.

———. *The Grimké Sisters from South Carolina: Pioneers for Women's Rights and Abolition*. Chapel Hill: University of North Carolina Press, 2004.

———, ed. *Black Women in White America: A Documentary History*. New York: Vintage Books, 1992.

Levine, Amy-Jill, ed. *"Women Like This": New Perspectives on Jewish Women in the Greco-Roman World*. Atlanta: Scholars Press, 1991.

Liefield, Walter L. "Women and Evangelism in the Early Church." *Missiology: An International Review* 15 (1987): 291–98.

Lindbeck, George. "Scripture, Consensus, and Community." In *Biblical Interpretation in Crisis*, edited by Richard J. Neuhaus. Grand Rapids, Eerdmans, 1989.

Lindley, Susan Hill. *"You Have Stept Out of Your Place": A History of Women and Religion in America*. Louisville, Ky.: Westminster John Knox, 1996.

Logan, James C. "Offering Christ: Wesleyan Evangelism Today." In *Rethinking Wesley's Theology for Contemporary Methodism*, edited by Randy L. Maddox. Nashville: Kingswood Books, 1998.

Lumpkin, Katharine Du Pre. *The Emancipation of Angelina Grimké*. Chapel Hill: University of North Carolina Press, 1974.

Lynch, James R. "Baptist Women in Ministry Through 1920." *American Baptist Quarterly* 13 (1994): 304–18.

Maddox, Randy L. *Responsible Grace: John Wesley's Practical Theology*. Nashville: Kingswood Books, 1994.

Maddox, Randy L., ed. *Aldersgate Reconsidered.* Nashville: Abingdon, 1990.

Malmgreen, Gail. "Domestic Discords: Women and the Family in East Cheshire Methodism, 1750–1839." In *Disciplines of Faith: Studies in Religion, Politics and Patriarchy*, edited by James Obelkevich et al. London: Routledge & Kegan Paul, 1987.

Marsden, George. *Fundamentalism and American Culture: The Shaping of Twentieth-Century Evangelicalism 1870–1925.* Oxford: Oxford University Press, 1980.

Martimort, Aime Georges. *Les Diaconesses: Essai Historique.* Rome: CLV Edizioni Liturgiche, 1982.

Martin, Dorothy. *Moody Bible Institute: God's Power in Action.* Chicago: Moody Press, 1977.

Martin, Earl. "Mary McLeod Bethune: A Prototype of the Rising Social Consciousness of the American Negro." Master's thesis, Northwestern University, 1958. Quoted in Clarence G. Newsome. "Mary McLeod Bethune and the Methodist Espiscopal Church North: In but Out." In *This Far By Faith: Readings in African-American Women's Religious Biography*, edited by Judith Weisenfeld and Richard Newman. New York: Routledge, 1996.

Mathews, Donald G. "Lynching Is Part of the Religion of Our People: Faith in the Christian South." In *Religion in the American South: Protestants and Others in History and Culture*, edited by Beth Barton Schweiger and Donald G. Mathews. Chapel Hill: University of North Carolina Press, 2004.

———. *Religion in the Old South.* Chicago: University of Chicago Press, 1977.

———. *Slavery and Methodism: A Chapter in American Morality 1780-1845.* Princeton: Princeton University Press, 1965. Reprint, Westport, Conn.: Greenwood Press, 1978.

May, Arthur J. *A History of the University of Rochester 1850–1962.* Rochester, N.Y.: University of Rochester Press, 1977.

McBeth, H. Leon. *The Baptist Heritage: Four Centuries of Baptist Witness.* Nashville: Broadman 1987.

McCants, David A. "Evangelicalism and Nineteenth-Century Women's Rights: A Case Study of Angelina E. Grimké." *Perspectives in Religious Studies* 14 (1987): 39–57.

McCluskey, Audrey Thomas, and Elaine M. Smith, eds. *Mary McLeod Bethune Building a Better World: Essays and Selected Documents.* Bloomington: Indiana University Press, 2001.

Meeks, M. Douglas, ed. *Portion of the Poor.* Nashville: Kingswood Books, 1995.

Mobley, Kendal. "The Ecumenical Woman's Missionary Movement: Helen Barrett Montgomery and The Baptist, 1920–30." In *Gender and the Social Gospel*, edited by Wendy Deichmann Edwards and Carolyn DeSwarte

Gifford. Urbana: University of Illinois Press, 2003.

Mugambi, J. N. K. "A Fresh Look at Evangelism in Africa." *International Review of Mission* 87 (1998): 342–60.

Newbigin, Lesslie. *The Open Secret: An Introduction to the Theology of Mission*, rev. ed. Grand Rapids: Eerdmans, 1995.

Newsome, Clarence G. "Mary McLeod Bethune and the Methodist Espiscopal Church North: In but Out." In *This Far By Faith: Readings in African-American Women's Religious Biography*, edited by Judith Weisenfeld and Richard Newman. New York: Routledge, 1996.

———. "Mary McLeod Bethune as Religionist." In *Women in New Worlds: Historical Perspectives on the Wesleyan Tradition*, vol. 1, edited by Hilah F. Thomas and Rosemary Skinner Keller. Nashville: Abingdon, 1981.

Nixson, Rosie. *Liberating Women for the Gospel: Women in Evangelism*. London: Hodder & Stoughton, 1997.

Noll, Mark A. *A History of Christianity in the United States and Canada*. Grand Rapids: Eerdmans, 1992.

———. *The Scandal of the Evangelical Mind*. Grand Rapids: Eerdmans, 1994.

Norwood, Frederick A. *The Story of American Methodism: A History of the United Methodists and Their Relations*. Nashville: Abingdon, 1974.

Omanson, Roger L. "Bible Translation: Baptist Contributions to Understanding God's Word." *Baptist History and Heritage* 31 (1996): 12–22.

Perry, Mark. *Lift Up Thy Voice: The Grimké Family's Journey from Slaveholders to Civil Rights Leaders*. New York: Viking, 2001.

Pope-Levison, Priscilla. *Turn the Pulpit Loose: Two Centuries of American Women Evangelists*. New York: Palgrave Macmillan, 2004.

Prochaska, F. K. *Women and Philanthropy in Nineteenth-Century England*. New York: Oxford University Press, 1980.

Purifoy, Lewis M. "The Methodist Anti-Slavery Tradition, 1784–1844." In *Abolitionism and American Religion*, edited by John R. McKivigan. New York: Garland, 1999.

Raboteau, Albert J. *African-American Religion*. Oxford: Oxford University Press, 1999.

Rauschenbusch, Walter. *Christianity and the Social Crisis*. New York: Macmillan, 1907.

Reis, Elizabeth. "African American Vision Stories." In *Religions of the United States in Practice*, edited by Collen McDannell. Princeton: Princeton University Press, 2001.

Richey, Russell E., Kenneth E. Rowe, and Jean Miller Schmidt, eds. *The Methodist Experience in America: A Sourcebook*, vol. 2. Nashville: Abingdon, 2000.

Robert, Dana Lee. *American Women in Mission: A Social History of their Thought and Practice*. Macon, Ga.: Mercer University Press, 1997.

———, ed. *Gospel Bearers, Gender Barriers: Missionary Women in the Twentieth*

Century. Maryknoll, N.Y.: Orbis Books, 2002.

Ruether, Rosemary Radford. *Women and Redemption: A Theological History*. Mineapolis: Fortress, 1998.

Russell, Letty M. "Liberation and Evangelization—A Feminist Perspective." *Occasional Bulletin of Missionary Research* (October 1974): 128–30.

Ruth, Lester. *A Little Heaven Below: Worship at Early Methodist Quarterly Meetings*. Nashville: Kingswood Books, 2000.

Schmidt, Jean Miller. *Grace Sufficient: A History of Women in American Methodism 1760–1939*. Nashville: Abingdon, 1999.

———. "Reexamining the Public/Private Split: Reforming the Continent and Spreading Scriptural Holiness." In *Perspectives on American Methodism: Interpretive Essays*, edited by Russell Richey et. al. Nashville: Abingdon, 1993.

Schwarz, Gerold. "The Legacy of Karl Hartenstein." *International Bulletin of Missionary Research* 8 (1984): 125–31.

Scott, Anne Firor. *Natural Allies: Women's Associations in American History*. Urbana: University of Illinois Press, 1991.

Scott, Waldron. "Karl Barth's Theology of Mission." *Missiology: An International Review* 3 (1975): 209–24.

Segal, Alan F. *Paul the Convert: The Apostolate and Apostasy of Saul the Pharisee*. New Haven: Yale University Press, 1990.

Sider, Ronald J., Philip N. Olson, and Heidi Bolland Unbuh. *Churches That Make a Difference: Reaching Your Community with Good News with Good Works*. Grand Rapids: Baker Books, 2002.

Siebert, Wilbur Henry. *The Underground Railroad From Slavery to Freedom*. New York: Macmillan, 1898.

Sigerman, Harriet. "An Unfinished Battle: 1848–1865." In *No Small Courage: A History of Women in the United States*, edited by Nancy F. Cott. Oxford: Oxford University Press, 2000.

Smith, Timothy Lawrence. *Revivalism and Social Reform in Mid-Nineteenth-Century America*. New York: Abingdon, 1957.

Speicher, Anna M. *The Religious World of Antislavery Women: Spirituality in the Lives of Five Abolitionist Lecturers*. Syracuse, N.Y.: Syracuse University Press, 2000.

Spruill, Julia Cherry. *Women's Life and Work in the Southern Colonies*. 1972. Reprint, New York: W.W. Norton, 1998.

Stanley, Susie C. *Holy Boldness: Women Preachers' Autobiographies and the Sanctified Self*. Knoxville: University of Tennessee Press, 2002.

Stott, John. "The Significance of Lausanne." *International Review of Mission* 64 (1975): 288–94.

Strong, Douglas. "The Crusade for Women's Rights and the Formative Antecedents of the Holiness Movement." *Wesleyan Theological Journal* 27 (1992): 132–60.

———. "The Doctrine of Christian Perfection Among Nineteenth Century

African American Preaching Women." Unpublished paper, n.d.

———. "A Real Christian is an Abolitionist: Conversion and Antislavery Activism in Early American Methodism." In *Conversion in the Wesleyan Tradition*, edited by Kenneth J. Collins and John H. Tyson. Nashville: Abingdon, 2001.

Stuard, Susan Mosher. "Women's Witnessing: A New Departure." In *Witnesses for Change: Quaker Women over Three Centuries*, edited by Elisabeth Potts Brown and Susan Mosher Stuard. New Brunswick, N.J.: Rutgers University Press, 1989.

Sweet, Leonard I. "The Female Seminary Movement and Woman's Mission in Antebellum America." *Journal of Church History* 54 (1985): 41–55.

Thomas, James S. *Methodism's Racial Dilemma: The Story of the Central Jurisdiction*. Nashville: Abingdon, 1992.

Thompson, Ernest Trice. "Black Presbyterians, Education and Evangelism after the Civil War." *Journal of Presbyterian History* 51 (1973): 174–98.

Tiainen-Anttila, Kaija. *The Problem of Humanity: The Blacks in the European Enlightenment*. Helsinki: Finnish Historical Society, 1994.

Tucker, Ruth. "Female Mission Strategists: A Historical and Contemporary Perspective." *Missiology: An International Review* 14 (1987): 73–89.

Turner, Bishop H. M. *The Genius and Theory of Methodist Polity, or The Machinery of Methodism. Practically Illustrated Through a Series of Questions and Answers*. Philadelphia: Publication Department, AME Church, 1885.

Tushnet, Mark V. *Slave Law in the American South: State v. Mann in History and Literature*. Lawrence: University Press of Kansas, 2003.

Valenze, Deborah M. *Prophetic Sons and Daughters: Female Preaching and Popular Religion in Industrial England*. Princeton: Princeton University Press, 1985.

Van Horne, John C. "Impediments to the Christianization and Education of Blacks in Colonial America: The Case of the Associates of Dr. Bray." *Historical Magazine of the Protestant Episcopal Church* 50 (1981): 243–69.

Wacker, Grant. *Religion in Nineteenth-Century America*. New York: Oxford University Press, 2000.

Walls, William. *The African Methodist Episcopal Zion Church: Reality of the Black Church*. Charlotte, N.C.: AME Zion Publishing House, 1974.

Warner, Laceye. "Reconsidering Evangelism: Lessons from Black Liberation and Womanist Theologies." In *Living Stones in the Household of God: The Legacy and Future of Black Theology*, edited by Linda E. Thomas. Minneapolis: Fortress, 2003.

Watson, David Lowes. *Class Leaders: Recovering a Tradition*. Nashville: Discipleship Resources, 1991.

Weeks, Stephen B. *Southern Quakers and Slavery: A Study of Institutional History*. Baltimore, Md.: The Johns Hopkins Press, 1896.

Wellman, Judith. *The Road to Seneca Falls: Elizabeth Cady Stanton and the First*

Woman's Rights Convention. Urbana: University of Illinois Press, 2004.

Westerhoff, John H. "Evangelism, Evangelization, and Catechesis." *Interpretation* 48 (1994): 156–65.

White, Charles. *The Beauty of Holiness: Phoebe Palmer as Theologian, Revivalist, Feminist, and Humanitarian*. Grand Rapids: Francis Asbury/Zondervan, 1986.

White, Ronald C., Jr. *Liberty and Justice for All: Racial Reform and the Social Gospel (1877–1925)*, rev. ed. Louisville, Ky.: Westminster John Knox, 2002.

White, Ronald, and C. Howard Hopkins. *The Social Gospel: Religion and Reform in a Changing America*. Philadelphia: Temple University Press, 1976.

Wilken, Robert L. *Remembering the Christian Past*. Grand Rapids: Eerdmans, 1995.

Williams, Delores S. *Sisters in the Wilderness: The Challenge of Womanist God-Talk*. Maryknoll, N.Y.: Orbis Books, 1993.

———. "Straight Talk, Plain Talk: Womanist Words about Salvation in a Social Context." In *Embracing the Spirit: Womanist Perspectives on Hope, Salvation, and Transformation*, edited by Emilie M. Townes. Maryknoll, N.Y.: Orbis Books, 1997.

Williamson, Harold F., and Payson S. Wild. *Northwestern University: A History 1850–1975*. Evanston, Ill.: Northwestern University Press, 1976.

Wills, Anne Blue. "Mapping Presbyterian Missionary Identity in *The Church at Home and Abroad*, 1890–1898." Pages 95–105 in *The Foreign Missionary Enterprise at Home: Explorations in North American Cultural History*, edited by Daniel H. Bays and Grant Wacker. Tuscaloosa: University of Alabama, 2003.

Wilmore, Gayraud S. *Black Religion and Black Radicalism: An Interpretation of the Religious History of Afro-American People*, rev. ed. Maryknoll, N.Y.: Orbis Books, 1993.

Woolman, John. "Some Considerations on the Keeping of Negroes Recommended to Professors of Christianity of Every Denomination" (1754). In *The Quaker Origins of Antislavery*, edited by J. William Frost. Norwood, Pa.: Norwood Editions, 1980.

Wright, Chris. "Mission as a Matrix for Hermeneutics and Biblical Theology." Paper presented at the University of St. Andrews: Scripture and Hermeneutics Seminar, August 2003.

Yoder, John Howard. *The Politics of Jesus: Vicit Agnus Noster*. Grand Rapids: Eerdmans, 1972.

Zikmund, Barbara Brown. "Biblical Arguments and Women's Place in the Church." In *The Bible and Social Reform*, edited by Ernest R. Sandeen. Philadelphia: Fortress, 1982.

Zilversmit, Arthur. *The First Emancipation: The Abolition of Slavery in the North*. Chicago: University of Chicago Press, 1967.

Zink-Sawyer, Beverly. *From Preachers to Suffragists: Woman's Rights and Religious Conviction in the Lives of Three Nineteenth century American*

INDEX